The Chortling Bard!

Caught'ya! Grammar with a Giggle for High School

(A method for teaching grammar, mechanics, usage, vocabulary, and literary devices with plots and vocabulary borrowed from Shakespeare)

Jane Bell Kiester

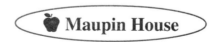
Maupin House

The Chortling Bard!

Editor: Jane Bell Kiester
Cover Design: David Dishman
Book Design: Billie J. Hermansen

Kiester, Jane Bell, 1945-.
    The chortling bard : Caught'ya! grammar with a giggle for high
schools / Jane Bell Kiester.
        p.   cm.
    Includes bibliographical references (p.   ).
    ISBN 0-929895-25-8
    1. English language--Grammar--Study and teaching (Secondary)
2. English language--Composition and exercises--Study and teaching
(Secondary) 3. Humor in education.   I. Title.
    LB1631.K463   1998
    428'.0071'2--dc21   97-52312
                                                              CIP

Maupin House Publishing, Inc.
PO Box 90148
Gainesville, FL 32607-0148
1-800-524-0634

This one is for Chuck, husband, lover, friend, and "terser" of verbose authors.

Yet do thy worst, old Time! Despite thy wrong,
My love shall in my heart ever live young.

(Modified from Shakespeare, Sonnet # XIX)

Acknowledgments

I couldn't write a book without my trusty in-home editors, my husband, Chuck Kiester, and my mother, Perra Bell. These two keep my books from being 1000 pages, clean up my mistakes, tell me where I am obtuse, laugh in the right places, keep me enthused and sane, and love me unconditionally. Most important of all for my writing, they are brutally (but lovingly) honest in their evaluation and suggestions. Thanks, you two. What would I ever do without you?

I would also like to thank once again, Mary Ann Coxe, Language Arts Supervisor for Alachua County Florida (recently retired) and friend. It seems I can't write a book without Mary Ann, either! Writing, like life, is definitely a communal effort. Mary Ann did the research (for all the English teachers in our district), enthused over my idea of using the Bard, and encouraged me to write when the pressures of teaching English and writing books overwhelmed me.

Another true friend, Cathy Berg, also has contributed to each book I have written. She teaches ninth-grade and eleventh-grade English and is known for her "dreaded mechanics and usage tests." Cathy is an outstanding (and exciting) teacher, and I trust her sense of our language completely. I would not dare publish an English book without Cathy's input and editing. She graciously agreed to proofread this book and find my errors. Thank you, Cathy, for the hours you spent and the wise suggestions you made, once again keeping the egg off my face.

Doris Farnbach, another friend, a "Grammar Guru," and a recently retired English teacher, is the only person I know for whom correct grammar is a hobby. Doris painstakingly spent hours going through this manuscript to make sure that few errors remained. I know it is impossible to produce an error-free book, but Doris will help me come close. She is picky and precise. She is wonderful. Thank you, Doris, for your time and your expertise. Doris, by the way, helped produce the Appendix found in my second book and reproduced at the end of this one.

Like serendipity, just as I was finishing up this book, I went to a local production of a Shakespearean play. There, inserted in the playbill was Michael Briggs's list of Shakespearean epithets. He kindly let me use them. Thank you, Michael, for agreeing with me that the teaching of grammar, not to mention Shakespeare, should be fun.

Finally, I wish to thank Maupin House, Inc., the writer-friendly publishing company that thinks more of helping teachers than of total profits. You make writing and publishing what it should be, an amicable partnership of friends.

Table of Contents

NOTE : Chapters 4, 5, and 6 include the following:

1. Corrected sentences of the Caught'yas for this story written together in a continuous fashion for easy perusing.

2. The vocabulary included in the Caught'yas, listed in the order that each word appears in the story.

3. A list of the literary devices and writing conventions used in this story, listed in alphabetical order alongside the numbers of the Caught'yas where they can be found.

4. One hundred twenty to one hundred twenty-four Caught'yas with the included vocabulary, literary devices and writing conventions, and grammar/ mechanics/usage skills listed beside each one.

5. A final exam and key.

Introduction

Rationale, Research, and Background

Rationale

While signing books at the publisher's table at a New Orleans conference two years ago, I couldn't help overhearing a conversation among several teachers who were standing nearby. The principal speaker was a middle school teacher who already enthusiastically used my two books, *Caught'ya! Grammar with a Giggle* and *Caught'ya Again! More Grammar with a Giggle*. She was trying to convince several high school teachers, who were questioning whether my books could be used at the upper levels, that the books were effective. It wasn't until she pointed out that there was a story in each book designed for use at the high school level, that they picked up the books to examine them. I don't know if they ever bought copies of the books, but the conversation remains vivid.

Since overhearing those teachers, I have spoken with many high school teachers who have said they needed to teach grammar, mechanics, usage, vocabulary, and literary devices and writing conventions to students in a way that would carry over into their students' writing. Because my first two books are so popular with middle and elementary level teachers, these high school teachers were unsure that the books also addressed the more sophisticated needs of ninth, tenth, eleventh, and twelfth graders.

I had to admit they had a point. While my other two *Caught'ya* books contain two stories ("Romeo and Juliet, Revisited and Revised," and "Charlie Excess Does It Again") that were designed for use at the high school level, many eighth-grade teachers have used these stories in their classes. They did so because the sixth- and seventh-grade teachers already had used the other stories available for the middle school level! Obviously more stories needed to be written.

Originally, I had included only two Caught'ya stories for each level because I believed that teachers would treat these stories like a recipe. After accustoming themselves to the method the first year and using my stories basically as written, they would thereafter want to branch out and write their own sentences based on stories that would appeal to their particular students (rural, inner city, small town, etc.). Indeed, many teachers have written their own stories (sometimes hilarious ones). Nonetheless, many others prefer to use mine; thus a dilemma has arisen.

Since I, too, was guilty of using both of the high school stories with my advanced eighth graders, I knew the time had come to write a *Caught'ya* book just for high school use. I sat in our hot tub with a canopy of north Florida greenery above me (definitely a place of inspiration). There, in the swirling, hot water, I wracked my brain for "G-rated" plots to use with high school students that still would appeal to them. In a flash of blind "je ne sais quoi," I came up with the idea of using the Bard himself. After I tempered his bawdiness and seventeenth century anti-feminist attitudes and adjusted the language to make it more palatable to teenagers, I ended up with soap-operas that appeal to young adults. I tried one of the stories with my gifted eighth graders this year, and they loved it!

What better way to find humorous plots, intrigue and action, good vocabulary, and great use of literary devices and writing conventions than to look to the source, Shakespeare? I hope the Bard (the seventeenth Earl of Oxford??) will forgive me for taking literary license with his plots and dialogue. After all, he "borrowed" from many ancient Greek, Italian, French, and other great authors. Turn about is, indeed, fair play.

This book gives you three *Caught'ya* stories, set out in the same manner as the stories in the other two *Caught'ya* books, but noting vocabulary and literary devices/writing conventions separately. As in all the other *Caught'ya* stories, each day's sentence contains at least one vocabulary word. This time, however, I used much of the vocabulary that Shakespeare himself used. Words purloined from Shakespeare have been marked with a heart (♥).

It is important to note that Shakespeare wrote for the common person and therefore kept his vocabulary fairly simple. After rejecting the archaic words that would not be useful for a modern student as well as words that in Shakespeare's day had entirely different meanings, I found fewer than one hundred words per play that would challenge high school students. Thus, I added a few of my favorite "$100 words" to the list.

The modernized, slightly revised (and cleaned up) stories of *Much Ado About Nothing, A Midsummer Night's Dream, Twelfth Night* – "Much Ado About Everything," "A Midsummer's Nightmare," and "Twelfth Night of Mischief or What You Will, Doubled" – are told in narrative style with dialogue rather than in play form. I did this in order to include all the grammar, mechanics, and usage skills contained in the traditional grammar books. In **Chapter 2**, there are also some very important notes pertaining to the use of these particular Caught'yas.

Chapter 3 might prove useful in introducing Shakespeare to your students in a way that will intrigue them — using Shakespearean epithets. Students love them! When students (and you) swear in seventeenth-century epithets, it takes the fear out of the sometimes strange language.

Please note that before writing the sentences, I made a list from *Warriner's English Grammar, Complete Course* (Warriner and Graham, 1957) and from *Houghton Mifflin English* (Haley-James and Stewig, 1988) of all the grammar, mechanics, and usage that high school teachers are expected to teach. Each skill is used at least twice in each story. Sticky points upon which my colleagues (who helped edit the book) and I disagreed were checked in *The Elements of Grammar* (Shertzer, 1996) and *A Writer's Reference* (Hacker, 1995).

In my second book, *Caught'ya Again! More Grammar with a Giggle*, an **Appendix** lists and explains, with examples and suggestions for further instruction, all the skills included in the Caught'ya sentences. Teachers have told me they have found it very useful, so I asked Maupin House Publishing, Inc. to repeat it in this book. It is the last section.

If you are not familiar with the *Caught'ya* method of teaching grammar, mechanics, usage, vocabulary, editing, and literary devices and writing conventions, you might want to read **Chapter 1** carefully. It is a condensed version of Chapters 1, 2, and 3 in *Caught'ya! Grammar with a Giggle* and similar to Chapter 1 in *Caught'ya Again! More Grammar with a Giggle*.

High school teachers **do** use my first two books with much success. But, I think a book devoted to high school students alone may help clear up the confusion, solve the problem of the dearth of stories left for the upper levels, and specifically address the more sophisticated needs and concerns of my high school colleagues.

Background and Research

In 1979, in a moment of desperation-led inspiration, I came up with the idea of the Caught'ya. I had observed in my students' weekly journals that nothing I did to try to teach grammar, mechanics, and usage (and I had tried every method that came down the educational pike) carried over into their writing. Something had to be changed.

I cautiously implemented the Caught'ya (then called the "Gotcha") method of teaching grammar, mechanics, usage, and vocabulary into my curriculum. It taught all the skills at the same time in the context of a story, *and* it taught the students how to edit. (This is really what we English teachers want our students to be able to do – edit, proofread, recognize the errors, and *correct* their own work!) I crossed my fingers and hoped for success.

After only a month of implementing this system with my students, I discovered that many of the errors that had plagued their papers had diminished considerably! During "editing time," students actually were editing and correcting. They had become aware of their own errors and were able to correct quite a few of them. I was seeing the results I had not seen when using any other method. Finally, something worked!

I changed schools and grade levels. At the middle school level, I taught English using the Caught'ya method, and I saw even better results in my students' improved writing. Then, one day the reading teacher came to me and asked what I was doing that the other English teachers were not. She had noticed that 100 percent of my students knew how to punctuate a quotation correctly, and she knew that I taught "regular" English. The students of other English teachers (including the ones in advanced classes) did not fare as well.

I was ecstatic. At the end of that year, the results of the California Achievement Test came back. Even my compensatory students had averaged an increase of two Stanines in language mechanics and usage from their previous test! That was all the proof I needed to abandon forever the traditional grammar book – far fewer errors in my students' writing *and* improved standardized test scores.

To put the cherry on top of the proverbial cake, students liked the method! It was short and fun. It required only ten minutes of each period, leaving the rest of the time to spend writing or reading and discussing literature. It began each period with a bang and a laugh, and it had the side effect of helping to bond me even tighter to my students, thus reducing discipline problems.

Then I heard about *Daily Oral Language*, a somewhat similar method self-published by two teachers in Wisconsin, Neil Vail and Joseph Papenfuss (Vail and Papenfuss, 1982). My method differed in that it contained vocabulary, required paragraphing discussions, and focused on the context of an actual story. Both methods stressed giving the reason for the correction and adapting the daily sentence to the skills needed by a particular class. Apparently we had invented similar techniques simultaneously!

At this point, like a gift from the heavens, a summary of the grammar-teaching research of the past seventy-eight years arrived in the truck mail at school. It had been sent by Mary Ann Coxe, the (recently retired) Language Arts Supervisor for Alachua County Schools, Florida. Mary Ann is a friend and a former wonderfully inventive high school teacher who proves the adage – "You can take the English teacher out of the classroom, but you can't take the classroom out of the English teacher." In 1984, concerned with what was (or more precisely what was not) going on in some English classes in our county, she conducted the research that the rest of us still in the classroom did not have time to do.

Mary Ann then summarized the results and sent them, along with the revised curriculum, to English teachers in the county. It was a subtle hint for a few, but to the rest of us, it was confirmation that our instincts had been right when we had abandoned the traditional grammar texts. In the next few paragraphs I offer you the results of Mary Ann's research.

Society assumes that schools should teach grammar and that learning grammar will help make students write better, yet much research has challenged that assumption. Hoyt (1906) concluded from his research, and many others since have corroborated him, that the teaching of grammar divorced from actual writing is useless.

Researchers also found that the writing of students who had had formal grammar teaching did not differ from the writing of those who had not studied any grammar at all (Elley, et al, 1979 and Sherwin, 1969). Recent research has not changed these conclusions.

A few years ago a former student of mine innocently put it quite succinctly: "Mrs. Kiester, I know what they're asking for in the grammar book. They ask for only one skill at a time. When I write, I use all the skills and rules at the same time. It's totally different." (Kevin Ho, at age 13) Why, then, given all this research and the knowledge that students think grammar books and their exercises were designed to bore them, have most schools continued to teach grammar directly from grammar books?

They do because we English teachers want to get rid of all those egregious errors in students' writing, and most of us know no better way to do it. That was the boat in which I had been floating in 1979. That was the spark that led to the invention of the Caught'ya technique.

With consistent success, I continued to use the Caught'ya method in my classroom. Indeed, I am *still* using it in my English classroom and am *still* getting results. One year, just to make sure I was including all the skills my county expected me to teach, I recorded lesson content. Without ever opening the grammar or vocabulary books provided, I taught (and am still teaching) the following:

> more than 300 vocabulary words
> paragraphing
> punctuation, including quotations
> subjects and predicates
> eight parts of speech
> subject/verb agreement
> collective nouns
> who/whom/that/which
> titles and how to write them
> avoidance of passive voice
> active verbs
> verb tense agreement and consistency
> correct forms of many verbs
> all nine comma rules
> common homophones
> basic spelling rules
> diagramming sentences
> conjunctions, memorization and proper use thereof
> prepositions and prepositional phrases as adjectives and adverbs
> use of infinitives
> common and proper nouns
> pronoun use and overuse
> antecedent/pronoun agreement
> proper use of pronouns
> run-on sentences and fragments (avoidance of)
> simple, compound, complex, and compound-complex sentences (composition
>   thereof and punctuation therein)
> letter writing format
> modifier agreement
> irregular verbs (especially "lie/lay" and sit/set")
> use of gerunds

parallel construction
direct and indirect objects
recognition of phrases and clauses
subordinate clauses and punctuation therein
participial phrases
analogies
bibliographical forms
common literary devices and writing conventions such as use of metaphor and
    similes and description within dialogue
various types of writing (descriptive, etc.)
effective adjective and adverb use
editing
proofreading
the writing process

Two years ago, Mary Ann Coxe sent out another piece of her research. R. Noguchi, who read 3,000 essays for his research (sounds like a typical year of teaching English), isolated twenty most common errors in student writing: punctuation, especially commas and apostrophes; verb use, especially irregular verbs; and pronoun use and reference (quoted in Connors, R.J. and Lunsford, A.A., 1988, also quoted by Shuman, Baird, 1992). Sound familiar?

In 1989, before I even knew about Noguchi's results, I had conducted some informal research on my own. I wanted to confirm the skills that were important to emphasize in my first two Caught'ya books. That year when I read my students' writing efforts, I kept track of the errors they consistently made in their writing. I did this on my desk calendar. Although the errors diminished in frequency as the year progressed, my results paralleled Noguchi's conclusions. The only difference was that I added common spelling errors to the list.

After the first two Caught'ya books were published and distributed, the publisher received many letters from happy teachers who had experienced success with the method. One young teacher startled her county by having her students test twenty-two percentage points higher on the mechanics part of a test than any other teacher in the county, a fact she credited to the use of Caught'yas in her classroom. She even won a trip!

"Is this snake oil or a new grammar book?" you ask. Read on and find out how the Caught'ya method works and why many teachers from grade one to junior college swear by it.

Chapter 1

How to implement successfully
the Caught'ya method of teaching
grammar, mechanics, usage, editing
literary devices and writing
conventions, and vocabulary.

What is included in this chapter:

Overview of method—Introduction

Even if you have already read *Caught'ya! Grammar with a Giggle or Caught'ya Again! More Grammar with a Giggle,* you still might want to skim this chapter before going on to the stories. While I do repeat the basic information necessary to implement the Caught'ya method in your classroom, I have added a few embellishments and alternative methods of execution that might help high school teachers make this non-traditional method more palatable for high school students, a much more discerning, critical, and cynical group than their younger counterparts.

The Caught'ya method is an integrated approach to teaching language skills in context. Essentially, it is a sentence or two of an ongoing, funny Shakespearean story taught from a blackboard or overhead projector three to five days a week. Each sentence is laced with errors that the teacher wishes to eliminate in students' writing. Each sentence also includes at least one challenging word that should be new to most students. Many also contain literary devices and writing conventions. The teacher introduces and elicits the meaning of the word(s), reads the sentence dramatically, and initiates a discussion as to whether the sentence begins a new paragraph in the story.

Students then write the Caught'ya as correctly as they can. Meanwhile, the teacher walks around the room and gives immediate, tinged-with-humor feedback to individual students, providing mini-lessons and urging or challenging students to find the errors on their own. Please note that a teacher can get around to each student in a class of thirty-five or more in fewer than five minutes by glancing at each paper, looking for one particular error. Only if the teacher finds that error corrected does he or she read the rest of the Caught'ya sentence for that student.

When nearly all of the students have completed the sentence and received a comment from the teacher, the teacher returns to the board or overhead. The meaning of the vocabulary word(s) is elicited and discussed again. Any literary devices or writing conventions used in the sentence are noted and discussed. The whole class, with the teacher presiding, then reviews the errors in the Caught'ya, discussing the *reasons* and the *rules* for each correction. Students take notes on their papers and use proofreading symbols to mark errors that were missed.

When the entire sentence has been corrected communally, corrections discussed thoroughly, and most importantly, the reasons of each noted on the students' papers, students count the errors they missed the first time - i.e., when they attempted to correct the sentence on their own. They then indicate the number of their initial errors in the margin of their paper. Several skills have been introduced, reinforced, or practiced, a new word has been learned, and maybe the class has enjoyed a giggle from the story, the vocabulary word, or the antics of the teacher as he or she cavorted around the room.

The evaluation of the Caught'ya sentences is equally important. It is based on whether students catch the errors and mark them on their papers when the whole class reviews the Caught'ya, *not* on the number of errors made the first time when students attempted to correct the sentence on their own. This way students, no matter how weak they have been in English skills, can experience success with the Caught'ya. Even the students with poor skills can get an "A + " if they listen and correct carefully, a wonderful inducement to pay attention.

A teacher can use a Caught'ya every day or only three or four times a week as long as the story line is not lost or forgotten. Skills can be repeated *ad nauseam* until every student in the class masters them or begs for mercy.

Students soon get used to entering the classroom and immediately settling down to write the Caught'ya sentence(s). The Caught'ya routine shortens the "waste time" at the beginning of every period. Because students, no matter how old, crave the individual feedback their teacher gives while they are working on the Caught'ya sentences, they usually get to work very quickly. It also has been noted that high school students in particular get started quickly in order to "get it over with" because the entire process is brief. Honest students have confessed during weak moments of confidence that they really *do* enjoy doing the Caught'yas. Almost all students admit that they learn from them.

Sometimes students help each other with the errors. You may hear whispered debates about whether and why a comma should be put in a certain spot. You may overhear disagreements about the part of speech of a certain word, music to any English teacher's ears. Later in this chapter you will find suggestions on how to "hype" the Caught'ya method in order to direct your students' attention toward correct English skills.

Students who are weak in English skills, such as those who are in the compensatory- or basic-skills classes, especially love the Caught'ya method because it eliminates any feeling of failure and frustration previously associated with language arts. Since the Caught'ya is short, it can be completed even by those students with short attention spans. If you have an easy Caught'ya sentence on the board, it is a good idea to check the weakest of your students first so you can praise him/her for making no errors that day. Teachers who use the Caught'ya method with basic-skills students note a marked increase in their standardized test scores in the areas of mechanics, usage, and reading, sometimes as much as three Stanines!

It is important to grab your students' interest in these quick "mini-bites" of English skills. You want your students to see that these are useful. High school students, in particular, object to learning something that is not "useful" to them (in the practical sense) or something that does not keep them amused.

It does not matter what grade you teach; this system works at any level as long as your students can read. It is up to you to change and modify the details to fit the needs of *your* students. (More about that later.)

Do not worry if you are an introvert, are not naturally a ham, or know that your students prefer you to be serious and scholarly. Caught'yas will succeed in your classroom if *you* are at all enthusiastic about them and about the subsequent improvement in your students' writing. If it is not your style to cavort around the room, or if your students are in that stage of being too sophisticated to be silly, your being serious as you go around the room will work just as well. All of us want feedback, and high school students are no exception. You simply have to modify the method to fit *your* personality and *your* students' likes and dislikes.

Remember, many teachers have used the Caught'ya method with great success, and all have different personalities. No two teachers present the Caught'yas in exactly the same way.

The Caught'ya is perfect for a daily mini-skill lesson before getting into the literature or writing for the rest of the period. You can modify the daily sentences very easily to include more examples of the errors you note in students' writing. The most important elements of the method are humor, enthusiasm, and the class discussion about the "why" of each correction. I have reduced the method of implementing a Caught'ya to ten easy steps.

Ten easy steps to a successful Caught'ya

> 1. Outline your own plot or choose a story from this book.
> 2. Decide on skills and vocabulary words you want to be sure to include and choose one of the following:
>   a. Compose your own sentences,
>   b. use the sentences already written in Chapters 4, 5, and 6 of this book, or
>   c. change the sentences in Chapters 4, 5, and 6 of this book to suit the particular skill needs of your students.
> 3. Write sentence(s) incorrectly on the board or overhead.
> 4. Read the sentence(s) dramatically; review the vocabulary word; warn of a difficult skill; ask students to identify parts of speech; or challenge students to find a literary device.
> 5. Students then write the Caught'ya as correctly as they can.
> 6. Walk around the room, commenting on each student's effort.
> 7. Go to the board or overhead and check the Caught'ya with the class, eliciting answers from students.
> 8. Students mark mistakes with proofreading symbols and take notes.
> 9. Students count and indicate the number of errors.
> 10. Collect one paper per student after five Caught'yas have been completed and grade only one Caught'ya per paper, noting the errors still missed so that the skills can be repeated in subsequent Caught'yas.

Step 1 **Choose a story from this book (or write your own).**

Assuming that you choose one of the tales in this book, I advise you to consult with your fellow English teachers at your high school to make certain you divvy up the stories by grade level. All three stories are equally appropriate for grades nine, ten, eleven, and twelve because the skills do not change with the grade level. Ninth-grade teachers may want to take a look at "Romeo and Juliet, Revisited and Revised," in *Caught'ya! Grammar with a Giggle* since many school systems require reading that Shakespeare story that year.

Once you choose a story, skim the sentences to see how they differ from Shakespeare's. At the beginning of each chapter of Caught'yas, I have included the entire story that has been broken out into daily Caught'ya sentences in the rest of that chapter. If it has been several years since you read the actual play, a quick review of it wouldn't hurt. This should help your students as well because sometimes Shakespeare's convoluted, soap-opera-type plots can be difficult to follow. It wouldn't hurt either to show the movie. Hollywood conveniently has produced recent, excellent versions of each of the three plays used in this book.

Decide on skills and vocabulary words you want to be sure to include and do one of the following: a) Compose your own sentences, b) use the sentences already written in Chapters 2, 3, and 4, or c) change these sentences to suit the particular skill needs of your students.

Step 2

At the beginning of each story, I have included a list of the vocabulary words in the order they appear in the Caught'ya sentences. The ones taken directly from Shakespeare are marked with a small heart (❤). Also listed are the literary devices and writing conventions used therein, arranged alphabetically. You will find at the left of each sentence all the skills used as the story unfolds. These pre-made sentences are generic and are designed for the average to slightly above-average high school student. If you teach advanced placement, high-honors, or basic-skills classes, you may want to make the sentences more or less difficult according to the needs of your students.

Changing the existing sentences or composing a few more of your own is easy. Check your students' writing efforts to see which skills need more practice. For example, let's say your advanced placement students need more work in the use of satire or more practice in the avoidance of dangling modifiers. Keeping loosely to Shakespeare's plot, simply add to the story a few sentences that demonstrate satire for your students or that dangle a modifier for them to correct.

On the other hand, students in basic-skills classes may need to keep working on the nine comma rules or the use of similes. You can simplify the existing sentences to use with your students. You also could add some sentences to give your students more practice in the basics. There are 120 to 124 sentences per story so that you can add some of your own after you determine the skills students need to practice.

Remember, however, that if you write your own sentences, you need to insert a vocabulary word in each sentence. The difficulty of the word doesn't matter. Just write the sentence and then find a good place in that sentence to substitute a more sophisticated word. One of those little electronic thesauruses is perfect for finding delicious synonyms.

Write sentence(s) incorrectly on the board or overhead.

Step 3

Personally, I dislike using any audio-visual device of any kind, even one as simple as an overhead. The cord trips you, the bulb burns out just as your most difficult class enters the room, and the squirt bottle (or else you have to use spit) is a tempting weapon for students to use on each other. Even more importantly, the uncorrected sentence needs to be written on the transparency in permanent marker so that you can use an erasable overhead marker when you correct the sentence and not erase the uncorrected sentence needed for the next period. Once written in permanent marker, the sentences cannot be changed to play with verb tense or to add another phrase with a comma or two. Thus, they no longer can be individualized for each group of students.

Once I used the same story and same daily sentences with a basic-skills class and with an advanced class. I wrote the daily Caught'ya on the blackboard and changed it slightly before each period, depending on the class about to enter. When you use the overhead, you lose this flexibility. On the other hand, you do have the sentences already copied for subsequent years and time for a few more sips of coffee and deep breaths before the bell rings for the next period. The choice (and dilemma) is yours.

When you put the sentences on the board or overhead (Use the sentences in Chapters 4, 5, or 6 that are marked "B" for board.), list beside them, or on the board somewhere, what you want your students to do with the sentence(s). At first, you may ask them only to correct it. The second grading period, you may require that they also indicate the reasons for each correction. You may want your students to write down the literary device (if any) in the sentence. You may even require that they change the sentence to *add* a certain literary device. Students could be asked to write a synonym or two for one or more of the words or to define the vocabulary word. What do *your* students need to practice?

Teaching note:

*At the lower grade levels it is always the teacher who directs all ten steps. At the high school level, however, some teachers have found it extremely effective to assign each student a Caught'ya or two and make it his or her responsibility to teach **Steps 4 through 10**. Students must prepare lesson plans and notes beforehand and then teach the assigned Caught'ya(s) on the appointed day(s). Teachers simply make copies of the assigned Caught'yas and the **Ten Easy Steps** to aid their students in their task.*

Of course, you cannot begin doing this until after you yourself have modeled teaching the Caught'ya for at least a month, showing your students some of the effective techniques of teaching a Caught'ya. When they are involved in their own learning process, students learn more and buy into it.

As an alternative to using individual students to teach only one Caught'ya sentence each, you could assign a small group of students (a response group?) to teach a week's worth of Caught'ya sentences. In this way, each student in the group must learn many skills really well in order to explain and teach them to his or her peers. Working in groups helps the weaker students and makes it easier for the shyer ones to stand in front of the class. This method of instruction involves your students in the evaluative process as well and has the added attraction of freeing you from grading the Caught'yas.

Step 4 **Read the sentences dramatically; review the vocabulary word; warn of a difficult skill; ask students to identify parts of speech; or challenge them to find a literary device.**

This is where it is especially important to challenge your students to correct the sentences. Dare them, make bets with them, do whatever it takes to intrigue your students enough to work hard to correct the sentences, find the literary device, and learn the vocabulary word(s) well enough to recall them when writing their own compositions.

It is a good idea to read the sentences dramatically, review what happened previously in the story (for those who have been absent), elicit the meaning of the vocabulary word in a way that will make your students remember it for more than five minutes (or make someone look it up for the class), and warn of any difficult skill that is included. A discussion of "to paragraph or not to paragraph" might be in order if you teach "regular" or below-level students.

Teaching note: ....

This year my students are keeping "Vocabulary Notebooks" in a spiral notebook. As they complete each Caught'ya, they write the vocabulary words, their meaning, and the part of speech. Students find these notebooks very useful when writing.

Students write the Caught'ya as correctly as they can.

Step 5

After you or one of your pupils instructs your students to write the Caught'ya on their own papers as correctly as they can, you should see them hard at work. First students should indicate the day of the week (to practice spelling) and the number of the Caught'ya above it. Encourage students to read and reread the sentences as they do when they edit and proofread their own papers to try to catch all the errors.

I have found that regular students like to know how many errors are in the Caught'ya sentences. They maintain that it helps them find the errors. I sometimes oblige them for a few weeks; however, I never seem to count correctly, and it only frustrates the perfectionists.

In contrast, the students in my honors classes become nervous when they know the number of errors they should find in a sentence. These high achievers become upset if they cannot find the total number of necessary corrections. I have learned from painful experience to forgo an error count for these students, no matter how earnestly they plead.

I suggest again that, during the second half of the year, your students should be capable of identifying the reason behind each correction in the margin of the paper. This extra requirement would help cement the skill. If students know *why* they need to put a comma in a compound sentence, for example, and write the rule that applies, there is a better chance they will remember that rule as they write their own compositions.

The basic technique asks students to correct the sentence and list any literary device or writing convention used. In addition, you could require your students either to list the parts of speech of each word or phrase or to diagram some of the sentences. As both a French teacher and an English teacher, I know well the necessity of teaching students the eight parts of speech. Some may scoff at diagramming sentences, but in my experience I have found that it helps students to visualize the form of the sentence. Diagramming appears to make the parts of a sentence (especially the modifiers) clearer, and the punctuation and parts of speech then make more sense. I do not suggest diagramming every Caught'ya sentence. This would get onerous for your students. One every week or two would suffice to keep them in practice and to help their visualization.

Walk around the room, commenting on each student's effort.

Step 6

As students write the corrected Caught'ya, you or the pupil(s) assigned to that day's Caught'ya, walk around to each student to tease, issue a challenge, goad a student good-naturedly, offer individual encouragement, or provide a ten-second mini-lesson. Time yourself very carefully. You do not want to spend more than five minutes doing this. After practice, you will find it takes about four minutes to circulate around a class of thirty-five students. There is, however, a trick to this -- several tricks in fact.

If your classes are large, as is usually the case in high school, you will see only part of a Caught'ya sentence in the first papers you examine. You cannot wait until all your students have completed the sentence to begin circulating around the many desks, or you will have pandemonium and boredom on your hands (not to mention wasted time). Simply glance at the first few and praise those who have not yet made errors. Then, as students' sentences are more and more complete, look for only *one* error.

Choose the most difficult correction in the sentence so that many of your students probably will miss it at first glance. If that error still exists in a student's paper, tease quickly (I say, "Caught'ya.") and move on. If, on the other hand, a student has found and corrected the targeted error, take a few more seconds to check the rest of the sentence. In this way, you can move very quickly around the room. I sometimes hum a tune (one at least twenty years old) as I circulate, stopping only occasionally to praise a student whose Caught'ya has no errors. My students especially hate my hummed rendition of "She'll Be Coming Round the Mountain."

It is a good idea to time yourself for the first few weeks or so to ensure that you don't spend too much time with this step. Of course, when individual students teach the Caught'ya sentences, you can help them by taking half of the room. With groups of students teaching the Caught'ya, obviously there is no problem since there are fewer student papers for each individual to examine.

Another trick that works especially well is to ask students on whose papers you find no errors to join you in checking their peers' work. Assign each student a row or a table, depending on how your room is arranged. In this way, the number of checkers increases as you move around the room, sort of like a chain letter.

One important point, however, that you must keep in mind is to vary where you begin checking the papers. I start at the right side of the room for even-numbered Caught'yas and the left side of the room for odd-numbered ones. This keeps me straight and the feedback fair considering that the first few I check never have the sentence completed.

It is also a good idea to have the day's assignment posted so that as students finish correcting the Caught'ya sentence, they can put it aside for a few minutes and begin writing or reading until you make it around the entire classroom. If you have a particularly rowdy or large class, give feedback to only half of the class each day, again varying the side so that each student gets feedback once every two days.

In my experience, however, students dislike this practice and will find something constructive to do so that I can complete my rounds of the class every day. Of course, my current students are gifted eighth graders who, though very bright, still are young enough to fall into line with the old ploy: "I like the way John is working quietly..." Students at the upper levels are less malleable.

Step 7   Go to the board or overhead and check the Caught'ya with the class, eliciting answers from students.

After the students have written the Caught'ya sentence as correctly as they can and noted the literary device (if any) in the sentences, and after you and/or some of your students have given them feedback, return to the blackboard or overhead and elicit the corrections from the class.

As students point out each correction, make the appropriate proofreading symbols on the board or overhead and review the *why* of each correction. If a mini-lesson is in order, give one. To the left of each sentence in **Chapters 4, 5 and 6** of this book, you will find the "why" listed for each correction. If a plethora of your students missed a certain skill (for example mixing up "lay" and "laid") you can launch into more explanation.

A few suggestions on how to teach some of the hard-to-teach points with humor, as well as simple-to-understand explanations and examples that you can use to supplement your own, can be found in the **Appendix** of this book. Many more suggestions, all classroom tested, can be found in Chapter 4 "Mini-lessons" in the book *Caught'ya Again! More Grammar with a Giggle.*

Since I teach eighth grade, I hear about my former students from colleagues at the high school. They tell me my students know things like subordinate clauses and how to recognize them and correctly punctuate them, but they ask me if I have to inject learning devices such as the renaming of the subordinating conjunctions "white bus words" to fit the acronym. And why, they ask, do we have to sing the helping verbs? Why? It's a very effective way to learn and helps students retain the information for many years!

It is always a good idea to use something different (especially humor) in your explanations. For example, I teach the difference between "lie" and "lay" by giving the usual spiel about transitive and intransitive verbs, complete with writing charts on the blackboard. I end my explanation by informing my fourteen-year-old students (who have sex on the brain, not correct English) that in the past tense, "Something has to get *laid.*" They titter, think about it for a moment, and then I see the comprehension begin to light up their faces. The difference between transitive and intransitive verbs suddenly becomes clear to them. They still have sex on the brain, but the next time in their writing, they might use the correct form of the verb and even smile as they do it.

I use mnemonic devices that sometimes annoy the teachers who inherit my students in subsequent years. I teach French as well as English, and I find that students learn faster with mnemonics and songs. (In French classes, we sing a different ditty for each irregular verb - "Row Row Row Your Boat," "Frère Jacques," "Jingle Bells," etc.) Sally Larson, a wonderfully inventive eighth-grade English teacher, pointed out to me that the main subordinating conjunctions can fit into the mnemonic "a white bus." My students memorize them that way and, once memorized, the conjunctions can be remembered, used more easily, and punctuated correctly in papers. Think about it: **A** after, although, as; **W** when, while, where; **H** how; **I** if; **T** than; **E** even though; **B** because, before; **U** until, unless; **S** since, so that.

I am sure you already use all kinds of similar techniques to wrest your students' attention from their bodies and friends to teach them English. (I was told by one teacher that he has students sing an opera of the irregular verbs!) This is the **Step** where you put such innovative ideas to good use. Because of the Caught'ya, you already should have their attention. My only advice (which comes from painful experience) is to keep it bizarre, funny, and *short.* Teach no more than one point a day and keep it to fewer than two minutes, even in your most advanced classes. Absorbing correct English usage, mechanics, and grammar must be done in short but intense bursts if retention and carry-over are to take place.

Repetition is the key. Keep on plugging, a little bit each day, and keep on repeating *ad nauseam* until your students get the point and, most importantly, begin to use it correctly in their writing. I think that the much used quote about "All's fair in love and war" should be amended to say, "All's fair in love, war, and the teaching of English to teenagers."

If you choose to let students teach the Caught'yas, it is a good idea to require lesson plans to be sure that the youthful "teachers" understand the points they are trying to get across to their peers. You always can step in and reteach a skill yourself on the days you direct the proceedings. Challenge students to come up with a weird and different way to teach the skills assigned. They can be very inventive!

Step 8 Students mark mistakes with proofreading symbols and take notes.

As you (or one of your students) go over the Caught'ya sentence at the board or overhead, students, if they have not already done so, should note by their Caught'ya sentences the reason for each correction. They also should use proofreading symbols to correct any error they did not catch on their own. Encourage them to mark the corrections with a colored pencil, pen, or marker of a different hue from the one with which they wrote the sentences. Thus, they easily can study the errors they did not catch so they do not miss them in future Caught'yas, in their writing, or on future Caught'ya tests.

Since I mentioned them, I'd better explain about Caught'ya tests. At the end of each story in **Chapters 4, 5, and 6**, I have included a final exam. I use the same exam as a pretest at the beginning of the year to see where my students stand.

It is also a good idea to give at least half a dozen Caught'ya mini-tests each semester. This is very easy. Simply use the next uncorrected Caught'ya (or several of them) as a test or, better yet, write a new uncorrected sentence that includes many of the skills that you and the Caught'yas have taught up to that point. In each story, I have noted which sentences would be appropriate for use in a mid-term test.

In all three stories, I covered all nine comma rules within the first fifteen Caught'yas. At this point a quickie quiz of most of them would be appropriate. (The comma rules, by the way, will be repeated constantly in subsequent sentences.) These one-to-five-sentence tests can be graded as harshly or easily as you wish. One ninth-grade teacher I know grades the tests of her high-honors class with a hundred, a fifty, or a zero. The students hate this, but it gets their attention.

Listed below are a few of the most commonly used proofreading symbols.

Indent	¶	take out indent	¶
add words here	∧	take out, delete	ℓ
capitalize	≡	make a small letter	A̸
move word	→	reverse order	and he
add punctuation (whatever is inside circle)	◯		

Step 9 Students count and indicate number of errors.

Students count the number of errors they did not catch when they attempted to correct the sentence on their own. They indicate the number in the right-hand margin. This process has two advantages. It makes students leave a good, healthy, right-hand margin, and it provides them with immediate feedback. Remind students to make all notations in a color different from the one they used to write the sentence itself. This study technique makes it easier to see where they need to concentrate.

Encourage, cajole, forbid, threaten, or do anything you can think of to keep your students honest. Since the grade they receive on the Caught'ya has nothing to do with the number of errors they made when they attempted to write the sentence on their own, it would be pointless to try to hide errors and correct them surreptitiously while the answers are divulged. Moreover, cheating only would hinder a student from learning from his/her mistakes.

What finally worked with my students (even the perfectionists) was to warn in an ominous tone that anyone who *never* (or rarely) missed anything on the Caught'yas also had to earn an "A+" on all the Caught'ya tests I planned to give that year. Since no student ever makes a perfect score on the pretest that they take at the beginning of the year, my students heed the warning.

Collect one paper per student after five Caught'yas have been completed and grade only one Caught'ya per paper, noting the errors still missed so that the skills can be repeated in subsequent Caught'yas.

Step 10

It is a good idea at the high school level to require that five Caught'ya sentences be kept on one sheet of paper. This helps your students organize themselves and hang onto a paper they use daily. It also helps you because you have only one sheet to grade per student.

The paper should have the heading you usually require (name, period, date) and a title. I require the latter to accustom my students to writing a title with correct capitalization and without quotations or underlining. A two- or three-word title works best for this purpose. My students use the title, "Caught'ya Sentences #_____ - _____," but I'd like to have a preposition in there somewhere for practice in not capitalizing. How about using the title of the Caught'ya story?

Students who have been absent should simply write the day(s) of the week they missed and write the word "absent" underneath. Since there are no student texts for this method, it is difficult for students to make up missed Caught'yas. One teacher I know, however, does require that students make up missed Caught'yas by copying from a peer's paper. She exhorts her students to be careful. Any error the peer missed also counts against the copying student.

Refer to the quick-reference lesson plan on the following page (without the extra comments) to use as you (or your students) teach the basic Caught'ya lesson. It won't be long, though, until you (and your students) no longer need it.

Lesson plan for the Caught'ya

This plan assumes that you already have completed Steps 1 and 2.

✎ Before school, write the sentence(s) for the day on the board, box the vocabulary word, and beside it or on the board, list what you want students to do with it. (Sample directions: correct; put the reasons and correct; diagram; list literary devices; put meaning and a synonym or two for the vocabulary word(s); rewrite to include something; list parts of speech; etc.)

✎ When the bell rings, read the sentence to the class with a dramatic flair, reviewing the story thus far, eliciting the meaning of the vocabulary word (if you choose), and discussing the need for a paragraph if you feel your students still need to be walked through this debate.

✎ Instruct students to copy the sentence as correctly as they can and follow the required guidelines you listed on the board. Students may wish to keep a "Vocabulary Notebook" with the vocabulary words they do not know.

✎ Walk around the room, giving students individual feedback. Say "Caught'ya" or something comparable if you catch a student with an error. Praise or challenge a student who has caught all of the errors up to the moment you glance at his/her paper.

✎ Go back to the blackboard or overhead and check the Caught'ya sentence out loud with your class. Elicit answers from the students. Be sure to discuss the reason for each correction. Use the **Appendix** at the back of this book for simple explanations and other examples. Using proofreading symbols and a pen of a different hue, correct the Caught'ya on the board or overhead as your students do the same with any error they did not catch. Remind students to take notes.

✎ Discuss the literary device in the sentence and conduct a mini-lesson in whatever skill you think needs more reinforcement. Keep it short!

✎ Instruct students to be sure that they put the day of the week and the number of the Caught'ya right above the sentence and to count their errors and indicate them in the right-hand margin.

✎ Collect five corrected Caught'yas and grade one Caught'ya to keep students honest.

Three steps to evaluate the Caught'ya

Introduction

Evaluating the Caught'ya is just as important as the process of doing one. The Caught'ya is designed to eliminate the feeling of failure and to foster success in language arts for "regular" and below-level students and to challenge high-honors students to new heights. We English teachers need to change the image of English classes. We need to improve the PR for our subject. The evaluation of the Caught'yas can help!

The most important thing to remember about evaluating the Caught'yas is that the sentences are *not* graded on how well a student initially grasps the English language when he/she corrects the sentence on his/her own but on how carefully that student corrects the sentence when you and the class review the Caught'ya at the blackboard or overhead.

A student can make one or twenty errors in any Caught'ya and still earn an "A" *if* that student has caught all of those errors and corrected them, complete with notes as to the reason or rule for each correction. This is the secret. You are only grading the Caught'yas to spark your students to pay close attention when you do the Caught'yas and to keep them honest. Evaluation of students' progress can be made through frequent, short Caught'ya tests.

The title of this book promises you "grammar with a giggle." Well, get ready to have a giggle yourself! A week's worth of Caught'yas takes only ten minutes a week to grade for a class of thirty-five students. Those of you who, like me, teach public school will have up to 180 Caught'ya papers a week to grade. The following three steps reduce the grading time for those 180 students to fewer than fifty minutes each week! I promise.

This grading requires that your students follow a certain format. Insist that your students put five Caught'ya sentences on one sheet of paper to reduce your paper shuffling time. *You* have to decide on the format that you like and insist on it. You probably will want to include the following:

✎ Student's full name

✎ Full date written out underneath the name for subtle spelling practice (February)

✎ A two- or three-word title for capitalization practice

✎ A fairly even margin on the left and a margin that leaves space on the right where the number of errors missed should be indicated

✎ Use of different colored ink for corrections, clearly marked so that you (and the student when he/she studies it) can tell at a glance what has been missed and then corrected by the student.

✎ Notes alongside many of the corrections that clearly indicate the reasons or rule for the correction

Now get out your green and purple pens. You are ready to grade the Caught'yas. The following three steps assume that you have a paper in front of you. If you do not, look at the sample paper at the end of this section and use it for clarification as you note the steps.

Step 1 — Check the format

Glance at the paper to see if the student has faithfully followed the format you require. Except for uneven margins, which are worth five points each, and the failure to use a different color, which should not count against a student, each error in the format deducts ten points. This may seem harsh, but it encourages students to be careful.

- ✎ Name written out and capitalized (10)

- ✎ Date written out correctly with month spelled out correctly (10)

- ✎ Title correctly spelled and capitalized (10)

- ✎ Number of uncaught errors indicated and circled to the right of each Caught'ya (10)

- ✎ All five Caught'yas on the same sheet of paper (10)

- ✎ Margins large enough and an even left margin (5 each margin)

Mark all errors clearly in a pen that is a color different from the two hues your student used. It is always helpful to keep an array of colors handy as you grade. Because of arthritis, I like to use those big "Crayola" markers. A box of them provides eight colors.

Step 2 — Check the content of one Caught'ya sentence.

Choose one of the week's Caught'ya sentences. This is what really saves you time. I assure you that if you read all of the sentences each week for each of your students, the final grade would be about the same (if you take off only three to five per error instead of ten).

For six years I graded every sentence of every student every week, but it got to be such a chore that I grew to dread the weekends. I struggled to keep positive about the Caught'yas because my students really were learning. Then I noticed that if I increased the number of points per error to ten and graded only one Caught'ya per student per week, the grade almost always came out the same. The careless students were consistently careless, and the careful students continued to be careful. In fact, some of the careless students (perhaps because I was taking off more points per error) became more careful.

When Carol Harrell, a colleague who used Caught'yas, independently came to the same conclusion, we talked it over, pooled our collective guilt at not reading every sentence, and chucked it out our classroom doors with glee at the extra hours per week we were giving ourselves.

Do not tell students which Caught'ya sentence you plan to grade. This makes them careful with all of the sentences. Do not always choose the most difficult sentence. In this way you will keep your students always hopping.

Another important point is that you can individualize the evaluation of the Caught'yas, grading an easier one for your slower students or classes. Remember, you want to *encourage* your students to like editing and to think of it as a fun game rather than an onerous, teacher-imposed chore only to be done when pressed. You *want* your students to receive high grades on the Caught'yas. By the way, you will find that the test scores on the mini-Caught'ya tests also rise as students feel better about English and editing.

After you choose the Caught'ya you wish to grade for the week, focus on it. Ask yourself the following questions. Each "No" answer deducts ten points from the score.

✎ Did the student clearly mark the errors with the proof-reading symbols you want him/her to use?

✎ Did the student take notes as to the reasons for the corrections?

✎ Did the student catch every error? These are worth ten points each.

✎ Is the number of errors indicated in the right-hand margin?

✎ Are all the words (including vocabulary word) spelled correctly? Take ten points off per word misspelled.

✎ Is the sentence copied correctly from the board or overhead?

✎ Have any words been left out?

✎ Are there any extraneous capital letters?

Take ten points off for each error you find that has not been marked by the student or does not have the correction written above it. Each tiny error is worth ten points. After all, you gave them all the answers! You will be pleasantly surprised at the results. Even your poorest student can earn an "A + ." In fact, I find that my "regular" and basic-skills students often earn higher grades than my honors students. Although they may miss more the first time around, "regular" and basic-skills students are more careful about checking each sentence. They tend to be less cock-sure than the honors, high-honors, and advanced-placement students, and the chance to earn an easy "A + " on a paper in language arts is exciting to them.

After you have added the number of points lost for errors in the format of the entire paper to the points lost for errors not caught in the one Caught'ya you checked, subtract the total from one hundred. Put that grade at the top of the student's paper with an encouraging or positive comment. Since you grade only one sentence per week per student, you have the luxury of making a brief, private comment on each paper. This is especially important in "regular" and basic-skills classes.

Take notes. Give rewards.

Step 3

As you grade the Caught'yas, it is important that you take notes somewhere. I like to use the big calendar blotter on my desk because it is always handy and because I never lose it as I do a piece of paper. A small spiral notebook also works well. I note errors frequently missed by students. In this way, I can concentrate on the errors they still make and not harp on already-mastered skills. I also make a weekly check on common English errors made by my students.

Each year different errors repeat themselves. Two years ago I struggled all year with improper verb tenses. This past year students rarely made verb tense errors in the Caught'yas and did not do so in their writing after about November, but they had a terrible time with pronouns! I wonder what it will be next year.

One of the reasons the Caught'ya system is so successful and popular with students is that it makes them feel good about themselves. There is always something positive you can say (no student will miss every error). Public displays of success are more important at the lower grade levels. At the high school level, the grade or the comment itself usually suffices. If, however, you teach a basic-skills class, your students will need added reinforcement.

Teachers of students with learning or behavioral problems (the two are usually linked) have told me repeatedly how well the Caught'ya technique works with their students because this is one of the few areas in which they can experience success. These teachers play up the reward system to the hilt to capitalize on that feeling of success.

After trying other less successful methods of publicizing student success, I experimented with a Caught'ya lottery in my classroom. This did the trick. It was little work for me, and my students loved it. The lottery is simple. When you pass back the Caught'ya papers, give 1/4 of a 3 x 5 card to each student who earned an "A + " on his/her paper. Announce the "A + " students publicly with a challenge, a grin, or some comment designed to bring notice to the student to be rewarded.

The students who receive a card write their own names, date, and class period on the card. Rather than just collecting the cards, make each "A + " student walk to the front of the classroom in full view of the rest of the class. Relishing the moment of public recognition, the student deposits the card in a box. Once a month open the box and draw out one card from each class. Those students receive a prize: a candy bar, a lunch period in your room with three friends, a coupon for something, etc.

An example of a corrected paper follows. The teacher's marks and comments are indicated by dark black lines. The sentences are from the story in **Chapter 4** of this book. Note that there is one format error.

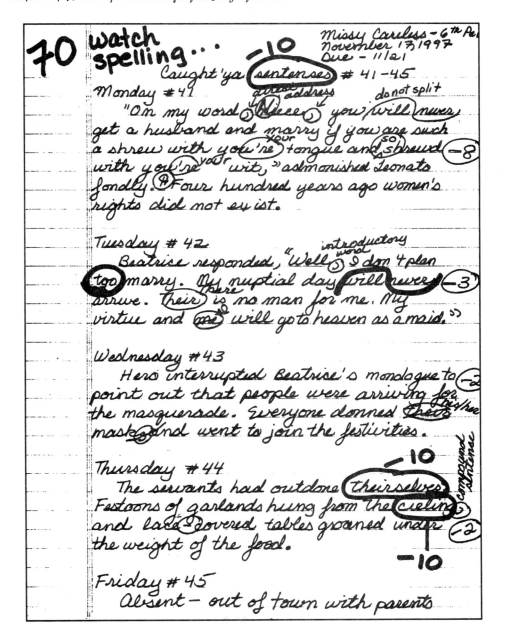

A sample Caught'ya paper. The thick dark marks are the teacher's.

Notes:

1. Format -10 (Missy did not capitalize the "s" in "Sentences" in the title and misspelled it as well.)

2. The teacher checked Thursday's Caught'ya and marked -20 for the two errors in spelling that Missy did not catch.

3. Although Missy also misspelled "to" in Caught'ya #4 and left the verb split, it does not count against her because the teacher only grades one Caught'ya per week.

4. Note that when Missy was absent, she did not have to complete the Caught'ya.

Important notes and advice about using these particular Caught'yas with your students

What is included in this chapter

How to adjust Caught'yas for your students' needs

"**B**" designates the suggested uncorrected sentences to put on the board. "**C**" indicates the corrected sentences on which to base your discussion. As I stated earlier, feel free to modify these sentences to fit the needs of your class. Ninth-grade teachers of "regular" or basic-skills English may wish to simplify some of the Caught'yas, making them shorter and less complex. Conversely, teachers of honors, high-honors, or advanced-placement English at the twelfth-grade level may want to make the sentences more sophisticated by adding clauses and phrases.

Make it easier. Make it harder. Split a long Caught'ya to make it two shorter ones. Put back in some of the hyphens (or commas, etc.) if you wish. Change the verb tense to keep your students on their toes. Misspell a word. Misplace a modifier. Play with a homophone. Only *you* know what your students need to learn and how much they are capable of learning.

I do need to add a word of caution here that comes from experience. If you do put back in some of the punctuation, either always make it correct or vary between making it correct and making it incorrect in a random fashion. One year I sometimes inserted extraneous commas and apostrophes in the Caught'yas. My students quickly figured out that if any punctuation was in the Caught'ya, then it was wrong.

Please note that I have reduced each modernized and slightly revised tale of Shakespeare's to 120 or 124 Caught'yas, enough for four per week for an entire year. However, if you plan to do a Caught'ya every day (which many teachers do), you'll need to add more sentences. If you want to do them less frequently, combine Caught'yas or skip some, simply reading them to your students for story continuity. The second half of the year, my students and I like to write one Caught'ya and then do a second orally, completing two in one day.

It is relatively easy to add more sentences at certain spots in the story. Get out your Shakespeare and add to a conversation or flesh out the story with more detail. In this manner, you can provide your students with more practice in the skills *they* need. Consult your students' writing to determine which skills need more repetition for mastery and carryover into their own work. It is a good idea to keep track of the errors they still are consistently making in their writing.

What is included

Grammar, mechanics, and usage

Almost all of the skills that your traditional grammar book teaches have been included in these Caught'yas. The only skills not covered are common abbreviations (like the states), analogies, bibliographical forms, business letters, footnotes, and writing in dialect. It was impossible to include these skills because Shakespeare's stories take place in the late sixteenth and early seventeenth centuries. You can, however, cover these few skills in a couple of short lessons, taught immediately after the Caught'yas. Skills such as diagramming can be taught by using a Caught'ya sentence as a base.

Format, vocabulary

In almost every Caught'ya, students are required to capitalize the first letter of each sentence, capitalize proper nouns, and supply end punctuation. Therefore, these skills are not listed each time to the left of the sentences.

There are usually several vocabulary words in each Caught'ya, and many are repeated throughout the story in subsequent Caught'yas. Sometimes I changed the form or the spelling of an original Shakespearean term ("earthlier" to "earthy," for example) to the modern version. You might want to give extra credit for the correct use of these vocabulary words in students' subsequent writing efforts. Ask them to box the vocabulary words during their final editing session (so you can see them more easily). If they are correctly used, add a few points to the total score; if incorrectly used, deduct a few points.

Listed skills, teaching suggestions, notes, tests, etc.

Periodically, I have made suggestions about how to teach a particular skill. These are located either to the left of each Caught'ya, mixed in with the reasons for each error in that Caught'ya, or in between Caught'yas. I tried, for example, to pick auspicious points in the story to teach various things (such as subordinating conjunctions and subordinate clauses) and to make suggestions accordingly. In addition, you will notice the ➡ **SUGGESTION** signs scattered throughout the Caught'yas. These also offer ideas for teaching and reviewing various skills. For example, periodically, when the previous Caught'ya embodies all eight parts of speech, I suggest reviewing them and their respective functions

The suggested final exam uses many of the skills and wraps up the story. The frequent informal Caught'ya tests evaluate students' progress officially. Unofficially, you will have the improvements in their writing.

A word of caution, a bit of advice, and a request

Words of caution

It is important to keep in mind that English rules are not always hard and fast! In fact, many of the rules of English are debatable. I, for example, always put the comma before the "and" in a series of three or more. Others do not. Some paragraphing is personal as, for example, in a long introduction to a quote. Optional commas after introductory adverbs abound.

In other words, do not spend one single anguished moment if you disagree with me when I give the reasons to the left of the Caught'ya sentences. You almost always can find a source that agrees with your position. I remember being in a room of English teachers debating something as simple as writing numbers: should we use words only up to ten, up to one hundred, or as far as one hundred twenty-one? Where does the use of digits begin? Each of us pulled out a trusty grammar book to support our argument. All of the sources gave a different number. We compromised although someone suggested flipping a coin.

My mother and I have debated fiercely for more than twenty-five years about splitting verbs with the adverb. (I would have preferred to have phrased it: "My mother and I have fiercely debated.") She is *technically* correct ("*technically* is correct??"), but common usage has changed the order so that it sounds wrong and somewhat awkward.

Another debatable point is the use of conjunctions to begin sentences. Technically, this is frowned upon, but all modern authors (this one included) begin sentences with "and," "but," "so," "yet," "for," and "or" for effect. I tell my students not to do so since they are learners and, therefore, are not yet ready to take such liberties. Since a number of my students still begin every sentence with "and," "so," or "but," my goal is to inhibit this practice. About January, if a student is a proficient writer, I allow judicious use of conjunctions to begin sentences.

Similarly, I try to limit the practice of ending a sentence with a preposition, but I do recall Winston Churchill's famous comment, "That is something up with which I will not put!" Obviously, we do not need to carry this rule to unreasonable lengths.

And, then we arrive at pronouns. Does one use subject or object with verbs of being? "*It is he*" is correct, but how many of us say that correctly? "Does everyone have *his or her* paper?" sounds so awkward, but it is correct. "Their" refers to plural nouns or pronouns and "everyone" is singular. "That" should never refer to people, but the news media ignore this rule all the time. (The local newspaper in Gainesville, Florida, seems to have abandoned the use of "whom.") I rest my case.

I read in a current grammar book (the one in my classroom that sits unused except as a reference) that "slow" and "fast" could be adverbs! They cited common usage as the reason why this was now allowed. Being somewhat old-fashioned, neither my colleagues nor I agree with that book, so we ignore this latest rule. In other words, use the rules with which you and your colleagues feel comfortable as long as you are consistent. It is important to be consistent within a school so that students do not get confused.

Three pieces of advice

1) Show the Shakespearean movie to your students early in October after you have titillated their interest in the story. Hollywood and the BBC have produced some excellent versions of all three of the plays used in this book. After watching the movie, students will recognize the direct quotes from Shakespeare as they appear in the Caught'yas, and, more importantly, they will not have any difficulty understanding the plot. Since, in Caught'yas, the plot is only revealed a few sentences a day, comprehension of the entire story line can be a problem. The movie, indeed, heightened my students' interest in the Caught'yas and even sparked some of them to read the play on their own.

2) Since you explain the "why" of all the corrections when you review the Caught'ya, you don't want to go beyond what your particular students can learn. By using the fundamental eight parts of speech, you easily can explain all the essential grammar and usage without using the more technical terms and "turning off" students. This tool is especially useful in teaching "regular" and basic-skills classes. For example, you can explain a participial phrase by identifying it as a phrase that has a verb in it that is used as an adjective. Follow that up with more examples to illustrate the use of commas to set off the phrase. Elicit more samples from students.

You also need to keep in mind that the end result is not to learn the terms, but to write correctly. Who cares if some time in the future your students can recognize and label subordinate clauses? Only English teachers and professional editors need to know how to recognize participial phrases and other technical terms by name. However, everyone needs to know how to punctuate them and to position them correctly as modifiers. Future employers do care that their employees can punctuate them correctly when writing.

3) Finally, I wish to reiterate — feel free to disagree with me. I am not even the "absolute word" in my own classroom. My students and I have hot debates over paragraphing and optional comma use, for example. By the way, just so you know how far I do go in order to be comfortable with the rules — the apostrophe in Caught'ya is a contraction of the made-up word, "caughtchya."

Request

Now for the request. Even though each set of Caught'yas has been proofread carefully by many people, I know a few errors probably still lurk among the sentences and lists of skills. Please, if you spot one, especially an egregious mistake that is not debatable, write to me via the publisher, at the address listed on the copyright page.

Conclusion

After you have read this book, begin the suggested warm-up with Shakespeare's epithets that follow in **Chapter 3**. Then relax and use the Caught'ya sentences to forge a partnership with your students which will result in improved writing, increased vocabulary, and maybe a few shared laughs. Enjoy!

Chapter 3

A fun, painless activity to introduce the idea of learning grammar with Shakespeare that makes the venerable Bard less daunting.

What is included in this chapter:

Introduction

To be honest, using Shakespeare's stories for Caught'yas proved more difficult than I thought it would be. It was very tricky to include all of the skills because I was constrained by the confines of someone else's story. When I use my own, it is easy to change the story to fit the skills I need to include.

Shakespeare also is antiquated and sometimes downright insulting where today's mores are concerned. Fathers retain absolute power over their daughters. Women possess zero rights and are considered inferior in every way. People of illegitimate birth are cast-offs and villains. (Think how many illegitimate children you may have in your classroom — probably one-third.) If a girl loses her virginity, she is a harlot and is disowned and thrown out of the house. (Don't the statistics show that by eleventh grade forty percent of female students in the United States have experienced sex?)

I toned down somewhat the seventeenth-century English mores, making a bastard just a half-brother, skipping lightly over the virgin parts, and making rude narrator comments about the "machismo" attitude of the men. In truth, if you look at the originals of the stories I used in this book, you might find fertile grounds for discussions of moral values, not to mention lots of ideas for papers — comparative essays, opinion essays, what-would-you-do? papers, research papers, persuasive essays, expository essays (these last two so necessary for the Writing Assessment Test), and creative writing stories.

In addition, it was frustrating not to be able to use much of Shakespeare's beautiful language. After all, it is the language, not the often insipid plots, that makes Shakespeare's plays so wonderful: the double entendres, the word plays, the repartée. Obviously, in one hundred twenty Caught'yas that necessarily have to be kept short and which are designed to teach most of the rules of modern English, much of the original wording cannot be included. However, whenever it was possible in the quotes, I used Shakespeare's clever verbiage.

Another problem was keeping the Caught'yas interesting so that they would appeal to teenagers. The idea of the original Caught'ya books was to amuse and intrigue students while teaching them those boring skills that we all need to learn. Shakespeare's language, however delightful it is to *us* as educated adults, is 400-year-old "bat-fowling, rump-fed ratsbane" (to use Shakespeare's words) and therefore possibly not interesting or relevant to today's teenagers.

Therefore I propose intriguing your students in a way that might just get them interested in the Bard — interesting "swear" words. You could have an epithet-of-the-day on the board. You could swear frequently (at least three times a period), Shakespearean style, at your students. You could give students a list of Shakespearean insults (included after this introduction) and encourage their use. As students become comfortable with them, you even can insert the most popular ones into the Caught'yas. Play with them. Spend a day with some big dictionaries and find out what they really mean. (**Warning:** some are *really* risqué.) Make them the "in" thing with your students. You might be pleasantly surprised to hear Shakespeare instead of four-letter epithets in the halls.

I found these wonderful insults at a local production of "Much Ado about Nothing." Michael Briggs, the producer and a Shakespearean scholar, teaches Shakespeare at a local junior college. He compiled the Shakespearean "swear words" from various sources, including the Internet, and currently uses them with his own students. He tells me that his students *love* using them with their peers. The epithets take the age out of 400-year-old language and make it fun. They also set students up to enjoy Shakespeare's plays upon words.

 I had fun adding one or two insults that Michael had missed. I bet you can find more... Anyway, on the following two pages is a reproducible list of Shakespearean "swear words." Use these epithets as you will and enjoy the fun.

Shakespearean Insults

Tired of the same old swear words?
Expand your vocabulary and use these epithets.

Directions:

1) Combine one word from each of the three columns below. Preface your insult with the word "thou" as in "Thou goatish, rump-fed varlet" and feel good, for if you find out what those words really mean, you have insulted the dewberry out of someone.

2) Use these 400-year-old swear words and be able to say something really crude right in front of adults without getting into trouble. (Most people don't know the true meaning, and English teachers are so thrilled that you are using Shakespeare that they won't mind.) When you write these epithets, don't forget the comma between the two adjectives. The adjectives and nouns are listed in alphabetical order. Just mix them up for great sounding (and really rude) swear words.

Adjectives	*Adjectives*	*Nouns*
artless	base-court	apple-john
bawdy	bat-fowling	baggage
beslubbering	beef-witted	barnacle
bootless	beetle-headed	bladder
churlish	boil-brained	boar-pig
cockered	clapper-clawed	bugbear
clouted	clay-brained	bum-baily
craven	common-kissing	canker-blossom
currish	crook-pated	clack-dish
dankish	cross-gartered	clotpole
dissembling	dismal-dreaming	coxcomb
droning	dizzy-eyed	codpiece
errant	doghearted	death-token
fawning	dread-bolted	dewberry
fobbing	earth-vexing	flap-dragon
froward	elf-skinned	flax-wench
frothy	fat-kidneyed	flirt-gill
gleeking	fen-sucked	foot-licker
goatish	flap-mouthed	fustilarian
gorbellied	fly-bitten	giglet
impertinent	folly-fallen	gudgeon
infectious	fool-born	haggard
jarring	full-gorged	harpy
loggerheaded	guts-griping	hedge-pig
lumpish	half-faced	horn-beast
mammering	hasty-witted	hugger-mugger
mangled	hedge-born	jolthead
mewling	hell-hated	lewdster
pribbling	idle-headed	maggot-pie

(continued on next page)

Adjectives	*Adjectives*	*Nouns*
puking	ill-nurtured	malt-worm
puny	knotty-pated	mammet
qualing	mile-livered	measle
rank	motley-minded	minnow
reeky	onion-eyed	miscreant
roguish	plume-plucked	moldwarp
ruttish	pottle-deep	mumble-news
saucy	pox-marked	nut-hook
shrewish	reeling-ripe	pigeon-egg
spleeny	rough-hewn	pignut
spongy	rude-growing	ratsbane
surly	rump-fed	strumpet
tottering	shard-borne	tosspot
villainous	tickle-brained	varlet

—Compiled by Michael Briggs
—Adapted by Jane Bell Kiester

Now look through Shakespeare and find others. There are more where these came from!

Chapter 4

Much Ado About Everything

What is included in this chapter:

Much Ado About Everything
As told in Caught'ya sentences

Below is the story shown in its entirety (not broken up into individual Caught'yas), exactly as it appears in the corrected Caught'yas (**C**). This should give you a quick look at the complexity of the sentences, at the vocabulary (in bold), and at the skills addressed in the Caught'yas of this story so that you can see if it is appropriate for your students. You will notice, for example, that the Caught'yas for this story are a tad simpler than the Caught'yas of the other two stories.

Please note that this story has been written in the past tense instead of the historic present as many teachers of honors and advanced placement classes espouse when students write about literature. I did this for four reasons. One, this is not intended as a summary, but rather as an original story. Two, in my opinion, the story was clearer in the past tense. Three, having the story in the past tense let me use the present tense in quotes and in narrator asides and the pluperfect in references to past actions. And four, and most significant, this story is a teaching tool for grammar, mechanics, and usage, not for literary style, and all the verb tenses needed to be represented for recognition and practice.

It is assumed that your students can recognize proper nouns, common capitalizations, regular verbs, and end punctuation. Therefore, in the interests of space, these are not mentioned in the list to the left of each Caught'ya.

I suggest that you begin the year by showing the movie or reading the story on the next few pages. Because this tale is broken up into daily sentences and because Shakespeare's plots tend to be more convoluted than the most enigmatic soap opera, students need to know where the story is headed. I piloted this story with my gifted eighth graders, and they loved it. After a month of doing Caught'yas and swearing in "Shakespearean," they begged to see the movie (I, of course, acquiesced). After seeing the movie (and loving it), about a third of my students bought the book on their own and read it for pleasure! As one enthusiastic student put it, "Shakespeare rules!"

Much Ado About Everything

This is the story of a battle of the sexes, of two love affairs **fraught** with obstacles, and of **chicanery**. It's a romantic comedy set in Messina, Italy, centuries ago when men held all the power, and women were **subjugated** to their will. The convoluted soap opera of peace battles began at the end of a foiled rebellion. Don Pedro, Prince of Aragon, Spain, had just defeated his **amoral** half-brother, Don John. The latter had been the **malefactor** who had staged the rebellion. Don Pedro and two of his **gallants**, Claudio, **a stalwart stripling** from Florence, Italy, and Benedick of Padua, Italy, were returning home from the war. When they reached Messina, Italy, they were to become the guests of Leonato, the governor of Messina.

Now Leonato had a **comely** daughter who was named Hero. Not only was Hero beautiful, but she was **dulcet** and **virtuous** as well. In addition to his dulcet, virtuous daughter, Leonato also was rearing his only niece, the **witty** Beatrice. She was as **caustic** as her cousin Hero was dulcet.

On the **momentous** day when our tale **commences**, Leonato received a letter from Don Pedro's messenger. It read:

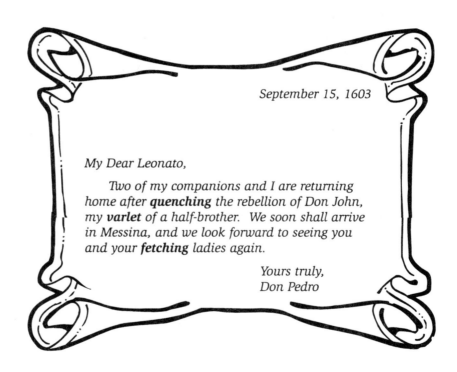

September 15, 1603

My Dear Leonato,

*Two of my companions and I are returning home after **quenching** the rebellion of Don John, my **varlet** of a half-brother. We soon shall arrive in Messina, and we look forward to seeing you and your **fetching** ladies again.*

Yours truly,
Don Pedro

In the spacious and **well-appointed** living room of his estate, Leonato read the letter to his **doting** daughter and niece.

"Is Signior Mountanto returning with him?" asked Beatrice who was trying to appear **nonchalant** as she sat on a green, high-backed couch.

"For whom are you asking, Niece?" **queried** Leonato **amiably**.

"My cousin means Signior Benedick of Padua," Hero said with a wink, a smile, and a pat for Beatrice.

The messenger who had brought the letter replied without **rancor**, "Oh, Sir Benedick returns with Don Pedro, and he is as pleasant as ever with his **barbs** and **quips**.

"How many enemies has he killed and eaten in the war? When he was last in Messina, Benedick fancied himself an **amorous** lady killer. He **feigned** love," Beatrice continued, "and challenged Cupid himself with his **disdain** for marriage."

"Ah, Beatrice, my dear, caustic niece, **bide** your tongue. He has done well for Don Pedro. He will be with us soon enough, and you can **utter** your barbs directly to Benedick himself," counseled Leonato.

"Yes, he is a good soldier, my lady, and a better friend. Sir Benedick — his bat-fowling mouth nonetheless — is a **valiant** man," replied the messenger **wryly**.

"Watch your food supply, Uncle Leonato," teased Beatrice, "for Benedick is known for his excellent stomach. In other words, he is not **frugal** with his fork."

Hero giggled at her cousin's implications but said nothing.

Leonato addressed the messenger. "You must not, Sir, mistake my niece. There is a kind of merry war going on between Signior Benedick and her. Whenever they meet, he and she have an **exemplary verbal** battle of **wits** worse than two lawyers in court."

Now, in those days of long ago, letters were slow to arrive. Soon after the messenger left Leonato's **abode**, Don Pedro and his two gallants entered the tall, stone gates of Messina. When Benedick, Don Pedro, and Claudio, the handsome, young, immature lord of Florence, Italy, arrived at Leonato's estate, Leonato invited them to stay. Benedick and Beatrice began their usual **mordacious repartée**.

"It's a good thing, Signior Leonato, that you are not Beatrice's father," said Benedick, not wasting any time in his **baiting** of Beatrice. "If your niece were your daughter, you would be in trouble. You two are too much alike."

"What? Are you observant, Sir Benedick?" **retorted** Beatrice.

"Ah, my 'Lady Disdain,' you speak," said Benedick.

"You call me 'Lady Disdain,' and yet you disdain all the ladies."

"The ladies love me — all except you, my 'loving' Beatrice."

"You love no one, you **pernicious**, unsuitable suitor."

"I wish my horse were as fast as your tongue."

"Keep quiet now, for no one is listening to you," Beatrice concluded.

Don Pedro **interjected**, "There is the sparring match. End round one! My dear Leonato, we will be staying here at least a month. These two will have **a plethora of** time to **spar** further."

While this repartée was going on, Claudio became **enraptured** by the silent Hero. The mere sight of her affected his heart. Her long black hair hung to her tiny waist, and her shy smile effected a quickening of his breathing.

As Leonato led his guests to their rooms, Claudio and Benedick **discoursed**.

"Hero is the sweetest lady I have ever seen," shy Claudio sighed.

"Everyone to his own taste," retorted Benedick sarcastically. "Well, I don't see anything in her," Benedick continued honestly, "but that cousin of hers would be comely if she were not a spitting **civet**."

"Are you casting asparagus on my feelings? Do you think my love is not complete like a half-formed wish?" babbled a frustrated Claudio.

"No, I am not casting **aspersions** on your feelings. I know that a half-warmed fish is less complete than they," Benedick **blithely** corrected his friend.

Claudio **taunted** Benedick for his views on love and marriage. Benedick warned Claudio that if he weren't careful, he would soon be a husband. Benedick then went on and on about how he would never, never fall in love nor marry. **Perdition** would freeze over before that would happen.

"Like you, my friend, I swore I'd never marry. If it were Hero who would be my wife, though, I would **succumb** to Cupid's arrows," **acceded** Claudio.

"Never in a million years!" **vociferated** Benedick. "Not I. I shall die a bachelor."

Little does the arrogant, **dogmatic**, and **cocksure** Benedick know what is in store for him! Will his wit rise to the occasion as D'Artagnan's did in <u>The Three Musketeers</u>?

Don Pedro entered the discussion and **upbraided** Benedick for his stand. "Before I die, Benedick, I predict that I shall see you a victim of Cupid's arrow." Don Pedro then offered to **woo** Hero for the timid Claudio, who was too shy to do so himself.

A servant overheard this conversation and reported it to Leonato's **venerable** older brother, Antonio. Antonio himself informed Leonato of the "news" as if he were a reporter for the <u>New York Times</u>. The only problem was that this **minion** *thought* that he heard Don Pedro say that he was going to woo the fair Hero for himself.

The plot thickens like gravy burbling on the stove. It thickens even more as the **infamous** Don John, who already had staged one rebellion against his half-brother, Don Pedro, arrived in town and lay in wait to plot nastily.

Although he had been defeated, Don John was by no means powerless. He was possessed of more **knavery** than Iago, that **arrant** villain who had preyed **nefariously** upon Othello. Accompanying Don John were his two equally **vile** associates, Borachio and Conrade. This **diabolical** trio, having heard the **fallacious** rumor concerning Don Pedro and Hero, plotted ways to break up the romance.

"If I can cross my brother in any way," said Don John with **antipathy**, "I'll do it. I'd like to get even with that **upstart** Claudio, too. He got all the glory for defeating me. It was I who should have won."

Meanwhile, at Leonato's **domicile**, Hero, Beatrice, Leonato, and his elderly brother, Antonio, were waiting for a masquerade dance to begin. Beatrice **regaled** the assembled company with her idea of the "ideal suitor."

"The perfect man (and there are fewer of them than men would like to think) would be somewhere between the grim, **churlish** Don John and the overly **presumptuous canker**, Benedick," Beatrice mused.

"Then half Signior Benedick's words in Don John's mouth and half Don John's **melancholy** in Signior Benedick's face would be your ideal mate?" teased Leonato.

"With a **virile** leg and a good foot, Uncle, and money in his pocket, too," continued Beatrice as if she had not been interrupted. "A man such as he would win any woman in the world — if he could get her to **accede**.

"I don't want anyone who has a beard on his face, either," Beatrice warmed up to her **diatribe**. "He who has a beard is more than a youth. He who has no beard is less than a man. He who is more than a youth is not for me; he who is less than a man, I am not for him."

"On my word, Niece, you never will get a husband and marry if you are such a **shrew** with your tongue and so **shrewd** with your wit," **admonished** Leonato fondly.

Four hundred years ago women's rights did not exist.

Beatrice responded, "Well, I don't plan to marry. *My* **nuptial** *day never will arrive. There is no man for me.* My virtue and I will go to heaven as a maid."

Hero interrupted Beatrice's monologue to point out that people were arriving for the masquerade. Everyone **donned** a mask and went to join the festivities.

The servants had outdone themselves. **Festoons** of **garlands** hung from the ceiling, and lace-covered tables groaned under the weight of the food. A **throng** of townspeople, dressed in an **array** of bright colors, each wearing a mask, danced around on the shiny wood floor like dream dancers swaying to imaginary music. It was a picturesque scene.

Soon the entire crowd was dancing. Benedick, who recognized Beatrice, danced with her. Beatrice, however, did not **discern** Benedick who, like D'Artagnan, **covertly** hid behind his mask. Much to the young man's surprise and dismay, Beatrice, thinking him a stranger, talked about Benedick.

"He is the Prince's jester," she said, "a very witty fool. His only gift is **devising** impossible and **odorous slanders**. His quips are cleverer than he," Beatrice ranted.

"When I **descry** the gentleman of whom you speak, I will tell him what you said," offered Benedick as they continued to dance closely and to exchange barbs.

Claudio danced with Hero, each gazing into the other's eyes. The two wrapped around each other like pigs in a blanket, oinking their **beatitude**.

Well, Don John and Borachio also were at the masquerade. They spread a lot of **dissension** and deceit instead of dancing. The two **infamous** varlets cornered Claudio and, pretending to be fooled by his disguise, **disseminated** their lie that Don Pedro planned to marry Hero that night.

As you can imagine, this lie **singularly** affected poor Claudio who thought that it was he who was going to wed Hero. Claudio was really **perturbed**. Don John, on the other hand, **reveled** in his **villainy** and delighted in getting revenge. He had no sense of humor and never smiled when he could frown. What a **motley**-minded loser!

But wait! Don John was **foiled** again. Don Pedro cleared up Claudio's **misconception** and **woe**. Don Pedro assured Claudio that Hero was his.

"Rest easy, my friend, I have wooed Hero in your name, and fair Hero is yours. Name the day she and you wish to marry."

Leonato, Hero's father, (and a typical **chauvinist** pig of the time) added further, "Take my daughter, who loves you a lot, and with her my fortune. When you marry, I hope that you and she will be very happy and that all ends well."

As the men conversed further, they walked outside into the garden. A full moon illuminated the scene. Graveled walkways, dotted by trees every few feet, wandered through beds of flowers. The men, however, were oblivious as they **meandered** farther down one of the paths. The topic of the men's conversation was Beatrice. Don Pedro thought that she was **predestined** to be Benedick's wife. After all, the two talked of nothing but the other except when they were lying asleep in their separate beds.

"Oh, my word," said Leonato, "if they, being who they are, were married for a week, they would **prattle** themselves mad! Let's get the two of them together."

"It would be a Herculean labor to bring Benedick and Beatrice together in a mountain of affection for each other," **proffered** Don Pedro. "Let's do it! Who's with me?"

The men debated how to get two young people to realize their love for each other, two young people who **abhorred** the following: marriage, love, the opposite sex, and anyone whose name began with a "B."

Just then, Hero, whose head was always in the clouds, wandered into the garden. She walked up to her father. When she heard the news of her **imminent** marriage to the **dapper** Claudio, she was elated.

Claudio, **besotted** by Hero, **beseeched** Leonato to hasten their marriage day. "Time goes on crutches until Love's rites take place. I can't wait to marry my beautiful, comely, superlative, **unrivaled** love."

After being reassured that their marriage was to take place that very week, Claudio and Hero joined the conspiracy in its plot to make the two non-**amorous** young people **amorous** of each other.

The assembled group hatched its plot. When they knew that Beatrice was eavesdropping, Hero and her ladies talked about Benedick, **lauding** him and giving him all the virtues that Beatrice liked. They also **ostentatiously** insisted that Benedick **pined** with love for Beatrice.

"That should get her," said Hero, who was standing among the ladies.

At the same time, the group of men made its plans to do the same to the **intemperate** Benedick. When Benedick could overhear them, the men planned to have a conversation **extolling** Beatrice's virtues and her **abiding** love for Benedick.

"Among those whom I know, Benedick is not the worst prospect for a husband," concluded Don Pedro. "He is honest and **meritorious**. Beatrice should fall in love with him and he with her. If we can pull this off, we will be truly Cupid's henchpeople."

Unsuccessful in his first attempt to **thwart** Claudio's and Hero's nuptials, Don John, Don Pedro's **contemptible** half-brother, and his **sycophant** Borachio devised another scheme. Borachio badly wanted to impress his boss. He proposed a **covert** plan. It seemed that Borachio had been dating the girl Margaret, Hero's maid. Margaret would do anything Borachio asked. Borachio proposed that they take advantage of Claudio's **quirks**, namely that the latter was quick to judge, to get riled, and to jump to conclusions. In other words, Claudio suffered from the **impetuousness** of youth — he did not look before he leaped.

Borachio's diabolical plan included the following: the night before Claudio's and Hero's nuptials, Borachio would talk with Margaret at Hero's bedroom window, calling her Hero; Margaret would wear Hero's clothes; he would insure that Claudio and Don Pedro witnessed the **rendezvous**; Claudio and Don Pedro would think that Hero had **cuckolded** Claudio; and Claudio would break off the wedding.

Don John **sanctioned** Borachio's plan. "I will learn their day of marriage so that we can put this plan into effect."

Meanwhile, in the garden, Benedick sat on a bench and **cogitated** on his friend's impending marriage. "What **folly**!" he thought out loud. "Claudio is usually a reasonable man. I'll never fall as he did. Ah, I hear my friends' voices. I'll hide in this **arbor**."

What **transpired** then was a masterpiece of theater, a dialogue worthy of Shakespeare.

Don Pedro, Leonato, and Claudio **clandestinely** followed Benedick to the park and, seeing him hide in a nearby arbor, winked at each other and began their **discourse**.

Don Pedro wasted no time. "Didn't you tell me, Leonato, that your outspoken niece, Beatrice, is in love with Benedick?"

"Yes, my friend. I'm so glad that she **dotes** on Benedick, a man whom, to outward appearances, she seems to **abhor**.

Leonato continued, "Beatrice loves him with an enraged affection."

"Maybe she only **counterfeits** her passion," suggested Don Pedro with a grin. "How do you know this?"

"Why, my **chaste** daughter, Hero, confided in me," Leonato answered. "Hero says that Beatrice rises twenty times a night, sits there in her nightgown, and writes the words 'Benedick and Beatrice' over and over on a piece of paper."

The conspirators went on and on in such a vein, talking about Beatrice's "love" for Benedick and periodically checking **surreptitiously** to make sure that Benedick still was listening **furtively**. They concluded their charade by "deciding" not to tell Benedick of Beatrice's supposed love because he would mock her. Benedick heard it all and bought his friends' act hook, line, and **soliloquy**.

Suddenly Benedick saw Beatrice in a new light. "She is quick with **badinage** and humor, and she is **pulchritudinous**. When I said I would die a bachelor, I did not consider Beatrice."

When, a few minutes later, Beatrice came to call Benedick in to dinner, Benedick interpreted everything Beatrice said and did as a **portent** of her love.

That very evening, Hero, a gentlewoman named Ursula, and Margaret, Hero's maid (the one who **was in cahoots with** Borachio) lured Beatrice into the garden. In a few minutes, the ladies arrived outside. When Beatrice heard her friends' voices, she hid in the **bracken**. As Beatrice listened from her hiding place, Hero embroidered a tale about Benedick's passion for Beatrice.

"He is wasting away from his love for Beatrice," she **avowed**. "Benedick is consumed with sighs. He is so noble, young, and handsome. Beatrice would make fun of him if she knew of his **ardor**," Hero continued, occasionally glancing at the bracken behind which Beatrice was hiding.

Hero and her ladies talked of how kind Nature had been to Benedick; how fair were his features; how witty he was; how honest, **valorous**, and gentlemanly he was; and how he really adored Beatrice. Hero and her ladies then exited the garden, **prattling** about Hero's and Claudio's wedding, an event that was scheduled to occur the following day.

Beatrice, who should have known better, had fallen for the **ruse** her friends' clever **cerebrums** had devised. "Ah, Benedick, love on. I will return your love, and my wild, **feral**, untamed heart will be tamed to your loving hand."

Meanwhile Benedick really was pining away for Beatrice although he **asserted** that a toothache distressed him. Benedick's friends taunted him about being in love. They were as **roguish** as he.

"If Hero and Margaret have done their parts with Beatrice, then the two bears will not bite one another when they meet," observed Claudio quietly to Don Pedro.

Just as Benedick summoned the courage to speak to Leonato for his niece's hand in marriage, the **mendacious** Don John appeared with an **insidious** lie about poor, innocent Hero.

Don John **prevaricated**, "I came to tell you that she is disloyal."

"Who?" asked Claudio. "Hero?"

"Leonato's Hero, your Hero, every man's Hero," Don John said insidiously. "If you don't believe me, come tonight under her chamber window, and you will see for yourself that no woman is more **perfidious** than she," finished Don John.

Claudio, who was **direly** and disastrously distressed, decided to meet with Don John that night. They were to **congregate** at midnight under Hero's window so that Claudio could see for himself that Don John had spoken the truth.

What Claudio thought he saw from his hiding place under Hero's window that night convinced him of Hero's **culpability**. The **callow** fool never even questioned the infamous Don John's motives in leading him to the scene.

The following day, while Hero teased her friend Beatrice and innocently got ready for her wedding, Borachio and Conrade, Don John's evil henchmen, were celebrating **inebriatedly** the success of their nefarious plan. **Unbeknownst** to the two **miscreants**, two watchmen (who were not really watchman since they were unwilling to do anything if offered resistance) overheard their drunken conversation. Borachio had just **regaled** Conrade with the tale of how Claudio and friends thought that Margaret was Hero when he and his companion were seized by the watchmen, who dragged them to Leonato's house.

There, the watchmen, not **articulate** at the calmest of times, bumbled their attempt to explain what they had overheard and their **subsequent** arrest of Borachio and Conrade. Conrade called Dogsberry, one of the watchmen, a donkey's **derrière**. **Calamitously**, the rather **inarticulate** watchmen failed to communicate, and Leonato left for the church without hearing the truth about his daughter.

At the church, the wedding ended before it began when the **friar** asked Claudio, "Do you come here to marry this lady?"

"No," answered Claudio simply and **candidly**.

At that point, all perdition broke loose. Claudio denounced Hero.

"Leonato, take her back. Do not give this rotten orange to a friend. She has not been faithful to me," Claudio **expounded**.

At first Leonato was **incredulous**. *His* daughter never would be unfaithful. Finally Claudio, Don Pedro, and the **incorrigible** liar, Don John, convinced him otherwise; Don Pedro thought badly of his own daughter. Although Hero protested her innocence, none of the men except the friar believed her. When her perturbed father wished to be dead rather than have such a "dishonorable" daughter, Hero **swooned** as if she were dead and lay pale on the floor. Don John, Don Pedro, and Claudio left the church, thinking among themselves that Hero had passed away instead of fainting from the shock at being found out in her **perfidy**.

The friar, who was convinced of Hero's innocence, **prevailed** upon Leonato not to be so harsh with his daughter. The noble man of the cloth was certain that Hero's **demeanor** was that of an innocent who had been unjustly accused. He also felt that there was a **heinous** plot **afoot** against Hero. When Benedick agreed with him, reminding all of Don John's perfidy and Claudio's penchant to accept things at face value without investigation, they laid a counter plot.

The **sage** friar suggested, "Let's let it be known that Hero died. Let's mourn and **lament**. Keep Hero hidden in your house and let no one know that she lives." To Hero he said, "Come die, lady, to live. Have patience. Your wedding day is but postponed."

Beatrice and Benedick were left alone in the church. Their former **animosity** gone, they avowed their love for each other.

"Come, ask me to do anything for you, my love," offered Benedick.

"Kill Claudio!" Beatrice **succinctly** replied.

"I will challenge him. I will kiss your hand, and then I will leave you. I promise that Claudio will **atone** for his **repudiation** of your cousin," Benedick promised.

The friar's **counterplot** worked. Everyone believed that Hero had "died of shame." The watchmen then showed up at the church with their captives, Borachio and Conrade. There, in **unintelligible** and **garbled** English, the watchmen managed to tell their tale.

The watchmen then went with the prisoners to Leonato's **domicile**. They found Claudio, Don Pedro, Leonato, Antonio (Leonato's brother), and Benedick already there. Leonato and Benedick **glowered** in anger. Benedick was **choleric** because he believed that Claudio, with his rejection of Hero, had shown disrespect for the lady.

"You have killed a very sweet lady, and her death shall be on your conscience," he lied.

The watchmen forced Borachio to tell Don Pedro how Don Pedro's own half-brother, Don John, **incensed** him to **slander** Lady Hero.

Needless to say, Don Pedro was shocked. Claudio was **wracked** with a plethora of guilt for not believing Hero. Leonato blamed Claudio for his daughter's "death" and offered him an unknown niece's hand in marriage. Claudio, stunned, accepted. Leonato wanted to punish Margaret for her role in the **calumnious** deception, but Borachio convinced him of her **inculpable** participation in the plot. Dogsberry, a watchman, requested that Conrade be brought to task for calling him a donkey's posterior.

Later, at the church, Claudio and Don Pedro paid their respects at Hero's "tomb." Claudio laid flowers, read a poem, and promised to return each year to pay **homage** to the woman whom he had **defiled**.

He **intoned**, "Now unto thy bones good night! Yearly, I will do this **rite**."

That same day, at the designated hour, Leonato arrived at the church with two **shrouded** ladies. Who is the unknown niece? Was one of the masked ladies Hero? Did Hero still want the fickle Claudio? Will Beatrice and Benedick get together at last? What will happen to Don John? Will he get his just deserts? You will have to take the final exam to find out the end of this tale of love and trickery.

Teachers, see page 82 (End-of-the-year Caught'ya Test key) for the dénouement of this tale.

Vocabulary used in this story

1. fraught, chicanery, subjugated
2. amoral, ❤ malefactor
3. ❤ gallants, stalwart, stripling
4. ❤comely, dulcet, ❤ virtuous
5. ❤ witty, caustic
6. momentous, ❤ commences
7. ❤ quenching, ❤ varlet, fetching
8. well-appointed, ❤ doting, nonchalant
9. queried, ❤ amiably
10. barbs, quips, ❤ rancor
11. amorous, ❤ feigned, ❤ disdain
12. ❤ bide, ❤ utter
13. ❤ valiant, wryly
14. ❤ frugal
15. exemplary, verbal, ❤ wits
16. abode
17. mordacious, repartée
18. baiting
19. retorted
20. ❤ pernicious
21. interjected, a plethora of, spar
22. enraptured
23. ❤ discoursed,
24. ❤ civet
25. aspersions ❤ blithely
26. taunted, perdition
27. succumb, acceded, vociferated
28. dogmatic, cocksure
29. upbraided, ❤ woo
30. venerable
31. minion
32. ❤ infamous
33. ❤ knavery, ❤ arrant, nefariously
34. ❤ vile, diabolical, fallacious
35. antipathy, upstart
36. domicile, ❤ regaled
37. churlish, presumptuous, ❤canker
38. melancholy
39. ❤ virile, accede
40. diatribe
41. ❤ shrew, ❤ shrewd, admonished
42. ❤ nuptial
43. donned
44. festoons, ❤ garlands
45. throng, array
46. discern, ❤covertly
47. ❤ devising, ❤ odorous, ❤ slanders
48. descry
49. beatitude
50. dissension
51. ❤ infamous (infamy), disseminate
52. singularly, ❤ perturbed
53. ❤ reveled, villainy, ❤ motley
54. foiled, misconception, ❤ woe
55. chauvinist
56. meandered
57. predestined
58. prattle
59. proffered
60. abhorred

61. imminent, dapper
62. besotted, ❤ beseeched, unrivaled
63. ❤ amorous
64. lauding (to laud)
65. ostentatiously, pined
66. ❤ intemperate, extolling, ❤ abiding
67. meritorious
68. ❤ thwart, ❤ contemptible, sycophant
69. ❤ covert
70. ❤ quirks, impetuousness
71. rendezvous, ❤ cuckolded
72. sanctioned
73. cogitated, ❤ folly, ❤ arbor
74. transpired
75. clandestinely, ❤ discourse
76. ❤ dotes, ❤ abhor
77. ❤ counterfeits
78. chaste
79. surreptitiously, furtively
80. soliloquy
81. badinage, pulchritudinous
82. portent
83. in cahoots with
84. bracken
85. avowed
86. ardor
87. ❤ valorous
88. prattle
89. ruse, cerebrums, feral
90. asserted
91. roguish
92. mendacious, insidious
93. prevaricated
94. perfidious
95. direly, congregate
96. culpability, callow
97. inebriated
98. unbeknownst, miscreants
99. regaled
100. articulate, subsequent, derrière
101. calamitously, inarticulate
102. friar, candidly
103. expounded
104. incredulous, incorrigible
105. swooned
106. perfidy
107. prevailed, demeanor
108. heinous, afoot
109. sage, lament
110. animosity, succinctly
111. atone, repudiation
112. counterplot, unintelligible, garbled
113. domicile, glowered
114. choleric
115. ❤ incensed, ❤ slander
116. wracked
117. calumnious, inculpable
118. homage, ❤ defiled
119. intoned, ❤ rite
120. shrouded (to shroud)

Literary devices and writing conventions used in this story

Alliteration #3, 14, 17, 18, 41, 45, 50, 95

Anadiplosis #26, 27, 28, 30, 60

Anecdote #78

Anthropomorphism #42, 44, 62

Aphorism (cliché) #26, 27, 49, 55, 70, 81

Building suspense and/or foreshadowing #28, 31, 68, 69, 71, 78, 82, 95, 109

Conversation #19, 20

Description #22, 44, 45, 56

Description within action or dialogue #8, 16, 53

Double entendre #14, 34, 39, 93

Euphemism #26, 100, 106

Establishment of setting and motif #1, 2, 3

Use of foreign language for effect #17, 22, 71, 100 (for humor)

Humor #11, 12, 13, 19, 28, 40, 58

Hyperbole #62

Idiomatic expression #61, 107, 108, 117, 118, 120

Irony #33, 64, 66, 74, 76

Literary allusion or reference #33, 46, 74

Use of made-up word #31

Malapropism #25

Metaphor #24, 27, 37, 40, 55, 59, 61, 62, 67, 89, 91, 92, 103, 119

Monologue #39, 40

Allusion to mythology #11, 27, 29, 34, 59, 67

Narration #30, 32, 34, 36, 45, 46, 51, 57, 60, 61, 64, 69, 71

Narrator aside #28, 31, 41, 52, 53, 55, 96, 120

Naturalistic detail #56

Onomatopoeia #31, 49

Oxymoron #2, 15, 47, 77

Personification #13, 32, 47, 56, 62, 87, 89

Play on words #11, 19, 20, 23, 41, 47, 63, 69, 109

Pun #39, 74

Repartée #17, 19, 20

Use of rhyme for effect #119

Sarcasm #10, 13, 14, 19, 20, 23, 36, 49, 54, 59, 91

Satire #38

Scene setting #3

Simile #15, 20, 25, 30, 31, 33, 45, 46, 49

Soliloquy #73

Spoonerism #25, 80

Subplot #32, 35, 50, 66, 68, 69

Summary for clarification #1, 2

Synecdoche #14, 89, 119

Repeated use of synonyms to make a point #89

Use of symbol #29

Repeated use of a word for effect #63

Caught'ya sentences for Much Ado About Everything

1. fraught, chicanery, subjugated ●

LD - establishing setting and motif; summary for clarification

Paragraph - beginning of story

Commas - series prepositional phrases; the country or state after a city; complex sentence with 2 independent clauses

Plural rule - if a word ends in "s," "x," "ch" or "sh," add "es" to make it plural

Numbers - write out to 99

Homophones - its/it's, their/there/they're

Irregular verbs - sit/sat/has sat and set/set/has set

Passive voice - to avoid if possible

Parallel construction - "of...of....of..."

Possessive pronouns - my, your, his, her, its, our, their

NOTE - present tense of narrator introduces story

B - this is the story of a battle of the sexes of 2 love affairs **fraught** with obstacles and of **chicanery**. its a romantic comedy set in messina italy centuries ago when men held all the power and women were **subjugated** to there will

C -   This is the story of a battle of the sexes, of two love affairs **fraught** with obstacles, and of **chicanery**. It's a romantic comedy set in Messina, Italy, centuries ago when men held all the power, and women were **subjugated** to their will.

➥ SUGGESTION:

The common homophones like "their/there/they're" will sometimes be misspelled, sometimes spelled correctly. I do this to keep students on their toes. My students complain that they have to think. They never know if I'm going to misspell a homophone or not. Once, after misspelling "their" in at least five previous Caught'ya sentences, I spelled it correctly. My students were upset. But, by that time, most of them were using that particular homophone correctly in their writing!

2. amoral, ❤ malefactor ●

LD - oxymoron ("peace battles"); establishing setting and motif; summary for clarification

No paragraph - continuation

Commas - appositive; around name of country after city; non-restrictive modifier

Homophone - peace/piece

Hyphen - 2 words acting as one

Often confused words - former/latter

Verb tense - need for pluperfect tense to refer to action previous to this story (the rebellion) - "had staged"

NOTE - Present tense of narrator introduces story, but story itself is in the past tense.

B - the convoluted soap opera of piece battles begins at the end of a foiled rebellion. don pedro prince of aragon spain had just defeated his **amoral** half brother don john. the latter had been the **malefactor** who staged the rebellion

C - The convoluted soap opera of peace battles began at the end of a foiled rebellion. Don Pedro, Prince of Aragon, Spain, had just defeated his **amoral** half-brother, Don John. The latter had been the **malefactor** who had staged the rebellion.

***B** = suggested sentence for the board or overhead   **C** = sentence written correctly   **LD** = literary device*

3. ❤ **gallants, stalwart, stripling** ●

LD - alliteration (s...s); **scene setting** No paragraph - continuation Commas - appositives; city, country/state; city, country/state; subordinate clause at beginning of sentence; appositive (non-restrictive modifier - not necessary) Numbers - write out to 99 Homophone - to/too/two **NOTE - Begin to teach the prepositions and what you can and cannot do with them**	**B** - don pedro and 2 of his **gallants** claudio a **stalwart stripling** from florence italy and benedick of padua italy were returning home from the war. when they reached messina italy they were to become the guests of leonato the governor of messina **C** - Don Pedro and two of his **gallants**, Claudio, a **stalwart stripling** from Florence, Italy, and Benedick of Padua, Italy, were returning home from the war. When they reached Messina, Italy, they were to become the guests of Leonato, the governor of Messina.

➥ **SUGGESTION:**

It is often a good idea to have students memorize the main prepositions (there are over forty of them). You can do this painlessly, memorizing a few each day until the entire list is learned. My students make up a dance to them. Once learned, prepositions can be used correctly in places like titles. In addition, students find it easier to understand that prepositional phrases are really adjectives and adverbs.

4. ❤ **comely, dulcet,** ❤ **virtuous** ●

Paragraph - new subject Commas - compound sentence Relative pronouns - who/whom/that/which ("That" refers only to things and can be subject or object; "who" is needed here as subject — nominative case; "whom" is always the object — objective case; "who" is always used with verbs of being.) Sentence structure - inverted sentence order Adverb vs. Adjective - "well" (adverb) and "good" (adjective) Coordinating conjunctions - (**f**or, **a**nd, **n**or, **b**ut, **o**r, **y**et, **s**o — FAN BOYS). There are only two instances when a comma precedes them: a series and a compound sentence. Compound sentence - teach what it is and how to recognize it Correlative conjunctions - "not only.....but also"	**B** - now leonato had a **comely** daughter that was named hero. not only was hero beautiful but she was **dulcet** and **virtuous** as well **C** - Now Leonato had a **comely** daughter who was named Hero. Not only was Hero beautiful, but she was **dulcet** and **virtuous** as well.

➥ **SUGGESTION:**

This is a good point to teach the coordinating conjunctions. Students can easily memorize them by chanting them in the order of the acronym FANBOYS. Once students memorize these, they can learn the two instances where a comma is needed before them, not to capitalize them in a title, and never to begin a sentence with one. This is also a good point to teach the three sentence types and how they are constructed.

5. ❤ **witty, caustic** ●

No paragraph Commas - 2 adjectives where 2nd is not age, color, or linked to noun; long introductory phrase; appositive (non-restrictive modifier - "his only niece") Transitive vs. intransitive verbs (This will be discussed many times in subsequent Caught'yas.) Spelling rule - "i" before "e" except after "c" and neighbor and weigh are weird Splitting verbs - Do not split helping verb and verb if at all possible.	**B** - in addition to his dulcet virtuous daughter leonato was also rearing his only niece the **witty** beatrice. she was as **caustic** as her cousin hero was dulcet **C** - In addition to his dulcet, virtuous daughter, Leonato also was rearing his only niece, the **witty** Beatrice. She was as **caustic** as her cousin Hero was dulcet.

B = suggested sentence for the board or overhead   *C = sentence written correctly*   *LD = literary device*

6. momentous, ♥ commences •

Paragraph - subject change

Comma - introductory subordinate clause of sentence (long introductory adverbial phrase)

Homophones - are/our, tail/tale

Run-on sentence - no punctuation

Verb-tense switch - correct use in this sentence

Spelling rule - "i" before "e" except after "c" and neighbor and weigh are weird

Possession - singular noun

Colon - use to denote break before letter (could use dash)

NOTE - Teach subordinating conjunctions (after, although, **a**s — **w**hen, **w**hile, **w**here — **h**ow — **i**f — than — **e**ven though — **b**ecause, **b**efore — **u**ntil, **u**nless — since, **s**o that - A White Bus

NOTE - Teach what a complex sentence is and how it is formed

B - on the **momentous** day when are tail **commences** leonato recieved a letter from don pedros messenger it read

C -   On the **momentous** day when our tale **commences**, Leonato received a letter from Don Pedro's messenger. It read:

➥ **SUGGESTION:**

It is also a good idea to have your students memorize the subordinating conjunctions early in the year. It is not hard. Use the suggested acronyms, put the words to a beat, and students will learn them quickly. Simply repeat them each time one shows up in a Caught'ya. In this painless manner, the conjunctions will be memorized. Once the conjunctions are memorized, students then can learn comma placement and the difference among a simple, a compound, a complex, and a compound/complex sentence.

---

7. ♥ quenching, ♥ varlet, fetching •

Paragraph - body of letter

Commas - date; greeting; appositive; compound sentence; closing

Friendly letter format

Numbers - write out to 99

Homophones - to/too/two; your/you're

Pronouns - "I" is subject and used with verbs of being; "me" is the object; word order (put yourself last)

Splitting verb - Do not split helping verb and verb if at all possible ("soon will arrive").

Hyphen - 2 words acting as one

Plural rule - consonant "y" changes to "ies"

Common spelling error - truly

B - september 15 1603 my dear leonato me and 2 of my companions are returning home after **quenching** the rebellion of don john my **varlet** of a half brother. we will soon arrive in messina and we look forward to seeing you and your **fetching** ladies again. yours truly don pedro

C -   September 15, 1603
My Dear Leonato,
    Two of my companions and I are returning home after **quenching** the rebellion of Don Juan, my **varlet** of a half-brother. We soon shall arrive in Messina, and we look forward to seeing you and your **fetching** ladies again.

                                                   Yours truly,
                                                   Don Pedro

B = suggested sentence for the board or overhead   C = sentence written correctly   LD = literary device

8. well-appointed, ♥ doting, nonchalant ●

LD - description within action and dialogue

2 Paragraphs - narrator then new person speaking

Commas - long introductory adverb with 2 prepositional phrases; 2 adjectives

Quotations - punctuation of quote that is a question

Hyphen - 2 words acting as one

Incorrect verb-tense switch - story in past tense

Spelling rule - "i" before "e" except after "c" and neighbor and weigh are weird

Relative pronouns - who/whom/whose/whoever/ whomever/that/which ("that" and "which" can be subject or object and are used only with objects and animals; "who" and "whom" are used with people; "who" is subject; "whom" is object)

Irregular verbs - sit/sat/have sat and set/set/ has set

Transitive and intransitive verbs - "set" and "sit;" go over differences

Hyphen - 2 words acting as one

B - in the spacious and **well-appointed** living room of his estate leonato reads the letter to his **doting** daughter and niece. is signior mountanto returning with him asked beatrice whom was trying to appear **nonchalant** as she set on a green high backed couch

C -   In the spacious and **well-appointed** living room of his estate, Leonato read the letter to his **doting** daughter and niece.

   "Is Signior Mountanto returning with him?" asked Beatrice who was trying to appear **nonchalant** as she sat on a green, high-backed couch.

9. queried, ♥ amiably ●

2 Paragraphs - new persons speaking

Commas - direct address; quote, noun list

Quotations - punctuation of quotation that is question

Relative pronouns - who/whom/that/which ("who" is subject; "whom" is object — here of a preposition; "that" and "which" are subject and object for things, not people)

Prepositions - avoid ending a sentence with a preposition if possible

Parallel construction - 3 nouns needed in series, not a verb ("patted")

B - who are you asking for neice **queried** leonato **amiably**. my cousin means signior benedick of padua hero said with a wink a smile and patted beatrice

C -   "For whom are you asking, Niece?" **queried** Leonato **amiably**.

   "My cousin means Signior Benedick of Padua," Hero said with a wink, a smile, and a pat for Beatrice.

10. barbs, quips, ♥ rancor ●

LD - sarcasm

Paragraph - narrator's introduction to quote

Commas - interjection; compound sentence; quote

Quotation

Relative pronouns - who/whom/that/which ("That" and "which" refer only to things; "who" is needed here as subject; "whom" is always the object; "who" is always used with verbs of being.)

Prepositions - review them here

B - the messenger that had brought the letter replied without **rancor** oh sir benedick returns with don pedro and he is as pleasant as ever with his **barbs** and **quips**

C -   The messenger who had brought the letter replied without **rancor**, "Oh, Sir Benedick returns with Don Pedro, and he is as pleasant as ever with his **barbs** and **quips**. *(To be continued in the next caught'ya.)*

B = suggested sentence for the board or overhead   C = sentence written correctly   LD = literary device

11. amorous, ❤ feigned, ❤ disdain ●

LD - play on words ("killed," "eaten"); **allusion to mythology** ("Cupid"); **humor**

Paragraph - new person speaking

Commas - introductory word ("so" as an interjection); subordinate clause at beginning of sentence; interrupted (continued) quote

Quotation - continued or interrupted

Run-on sentence (no periods)

Coordinating conjunctions - Do not begin a sentence with a coordinating conjunction unless it is treated as an interjection

Punctuation - need question mark for interrogative

Plural rules - consonant "y" changes to "ies"

Incorrect verb-tense switch - story in past tense

Compound predicate

Complex sentence - subordinate clause

B - so how many enemys has he killed and eaten in the war when he was last in messina benedick fancied himself an **amorous** lady killer he **feigned** love beatrice continues and challenged cupid himself with his **disdain** for marriage

C -   "*(So, how many.....or)* How many enemies has he killed and eaten in the war? When he was last in Messina, Benedick fancied himself an **amorous** lady killer. He **feigned** love," Beatrice continued, "and challenged Cupid himself with his **disdain** for marriage."

12. ❤ bide, ❤ utter ●

LD - humor

Paragraph - new person speaking

Commas - interjection; direct address; 2 adjectives where the 2nd is not age, color, or linked to noun; quote

Quotation

Adjective vs. Adverb - "good" as adjective and "well" as adverb

Spelling rule - "i" before "e...."

Often confused prepositions - between/among

Homophones - your/you're and to/too/two

Reflexive pronouns - myself, yourself, himself, herself, itself, ourselves, yourselves, themselves; use correct form

B - ah beatrice my dear caustic niece **bide** your tongue. he has done good for don pedro. he will be between us soon enough and you can **utter** youre barbs directly too benedick himself counseled leonato

C -   "Ah, Beatrice, my dear, caustic niece, **bide** your tongue. He has done well for Don Pedro. He will be among *(or with)* us soon enough, and you can **utter** your barbs directly to Benedick himself," counseled Leonato.

➡ SUGGESTION:

This is a good spot to go over and/or teach the eight parts of speech and their various functions since all eight are represented in Caught'ya #12. You might want to repeat this exercise every time you find a Caught'ya in which all eight parts of speech are included. I use the acronym NIPPAVAC.

13. ❤ valiant, wryly ●

LD - humor and personification ("bat-fowling" mouth); **sarcasm**

Paragraph - new person speaking

Commas - introductory word; direct address; quote

Quotation

Adjective vs. adverb - "good" as adjective

Comparatives - good/better/best

Spelling rule - "i" before "e..."

Hyphen - 2 words acting as one

Dash vs. parentheses - one or the other needed to denote break in the sentence for narrator's aside

B - yes he is a good soldier my lady and a better friend. sir benedick his bat fowling mouth nonetheless is a **valiant** man replied the messenger **wryly**

C -   "Yes, he is a good soldier, my lady, and a better friend. Sir Benedick — his bat-fowling mouth nonetheless — is a **valiant** man," replied the messenger **wryly**.

B = suggested sentence for the board or overhead   C = sentence written correctly   LD = literary device

14. ❤ **frugal** • ❤ • • • •

LD - sarcasm and double entendre ("excellent stomach"); **alliteration** (f,f); **synecdoche** ("fork" as part standing for the whole - food being the whole)

2 paragraphs - new person speaking then narrator

Commas - direct address; interrupted (continued) quote; introductory phrase; no comma before "but" as it does not begin a compound sentence

Quotation - interrupted quote

Possession - singular noun

Double negative - avoid use

B - watch your food supply uncle leonato teased beatrice for benedick is known for his excellent stomach. in other words he is not **frugal** with his fork. hero giggled at her cousins implications but didnt say nothing

C - "Watch your food supply, Uncle Leonato," teased Beatrice, "for Benedick is known for his excellent stomach. In other words, he is not **frugal** with his fork."

Hero giggled at her cousin's implications but said nothing. *(or — didn't say anything)*

15., exemplary, verbal, ❤ wits •

LD - oxymoron ("merry war"); **simile**

Paragraph - new person speaking

Commas - direct address; introductory subordinate clause

Quotation

Homophone - their/there/they're

Capitalization - Capitalize "Sir" as it refers to Don Pedro and is used as a name.

Often confused words - between (only 2)/among (more); then/than ("Then" is an adverb; "than" is a conjunction used to compare.)

Pronouns - "she" is subject and "her" is object or shows possession

Spelling rule - "i" before "e..."

Irregular comparatives - bad/worse/worst

Numbers - write out to 99

B - leonato addressed the messenger you must not sir mistake my neice. there is a kind of merry war going on among signior benedick and she. whenever they meet she and him have an **exemplary verbal** battle of **wits** worser then 2 lawyers in court

C - Leonato addressed the messenger. "You must not, Sir, mistake my niece. There is a kind of merry war going on between Signior Benedick and her. Whenever they meet, he and she have an **exemplary verbal** battle of **wits** worse than two lawyers in court."

16. abode •

LD - description in action

Paragraph - narrator

Commas - introductory word; long introductory adverb with 2 prepositional phrases; introductory subordinate clause; 2 adjectives where 2nd is not age, color, or linked to noun

Quotation

Prepositional phrases - discuss use of as adverbs and adjectives

Possession - singular noun

Possessives vs. plurals - Discuss difference and use of each.

Wrong word use - never use "is when" (using "when" as a verb which it is not)

Numbers - write out to 99.

Incorrect verb-tense switch - story in past tense

B - now in those days' of long ago letter's were slow to arrive. soon after the messenger left leonatos' **abode** is when don pedro and his 2 gallants' enter the tall stone gate's of messina

C - Now, in those days of long ago, letters were slow to arrive. Soon after the messenger left Leonato's **abode**, Don Pedro and his two gallants entered the tall, stone gates of Messina.

➡ **SUGGESTION:**

You may wish to put in an extraneous apostrophe or two whenever possible in order to foster frequent discussions about the difference between possessives and plurals until your students no longer confuse them.

---

17. **mordacious** (note Latin prefix - "mord" meaning "to bite"), **repartée** •

LD - alliteration (b,b,b); **use of foreign word; repartée**

No paragraph - continuation

Commas - noun series; appositive; adjective series; city, state; subordinate clause at beginning of the sentence

Coordinating conjunctions - Do not begin a sentence with a coordinating conjunction unless it is used as an interjection.

Possessive pronouns - my, your, his, her, its, our, their

Possession - singular noun

Homophone - their/there/they're

Compound subject in last sentence

Use of strong, active verbs

B - and when benedick don pedro and claudio the handsome young immature lord of florence italy arrived at leonatos estate leonato invited them to stay. benedick and beatrice began there usual **mordacious repartée**

C - When Benedick, Don Pedro, and Claudio, the handsome, young, immature lord of Florence, Italy, arrived at Leonato's estate, Leonato invited them to stay. Benedick and Beatrice began their usual **mordacious repartée.**

18. **baiting** •

LD - alliteration ("baiting of Beatrice")

Paragraph - new person speaking

Commas - direct address; quote; participial phrase introductory subordinate clause

Quotation - capitalization and punctuation in interrupted (continued) quote

Adjectives vs. adverbs - "good" as adjective

Homophone - its/it's, your/you're, to/too/two

Indirect quotation - avoidance of quotes with "that" used as a conjunction

Possession - singular noun

Spelling rule - "i" before "e..."

Verb tense - need for subjunctive mood in "if" clause

Spelling rule - discuss rule that makes "batting" and "bating" different (If a word ends in consonant/vowel/consonant, you must double the last consonant if you add a suffix.)

B - its a good thing signior leonato that you are not beatrices father said benedick not wasting any time in his **baiting** of beatrice. if youre neice was your daughter you would be in trouble. you to are to much alike

C -   "It's a good thing, Signior Leonato, that you are not Beatrice's father," said Benedick, not wasting any time in his **baiting** of Beatrice. "If your niece were your daughter, you would be in trouble. You two are too much alike."

➥ **SUGGESTION:**

Since all nine comma rules have been introduced in the previous Caught'yas, this might be a good point to pause and review them all together. You can find a list of them under "Comma Rules" in the Appendix of this book. I distribute a copy to my students, and they write examples to fit every rule. They enjoy doing this in groups.

19. **retorted** •

LD - repartée; conversation; sarcasm; humor; play on word ("disdain")

4 Paragraphs - conversation

Commas - direct address; interjection; quote; compound sentence; direct address

Quotations

Paragraphs - use of indentation only in order to denote different person speaking

Punctuation - use of dash to indicate break (comma would also be acceptable)

Often confused words - accept/except

Punctuation - quotation marks needed around falsehood ('loving'); quote within a quote to denote sarcasm

B - what. are you observant sir benedick **retorted** beatrice. ah my lady disdain you speak said benedick. you call me lady disdain and yet you disdain all the ladies the ladies love me all accept you my loving beatrice

C -   "What? Are you observant, Sir Benedick?" **retorted** Beatrice.

"Ah, my 'Lady Disdain,' you speak," said Benedick.

"You call me 'Lady Disdain,' and yet you disdain all the ladies."

"The ladies love me — all except you, my 'loving' Beatrice."

B = *suggested sentence for the board or overhead*   *C* = *sentence written correctly*   *LD* = *literary device*

20. ❤ **pernicious** •

LD - repartée; conversation; play on words ("unsuitable suitor"); **sarcasm; simile**

NOTE: Warn students that two people are speaking.

3 Paragraphs - conversation between two people

Commas - direct address; 2 adjectives where 2nd is not age, color, or linked to noun; compound sentence; quote

Quotations

Common spelling error - "no one" is 2 words.

Homophone - your/you're

Often confused words - quiet/quit/quite

As vs. like - need to use "as" instead of "like" because "like" is used only with nouns and "as" is needed in comparatives - "as fast as"

Verb tense - need for subjunctive mood in clause of wishing

B - you love no one you **pernicious** unsuitable suitor. i wish my horse was fast like your tongue. keep quite now for noone is listening to you beatrice concluded

C -   "You love no one, you **pernicious**, unsuitable suitor."

"I wish my horse were as fast as your tongue."

"Keep quiet now, for no one is listening to you," Beatrice concluded.

---

21. interjected, a plethora of, spar •

Paragraph - new person speaking

Commas - quote; direct address

Quotation

Homophones - their/there/they're, hear/here, to/two/too

Spelling rule - if a word ends in consonant/vowel/consonant you must double the last consonant if you add a suffix ("sparring")

Punctuation - need for exclamation mark for emphasis

Numbers - write out to 99

Splitting infinitives - Never split an infinitive. (*Star Trek* was wrong — "To boldly go.." should be "To go boldly..." -- "to spar further".

Often confused words - farther/further

B - don pedro **interjected** their is the sparring match. end round one. my dear leonato we will be staying hear at least a month. these 2 will have **a plethora of** time to farther **spar**

C -   Don Pedro **interjected**, "There is the sparring match. End round one! My dear Leonato, we will be staying here at least a month. These two will have **a plethora of** time to **spar** further."

---

22. enraptured •

LD - description; use of foreign word

Paragraph - narrator again

Commas - introductory subordinate clause; compound sentence (3rd one)

Incorrect verb-tense switch - story in past tense

Often confused words - affect/effect

Gerund - participle used as a noun ("breathing")

Homophones - waist/waste, site/sight

Pronouns - review possessive pronouns

Strong verbs - needed in description

Prepositions - review prepositions

B - while this repartée was going on claudio became **enraptured** by the silent hero. the mere site of her affected his heart. her long black hair hung to her tiny waste and her shy smile affected a quickening of his breathing

C -   While this repartée was going on, Claudio became **enraptured** by the silent Hero. The mere sight of her affected his heart. Her long black hair hung to her tiny waist, and her shy smile effected a quickening of his breathing.

B = *suggested sentence for the board or overhead*   *C* = *sentence written correctly*   *LD* = *literary device*

23. ♥ discoursed •

LD - sarcasm; play on words (referring to taste - food again)

3 Paragraphs - 3 people speaking (narrator, Claudio, Benedick)

Commas - introductory subordinate clause; quote; quote

Quotations

Regular comparisons - sweet/sweeter/sweetest

Possessive pronouns - my, your, his, her, its, our, their

Irregular verb - see/saw/has seen

Antecedent/pronoun agreement - "everyone" is singular so "their," which is plural, cannot be used

Collective nouns and pronouns - discuss common collective nouns (family, everyone, crowd, crew, group, etc.)

B - as leonato led his guests to their rooms claudio and benedick **discoursed**. hero is the sweetest lady i ever seen shy claudio sighed. everyone to their own taste retorted benedick sarcastically

C -   As Leonato led his guests to their rooms, Claudio and Benedick **discoursed**.

"Hero is the sweetest lady I have ever seen," shy Claudio sighed. *(or "I ever saw...")*

"Everyone to his own taste," retorted Benedick sarcastically.

➡ SUGGESTION:

This is a good point for a discussion of the difference between a phrase and a clause. See the Appendix for further explanation.

24. ♥ civet •

LD - metaphor (comparing Beatrice to a civet)

No paragraph

Commas - introductory word; interrupted (continued) quote

Quotation

Interrupted quote - punctuation and capitalization

Contraction - discuss commonest contractions

Adverb vs. Adjective - Discuss use of "well" as adverb.

Verb tense - need for subjunctive mood in "if" clause

Spelling rule - if a word ends in consonant/vowel/consonant and a suffix is added, the last consonant much be doubled ("spitting")

B - well i dont see anything in her benedick continued honestly but that cousin of hers would be comely if she was not a spiting **civet**

C - "Well, I don't see anything in her," Benedick continued honestly, "but that cousin of hers would be comely if she were not a spitting **civet**."

➡ SUGGESTION:

This is another good spot to go over and/or teach the eight parts of speech and their various functions since all eight are represented in Caught'ya #24. You might want to repeat this exercise every time you find a Caught'ya in which all eight parts of speech are included.

B = suggested sentence for the board or overhead   *C = sentence written correctly*   *LD = literary device*

25. aspersions; ❤ blithely ●

LD - malapropism ("casting asparagus"); **simile; spoonerism** ("half-formed fish")

2 Paragraphs - conversation

Commas - introductory word; quote

Run-on sentence - lack of punctuation

Question marks - needed in questions

Hyphen - 2 words acting as one

Homophone - no/know

Often confused words - then/than ("Then" is an adverb, and "than" is a conjunction used to compare.)

Pronouns - "They" (as a subject) must be used after "than" because "are" is implied ("than they *are*").

Spelling rules - "i" before "e..."; if consonant/vowel/consonant in root, you must double the last consonant when adding a suffix (spar - spa**rr**ing)

B - are you casting asparagus on my feelings do you think my love is not complete like a half-formed wish babbled a frustrated claudio. no i am not casting **aspersions** on your feelings. i no that a half warmed fish is less complete then them benedick **blithely** corrected his freind

C -   "Are you casting asparagus on my feelings? Do you think my love is not complete like a half-formed wish?" babbled a frustrated Claudio.

     "No, I am not casting **aspersions** on your feelings. I know that a half-warmed fish is less complete than they," Benedick **blithely** corrected his friend.

26. taunted, perdition ●

LD - aphorism ("hell would freeze over"); **anadiplosis; euphemism** (perdition instead of Hell)

Paragraph - narrator

Commas - subordinate clause before verb; repeated word

Coordinating conjunctions - Do not begin a sentence one.

Verb tense - need for subjunctive mood in "if" clause

Contraction - review common contractions

Often confused words - then/than ("Then" is an adverb, and "than" is a conjunction used to compare.)

Negatives - "never" necessitates the conjunction "nor"

Verb tense - correct use of conditional tense (Students often misuse instead of past tense. Point out the difference if this is a problem with your students.)

B - and claudio **taunted** benedick for his views on love and marriage. and benedick warned claudio that if he wasnt careful he would soon be a husband. benedick then went on and on about how he would never never fall in love or marry. **perdition** would freeze over before that would happen

C -   Claudio **taunted** Benedick for his views on love and marriage. Benedick warned Claudio that if he weren't careful, he would soon be a husband. Benedick then went on and on about how he would never, never fall in love nor marry. **Perdition** would freeze over before that would happen.

27. succumb, acceded, vociferated ●

LD - metaphor; allusion to mythology (Cupid); **anadiplosis; aphorism** ("Never...")

2 Paragraphs - conversation

Commas - direct address; introductory subordinate clauses; interrupter; quote

Quotation

Verb tense - need for subjunctive mood with "if" clause

Relative pronouns - who/whom/that/which ("who" needed as subject; "that" and "which never refer to people)

Possession - singular noun (discuss all possessive rules)

Often confused words - accede/exceed

Sentence structure - deliberate use of fragment

Pronouns - "I" is needed in fragment "Not I" since the following sentence picks it up as a subject

Italics - emphasis

Splitting verbs - avoid splitting helping verb and verb.

B - like you my friend i swore id never marry. if it was hero that would be my wife though i would **succumb** to cupid's arrow's **acceded** claudio. never in a million year's **vociferated** benedick. not me. i shall die a bachelor

C -   "Like you, my friend, I swore I'd never marry. If it were Hero who would be my wife, though, I would **succumb** to Cupid's arrows," **acceded** Claudio.

     "Never in a million years!" **vociferated** Benedick. "Not I. I shall die a bachelor."

B = *suggested sentence for the board or overhead*   **C** = *sentence written correctly*   **LD** = *literary device*

28. dogmatic, cocksure •

LD - foreshadowing and building suspense; narrator aside; humor; anadiplosis

Paragraph - narrator aside

Commas - adjective series

Verb tense switch - correct use of present tense to indicate narrator aside

Run-on sentence - lack of punctuation

Punctuation - need for exclamation mark (dramatic statement)

Like vs. as - "Like" cannot be used since it is followed by a verb at the end of the phrase ("as D'Artagnan's did"). "Like" can only be followed by a noun as in "like water."

Possession - singular noun

Numbers - write out to 99

Underlining vs. quotation marks - Underline titles of books. Discuss rules for underlining vs. putting quotation marks around titles - whole longer works like books, magazines, and record albums are underlined and smaller parts of the whole that are shorter like poems, articles and songs are put into quotes.

Punctuation - need for question mark

Irregular verb - rise/raise/has risen

B - little does the arrogant **dogmatic** and **cocksure** benedick know what is in store for him will his wit rise to the occasion like d'artagnans did in the 3 musketeers

C - Little does the arrogant, **dogmatic**, and **cocksure** Benedick know what is in store for him! Will his wit rise to the occasion as D'Artagnan's did in <u>The Three Musketeers</u>?

29. upbraided, ♥ woo •

LD - use of symbol and allusion to mythology ("Cupid's arrow")

Paragraph - new person speaking (Two paragraphs also would be correct, the second after "arrow.")

Commas - introductory subordinate clause; direct address; non-restrictive modifier

Possession - singular noun

Often confused words - then/than ("Then" is an adverb and needed here; "than" is a conjunction used to compare.)

Homophone - to/too/two

Relative pronouns - who/whom/that/which ("who" needed here as subject; "that" and "which" never used with people.)

Reflexive pronouns - correct form of reflexive pronoun needed - "himself"

Infinitives - discuss uses of infinitives and how they should not be split

B - don pedro entered the discussion and **upbraided** benedick for his stand. before i die benedick i predict that i shall see you a victim of cupids arrow. don pedro than offered to **woo** hero for the timid claudio that was to shy to do so hisself

C - Don Pedro entered the discussion and **upbraided** Benedick for his stand. "Before I die, Benedick, I predict that I shall see you a victim of Cupid's arrow." Don Pedro then offered to **woo** Hero for the timid Claudio, who was too shy to do so himself.

➡**SUGGESTION:**

I found that # 29 was a perfect quickie Caught'ya Quiz since it includes many of the errors in the previous five Caught'yas. I like to give these quizzes about once a month or so as a check on my students' progress. They don't seem to mind since the grades tend to be good!

B = *suggested sentence for the board or overhead*   ***C*** = *sentence written correctly*   ***LD*** = *literary device*

30. venerable •

LD - anadiplosis; simile; narration

Paragraph - subject change

Commas - appositive (non-restrictive modifier, although some people put no comma with a single word); no comma needed after "venerable" since "older" denotes age and no comma after conversation as it is not a compound sentence, only a compound verb

Incorrect use of verb-tense switch - story in past tense

Possession - singular noun

Run-on sentence - lack of punctuation

Punctuation - use of quotes to indicate a falsehood

Like vs. as - "Like" must be followed by a noun in a straight comparison.

Verb tense - need for subjunctive mood in "if" clause

Underlining vs. quotation marks - Underline titles of newspapers and books. Discuss rules for underlining vs. putting quotation marks around titles - whole longer works like books, magazines, and record albums are underlined and smaller parts of the whole that are shorter like poems, articles and songs are put into quotes.

Strong verbs - good description of action

B - a servant overhears this conversation and reports it to leonatos **venerable** older brother antonio antonio himself informed leonato of the news like he was a reporter for the new york times

C -   A servant overheard this conversation and reported it to Leonato's **venerable** older brother, Antonio. Antonio himself informed Leonato of the "news" as if he were a reporter for the New York Times.

31. minion •

LD - narrator aside; simile; onomatopoeia and **made-up word** ("burbling"); **building suspense**

No paragraph; paragraph - narrator aside

Pronouns - need for noun as there are too many pronouns for clarity

Indirect quotation - avoidance of quotes with the word "that" used as a conjunction

Italics - needed for emphasis (When you read this Caught'ya to your class, emphasize the word "thought.")

Homophone - herd/heard

Verb tense - correct use of present tense for narrator aside

B - the only problem was that this **minion** *thought* that he herd him say that he was going to woo the fair hero for himself. the plot thickens like gravy burbling on the stove

C - The only problem was that this **minion** *thought* that he heard Don Pedro say that he was going to woo the fair Hero for himself.

  The plot thickens like gravy burbling on the stove.

B = *suggested sentence for the board or overhead*   **C** = *sentence written correctly*   **LD** = *literary device*

32. ❤ infamous •••

LD - subplot introduced here; personification (plots cannot thicken); **narration**

No paragraph

Commas - appositive and adjective clause with relative pronoun

Coordinating conjunctions - Do not begin a sentence with one.

Hyphen - 2 words acting as one

Relative pronouns - who/whom/that/which ("who" needed here as subject)

Splitting verbs - avoid splitting helping verb and verb if possible.

Irregular verbs - lie/lay/has lain and lay/laid/has laid

Transitive vs. intransitive verbs - Discuss transitive (lay/laid) vs. intransitive verbs (lie/lay). I tell my students that since "laid" is part of a transitive verb, something always has to get "laid." They laugh and hoot, but they learn it.

Splitting Infinitives - avoid (*Star Trek* was wrong — "To boldly go.." should be "To go boldly...")

B - and it thickens even more as the **infamous** don john whom had already staged one rebellion against his half brother don pedro arrived in town and laid in wait to nastily plot

C - It thickens even more as the **infamous** Don John, who already had staged one rebellion against his half-brother, Don Pedro, arrived in town and lay in wait to plot nastily.

33. ❤ knavery, ❤ arrant, nefariously ••

LD - literary allusion; simile; irony; narration

Paragraph

Commas - introductory subordinate clause; appositive

Verb tense - need for pluperfect tense to refer to previous action

Often confused words - then/than ("Then" is an adverb, and "than" is a conjunction used to show comparison.)

Relative pronouns - who/whom/that/which ("who" needed as subject of "had preyed")

Homophones - no/know, pray/prey

B - although he was defeated don john was by no means powerless. he was possessed of more **knavery** then iago that **arrant** villain that **nefariously** prayed upon othello

C - Although he had been defeated, Don John was by no means powerless. He was possessed of more **knavery** than Iago, that **arrant** villain who had preyed **nefariously** upon Othello.

34. ❤ vile, diabolical, fallacious ••

LD - double entendre and allusion to mythology (the name "Borachio" which alludes to debauchery, drunkenness, and lecherous behavior); **narration**

No paragraph

Commas - non-restrictive modifier; participial phrase as interrupter

Subject/verb agreement - plural subject located in predicate

Homophones - herd/heard, brake/break

Numbers - write out to 99

Spelling rule - if a word ends in consonant/vowel/consonant and a suffix is added, the last consonant much be doubled ("plotting")

B - accompanying don john was his 2 equally **vile** associates borachio and conrade. this **diabolical** trio having herd the **fallacious** rumor concerning don pedro and hero ploted ways to brake up the romance

C - Accompanying Don John were his two equally **vile** associates, Borachio and Conrade. This **diabolical** trio, having heard the **fallacious** rumor concerning Don Pedro and Hero, plotted ways to break up the romance.

B = *suggested sentence for the board or overhead*   *C* = *sentence written correctly*   *LD* = *literary device*

35. antipathy, upstart •

LD - subplot

Paragraph - new person speaking

Commas - continued (interrupted) quote; "too" always has to be set off by commas if it means "also;" no comma after "upstart" since it is a restrictive modifier

Quotation

Verb tense - need for subjunctive mood, future, or conditional tense with "if" clause

Contractions

Word use error - "gots" is not a word

Homophone - to/two/too

Pronouns - "I" must be used with a verb of being since it is simply the subject placed after the verb

Relative pronouns - who/whom/that/which ("who" needed as subject; "whom" as object)

Word use error - "Should have" not "should of" should be used since "should" needs to be followed by a helping verb, not a preposition; "of" makes no sense here as there is no object.

B - if i can cross my brother in any way said don john with **antipathy** ill do it. id like to get even with that **upstart** claudio too. he gots all the glory for defeating me. It was me who should of won

C -   "If I can cross my brother in any way," said Don John with **antipathy**, "I'll do it. I'd like to get even with that **upstart** Claudio, too. He got all the glory for defeating me. It was I who should have won."

36. domicile, ❤ regaled •

LD - narration; sarcasm

Paragraph - place change

Commas - optional for introductory one-word adverb; after 2 introductory adverbs; list of nouns; non-restrictive modifier (only one elderly brother)

Punctuation - need for quotes around falsehood (Beatrice wants no suitor)

Incorrect verb-tense switch - story in past tense

B - meanwhile at leonatos **domicile** hero beatrice leonato and his elderly brother antonio are waiting for a masquerade dance to begin. beatrice **regaled** the assembled company with her idea of the ideal suitor

C -   Meanwhile, at Leonato's **domicile**, Hero, Beatrice, Leonato, and his elderly brother, Antonio, were waiting for a masquerade dance to begin. Beatrice **regaled** the assembled company with her idea of the "ideal suitor."

37. churlish, presumptuous, ❤ canker •

LD - metaphor (Benedick as a canker sore)

Paragraph - new person speaking

Commas - 2 adjectives; non-restrictive modifier; quote

Quotation

Punctuation - use of parentheses for aside comment to herself

Often confused words - fewer/less ("fewer" can be counted, "less" compares); then/than ("than" needed here to compare.)

Often confused prepositions - among/between

B - the perfect man and there are less of them then men would like to think would be somewhere among the grim **churlish** don john and the overly **presumptuous canker** benedick beatrice mused

C -   "The perfect man (and there are fewer of them than men would like to think) would be somewhere between the grim, **churlish** Don John and the overly **presumptuous canker**, Benedick," Beatrice mused.

B = *suggested sentence for the board or overhead*   *C* = *sentence written correctly*   *LD* = *literary device*

38. melancholy •

LD - satire

Paragraph - new person speaking

Quotation

Possession - singular nouns

Redundancy - "Of" is redundant after "half."

Often confused words - then/than ("Then" is needed here as an adverb.)

Homophone - your/you're

Punctuation - need for question mark in question

Verb tense - correct use of conditional (Warn students to use conditional tense only if the action has not yet happened. Do not substitute for the past tense.)

B - than half of signior benedicks words in don johns mouth and half of don johns **melancholy** in signior benedicks face would be youre ideal mate teased leonato

C - "Then half Signior Benedick's words in Don John's mouth and half Don John's **melancholy** in Signior Benedick's face would be your ideal mate?" teased Leonato.

39. ❤ virile, accede •

LD - pun (The French word "foutre," a very crude word meaning "to fornicate" sounds somewhat like the English word "foot." Shakespeare used this pun to mean that Beatrice's ideal man was also a good lover. Audiences of Shakespeare's day, who all knew French, would pick up on this pun immediately.)**; double entendre** (Shakespeare also probably meant the word "leg" to refer to the male organ. There are many sexual puns and references in this play.)**; monologue**

Paragraph - new person speaking

Commas - direct address; "too" meaning "also"

Quotation

Coordinating conjunctions - Do not begin a sentence with one.

Homophone - to/too/two

Verb tense - need for pluperfect to refer to action that precedes this paragraph

Like vs. as - "Like" should be used only with a noun or pronoun standing for a noun in a direct comparison; "as if" must be used here because it is not a comparison.

Pronouns - "he" needed because it is the subject of an implied verb ("is")

Punctuation - dash (or commas) needed to denote break; no quotation marks at end as continued in next Caught'ya (and quotation) continued in next paragraph

B - and with a **virile** leg and a good foot uncle and money in his pocket to continued beatrice like she wasnt interrupted. a man such as that would win any woman in the world if he could get her to **accede** *(to be continued in the next Caught'ya...)*

C - "With a **virile** leg and a good foot, Uncle, and money in his pocket, too," continued Beatrice as if she had not been interrupted. "A man such as he *(like him)* would win any woman in the world — if he could get her to **accede**. *(to be continued in the next Caught'ya...)*

B = suggested sentence for the board or overhead   *C = sentence written correctly*   *LD = literary device*

40. diatribe •

LD - monologue; humor; metaphor ("beard" for "youth")

NOTE: Discuss the meaning of this confusing monologue. Shakespeare loved to play with words and riddles, and this is a sterling example

Paragraph - slight subject change (debatable)

Commas - quote; odd word order ("I am not for him"); extra word

Quotation

Contraction

Correlative conjunctions - "either" needed here, for there is no negative

Relative pronouns - who/whom/that/which ("who" needed in all 5 places as the subject; "that" or "which" never used with people)

Often confused words - then/than ("than" for comparisons here); fewer/less

Punctuation - use of semicolon in compound sentence

NOTE: This is a good place to discuss 3 uses of semicolons - in a series of independent clauses, in a compound sentence instead of a conjunction, and after a colon (for clarity) if the list uses commas.

B - and i dont want anyone that has a beard on his face neither beatrice warmed up to her **diatribe**. he that has a beard is more then a youth. he which has no beard is less than a man. he that is more than a youth is not for me he that is less then a man i am not for him

C -   "I don't want anyone who has a beard on his face, either," Beatrice warmed up to her **diatribe**. "He who has a beard is more than a youth. He who has no beard is less than a man. He who is more than a youth is not for me; he who is less than a man, I am not for him."

41. ❤ **shrew,** ❤ **shrewd, admonished** • ❤ • • • • •

LD - alliteration; play on words; narrator aside

2 Paragraphs - new person speaking; narrator aside

Commas - interjection; direct address; quote; optional comma after "ago" for introductory adverb

Quotation

Capitalization - Capitalize "niece" since it used as a name.

Splitting verbs - avoid

Spelling rule - "i" before "e" except after "c..."

Parallel construction - noun/verb ("a shrew ...and shrewd") or rewrite

Numbers - write out up to 99 unless they begin a sentence

Possession - plural noun that does not end in "s" (discuss what to do with plural nouns that *do* end in "s")

B - on my word niece you never will get a husband and marry if you are such a **shrew** with your tongue and so **shrewd** with your wit **admonished** leonato fondly. 400 years ago womens rights did not exist

C -   "On my word, Niece, you never will get a husband and marry if you are such a **shrew** with your tongue and so **shrewd** with your wit," **admonished** Leonato fondly.

         Four hundred years ago women's rights did not exist.

➥ **SUGGESTIONS:**

This is another good place to go over the parts of speech since all eight are represented in Caught'ya #41. This is also a good place to review the differences among a simple, a compound, and a complex sentence.

---

42. ♥ nuptial •

LD - anthropomorphism (making her virtue human)

Paragraph - new person speaking

Commas - quote; introductory word

Quotation

Contraction

Run-on sentence - lack of punctuation and overuse of "and"

Splitting verbs - avoid

Pronouns - "I" as subject and "me" as object; word order (put yourself last)

Prepositions - Do not end a sentence with a preposition if at all possible.

Homophone - their/there/they're

Subject/verb agreement - "man" requires singular verb

Italics - emphasis of word

B - beatrice responded well i dont plan to marry and *my* **nuptial** day will never arrive and there are no man for I and me and my virtue will go to heaven as a maid

C -   Beatrice responded, "Well, I don't plan to marry. *My* **nuptial** day never will arrive. There is no man for me. My virtue and I will go to heaven as a maid."

43. donned •

Paragraph - narrator with subject change

No commas - none needed after "mask" as it is not a compound sentence, only a compound predicate.

Possession - singular noun

Indirect quotation - use of "that" to avoid quotes

Antecedent/pronoun agreement - "everyone" is singular and needs a singular pronoun

Collective noun - use singular form of verb

B - hero interrupted beatrices monologue to point out that people were arriving for the masquerade. everyone **donned** there mask and went to join the festivities

C -   Hero interrupted Beatrice's monologue to point out that people were arriving for the masquerade. Everyone **donned** a *(or his/her)* mask and went to join the festivities.

44. festoons, ♥ garlands •

LD - anthropomorphism (making tables like humans who groan under a heavy weight); **description**

Paragraph - subject change; place change

Comma - compound sentence

Reflexive pronouns - must use correct form of reflexive pronoun

Relative pronouns - who/whom/whose/whoever/whomever/that/which ("that" and "which" can be subject or object and are used only with objects and animals; "who" and "whom" are used with people; "who" is subject; "whom" is object)

Spelling of common word - "weight"

Hyphen - 2 words acting as one adjective

Strong, active verbs - needed in description

NOTE: This would be a good place to review prepositions.

B - the servants had outdone theirselves **festoons** of **garlands** hung from the ceiling and lace covered tables groaned under the weight of the food

C -   The servants had outdone themselves. **Festoons** of **garlands** hung from the ceiling, and lace-covered tables groaned under the weight of the food.

---

45. throng, array •

LD - narration; description; alliteration; simile

No paragraph

Commas - participial phrases

Articles - use "an" only before a noun or adjective that begins with a vowel or a silent "h" as in "hour"

Antecedent/pronoun agreement - "throng" is a collective noun and therefore singular; "each" is short for "each one" and also is singular; "their" is plural

Collective nouns and pronouns - Discuss common collective nouns - family, everyone (indefinite pronoun), crowd, crew, group, etc.

Strong, active verbs - needed in description

B - an **throng** of townspeople dressed in a **array** of bright colors each wearing their mask danced around on the shiny wood floor like dream dancers swaying to imaginary music. it was a picturesque scene

C - A **throng** of townspeople, dressed in an **array** of bright colors, each wearing a *(or his/her)* mask, danced around on the shiny wood floor like dream dancers swaying to imaginary music. It was a picturesque scene.

46. discern, ♥ covertly •

LD - narration; simile; literary reference

NOTE: Warn students of the need to rewrite.

Paragraph - action change

Commas - adjective clause with relative pronoun as non-restrictive modifier; interrupter; comparative as interrupter

Subject/verb agreement - collective noun "crowd" is singular

Collective nouns and pronouns - Discuss common ones — family, everyone, crowd, crew, group, etc.

Relative pronouns - who/whom/that ("who" needed here as subject of "recognized and "hid")

Misplaced modifier - Benedick was like D'Artagnan, not his mask.

Like vs. as - "like" needed in a direct comparison

B - soon the entire crowd were dancing. benedick whom recognized beatrice danced with her. beatrice however did not **discern** benedick who **covertly** hid behind his mask like d'artagnan

C -   Soon the entire crowd was dancing. Benedick, who recognized Beatrice, danced with her. Beatrice, however, did not **discern** Benedick who, like D'Artagnan, **covertly** hid behind his mask.

47. ♥ devising (to devise)**, ♥ odorous, ♥ slanders** •

LD - oxymoron ("witty fool")**; play on words** ("fool" as a jester and as a real idiot)**; personification** (as if quips could do something)

No paragraph; paragraph when Beatrice speaks

Commas - long introductory adverbial phrase; participial phrase; interrupted quote; quote

Quotation

Possession - singular nouns

Often confused words - then/than (need "than" as comparative here)

Improper verb-tense switch - story in past

Pronouns - "he" as subject of the verb "to be" ("he *is*" where "is" is implied)

B - much to the young mans surprise and dismay beatrice thinking him a stranger talks about benedick. he is the princes jester she said a very witty fool. his only gift is **devising** impossible and **odorous slanders**. his quips are cleverer than him beatrice ranted

C - Much to the young man's surprise and dismay, Beatrice, thinking him a stranger, talked about Benedick.

"He is the Prince's jester," she said, "a very witty fool. His only gift is **devising** impossible and **odorous slanders**. His quips are cleverer than he," Beatrice ranted.

---

48. descry •

Paragraph - new person speaking

Commas - introductory subordinate clause; quote

Relative pronouns - who/whom/that/which ("whom" needed as object of preposition)

Parallel construction - "*to* dance" and "*to* exchange"

Splitting infinitives - never split infinitives (*Star Trek* was wrong — "To boldly go.." should be "To go boldly...")

B - when i **descry** the gentleman who you speak of i will tell him what you said offered benedick as they continued to closely dance and exchanged barbs

C - "When I **descry** the gentleman of whom you speak, I will tell him what you said," offered Benedick as they continued to dance closely and to exchange barbs.

49. beatitude •

LD - aphorism; simile; onomatopoeia ("oinking"); sarcasm

Paragraph - narrator speaking

Commas - participial phrase; participial phrase

Numbers - write out to 99

Plural vs. possessive nouns

Possession - singular noun

Incorrect verb-tense switch - story in past tense

Spelling rule - if a word ends in consonant/vowel/consonant and a suffix is added, the last consonant much be doubled ("wrapped")

Homophone - their/there/they're

Possessive pronouns - my, your, his, her, its, our, their

Prepositions - Note use of them here and review them if needed.

B - claudio danced with hero each gazing into the other's eye's. the 2 wraped around each other like pigs' in a blanket oinking there **beatitude**

C - Claudio danced with Hero, each gazing into the other's eyes. The two wrapped around each other like pigs in a blanket, oinking their **beatitude**.

➥ **SUGGESTION:**

This would be a good point for a midterm exam. You can type up as a test Caught'yas #50 - #55 for a good review of much of what your students have been practicing up to this point. Type them together, without numbers, as one, long Caught'ya.

50. dissension •

LD - narrative; subplot; alliteration

Paragraph - narrator

Comma - introductory word

Spelling rules - "i" before "e" except after "c..."

Incorrect verb-tense switch - story in past tense

Common spelling error - "a lot" is two words

Compound subject

B - well don john and borachio also were at the masquerade. they are spreading alot of **dissension** and deciet instead of dancing

C - Well, Don John and Borachio also were at the masquerade. They spread a lot of **dissension** and deceit instead of dancing.

---

51. ♥ **infamous (infamy), disseminate** •

LD - narration

No paragraph - continuation

Commas - participial phrase as interrupter; no comma before "and" as not a compound sentence (no subject)

Numbers - write out to 99

Possessive pronouns - my, your, his, her, its, our, their

Spelling rule - if a word ends in consonant/vowel/consonant and a suffix is added, the last consonant much be doubled ("planned")

Homophone - their/there/they're

Strong verbs - needed to describe action

Incorrect word use - You cannot use "tonight" in a story in the past tense when the narrator is relating events.

B - the 2 **infamous** varlets cornered claudio and pretending to be fooled by his disguise **disseminated** there lie that don pedro planed to marry hero tonight

C - The two **infamous** varlets cornered Claudio and, pretending to be fooled by his disguise, **disseminated** their lie that Don Pedro planned to marry Hero that night.

52. **singularly,** ♥ **perturbed** •

LD - narrator aside

Paragraph - narrator aside

Commas - introductory subordinate clause

Use of second person in a narrator aside - Narrator is stepping out of the story.

Relative pronouns - who/whom/that/which ("who" both times needed as subject; never use "that" or "which" to refer to people.)

Run-on sentence - "and"

Often confused words - affect/effect

Pronouns - "he" needed here as subject of "was"

Italics - emphasis of word

Intensifiers - "really" (Go over uses of intensifiers.)

B - as you can imagine this lie **singularly** effected poor claudio whom thought that it was *him* that was going to wed hero and claudio was really **perturbed**

C -   As you can imagine, this lie **singularly** affected poor Claudio who thought that it was *he* who was going to wed Hero. Claudio was really **perturbed**.

53. ♥ **reveled, villainy,** ♥ **motley** •

LD - narrator aside; description within action

No paragraph - slight subject change but narrator still speaking

Commas - interrupter; no comma after "humor" as it is not a compound sentence (no subject)

Run on sentence

Homophone - no/know

Hyphen - 2 words acting as one

Sentence structure - deliberate use of fragment for narrator aside.

Punctuation - need for exclamation in fragment for emphasis

B - don john on the other hand **reveled** in his **villainy** and delighted in getting revenge and he had know sense of humor and never smiled when he could frown and what a **motley** minded loser

C - Don John, on the other hand, **reveled** in his **villainy** and delighted in getting revenge. He had no sense of humor and never smiled when he could frown. What a **motley**-minded loser!

B = *suggested sentence for the board or overhead*   ***C*** = *sentence written correctly*   ***LD*** = *literary device*

54. foiled, misconception, ♥ woe ●

LD - sarcasm

2 Paragraphs - narrator and then Don Pedro

Commas - direct address; compound sentence

Sentence structure - deliberate use of fragment.

Punctuation - need for exclamation mark in fragment

Possession - singular noun

Imperative sentence - subject is implied

Often confused words - assure/insure

Spelling rule - "i" before "e..."

Homophone - your/you're

Pronouns - "She" is needed as subject of "wish" (subjective case in the predicate); word order (put yourself last).

B - but wait. don john was **foiled** again. don pedro cleared up claudios **misconception** and **woe**. don pedro assured claudio that hero was his. rest easy my freind i have wooed hero in youre name and fair hero is yours. name the day you and her wish to marry

C -   But wait! Don John was **foiled** again. Don Pedro cleared up Claudio's **misconception** and **woe**. Don Pedro assured Claudio that Hero was his.

"Rest easy, my friend, I have wooed Hero in your name, and fair Hero is yours. Name the day she and you wish to marry."

55. chauvinist ●

LD - narrator aside; metaphor and aphorism ("chauvinist pig")

Paragraph - new person speaking

Commas - appositive; quote; adjective clause with relative pronoun; introductory subordinate clause

Quotation

Punctuation - use of parentheses for narrator aside

Imperative sentence - subject implied

Misplaced modifier - daughter loves a lot, not fortune

Often confused words - farther/further

Common spelling errors - "a lot" is 2 words, so are "all right" and "no one"

Pronouns - Use "she" because it is the subject of "will be."

Adjective vs. adverb - "Good" is an adjective and "well" is an adverb .

B - leonato heros father and a typical **chauvinist** pig of the time added further take my daughter and with her my fortune who loves you alot. i hope that you and her will be very happy and that all ends good

C -   Leonato, Hero's father, (and a typical **chauvinist** pig of the time) added further, "Take my daughter, who loves you a lot, and with her my fortune. When you marry, I hope that you and she will be very happy and that all ends well."

56. meandered ●

LD - personification (walkways cannot wander); **naturalistic detail; description**

Paragraph - narrator again

Commas - introductory subordinate clause; participial phrase; interrupter

Dangling participle - the flowers were not dotted by trees

Often confused words - further/farther ("farther" refers to a measurable distance)

Strong verbs - needed in description

Compound and complex sentences - review

B - as the men conversed farther they walked outside into the garden. a full moon illuminated the scene. graveled walkways wandered through beds of flowers dotted by trees every few feet. the men however were oblivious as they **meandered** farther down one of the paths

C -   As the men conversed further, they walked outside into the garden. A full moon illuminated the scene. Graveled walkways, dotted by trees every few feet, wandered through beds of flowers. The men, however, were oblivious as they **meandered** farther down one of the paths.

B = suggested sentence for the board or overhead   *C = sentence written correctly*   *LD = literary device*

57. predestined •

LD - narration

No paragraph - continuation

Commas - introductory phrase

Possession - plural noun that does not end in "s" (Discuss possessive of plural nouns that *do* end in "s" as well.)

Possession - singular noun

Numbers - write out to 99

Often confused words - accept/except

Homophone - there/their/they're

Possessive pronouns - my, your, his, her, its, our, their

Irregular verbs - lie/lay/has lain/ lying and lay/laid/has laid/laying

Intransitive vs. transitive verbs - Discuss intransitive (lie/lay) and transitive (lay/laid) verbs

B - the topic of the mens conversation was beatrice. don pedro thought that she was **predestined** to be benedicks wife. after all the 2 talked of nothing but the other accept when they were laying asleep in their separate beds

C - The topic of the men's conversation was Beatrice. Don Pedro thought that she was **predestined** to be Benedick's wife. After all, the two talked of nothing but the other except when they were lying asleep in their separate beds.

58. prattle •

LD - humor

Paragraph - new person speaking

Commas - interjection; introductory phrase; interrupted quote; introductory subordinate clause

Quotation - continued quote needs no capital letter to begin continuation

Verb tense - use of conditional tense after "if" clause

Punctuation - need for exclamation mark

Contraction

Redundancy - eliminate redundant words ("with each other")

NOTE: This would be another good spot to go over the eight parts of speech.

B - oh my word said leonato if they being who they are were married for a week they would **prattle** themselves mad. lets get the two of them together with each other

C - "Oh, my word," said Leonato, "if they, being who they are, were married for a week, they would **prattle** themselves mad! Let's get the two of them together."

59. proffered •

LD - allusion to mythology; metaphor; sarcasm

Paragraph - new person speaking

Commas - quote

Quotation

Contractions

Often confused words - who's/whose

Punctuation - need for exclamation mark; need for question mark

B - it would be a herculean labor to bring benedick and beatrice together in a mountain of affection for each other **proffered** don pedro. lets do it. whose with me

C - "It would be a Herculean labor to bring Benedick and Beatrice together in a mountain of affection for each other," **proffered** Don Pedro. "Let's do it! Who's with me?"

B = *suggested sentence for the board or overhead*   *C* = *sentence written correctly*   *LD* = *literary device*

60. abhorred •••

LD - anadiplosis ("two young people"); **narration**

Paragraph - narrator speaking

Commas - repetition; noun series

Homophone - their/they're/there

Colon - colon needed for long series (a colon is not used before a verb.)

Numbers - write out to 99

Often confused words - who's/whose

Punctuation - need to put quotation marks around a single letter

B - the men debated how to get two young people to realize their love for each other 2 young people who **abhorred** the following marriage love the opposite sex and anyone whos name began with a b

C -   The men debated how to get two young people to realize their love for each other, two young people who **abhorred** the following: marriage, love, the opposite sex, and anyone whose name began with a "B."

61. imminent, dapper ••

LD - **narration; idiomatic expression** and **metaphor** (head in the clouds)

Paragraph - subject change

Commas - introductory adverb; relative clause; introductory subordinate clause

Often confused words - who's/whose

B - just then hero whos head was always in the clouds wandered into the garden. she walked up to her father. when she heard the news of her **imminent** marriage to the **dapper** claudio she was elated

C -   Just then, Hero, whose head was always in the clouds, wandered into the garden. She walked up to her father. When she heard the news of her **imminent** marriage to the **dapper** Claudio, she was elated.

62. besotted, ♥ beseeched, unrivaled •••••••••••••••••••••••••••••••

LD - metaphors and **personifications** ("time goes on crutches" and "Love's rites" meaning marriage); **hyperbole; anthropomorphism** (Love as a human)

NOTE: Warn students of the need to reword sentence.

Paragraph - new person speaking

Commas - participial phrase; quote; adjective series

Quotation

Homophone - their/there/they're

Possessive pronouns - my, your, his, her, its, our, their

Misplaced modifier - the day was not besotted, Claudio was

Possession - singular noun

Capitalization - need for capital "L" in "Love" since it is being referred to as a person

Contraction

B - claudio **beseeched** leonato to hasten there marriage day **besotted** by hero murmured time goes on crutches until loves rites take place. i can't wait to marry my beautiful comely superlative **unrivaled** love

C -   Claudio, **besotted** by Hero, **beseeched** Leonato to hasten their marriage day. "Time goes on crutches until Love's rites take place. I can't wait to marry my beautiful, comely, superlative, **unrivaled** love."

B = *suggested sentence for the board or overhead*   ***C*** = *sentence written correctly*   ***LD*** = *literary device*

63. ♥ **amorous** •

LD - playing with the word "amorous" and repeating it for effect

Paragraph - narrator

Commas - long introductory adverbial phrase; no comma after "non-amorous" since "young" denotes age

Homophone - their/there/they're

Intensifier - use of "very" as an intensifier (Discuss various uses of adverbs.)

Antecedent/pronoun agreement - "group" is a collective noun and therefore singular

Collective nouns - "the conspiracy" (need for singular verb)

Possessive pronouns - my, your, his, her, its, our, their

Incorrect verb-tense switch - story is in past tense

Numbers - write out to 99

Hyphen - 2 words acting as one

B - after being reassured that there marriage was to take place that very week claudio and hero join the conspiracy in there plot to make the 2 non **amorous** young people **amorous** of each other

C -   After being reassured that their marriage was to take place that very week, Claudio and Hero joined the conspiracy in its plot to make the two non-**amorous** young people **amorous** of each other.

64. lauding (to laud) •

LD - narration; irony

Paragraph - subject change

Commas - introductory subordinate clause; participial phrases

Antecedent/pronoun agreement - "group" is a collective noun and therefore singular

Collective nouns - "group" needs singular verb

Possessive pronouns - my, your, his, her, its, our, their

Plural rules - words that end in a consonant and "y" change "y" to "i" and add "es"

Verb tense - incorrect use conditional "would" as substitute for past tense

Relative pronoun - "that" used correctly

B - the assembled group hatched their plot. when they knew that beatrice was eavesdropping hero and her ladys would talk about benedick **lauding** him and giving him all the virtues that beatrice liked

C -   The assembled group hatched its plot. When they knew that Beatrice was eavesdropping, Hero and her ladies talked about Benedick, **lauding** him and giving him all the virtues that Beatrice liked.

65. ostentatiously, pined •

No paragraph - narrator is speaking; paragraph - Hero speaks

Commas - quote; non-restrictive relative pronoun clause

Quotation

Conditional tense - Avoid use of conditional "would" in a narration; it is not needed here.

Relative pronouns - "who" needed as subject of "was"

Often confused prepositions - among/between ("between" 2; "among" 3 or more)

Plural rule - consonant "y" changes to "i" and "es" is added

B - they would also **ostentatiously** insist that benedick **pined** with love for beatrice. that should get her said hero who was standing between the ladys

C - They also **ostentatiously** insisted that Benedick **pined** with love for Beatrice.

"That should get her," said Hero, who was standing among the ladies.

B = *suggested sentence for the board or overhead*   *C* = *sentence written correctly*   *LD* = *literary device*

66. ❤ intemperate, extolling, ❤ abiding •••

LD - building suspense; subplot; irony

NOTE: Warn students of need to reword sentence.

Paragraph - narrator

Commas - longish introductory adverbial phrase; introductory subordinate clause

Antecedent/pronoun agreement - "group" is a collective noun and therefore singular

Collective nouns - "group" needs singular possessive pronoun

Misplaced modifier - the conversation will extol

Possession - singular noun

B - at the same time the group of men made there plans to do the same to the **intemperate** benedick. the men planned to have a conversation when benedick could overhear them **extolling** beatrices virtues and her **abiding** love for benedick

C - At the same time, the group of men made its plans to do the same to the **intemperate** Benedick. When Benedick could overhear them, the men planned to have a conversation **extolling** Beatrice's virtues and her **abiding** love for Benedick.

67. meritorious •••

LD - allusion to mythology; metaphor

Paragraph - new person speaking

Commas - long introductory phrase; quote; introductory subordinate clause

Irregular comparatives - bad/worse/worst

Relative pronouns - who/whom/whose/whoever/ whomever/that/which ("that" and "which" can be subject or object and are used only with objects and animals; "who" and "whom" are used with people; "who" is subject; "whom" is object)

Pronouns - need to use "he" since "should fall in love with" is implied and therefore a subject is needed

Often confused words - among/between

Verb tense - need for future tense or subjunctive mood with "if" clause

Possession - singular noun

Commonly misspelled word - truly

B - among those that i know benedick is not the worst prospect for a husband concluded don pedro. he is honest and **meritorious**. beatrice should fall in love with him and him with her. if we can pull this off we are truely cupids henchpeople

C - "Among those whom I know, Benedick is not the worst prospect for a husband," concluded Don Pedro. "He is honest and **meritorious**. Beatrice should fall in love with him and he with her. If we can pull this off, we will be truly Cupid's henchpeople."

68. ❤ thwart, ❤ contemptible, sycophant •••••••••••••••••••••••••••••••••••

LD - subplot; building suspense

Paragraph - new topic

Commas - long modifier at beginning of sentence; appositive; no comma before or after Borachio since it is a restrictive modifier (Don Pedro has several sycophants — Borachio and conrade)

Possession - singular nouns

Hyphen - 2 words acting as one

Verb recognition - Have students find main verb (devised) in this sentence.

B - unsuccessful in his first attempt to **thwart** claudios and heros nuptials don john don pedros **contemptible** half brother and his **sycophant** borachio devised another scheme

C - Unsuccessful in his first attempt to **thwart** Claudio's and Hero's nuptials, Don John, Don Pedro's **contemptible** half-brother, and his **sycophant** Borachio devised another scheme.

69. ❤ covert •••

LD - subplot; play on words ("maid"); **narration; building of suspense**

No paragraph - narration continued

Comma - appositive

Possession - singular noun

Verb tense - correct use of conditional tense

Simple sentences - Ask students to pick out subjects and main verbs.

B - borachio badly wanted to impress his boss. he proposed a **covert** plan. it seemed that borachio had been dating the girl margaret heros maid. margaret would do anything borachio asked

C - Borachio badly wanted to impress his boss. He proposed a **covert** plan. It seemed that Borachio had been dating the girl Margaret, Hero's maid. Margaret would do anything Borachio asked.

B = *suggested sentence for the board or overhead*   ***C*** = *sentence written correctly*   ***LD*** = *literary device*

70. ♥ quirks, impetuousness ●

LD - aphorism ("look before you leap")

No paragraph - same topic

Commas - extra information; infinitive series; introductory phrase

Indirect quotation - use of "that" to avoid quotes

Parallel construction - all should be infinitive phrases

Often confused words - former/latter

Changing adjectives to nouns - use of "ness"

Punctuation - need for dash to denote break and for sentence to make sense

B - borachio proposed that they take advantage of claudios **quirks** namely that the latter was quick to judge got riled and to jump to conclusions. in other words claudio suffered from the **impetuousness** of youth he did not look before he leaped.

C - Borachio proposed that they take advantage of Claudio's **quirks**, namely that the latter was quick to judge, to get riled, and to jump to conclusions. In other words, Claudio suffered from the **impetuousness** of youth — he did not look before he leaped.

71. rendezvous, ♥ cuckolded (If you are uncomfortable using and defining this word, ● substitute "cheated on" or "went out on.")

LD - use of foreign word; building the suspense; narration

NOTE: Warn students that this is one sentence, improperly punctuated.

Paragraph - new subject

Commas - long introductory adverb; participial phrase

Run-on sentence - no punctuation

Colon - use of colon to set off list of sentences

Semicolons - use after a colon for clarity in a series

Possession - singular nouns

Common spelling error - clothes/cloths

Homophone - break/brake; insure/ensure

Verb tense - correct use of conditional in planned future actions

NOTE: If needed, discuss again the three uses of the semicolons - in a series of independent clauses, in a compound sentence instead of a conjunction, and after a colon (for clarity) if the list uses commas

B - borachios diabolical plan included the following the night before claudios and heros nuptials borachio would talk with margaret at heros bedroom window calling her hero margaret would wear heros cloths he would insure that claudio and don pedro witnessed the **rendezvous** claudio and don pedro would think that hero had **cuckolded** claudio and claudio would break off the wedding

C - Borachio's diabolical plan included the following: the night before Claudio's and Hero's nuptials, Borachio would talk with Margaret at Hero's bedroom window, calling her Hero; Margaret would wear Hero's clothes; he would insure that Claudio and Don Pedro witnessed the **rendezvous**; Claudio and Don Pedro would think that Hero had **cuckolded** Claudio; and Claudio would break off the wedding.

72. sanctioned ●

Paragraph - new person speaking

No commas - subordinate clause is at the end of the sentence

Quotation

Homophone - their/there/they're

Possession - singular noun

Possessive pronouns - my, your, his, her, its, our, their

Often confused words - affect/effect

B - don john **sanctioned** borachios plan. i will learn there day of marriage so that we can put this plan into effect

C - Don John **sanctioned** Borachio's plan. "I will learn their day of marriage so that we can put this plan into effect."

---

73. cogitated, ❤ folly, ❤ arbor ●

LD - soliloquy

Paragraph - new person speaking

Commas - two introductory adverbs (one a phrase); interjection ("Ah")

Quotation - You do need quotes if someone is thinking out loud.

Possession - singular noun

Punctuation - need for exclamation mark in deliberate fragment for emphasis

Possession - plural noun

Contraction

Pronouns - "Him" used in the nominative case is incorrect as "he did" is implied ("I'll never fall as he did").

Run-on sentences - lack of punctuation

Like vs. as - incorrect use of "like" ("Like" is used only in a direct comparison between two nouns or pronouns.)

B - meanwhile in the garden benedick set on a bench and **cogitated** on his friends impending marriage. what **folly** he thought out loud. claudio is usually a reasonable man. ill never fall like him. ah i hear my friends voices ill hide in this **arbor**

C -   Meanwhile, in the garden, Benedick sat on a bench and **cogitated** on his friend's impending marriage. "What **folly**!" he thought out loud. "Claudio is usually a reasonable man. I'll never fall as he did. Ah, I hear my friends' voices. I'll hide in this **arbor**."

74. transpired ●

LD - pun (Masterpiece Theater); **reference to literature; irony** ("a dialogue worthy of Shakespeare")

Paragraph - narrator speaking

Commas - appositive

Often confused words - then/than

B - what **transpired** then was a masterpiece of theater a dialogue worthy of shakespeare

C -   What **transpired** then was a masterpiece of theater, a dialogue worthy of Shakespeare.

75. clandestinely; ❤ discourse ●

Paragraph - new subject

Commas - noun series; participial phrase modifying Claudio

Homophone - their/there/they're

Possessive pronouns - my, your, his, her, its, our, their

Compound verb

B - don pedro leonato and claudio **clandestinely** followed benedick to the park and seeing him hide in a nearby arbor winked at each other and began there **discourse**

C -   Don Pedro, Leonato, and Claudio **clandestinely** followed Benedick to the park and, seeing him hide in a nearby arbor, winked at each other and began their **discourse**.

76. ❤ dotes, ❤ abhor ●

LD - irony

2 Paragraphs - 2 persons speaking

Commas - direct address; appositive; introductory word and direct address; appositive; aside as interrupter ("to outward...")

Quotation

Contractions

Homophone - your/you're

Spelling rule - "i" before "e"

Relative pronouns - who/whom/whose/whoever/ whomever/that/which ("that" and "which" can be subject or object and are used only with objects and animals; "who" and "whom" are used with people; "who" is subject; "whom" is object)

B - don pedro wasted no time. didnt you tell me leonato that youre outspoken niece beatrice is in love with benedick. yes my friend. im so glad that she **dotes** on benedick a man who to outward appearances she seems to **abhor**

C -   Don Pedro wasted no time. "Didn't you tell me, Leonato, that your outspoken niece, Beatrice, is in love with Benedick?"

    "Yes, my friend. I'm so glad that she **dotes** on Benedick, a man whom, to outward appearances, she seems to **abhor**.

---

77. ❤ **counterfeits** •

LD - oxymoron ("enraged affection")

2 Paragraphs - 2 persons speaking

Commas - quote; quote

Quotations

Incorrect verb tense switch - story in past tense

Punctuation - need for question mark

B - leonato continued beatrice loves him with an enraged affection. maybe she only **counterfeits** her passion suggests don pedro with a grin. how do you know this

C -   Leonato continued, "Beatrice loves him with an enraged affection."

"Maybe she only **counterfeits** her passion," suggested Don Pedro with a grin. "How do you know this?"

78. chaste •

LD - anecdote; foreshadowing by using the word "chaste"

Paragraph - new person speaking

Commas - interjection; appositive (non-restrictive); quote; verb series; no comma needed after "words" since what follows is necessary for clarity

Commas - introductory word; appositive; quote; verb series

Quotation

Irregular verbs - rise/rose/ has risen, raise/raised/has raised, sit/sat/has sat, and set/set/has set

Transitive vs. intransitive verbs - review difference

Numbers - write out to 99

Punctuation - quote within a quote

Homophone - piece/peace

B - why my **chaste** daughter hero confided in me leonato answered. hero says that beatrice raises up 20 times a night and sets there in her nightgown and writes the words benedick and beatrice over and over on a peace of paper

C -   "Why, my **chaste** daughter, Hero, confided in me," Leonato answered. "Hero says that Beatrice rises twenty times a night, sits there in her nightgown, and writes the words 'Benedick and Beatrice' over and over on a piece of paper."

79. surreptitiously, furtively •

Paragraph - narrator

Commas - participial phrase

Possession - singular noun

Punctuation - quotation marks needed around supposed falsehood

Homophone - vein/vain

Splitting verbs - don't

B - the conspirators went on and on in such a vein talking about beatrices love for benedick and periodically checking **surreptitiously** to make sure that benedick was still **furtively** listening

C -   The conspirators went on and on in such a vein, talking about Beatrice's "love" for Benedick and periodically checking **surreptitiously** to make sure that Benedick still was listening **furtively**.

80. soliloquy •

LD - spoonerism ("hook, line, and sinker")

No paragraph - continuation

Commas - noun series

Possessive pronouns - my, your, his, her, its, our, their

Homophones - their/there/they're; heard/herd

Punctuation - use of quotation marks to mark falsehood

Possession -singular and plural noun

B - they concluded their charade by deciding not to tell benedick of beatrices supposed love because he would mock her. benedick herd it all and bought his friends act hook line and **soliloquy**

C - They concluded their charade by "deciding" not to tell Benedick of Beatrice's supposed love because he would mock her. Benedick heard it all and bought his friends' act hook, line, and **soliloquy**.

B = suggested sentence for the board or overhead   C = sentence written correctly   LD = literary device

81. badinage (witty and clever repartée), pulchritudinous •

LD - aphorism

Paragraph - new person speaking

Commas - compound sentence; introductory subordinate clause

Quotation

Pronouns - too many pronouns make meaning unclear (use nouns)

Verb tense - correct use of conditional

B - suddenly he saw beatrice in a new light. she is quick with **badinage** and humor and she is **pulchritudinous**. when i said i would die a bachelor i did not consider her

C -   Suddenly Benedick saw Beatrice in a new light. "She is quick with **badinage** and humor, and she is **pulchritudinous**. When I said I would die a bachelor, I did not consider Beatrice."

82. portent •

LD - foreshadowing

Paragraph - time change

Commas - separate two adverbs and at the end of 2nd adverb; introductory subordinate clause

Pronouns - use of too many pronouns for clarity (replace with nouns)

B - when a few minutes later she came to call him in to dinner he interpreted everything she said and did as a **portent** of her love

C -   When, a few minutes later, Beatrice came to call Benedick in to dinner, Benedick interpreted everything Beatrice said and did as a **portent** of her love.

83. in cahoots with •

Paragraph - time change

Commas - introductory adverb (optional); noun series

Punctuation - parentheses or dashes needed to denote narrator clarification

Possession - singular noun

Relative pronouns - "who" needed as subject

B - that very evening hero a gentlewoman named ursula and heros maid the one who was **in cahoots with** borachio lured beatrice into the garden

C -   That very evening, Hero, a gentlewoman named Ursula, and Margaret, Hero's maid (the one who was **in cahoots with** Borachio) lured Beatrice into the garden.

84. bracken •

No paragraph - continuation

Commas - introductory adverb (optional); introductory subordinate clause

Plural rule - if a singular noun ends in consonant and a "y," drop the "y" and add "ies"

Homophone - heard/herd

Possession - plural noun

B - in a few minutes the ladys arrived outside. when beatrice heard her friends voices she hid in the **bracken**

C - In a few minutes, the ladies arrived outside. When Beatrice heard her friends' voices, she hid in the **bracken**.

85. avowed •

Paragraph - new person speaking

Commas - introductory subordinate clause; quote

Quotation

Strong verbs - embroidered; avowed

Possession - singular noun

Possessive pronouns - my, your, his, her, its, our, their

B - as beatrice listened from her hiding place hero embroidered a tale about benedicks passion for beatrice. he is wasting away from his love for beatrice she **avowed**

C - As Beatrice listened from her hiding place, Hero embroidered a tale about Benedick's passion for Beatrice.

    "He is wasting away from his love for Beatrice," she **avowed**.

B = suggested sentence for the board or overhead   C = sentence written correctly   LD = literary device

86. ardor ●

No paragraph - quote continued

Commas - adjective series; quote; participial phrase

Quotation

Possessive pronouns - my, your, his, her, its, our, their

Verb tense - correct use of conditional tense before "if" clause

Prepositions - avoid ending a sentence with one if at all possible.

B - benedick is consumed with sighs. he is so noble young and handsome. beatrice would make fun of him if she knew of his **ardor** hero continued occasionally glancing at the bracken beatrice was hiding behind

C - "Benedick is consumed with sighs. He is so noble, young, and handsome. Beatrice would make fun of him if she knew of his **ardor**," Hero continued, occasionally glancing at the bracken behind which Beatrice was hiding.

87. ♥ valorous ●

LD - personification ("nature")

Paragraph - narrator

Commas - adjective series

Plural rule - if a singular noun ends in consonant and a "y," get rid of the "y" and add "ies"

Capitalization - "nature" needs capital "N" since it is used as a person

Colons and semicolons - use of colon and semicolons in a list; never put a colon after a verb; discuss uses of

Possessive pronouns - my, your, his, her, its, our, their

B - hero and her ladies talked of how kind nature had been to benedick how fair were his features how witty he was how honest **valorous** and gentlemanly he was and how he really adored beatrice

C -   Hero and her ladies talked of how kind Nature had been to Benedick; how fair were his features; how witty he was; how honest, **valorous**, and gentlemanly he was; and how he really adored Beatrice.

88. prattle ●

No paragraph - continuation

Commas - participial phrase as interrupter; appositive

Plural rule - if a singular noun ends in consonant and a "y," get rid of the "y" and add "ies"

Possession - singular nouns

Commonly misspelled word - occur

Indefinite articles - use of "an" with nouns that begin with a vowel or silent "h" as in "an hour"

Incorrect word use - misuse of the word "tomorrow" in a story that takes place in the past tense

B - hero and her ladys than exited the garden **prattling** about heros and claudios wedding a event that was scheduled to ocurr tomorrow

C - Hero and her ladies then exited the garden, **prattling** about Hero's and Claudio's wedding, an event that was scheduled to occur the following day.

89. ruse, cerebrums, feral ●

LD - personification ("wild heart"); **synecdoche and metaphor** ("hand" as a part standing for the whole and meaning Benedick); **repeated use of synonyms for emphasis** ("wild/feral/untamed")

Paragraph - new person speaking

Commas - adjective clause with a relative pronoun ("who"); interjection; direct address; compound sentence; adjective series

QuotationRelative pronoun - "who" as subject

Possession - plural noun

B - beatrice who should have known better had fallen for the **ruse** her friends clever **cerebrums** had devised. ah benedick love on. i will return your love and my wild **feral** untamed heart will be tamed to your loving hand

C -   Beatrice, who should have known better, had fallen for the **ruse** her friends' clever **cerebrums** had devised. "Ah, Benedick, love on. I will return your love, and my wild, **feral**, untamed heart will be tamed to your loving hand."

B = *suggested sentence for the board or overhead*   **C** = *sentence written correctly*   **LD** = *literary device*

90. asserted ●

Paragraph - place change

Commas - optional comma after introductory adverb; subordinate clause in the predicate needs no comma

Italics -emphasis

Splitting verbs - don't

B - meanwhile benedick *was* really pining away for beatrice although he **asserted** that a toothache distressed him

C -   Meanwhile Benedick really *was* pining away for Beatrice although he **asserted** that a toothache distressed him.

91. roguish ●

LD - metaphor ("bears"); **sarcasm**

No paragraph - narrator talks and then paragraph when Claudio speaks

Commas - introductory subordinate clause; quote

Quotation

Possession - singular noun

Spelling rule - need for "u" in "roguish" to make "g" hard

Pronouns - need for nominative case "he" since the verb "is" has been implied ("as roguish as he *is*...)

Often confused words - then/than ("Then" is an adverb, and "than" is a conjunction used to compare.)

Verb tense - need for subjunctive mood, future, or conditional with "if" clause.

B - benedicks friends taunted him about being in love. they were as **roguish** as him. if hero and margaret have done their parts with beatrice then the two bears will not bite one another when they meet observed claudio quietly to don pedro.

C - Benedick's friends taunted him about being in love. They were as **roguish** as he.

"If Hero and Margaret have done their parts with Beatrice, then the two bears will not bite one another when they meet," observed Claudio quietly to Don Pedro.

92. mendacious, insidious ●

LD - metaphor

Paragraph - time change

Commas - introductory subordinate clause; two adjectives where the 2nd is not color, age, or linked to nounPrepositions - review

Spelling rule - "i" before "e" except after "c..."

Possessive pronouns - my, your, his, her, its, our, their

Possession - singular noun

Indefinite article - "an" before a vowel or silent "h"

B - just as benedick summoned the courage to speak to leonato for his nieces hand in marriage the **mendacious** don john appeared with an **insidious** lie about poor innocent hero

C -   Just as Benedick summoned the courage to speak to Leonato for his niece's hand in marriage, the **menda-cious** Don John appeared with an **insidious** lie about poor, innocent Hero.

93. prevaricated ●

LD - double entendre ("Leonato's.......every man's Hero")

3 Paragraphs - conversation

Commas - quote; noun series; quote

Quotations

Punctuation - need for question marks

Possession - singular nouns

Homophone - your/you're

B - don john **prevaricated** i came to tell you that she is disloyal. who asked claudio. hero. leonatos hero your hero every mans hero don john said insidiously

C -   Don John **prevaricated**, "I came to tell you that she is disloyal."

"Who?" asked Claudio. "Hero?"

"Leonato's Hero, your Hero, every man's Hero," Don John said insidiously.

---

94. perfidious •

No paragraph - continuation

Commas - introductory subordinate clause; compound/complex sentence; quote

Quotation

Contraction

Pronouns - The nominative pronoun "she" must be used since the verb "is" is implied.

Often confused words - then/than

B - if you dont believe me come tonight under her chamber window and you will see for yourself that no woman is more **perfidious** than her finished don john

C - "If you don't believe me, come tonight under her chamber window, and you will see for yourself that no woman is more **perfidious** than she," finished Don John.

95. direly, congregate •

LD - alliteration; foreshadowing ("disastrously")

Paragraph

Commas - adjective clause with relative pronoun; no need for comma before subordinate clause in predicate

Relative pronouns - who/whom (use of "who" as subject of clause)

Possession - singular noun

Verb tense - need for pluperfect tense to refer to a past action

B - claudio whom was **direly** and disastrously distressed decided to meet with don john that night. They were to **congregate** at midnight under heros window so that Claudio could see for himself that don john had spoken the truth

C - Claudio, who was **direly** and disastrously distressed, decided to meet with Don John that night. They were to **congregate** at midnight under Hero's window so that Claudio could see for himself that Don John had spoken the truth.

96. culpability, callow •

LD - narrator aside

Paragraph - time change

No commas

Noun phrase use as subject ("What Claudio thought he saw......")

Possessive pronouns - my, your, his, her, its, our, their

Possession - singular noun

Incorrect word use - use of "tonight" in a story in past tense

B - what claudio thought he saw from his hiding place under heros window tonight convinced him of heros **culpability**. the **callow** fool never even questioned the infamous don johns motives in leading him to the scene

C - What Claudio thought he saw from his hiding place under Hero's window that night convinced him of Hero's **culpability**. The **callow** fool never even questioned the infamous Don John's motives in leading him to the scene.

97. inebriated •

Paragraph - time change

Commas - introductory adverb; dependent adverbial clause (subordinate clause); appositive

Spelling rule - "i" before "e" except after "c"

Possession - singular noun

Splitting verbs

Homophone - their/there/they're

B - the following day while hero teased her freind beatrice and innocently got ready for her wedding borachio and conrade don johns evil henchmen were **inebriatedly** celebrating the success of there nefarious plan

C - The following day, while Hero teased her friend Beatrice and innocently got ready for her wedding, Borachio and Conrade, Don John's evil henchmen, were celebrating **inebriatedly** the success of their nefarious plan.

B = *suggested sentence for the board or overhead*   *C* = *sentence written correctly*   *LD* = *literary device*

98. unbeknownst, miscreants ●

No paragraph - narrator continues tale

Commas - introductory phrase; subordinate clause in predicate needs no comma

Incorrect verb-tense switch - story in past tense

Punctuation - parentheses or dash needed for parentheses around extra information supplied by narrator that is extraneous to the paragraph

Homophone - their/there/they're

B - unbeknownst to the two **miscreants** 2 watchmen that are not really watchman since they are unwilling to do anything if offered resistance overheard there drunken conversation

C - Unbeknownst to the two **miscreants**, two watchmen (who were not really watchman since they were unwilling to do anything if offered resistance) overheard their drunken conversation.

99. regaled ●

No paragraph

No commas - dependent subordinate clause; non restrictive modifier

Verb tense - need for pluperfect tense to refer to previous action

Homophone - tail/tale

Spelling rule - "i" before "e..." in "friends" but exception to rule in "seize"

Relative pronoun - who/whom/that (Never use "that" with people; "who" is needed as nominative case.)

Possessive pronouns - my, your, his, her, its, our, their

Possession - singular noun

B - borachio had just **regaled** conrade with the tail of how claudio and friends thought that margaret was hero when he and his companion were siezed by the watchmen that dragged them to leonatos house

C - Borachio had just **regaled** Conrade with the tale of how Claudio and friends thought that Margaret was Hero when he and his companion were seized by the watchmen, who dragged them to Leonato's house.

100. articulate, subsequent, derrière (French for "rear end") ●

LD - use of foreign language for humor; euphemism ("derrière" instead of "ass")

Paragraph - place change

Commas - introductory adverb; aside as extra information; appositive

Possession - singular noun

Homophone - there/their/they're

Comparatives - "most" not needed as the "est" in "calmest" indicates the superlative degree

B - there the watchmen not **articulate** at the most calmest of times bumbled there attempt to explain what they had overheard and there **subsequent** arrest of borachio and conrade. conrade called dogsberry one of the watchmen a donkeys **derrière**

C -   There, the watchmen, not **articulate** at the calmest of times, bumbled their attempt to explain what they had overheard and their **subsequent** arrest of Borachio and Conrade. Conrade called Dogsberry, one of the watchmen, a donkey's **derrière**.

101. calamitously, inarticulate ●

No paragraph

Comma - after introductory adverb for clarity; compound sentence

Possessive pronouns - my, your, his, her, its, our, their

B - calamitously the rather **inarticulate** watchmen failed to communicate and leonato left for the church without hearing the truth about his daughter

C - Calamitously, the rather **inarticulate** watchmen failed to communicate, and Leonato left for the church without hearing the truth about his daughter.

102. friar, candidly ●

2 Paragraphs - 2 persons speaking

Commas - after introductory adverb (prepositional phrase) for clarity; quote; introductory word (and quote)

Quotation

Punctuation - need for question mark in question

Homophone - here/hear

B - at the church the wedding ended before it began when the **friar** asked claudio do you come here to marry this lady. no answered claudio simply and **candidly**

C -   At the church, the wedding ended before it began when the **friar** asked Claudio, "Do you come here to marry this lady?"

    "No," answered Claudio simply and **candidly**.

B = suggested sentence for the board or overhead   C = sentence written correctly   LD = literary device

103. expounded

LD - metaphor ("rotten orange" to refer to Hero)

2 Paragraphs - narrator and Claudio speaking

Commas - optional comma after introductory adverb; direct address; quote

Run on sentence - lack of punctuation (You might want to put it on the board with commas instead of periods.)

Redundancy - get rid of "again"

Imperative sentence - subject implied

B - at that point all perdition broke loose claudio denounced hero leonato take her back again do not give this rotten orange to a friend she has not been faithful to me claudio **expounded**

C - At that point, all perdition broke loose. Claudio denounced Hero.

"Leonato, take her back. Do not give this rotten orange to a friend. She has not been faithful to me," Claudio **expounded**.

104. incredulous, incorrigible

Paragraph - narrator again

Commas - noun series; appositive

Possessive pronouns - my, your, his, her, its, our, their

Semi-colon - use in compound sentence

Italics - for emphasis

Splitting verbs - don't

Adjective vs. adverb - "badly" is adverb; "bad" is adjective.

B - at first leonato was **incredulous**. *his* daughter would never be unfaithful. finally claudio don pedro and the **incorrigible** liar don john convinced him otherwise and don pedro thought bad of his own daughter

C - At first Leonato was **incredulous**. *His* daughter never would be unfaithful. Finally Claudio, Don Pedro, and the **incorrigible** liar, Don John, convinced him otherwise; Don Pedro thought badly of his own daughter.

105. swooned

No paragraph

Commas - introductory subordinate clause of both sentences

Often confused words - accept/except

Punctuation - use of quotation marks to denote falsehood

Like vs. as - Use "like" only in direct comparison between nouns or pronouns.

Verb tense - need for subjunctive mood in "if" clause

Irregular verbs - lie/lay/has lain/ lying and lay/laid/has laid/laying

Transitive vs. intransitive verbs - review intransitive (lie/lay) and transitive (lay/laid) verbs

B - although hero protested her innocence none of the men accept the friar believed her. when her perturbed father wished to be dead rather than have such a dishonorable daughter hero **swooned** like she was dead and laid pale on the floor

C - Although Hero protested her innocence, none of the men except the friar believed her. When her perturbed father wished to be dead rather than have such a "dishonorable" daughter, Hero **swooned** as if she were dead and lay pale on the floor.

106. perfidy

LD - euphemism (passed away)

No paragraph

Commas - noun series; participial phrase

Often confused prepositions - between/among

Verb tense - need for pluperfect tense to refer to previous action

B - don john don pedro and claudio left the church thinking between themselves that hero had passed away instead of fainting from the shock at being found out in her **perfidy**

C - Don John, Don Pedro, and Claudio left the church, thinking among themselves that Hero had passed away instead of fainting from the shock at being found out in her **perfidy**.

107. prevailed, demeanor ●●

LD - idiomatic expression ("man of the cloth")

Paragraph - subject change

Commas - subordinate adjective clause with relative pronoun

Relative pronouns - "who" needed as nominative in both cases

Possession - singular noun

Possessive pronouns - my, your, his, her, its, our, their

Splitting verbs - don't

Verb tense - need for pluperfect tense as Hero had been accused before this paragraph

B - the friar whom was convinced of heros innocence **prevailed** upon leonato not to be so harsh with his daughter. the noble man of the cloth was certain that heros **demeanor** was that of an innocent who had unjustly been accused

C - The friar, who was convinced of Hero's innocence, **prevailed** upon Leonato not to be so harsh with his daughter. The noble man of the cloth was certain that Hero's **demeanor** was that of an innocent who had been unjustly accused.

108. heinous, afoot ●●

LD - idiomatic expression ("face value")

No paragraph

Commas - introductory subordinate clause; participial phrase

Homophone - their/there/they're

Possession - singular nouns

Often confused words - accept/except

Irregular verbs - lie/lay/has lain/ lying and lay/laid/has laid/laying

Intransitive (lie/lay) vs. transitive (lay/laid) verbs

B - he also felt that there was a **heinous** plot **afoot** against hero. when benedick agreed with him reminding all of don johns perfidy and claudios penchant to accept things at face value without investigation they lay a counter plot

C - He also felt that there was a **heinous** plot **afoot** against Hero. When Benedick agreed with him, reminding all of Don John's perfidy and Claudio's penchant to accept things at face value without investigation, they laid a counter plot.

109. sage, lament ●●

LD - building suspense and intrigue; play on words ("die to live")

Paragraph - new person speaking

Commas - quote; quote; direct address

Quotation

Contractions

Homophone - your/you're

Commonly misspelled word - "no one" is two words

B - the **sage** friar suggested lets let it be known that hero died. lets mourn and **lament**. keep hero hidden in youre house and let noone know that she lives.to hero he said come die lady to live. have patience. your wedding day is but postponed

C - The **sage** friar suggested, "Let's let it be known that Hero died. Let's mourn and **lament**. Keep Hero hidden in your house and let no one know that she lives."To Hero he said, "Come die, lady, to live. Have patience. Your wedding day is but postponed."

110. animosity, succinctly ●●●

3 Paragraphs - narrator then conversation

Commas - introductory phrase; 2 commands together with no coordinating conjunction; direct address; quote

Homophone - there/their/they're

Punctuation - need for exclamation mark to indicate passion of statement

B - beatrice and benedick were left alone in the church. there former **animosity** gone they avowed there love for each other. come ask me to do anything for you my love offered benedick. kill claudio beatrice **succinctly** replied

C - Beatrice and Benedick were left alone in the church. Their former **animosity** gone, they avowed their love for each other.

"Come, ask me to do anything for you, my love," offered Benedick.

"Kill Claudio!" Beatrice **succinctly** replied.

B = suggested sentence for the board or overhead   C = sentence written correctly   LD = literary device

111. atone, repudiation •

Paragraph - conversation continued

Commas - compound sentence; quote

Run on sentence - lack of punctuation

Verb tense - use of future tense to indicate definite future action

Often confused words - then/than

Possessive pronouns - my, your, his, her, its, our, their

B - i will challenge him i will kiss your hand and than i will leave you i promise that claudio will **atone** for his **repudiation** of your cousin benedick promised

C - "I will challenge him. I will kiss your hand, and then I will leave you. I promise that Claudio will **atone** for his **repudiation** of your cousin," Benedick promised.

112. counterplot, unintelligible, garbled •

Paragraph - new subject

Commas - appositive; for clarity in introductory adverb; introductory phrase

Capitalization - Names of countries and languages must always be capitalized

Punctuation - use of quotation marks to denote falsehood

Homophones - there/their/they're, tail/tale

B - the friars **counterplot** worked. everyone believed that hero had died of shame. the watchmen then showed up at the church with their captives borachio and conrade. there in **unintelligible** and **garbled** english the watchmen managed to tell there tail

C - The friar's **counterplot** worked. Everyone believed that Hero had "died of shame." The watchmen then showed up at the church with their captives, Borachio and Conrade. There, in **unintelligible** and **garbled** English, the watchmen managed to tell their tale.

113. domicile; glowered •

Paragraph - place change

Commas - noun series

Punctuation - parentheses needed around appositive as commas would confuse

Often confused words - then/than

Incorrect verb-tense switch - story in past tense

B - the watchmen then went with the prisoners to leonatos **domicile**. they found claudio don pedro leonato antonio leonatos brother and benedick already there. leonato and benedick **glowered** in anger

C - The Watchmen then went with the prisoners to Leonato's **domicile**. They found Claudio, Don Pedro, Leonato, Antonio (Leonato's brother), and Benedick already there. Leonato and Benedick **glowered** in anger.

114. choleric •

No paragraph - continuation; Paragraph - Benedick speaks

Commas - adjective phrase; compound sentence; quote; subordinate clause after verb needs no comma

Quotation

Possessive pronouns - my, your, his, her, its, our, their

Confused part of speech - "Disrespect" is a noun not a verb in standard English.

B - benedick was **choleric** because he believed that claudio with his rejection of hero had disrespected the lady. you have killed a very sweet lady and her death shall be on your conscience he lied

C - Benedick was **choleric** because he believed that Claudio, with his rejection of Hero, had shown disrespect for the lady.

"You have killed a very sweet lady, and her death shall be on your conscience," he lied.

115. ❤ incensed, ❤ slander •

Paragraph - new person speaking

Commas - appositive

Incorrect verb-tense switch

Possession - singular noun

Hyphen - 2 words acting as one

B - the watchmen force borachio to tell don pedro how don pedros own half brother don john **incensed** him to **slander** lady hero

C - The watchmen forced Borachio to tell Don Pedro how Don Pedro's own half-brother, Don John, **incensed** him to **slander** Lady Hero.

B = suggested sentence for the board or overhead   C = sentence written correctly   LD = literary device

116. wracked •

Paragraph - subject change

Commas - introductory phrase; participle

Possession - singular nouns

Possessive pronouns - my, your, his, her, its, our, their

Punctuation - use of quote to denote falsehood

Spelling rule - "i" before "e..."

Articles - use "an" before a word that begins with a vowel or a silent "h"

Often confused words - accept/except

B - needless to say don pedro was shocked. claudio was **wracked** with a plethora of guilt for not believing hero. leonato blamed claudio for his daughters death and offered him an unknown nieces in marriage. claudio stunned accepted

C - Needless to say, Don Pedro was shocked. Claudio was **wracked** with a plethora of guilt for not believing Hero. Leonato blamed Claudio for his daughter's "death" and offered him an unknown niece's hand in marriage. Claudio, stunned, accepted.

117. calumnious, inculpable •

LD - idiomatic expression (brought to task)

No paragraph

Commas - compound sentence; appositive

Possessive pronouns - my, your, his, her, its, our, their

Pronouns - discuss different types

Possession - singular noun

Confusion of plural and possessive case

B - leonato wanted to punish margaret for her role in the **calumnious** deception but borachio convinced him of her **inculpable** participation in the plot. dogsberry a watchman requested that conrade be brought to task for calling him a donkeys posterior

C - Leonato wanted to punish Margaret for her role in the **calumnious** deception, but Borachio convinced him of her **inculpable** participation in the plot. Dogsberry, a watchman, requested that Conrade be brought to task for calling him a donkey's posterior.

118. homage. ❤ defiled •

LD - idiomatic expression

Paragraph - time change

Commas - introductory adverbs in first sentence; verb series

Homophone - there/their/they're

Incorrect verb-tense switch - story in past tense

Irregular verbs - lie/lay/has lain/ lying and lay/laid/has laid/laying

Intransitive (lie/lay) vs. transitive (lay/laid) verbs

Possession - singular noun

Punctuation - use of quotation marks to denote falsehood

Relative pronoun - objective case must be used ("whom")

Verb tense - need for pluperfect tense for action that took place previous to this paragraph

B - later at the church claudio and don pedro paid there respects at heros tomb. claudio lay flowers read a poem and promises to return each year to pay **homage** to the woman who he had **defiled**

C - Later, at the church, Claudio and Don Pedro paid their respects at Hero's "tomb." Claudio laid flowers, read a poem, and promised to return each year to pay **homage** to the woman whom he had **defiled**.

119. intoned, ❤ rite •

LD - synecdoche and **metaphor** (bones as part of whole body); **rhyme**

Paragraph - new person speaking

Comma - quote; introductory adverb (for clarity)

Quotation

Punctuation - need for exclamation mark

Pronouns - use of "thy" in English (like the familiar in almost all other languages)

B - he **intoned** now unto thy bones good night. yearly i will do this **rite**

C - He **intoned**, "Now unto thy bones good night! Yearly, I will do this **rite**."

B = *suggested sentence for the board or overhead*   *C* = *sentence written correctly*   *LD* = *literary device*

120. shrouded (to shroud) ●

LD - idiomatic expression ("just deserts"); **narrator aside**

Paragraph - time change

Commas - long introductory adverb and prepositional phrase (adverb)

Plural rule - consonant "y" changes to consonant "ies" in the plural

Punctuation - need for question marks in questions

B - that same day at the designated hour leonato arrived at the church with two **shrouded** ladys. who is the unknown niece. was one of the masked ladies hero. did hero still want the fickle claudio. will beatrice and benedick get together at last. what will happen to don john. will he get his just deserts. you will have to take the final exam to find out the end of this tale of love and trickery

C -   That same day, at the designated hour, Leonato arrived at the church with two **shrouded** ladies. Who is the unknown niece? Was one of the masked ladies Hero? Did Hero still want the fickle Claudio? Will Beatrice and Benedick get together at last? What will happen to Don John? Will he get his just deserts? You will have to take the final exam to find out the end of this tale of love and trickery.

B = suggested sentence for the board or overhead   C = sentence written correctly   LD = literary device

End-of-the-year Caught'ya Test

Directions:

Be very careful. You will receive no hints for this test, except that there are twelve paragraphs, only one misplaced modifier, and three run-on sentences, one of which must be solved by a colon and semi-colons. Other than in the run-on sentence, all end punctuation has been provided.

Edit this story as best you can on this paper. Use the paragraph sign to indicate the need for a paragraph. Use proofreading symbols for mechanical corrections. Write in corrections of misspelled words. Rewrite sentences where the meanings are unclear. Then rewrite the entire test correctly on your own paper. This is what your teacher will grade.

When you reach the end of the test, do the following: write the numbers 1 to 20 on the back of your paper and tell the part of speech of each word in the last sentence of the story. After you have finished the entire test, go back and check your work several times. Good editors always do. Good luck! This is a difficult test with over one hundred errors to find.

the dénouement of the story

when leonato arrived at the church with the 2 masked ladies he and the ladys had poetic justice and happy endings on there minds. as soon as leonato entered the sanctuary benedick summons the courage to ask him for beatrices hand in marriage. leonato agrees without even consulting the lady in question a typical chauvinist of the day or farther questioning benedick. claudio and don pedro whom among them had noticed benedicks distress teased him about abandoning his vows of permanent bachelorhood. good day benedick said don pedro why whats the matter with you. you have a face full of storm and cloudiness. ah benedick is the noble beast in love a bull whos horns is about to be cliped taunted claudio. and you said youd never marry or fall in love. you should of stuck to youre vows and not of let this lady effect your better judgment. you my freind are a bleating calf and you are no gooder than me teased back benedick. claudio then replied i owe you one for that insult you did good with that one you are a better wit then me. now leonatos older venerable brother antonio had been waiting in the wings with the 2 masked ladys. he brought them out were the rest of the crowd waited with there apprehension hidden good since men of those times are not really allowed too show much emotion. claudio had sworn to blindly marry the bride of leonatos choice and he stood up to so do. the masked lady lay her hand in claudios. only after the ceremony had begun did hero reveal her face. another hero exclaimed claudio whom was not always a quick wit. no a hero from the dead laughed beatrice as she removed her mask too. her and me have been hiding. well the end of this tale was as follows claudio married hero that for some strange reason still wanted the jerk benedick and beatrice married as well and never stoped baiting each other everyone revealed there part in the plot to get benedick and beatrice together and all ended good for the lovers romances. as for evil mendacious don john he was banished from the country for no less than 20 years. we dont know if borachio ended up with poor margaret heros lady in waiting but for margarets sake we hope not. ah love certainly is a giddy thing with many twists and this absolutely marks the end of this convoluted story.

End-of-the-year Caught'ya Test Key

Teachers: *This is an extremely difficult test. It covers a year's worth of material. You might want to have a review before the test. On the day of the test, read the test out loud to your students to give them hints of where to paragraph and punctuate. Remind your students to number their papers from 1 to 20 on the back and write the part of speech of each word in the last sentence. Since there are over one hundred errors in this test, depending on how you count the misplaced modifier, you might want to grade it on a percentage basis.*

The Dénouement of the Story

When Leonato arrived at the church with the two masked ladies, he and the ladies had poetic justice and happy endings on their minds. As soon as Leonato entered the sanctuary, Benedick summoned the courage to ask him for Beatrice's hand in marriage. Leonato, a typical chauvinist of the day, agreed without even consulting the lady in question or further questioning Benedick.

Claudio and Don Pedro, who between them had noticed Benedick's distress, teased him about abandoning his vows of permanent bachelorhood.

"Good day, Benedick," said Don Pedro, "Why, what's the matter with you? You have a face full of storm and cloudiness."

"Ah, Benedick is the noble beast in love, a bull whose horns are about to be clipped," taunted Claudio. "You said you'd never marry nor fall in love. You should have stuck to your vows and not have let this lady affect your better judgment."

"You, my friend, are a bleating calf, and you are no better than I," teased back Benedick.

Claudio then replied, "I owe you one for that insult. You did well with that one. You are a better wit than I."

Now Leonato's older, venerable brother, Antonio, had been waiting in the wings with the two masked ladies. He brought them out where the crowd waited with its apprehension well hidden since men of those times really were not allowed to show much emotion.

Claudio had sworn to marry blindly the bride of Leonato's choice, and he stood up to do so. The masked lady laid her hand in Claudio's. Only after the ceremony had begun did Hero reveal her face.

"Another Hero!" exclaimed Claudio who was not always a quick wit.

"No, a Hero from the dead," laughed Beatrice as she removed her mask, too. "She and I have been hiding."

Well, the end of this tale was as follows: Claudio married Hero, who for some strange reason still wanted the jerk; Benedick and Beatrice married as well and never stopped baiting each other; everyone revealed his or her part in the plot to get Benedick and Beatrice together; and all ended well for the lovers' romances.

As for evil, mendacious Don John, he was banished from the country for no fewer than twenty years. We don't know if Borachio ended up with poor Margaret, Hero's lady-in-waiting, but for Margaret's sake, we hope not. Ah, love certainly is a giddy thing with many twists, and this absolutely marks the end of this convoluted story.

Chapter 5

A Midsummer's Nightmare

What is included in this chapter:

A Midsummer's Nightmare
As told in Caught'ya sentences

Below is the story shown in its entirety (not broken up into individual Caught'yas), exactly as it appears in the corrected Caught'yas **(C)**. This should give you a quick look at the complexity of the sentences, at the vocabulary (in bold), and at the skills addressed in the Caught'yas of this story so that you can see if it is appropriate for your students. You will notice, for example, that the Caught'yas for this story are slightly more complex and difficult than the *Caught'yas of Much Ado about Everything* in **Chapter 4**.

Please note that this story has been written in the past tense instead of the historic present as many teachers of honors and advanced placement classes espouse when students write about literature. I did this for four reasons. One, this is not intended as a summary, but rather as an original story. Two, in my opinion, the story was clearer in the past tense. Three, having the story in the past tense let me use the present tense in quotes and in narrator asides and the pluperfect in references to past actions. And four, and most significant, this story is a teaching tool for grammar, mechanics, and usage, not for literary style, and all the verb tenses needed to be represented for recognition and practice.

It is assumed that your students can recognize proper nouns, common capitalizations, regular verbs, and end punctuation. Therefore, in the interests of space, these are not mentioned in the list to the left of each Caught'ya.

I suggest that you begin the year by showing the movie or reading the story on the next few pages. Because this tale is broken up into daily sentences and because Shakespeare's plots tend to be more convoluted than the most enigmatic soap opera, students need to know where the story is headed. I piloted the Caught'yas of *Much Ado About Nothing* with my gifted eighth graders, and they loved the story and its heroes, heroines, and villains. After a month of doing Caught'yas and swearing in "Shakespearean," they begged to see the movie (I, of course, acquiesced). After seeing the movie (and loving it), about a third of my students bought the book on their own and read it for pleasure! As one enthusiastic student put it, "Shakespeare rules!"

A Midsummer's Nightmare

This is the **earthy** tale of love, impending **nuptials**, trickery, mistaken identities, passion, and celebration that involves fairies, sprites, noblemen, and **hard-handed** laborers. It takes place in the ancient kingdom of Athens, Greece, where men's words were the law, and women were **subjugated** to their will.

Our **jovial** and **mirthful** story **commences** when Theseus, the Duke of Athens, and his bride-to-be, Hippolyta, the **comely** Queen of the Amazons, were planning the **pageantry** of their forthcoming wedding. They were impatient, as would be any red-blooded middle-aged couple, for their **nuptial** day to arrive five days **hence**, on May 1, 1600. Theseus had just ordered Philostrate, his Master of Revelry, to **devise** some diversion to distract Hippolyta and him until their wedding day.

"Ah, Hippolyta, my **pert** and noble bride-to-be, let us marry with **pomp** and much **reveling**. In other words, let us have a jolly, good time of it, too."

"Yes, my wise and **noble** mate-to-be, you won me in battle. You **wooed** me with your sword. Let's make a merry, joyous thing of our wedding. Let's stop the **strife** and have a blast!"

Suddenly Theseus and Hippolyta were interrupted by the arrival of Egeus, an angry father who laid a **prodigious** problem before his ruler — his rebellious daughter and the two young men who professed to love her. As Egeus **waxed** angrier and angrier, he explained that his daughter Hermia, a **diminutive** ball-of-fire, was being **wooed** by two dudes, Lysander and Demetrius, and she would not accept his choice of the two.

"My noble lord, Lysander has bewitched my disobedient daughter Hermia," Egeus said. "This Lysander has sent her poems and love **tokens**. He has sung under her window, **feigning** love, and he has stolen her heart with presents and **cunning**," he continued. "In fact, he has sent Hermia so many **trinkets** she could open a gift shop and make a pretty penny. This **knave** so convinced her that she defied me and gave me this note," Egeus concluded his complaint as he **brandished** a short note under Theseus's nose.

The letter read:

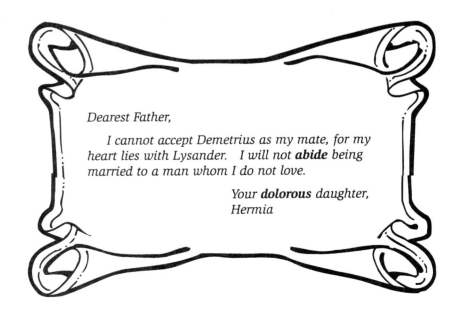

Dearest Father,

*I cannot accept Demetrius as my mate, for my heart lies with Lysander. I will not **abide** being married to a man whom I do not love.*

*Your **dolorous** daughter,*
Hermia

Then Egeus **audaciously supplicated** his ruler, "Ah, my Duke," he said, " I beg you to enforce the Athenian law which gives fathers absolute power over their **wayward** daughters. If Hermia does not wed Demetrius, I may, according to our law, put her to death."

"You wouldn't! Lysander and I love each other," sobbed Hermia in **palpable** distress. "You don't understand what is between him and me."

"What do you have to say for yourself, Hermia?" asked Theseus. "Your father, of course, should be like a god to you."

"I **entreat** your Grace to pardon me for loving and beg you to tell me what may **befall** me if I refuse to marry Demetrius. My family will not give me its approval, and I do not want to carry any unwished yoke," Hermia **beseeched**.

"Well, **audacious** Hermia, your father has the right to put you to death or to send you to a convent away from all men if you do not obey his will," returned Theseus. "You have until Hippolyta's and my wedding day to decide your own fate," he concluded.

"Hermia, if you do not accept the man of my choice," Egeus maintained, grasping at the Duke's second punishment, "then you will die unwed in a convent."

"Oh, **woe**," sobbed Hermia. "Lysander and I are like the classic tale of the star-crossed, **thwarted** lovers, Romeo and Juliet."

"The course of true love never did run smoothly," added Lysander.

Lysander politely argued that he was the equal of Demetrius and that, in fact, Demetrius first had wooed another fair maiden, Helena. Lysander continued to explain that Demetrius, after winning Helena, had jilted her like an **odorous cad** and then pursued Hermia. He abandoned poor Helena to her **unrequited** love.

This is worse than a soap opera like Days of Your Lives! Lysander loved Hermia. Demetrius loved Hermia. Helena adored Demetrius. Hermia's father was a pig-headed, opinionated, **austere** man where his daughters were concerned and would never bend. This group of Athenians was like a wild herd of warthogs with each animal running in its own direction.

Theseus then left with Hippolyta, Egeus, and Demetrius following him. He had heard enough of this **lamentable** family's squabble, and he wanted to discuss business with Egeus and Demetrius. Lysander and Hermia were left alone.

"Why are you so pale, my love?" asked Lysander of his **paramour**. "Between us we can solve this problem that affects us so profoundly. Your **visage** is so lovely."

"Oh, my sweet Lysander, woe is me. You and I cannot marry. My strict father will not allow it, and I do not love Demetrius. I am in the same position as Juliet," Hermia said, again referring to that classic tale, "Romeo and Juliet." "I shall have to marry someone I do not love or spend the rest of my life in a convent. If only I were a boy," she **uttered** with a sigh.

"I have an awesome idea," said the **intrepid, shrewd** Lysander. "My wealthy aunt has an **abode** outside the **jurisdiction** of Athenian law. Let's leave our respective homes in **stealth**, meet in the woods, and elope to my aunt's house to be married. We will effect our own future."

"Oh, my dearest, best, most wonderfully **gallant** love, I will meet you, and we will wed!" said Hermia.

Just then Helena, the poor young lady whose love for Demetrius had come to **naught**, appeared. Helena's lovely blond hair hung limp in her distress; her usually tall figure stooped in sorrow; and her natural **timidity** made her voice hesitant and faint.

Now Hermia was Helena's best friend. Helena, surprisingly, bore no **enmity** for her friend who was supposed to marry the man she herself loved. In fact, she beseeched Hermia and Lysander to tell her how to win Demetrius's love.

Hermia and Lysander tried to comfort Helena, informing her of their plans to elope.

"Perhaps when we are wed, Demetrius will turn his affection once again to you. If this does not work, maybe among the three of us we can come up with a plan to transform Demetrius into a **paragon** of a suitor," Hermia said.

Helena then decided to inform Demetrius of the impending elopement so that she could go with him in pursuit of the two lovers. The plot thickens.

While Theseus and Hippolyta anticipated their wedding celebration, while Hermia and Lysander planned their **clandestine** elopement, and while Helena plotted to win Demetrius's love, a meeting took place in town at the house of Peter Quince, the carpenter. Quince and his **cohorts**, Nick Bottom, Flute, Snug, Snout, and Robin Starveling, were **divvying up** parts and setting a time for a rehearsal for a short play they wished to perform in honor of Theseus's and Hippolyta's wedding. This troupe of would-be actors had trouble getting its act together. The planning of this amateurish play was hampered by the weaver Nick Bottom. He was the clumsy, offensively **bumptious** man not known for **lofty** thoughts who tried to take over the meeting. While Bottom was cast as the hero in this "most lamentable comedy," he also said that he could play the part of the heroine.

"Let me play the heroine, Thisbe," said Bottom, a man whose name fit his personality, in a lovely, **falsetto** voice. "I also can play the part of the lion," he growled, trying to show his **versatility** and **prowess** as an actor, for he badly wanted more parts. "Grrrr."

"No, Bottom, you will play no part but that of Pyramus, the hero. Pyramus is a sweet-faced man, a proper man, a most lovely, gentlemanly man. This is why only you can play the part, my **confrère**," confided Quince. "You will play it so well."

Finally, the parts in the play, the rehearsal time, and the rehearsal place (the very same woods where Lysander and Hermia planned to meet) were all resolved. The **rustic** actors themselves at last were in agreement. The play was to be based on the story "Pyramus and Thisbe," a classic tale of tragic misunderstandings. The **valorous** but **bucolic** actors, themselves, would make it a comedy.

As all this was taking place, the elves and fairies **frolicked** in the forest (Yes, it was the same forest where everyone else had planned to meet that evening.) They awaited the arrival of Titania, the Queen of the Pixies, and her court. Among the **convened** fairies in the forest was the seriously **waggish** elf, Puck, who liked to play tricks on **mortals** (non fairies) in order to amuse his king, Oberon. All was complicated by the fact that Oberon, the Pixie King, was about to arrive in that same forest, too.

"The king will frolic here tonight. We must be careful to keep the queen from his sight. Oberon is full of **wrath** for the queen and she for him," Puck warned the other pixies. "I don't know which one is angrier."

"You are that **knavish** sprite, Puck, from whom mortal maidens run in fear. You are the one whom the town blames for all its mishaps. Being bad is your favorite sport," one pixie said.

"That is I," boasted Puck. "Oh, we have to get our kicks somewhere, even with mortals. Mortals, as they tell **lugubrious** tales and then fall off their stools, provide a lot of laughs."

Now Puck was right. Titania and Oberon, her mate, were not exactly on the best of terms. In plain words, they were ticked at each other. In fact, Titania was barely speaking to Oberon except to yell at him. They blamed each other for the **discord** and for stealing an Indian boy.

Suddenly, just as Titania with her court entered the forest from one direction, Oberon and his **entourage** arrived from the opposite direction. The sparks began to fly, and the **tapestry** of a complicated tale became even more interwoven.

"You faithful **philanderer**," accused Titania. "You loved Hippolyta in all senses of the word. You were **amorous** with a tall, **lanky** foreigner, of all mortal women! You should have been devoted to me."

"For shame, Titania!" retorted Oberon. "How can you **chide** me for my **dalliance** with Hippolyta when you went after Theseus. You don't understand the relationship between her and me."

"Ah, jealousy, lies, and rumors," **taunted** Titania.

"How long do you plan to remain in these woods?" asked Oberon.

"**Perchance** fewer than five days; perhaps more. I may stay until after Theseus's wedding day," flung Titania as she and her entourage left the grove.

Oberon plotted his revenge against Titania. He recounted the old tale of Cupid to the **roguish** Puck. "One night, less than a year ago, I saw a strange and wonderful sight," he **chronicled**. "Cupid, that little sprite with a baby-bald **pate**, kept his bow taut and his arrow cocked. He flew between earth and the moon, trying to strike a young, beautiful mortal girl. He released the arrow, but it missed the heart of the girl. Instead, it struck a milk-white flower which turned purple with desire.

"From that time on, that flower was magical," Oberon continued to **regale** his listener, "and if its nectar is dropped onto the eyelids of a sleeper, mortal or fairy, it will make him or her fall instantly in love with the first living creature seen after awakening.

"Fetch me that flower so that I may play a trick on Titania."

"I'm gone," grinned Puck.

"I shall become invisible to watch Titania's **contrived antics**," said Oberon as he faded from sight. "She will not know where I am."

While Oberon was plotting his **witty** scheme to blackmail Titania, Demetrius, with Helena in hot pursuit right behind him, ran into the same clearing where Oberon was waiting for the **denouement** of his trickery. Fair and usually timid Helena still hoped to win Demetrius's love. Demetrius, on the other hand, planned to kill Lysander, capture Hermia, and lose the pesky Helena in the woods. Poor, misguided Helena still loved the **dastardly** Demetrius despite his **sinister** threats and obvious **disdain** for her.

What a lovesick fool! Demetrius is a **vile**, unfeeling **varlet**, but love is blind like the proverbial **wombat**. Perhaps she is as **daft** as he.

"Get away from me, you **vexatious** female. You make me sick when I look at you," **scoffed** Demetrius as he ran farther into the woods.

"Use me as your spaniel. **Spurn** me. Strike me. Let me be with you. I will change the story of Daphne and Apollo and will chase you. It will be the deer chasing the lion, the dove chasing the griffin. I'll follow you and make a heaven of my hell," huffed Helena as she chased Demetrius through the woods away from the **glen** where Oberon stood invisible.

"Oh, my poor, lovesick maiden, before this **idle** youth leaves this forest, I shall see to it that he will seek your love," promised Oberon as he observed this **debacle**. "He will be **enthralled** and madly in love with you before I am done with him," he chortled.

Puck then returned with the magical flower.

"You did well. Give it to me, Puck. I have much use for this blossom. I will find Titania this very night. She sleeps by a **knoll** where violets and lovely blooms grow. A canopy of woodbine and roses arches over her favorite spot," Oberon said. "There she will sleep. I'll put some of the juice of this in her eyes and make her worst nightmare come true.

"Puck, you go and find an Athenian youth in the forest. There will be a sweet lady near him. When this **canker** on the rear of humanity sleeps for the night, **anoint** his eyes so that when he wakes, he may fall in love with the maiden."

As Puck and Oberon left on their respective errands of **rascality**, Titania arrived at her favorite sleeping place with her entourage, sent away all her sprites, and lay down to sleep. Oberon **stealthily** entered and squeezed the flower juices on Titania's eyelids.

"Whatever you see when you awake, dear Titania, be it bear or cat or pig, you will love it with all your heart. Wake when some vile thing is near," Oberon taunted. "What is in store for you will amuse Puck and me."

Meanwhile, nearby in that very same woods, Lysander and Hermia met in secret. Exhausted by all the trauma of the day and the **keen** disappointment at being forbidden to marry, they pledged their **troth** to one another and lay down to sleep. In order to preserve her modesty, Hermia lay a few feet away from her love.

In fewer than two minutes after the two would-be lovers fell asleep, Puck, that **impish** sprite with a bizarre sense of humor, appeared on the scene.

"This must be the Athenian youth and maid of whom Oberon spoke. I will quickly put the flower juice in his eyes and return to Oberon with **alacrity**," he said as he dripped the potion by mistake onto Lysander's eyelids.

As Puck departed, Demetrius and poor Helena arrived, the **latter** still running after the **former**. Helena was out of breath and stopped. Demetrius, the **dissembling** cad, took advantage of her exhaustion and sped away. Lysander awoke at the noise, raised himself up, **espied** Helena, and fell head-over-heels in love with her.

Truly, this is worse than the worst soap opera! Lysander now loved Helena, and poor Hermia, in one mad moment, had lost her **beau**. This was not the end of the mischief, however. Oberon and Puck still had a **plenitude** of trouble to stir up that night.

"Oh, sweet, wonderful, comely, perfect Helena," **fawned** the newly lovesick Lysander, "I never saw a more desirable and lovely girl. You are the one whom I love," he said as he lustfully lunged for her.

"What is happening here?" Helena asked as she tried to push Lysander away. "What is this **mockery** of love?"

"Help me, Lysander, for I have had a terrible dream. Tell me that you still love me and not Helena," Hermia **beseeched** Lysander as she awoke and saw Helena lying in Lysander's arms.

While this switching of alliances was taking place, Titania slept on peacefully in her flowery **bower** — a disaster waiting to happen. Oberon had placed the potion on her eyelids. When Titania awoke, she would love the first creature she would see.

As Titania slept, the local **buffoons** arrived to practice their play. Unaware of her royal presence, Peter Quince and his troupe conducted their disastrous rehearsal of "Pyramus and Thisbe" as if they had the whole forest to themselves. No sooner had the rehearsal begun, when Bottom, the weaver, interrupted the proceedings — something he did **a plethora of** times.

"The refined, **patrician** ladies will be frightened when Pyramus raises his sword and kills himself," he protested.

"We'll leave that part out," reassured Quince.

"No, I have a better idea," **interjected** Bottom. "You write a prologue that will assure the audience that Pyramus is only I, Nick Bottom, and that it is an illusion that he kills himself."

The **redoubtable** Bottom and his cohorts launched objections such as this one, one after another: Wouldn't the lion frighten the ladies? Should someone play the moon? What should they do for the wall? The actors themselves made a comedy of this love tragedy.

Snout suggested adding yet another prologue to **elucidate** to the ladies that the lion was not *really* a lion. He also maintained that he didn't *feel* the part he had been assigned. Bottom added his "two cents" again by saying that Snout could be the wall through which Pyramus and Thisbe talked. The entire rehearsal was a **travesty** of errors.

While this **burlesque** of a rehearsal was being enacted, Puck, unseen to the actors, came on the scene. He listened to the **sham** of a play and plotted mischief. When Bottom made a grand, stage exit behind some bushes, Puck followed him. At the same moment that Flute (who played **dulcet** Thisbe) was **orating**, Puck transformed Bottom's **rotund, corpulent** head into that of an ass. This was certainly an appropriate transformation.

Unaware of the **metamorphosis** of his head, Bottom thought his fellow actors were playing a trick on him when they dispersed in fear at the sight of him. Singing loudly in order to demonstrate his fearlessness, he walked up and down. "Heehaw! Heehaw!"

This loud braying awakened Titania from her hidden bower. "What angel wakes me from my flowery bed?" she **pondered**, admiring the **ponderous** song.

Titania was, indeed, bewitched. The magical flower had done its work. The minute she saw Bottom, ass-head and all, Titania fell instantly and madly in love with him. Oberon had his revenge.

"Oh, my dear pixies, lead this gentle mortal to my bower and tend to his every need," Titania **enjoined** her entourage.

In another part of the wood, Puck, that **paradigm** of mischief, was regaling Oberon with the results of his various pranks.

"**Pulchritudinous** Titania is in love with a monster," Puck tittered. "I found a **bumpkin** who was trying to act the part of Pyramus in a play, and I turned his head into that of an ass." Puck continued with his recital. "Upon seeing this 'ass,' the other actors fled the scene faster than a flock of wild geese when it hears a gun's report."

"This is better than I could **devise**," said Oberon in delight. "What about the Athenian cad?"

"I put the juice in his eyes as he was sleeping," Puck **corroborated**.

"Wait! Here comes that same Athenian," whispered Oberon as Demetrius and Hermia appeared. "Let's listen to see if he has had a change of heart."

"This is the same woman, but it's not the same man," **rejoined** Puck. "This one is handsomer than he."

"What have you done with my Lysander?" asked Hermia.

"Why do you **rebuke** me who loves you so?" asked Demetrius.

"Where is he? Ah, good Demetrius, will you give him to me?"

"I would rather give his carcass to my hounds."

"Out, dog! Out, **cur**! You're trying my patience."

After Hermia accused Demetrius of killing Lysander, Demetrius assured her that Lysander was not dead. Hermia left in search of her lost love. Demetrius, heavy with a **surfeit** of woe, lay down and slept.

"Oh, Puck, you **misbegotten** excuse for an elf, what have you done?" asked Oberon angrily. "You have laid the love juice on the eyes of a *true* lover. Go back into the woods, find this Helena, and bring her here. I'll put 'wrong to right' to correct your **erring**."

As Puck left, Oberon put the juice in Demetrius's **orbs**. Puck soon returned with news of Helena who was nearby. He told Oberon of Lysander (the **erroneous** recipient of the love juice) who was pleading with Helena for her love. "What **nincompoops** these mortals are," observed Puck as Lysander and Helena arrived on the scene.

Puck and Oberon **expeditiously** stepped behind a tree to watch the proceedings happily. Puck was delighted that poor, bereft, lamentable Helena now would have two suitors instead of none. Indeed, as Lysander was wooing a **dispassionate** Helena, Demetrius woke up, saw Helena, tried to kiss her hand, and professed his love for her.

"Oh, my goddess, my nymph, my **divine** love, I want to give your beautiful lips a **buss**. Then I will be in bliss," **simpered** Demetrius

Confounded by all this professed love when recently there had been none, Helena doubted the sincerity of the two gentlemen.

"Oh, Hell! Oh, bat **guano**!" stomped Helena in anger. "You are all making fun of me. Do you hate me so much that you join to mock me? You, Lysander and Demetrius, both love Hermia, not me."

"Helena, my love, it's not so," protested Lysander.

"Helena, my beauty, I love you so," **reiterated** Demetrius.

At this moment, Hermia found them. "Why don't you love me anymore, Lysander?" Hermia **entreated** with palpable distress.

"My love is for the beauteous, **flaxen**-haired Helena. I hate the sight of you now," answered Lysander, wounding Hermia to the quick.

"Oh, she is one of this **confederacy**, too!" cried Helena. "Oh, my best friend, after all we have shared — the schooldays, the friendship, the sisters' vows, the childish games, and the childhood innocence." She continued, "You and I grew up together. We were like two berries molded on one stem, two bodies with one heart. How can you **deride** me so?"

Hermia did not understand what all this was about. She and her closest friend, Helena, were no longer on speaking terms. Hermia and her love were no longer going to be wed. Poor Hermia was **bereft** of her love and weary with sorrow.

Finally, Lysander called Hermia, who was very short, a "dwarf," a "**vixen**," and an "acorn." This was too much for Hermia to bear. She accused her former friend of stealing Lysander. Helena, who was usually **docile** and **acquiescent**, called Hermia a "puppet" of the two men. Hermia thought that her tall, fair ex-friend had been making fun of her **diminutive stature** by using the word "puppet," and she started to quarrel. Hermia, a real spitfire, was about to scratch Helena and to pull her hair, but timid Helena backed away.

Both **striplings** rushed to protect Helena. In doing this, they antagonized each other even more than usual, and Lysander, angry to the hilt, challenged Demetrius to a duel. They drew their swords and left the two ladies.

With the men gone, Hermia, that **volatile virago**, blamed Helena for the entire **fracas**. Helena, not wanting to get into a **fray**, ran off. Hermia was left alone in the glen, alone, that was, except for Puck and Oberon.

Oberon blamed Puck for **contriving** all the **strife** that had affected everyone's life. He was convinced there had been too much mischief-making.

"Please believe me, Oberon, King of Shadows, I made a mistake. You know how all these Athenians dress alike," Puck **implored**. "I must admit, though, that I enjoyed watching all the **petty** squabbles."

Oberon decided to set things right, both in his life with Titania and in the mortals' lives. He ordered Puck to lead Lysander and Demetrius around in circles until they were **enervated** enough to sleep. Then Puck was to put into Lysander's eyes an herb that would remove the spell of the love juice and let nature take its course. While Puck was performing his duties, Oberon, **simultaneously**, would release Titania from her infatuation with the ass-pated Bottom.

Puck flooded the glade with a dense, **impenetrable miasma** so that the lovers would dash about, blindly searching for each other until they tired themselves out. His **ploy** worked, and the four mortals lay down to sleep. It was at this point that Titania, her donkey-headed "love," and her elves entered the scene.

Titania was still **enamored** of Bottom. She crowned his head with flowers, kissed his long, rather hairy ears, and caressed him. Bottom wanted none of this, but he did like being waited upon by Titania's little elves and "hee hawed" his approval. Bottom, ever the **Philistine** in his tastes, asked for clattering music and hay. Suddenly he felt drowsy. He lay down and fell asleep in Titania's arms. Titania, her **"paramour" enfolded** in her arms, laid down her head and slept as well.

Oberon then arrived at this **bucolic** and placid scene. He felt remorse over the dispute of the possession of the Indian boy (a changeling) and pity for Titania, who now loved an ass.

"I will release the Fairy Queen," said Oberon as he put the antidote into Titania's eyes. "Now, my sweet Titania, awaken."

Titania awoke, saw Bottom in her arms, and said, "My Oberon, what visions I have seen. I dreamed that I was **enamored** of a donkey."

Oberon responded, pointing, "There lies your love."

"How did all this come to pass?" queried Titania. "Oh, how I **loathe** this ass's visage now. How could I have loved such a creature? Puck, take the ass's head off this bumpkin."

"Let us dance in the palace at midnight to bless the aristocrats' marriage. Let us now **cavort** here near where these sleepers lie," said Oberon as he took Titania's hand.

As dawn broke over the tops of the trees and the morning lark began to sing, the sound of a hunting horn **ululated** through the forest. Theseus, Hippolyta, Egeus, and the entire Athenian court passed through the place where the other mortals still slept and where the fairies had just celebrated the renewal of their **amity**. Theseus saw the sleeping girls, and Egeus recognized Helena and his **recalcitrant** daughter, Hermia.

"Ah, " said Theseus, "Isn't this the day Hermia must give me her decision about marrying Demetrius or about going to live in a convent?" he asked. "Hunter, awaken these **dauntless** maidens and their intrepid striplings with your horns," Theseus commanded.

The young people awoke and knelt before Theseus. He asked them how they came to be lying there together as if they were friends, without the enmity of the past.

Egeus demanded **reparation** from Lysander, saying that the latter had intended to steal his daughter from the man of her parents' choice. "This Lysander is against my daughter and me, no matter how much love he professes," he said.

In fewer than two heartbeats, Demetrius spoke up, his original love for Helena **forged** even stronger by the juice of the flower. "My love for Hermia melted as snow does from the fields in spring. I love Helena. She and I **doted** on each other in our childhood. My supposed 'love' for Hermia was but a temporary sickness," he said.

Theseus, desiring peace for his forthcoming nuptials, overruled Egeus and **issued his edict** that the two couples should join with him and Hippolyta in a triple wedding. Theseus and the court all left the forest and returned to Athens. The lovers followed him. They were still **disconcerted** by what had taken place in the forest during the night. It was as if a fog clouded their memories.

Meanwhile, the **hapless** Bottom, now **sans** ass-head, woke up alone in Titania's bower. He was only vaguely aware of what had occurred the previous night and thought that he was still awaiting his cue as Pyramus. Discovering that his cohorts in "drama crime" were missing, Bottom tried to recall the night's adventures. In true "Bottom" style, he thought that perhaps his friend Quince might want to make a **ballad** of his "dream" (to be called "'Bottom's Dream' because it had no bottom") to **bolster** his part in the play. Bottom, too, then departed the forest in pursuit of his fellow **thespians**.

At the aristocrats' palace, the triple marriage was conducted. That evening's entertainment was, of course, the play "Pyramus and Thisbe," performed by none other than Quince, Bottom, and company. Philostrate, the Master of Revels, recommended it as he had seen the play and had **shed** tears of **mirth** over the **ineptitude** of the dialogue and of the actors.

The play began with a **deplorable** prologue with Quince so nervous that he interrupted himself and said the opposite of what he intended. The characters then gave a short synopsis of the plot in **execrable** verse. Snug, as the Lion, reassured the audience that he was only Snug and that he would not bite them. Moonshine forgot his part and **avowed** that his lantern was the moon and that he was the man in the moon, etc.

From there the play progressed downhill in quality. At the end, after the double "suicide" of Pyramus and Thisbe, Bottom, performing an instant **resurrection**, leapt up from the "dead" to ask Theseus if he wanted to watch a dance or hear an epilogue. Theseus and the rest could take no more of this travesty of a play and opted for the dance. The three couples retired at last.

Teachers, see page 139 (End-of-the-year Caught'ya Test key) for the dénouement of this tale.

Vocabulary used in this story

1. ♥ earthy, ♥ nuptials (noun), ♥ hard-handed, subjugated
2. ♥ jovial, ♥ mirthful, ♥ commences, comely, ♥ pageantry
3. ♥ nuptial (adj.), ♥ hence
4. devise (verb)
5. ♥ pert, ♥ pomp, ♥ reveling (revel, revels), ♥ noble, ♥ woo, ♥ strife
6. ♥ prodigious
7. ♥ waxed, diminutive, ♥ wooed (past participial of "woo")
8. tokens, ♥ feigning, ♥ cunning
9. trinkets, ♥ knave (noun), brandished
10. ♥ abide, dolorous
11. audaciously, supplicated, wayward
12. ♥ palpable
13. ♥ entreat, ♥ befall, ♥ beseeched
14. ♥ audacious
15. woe, thwarted
16. ♥ odorous, cad, unrequited
17. ♥ austere
18. ♥ lamentable
19. ♥ paramour, ♥ visage
20. ♥ uttered
21. intrepid, ♥ shrewd, abode, jurisdiction, ♥ stealth
22. ♥ gallant
23. ♥ naught, timidity
24. ♥ enmity
25. ♥ paragon
26. clandestine
27. cohorts, to divvy up
28. bumptious, ♥ lofty
29. falsetto, versatility, prowess
30. confrère
31. rustic, ♥ valorous, bucolic
32. ♥ frolicked
33. convened, waggish, ♥ mortals
34. ♥ wrath, ♥ knavish (adj.)
35. lugubrious
36. discord
37. entourage, tapestry
38. philanderer, amorous, lanky
39. chide, dalliance
40. ♥ taunted, ♥ perchance
41. roguish, ♥ chronicled
42. ♥ pate
43. ♥ regale
44. ♥ contrived, antics
45. ♥ witty, denouement
46. dastardly, ♥ sinister, disdain
47. ♥ vile, ♥ varlet, wombat, daft
48. vexatious, scoffed
49. ♥ spurn, glen
50. ♥ idle (adj.), debacle, ♥ enthralled
51. knoll
52. ♥ canker, ♥ anoint
53. rascality
54. ♥ stealthily (adv.)
55. ♥ keen, ♥ troth
56. impish
57. alacrity
58. latter, former, ♥ dissembling
59. espied
60. beau, plenitude
61. ♥ fawned
62. ♥ mockery
63. ♥ beseeched
64. ♥ bower
65. ♥ buffoon
66. a plethora of, patrician
67. interjected
68. redoubtable
69. elucidate
70. travesty, burlesque, sham
71. dulcet, orating, rotund, corpulent
72. metamorphosis
73. pondered, ponderous
74. enjoined
75. paradigm, pulchritudinous, bumpkin
76. devise (verb)
77. corroborated, rejoined
78. ♥ rebuke, cur
79. ♥ surfeit
80. misbegotten, erring
81. orbs, erroneous
82. nincompoops
83. expeditiously
84. dispassionate
85. divine, buss, simpered
86. ♥ confounded
87. guano
88. reiterated
89. ♥ entreated (past participle), flaxen
90. ♥ confederacy
91. deride (verb)
92. bereft
93. vixen, docile, acquiescent
94. diminutive, stature
95. striplings
96. volatile, virago, fracas, fray
97. ♥ contriving, strife, implored, petty
98. enervated
99. simultaneously
100. impenetrable, miasma, ploy
101. enamored
102. Philistine, paramour, enfolded
103. bucolic
104. ♥ enamored
105. ♥ loathe
106. cavort
107. ululated, ♥ amity
108. recalcitrant
109. dauntless
110. reparation
111. forged, ♥ doted
112. to issue an edict
113. disconcerted
114. hapless, sans (French word - without)
115. ♥ ballad (in Shakespeare it is "ballet"), bolster
116. thespians
117. ♥ shed (verb), mirth, ineptitude
118. deplorable, execrable
119. avowed
120. resurrection

Literary devices and writing conventions used in this story

Action and description within dialogue #34
Alliteration #4, 6, 17, 46, 47, 61, 85, 96
Anadiplosis #35, 68, 96
Anecdote #9, 35, 41, 42, 43
Use of aphorism (cliché) - #8, 15, 25, 47, 59, 89
Biblical reference #102
Character development in action and dialogue #29
Conversation #13, 34, 40, 77
Description #23, 28, 29, 42, 107
Description within dialogue #34, 51
Double entendre - #5, 27, 38, 52, 75, 76, 93, 103
Establishment of setting and motif - #1
Euphemism - #87
Fantasy and unreality #32, 33
Use of foreign language for effect #30
Foreshadowing #25, 31, 54, 60, 64, 70
Historical reference #21, 102
Historical allusion - #5, 14, 38
Humor #30, 35, 70 (implied), #75, 101, 105 (tongue-in-cheek), #115
Hyperbole #22, 61, 83, 84, 85
Use of idiom - #8, 69
Idiomatic expression #9
Irony #27, 30, 73
Literary allusion #15, 20, 31, 49.
Metaphor #5, 13, 37, 49, 52
Monologue #49

Motif #1, 49
Allusion to mythology #49
Narrator aside #17, 25, 32, 47, 60, 71, 120
Naturalistic detail #51, 107
Deliberate use of non-sequator #19
Onomatopoeia #29, 72, 101
Oxymoron #28, 33, 38, 67, 68, 117
Paradox #49, 115
Personification #25, 37, 47, 52
Play on words #4, 13, 27, 44, 73, 77, 83, 95, 114, 117
Pun #115
Quote within a quote #49, 80, 115
Familiar quote slightly changed #82
Repartée #78
Use of rhyme for effect #34
Sarcasm #28, 30, 52, 71, 100, 115
Satire #25
Establishment of setting #1, 31, 45
Simile #12, 16, 17, 76, 91, 111, 113
Use of slang - #5, 7, 21, 36
Soliloquy #73
Subplot - #26, 27, 32
Repeated use of synonyms to make a point #70, 78
Substituting synonyms to avoid repetition #51, 52
Use of symbol #5, 13
Tale within a tale #41

Caught'ya Sentences for a Midsummer's Nightmare

1. ❤ earthy, ❤ nuptials, ❤ hard-handed, subjugated •

LD - establishment of setting and motif

Paragraph - beginning of story

Commas - list of nouns; list of nouns; commas between city and state (country) and after state and country (non-restrictive modifier); compound sentence

Verb tense - use of present tense (introduction to story); use of past tense to talk about "ancient kingdom"

Run on sentence - make several shorter sentences for clarity

Adjective clause -"where"

Plural rules - fairies, sprites, men, laborers

Possession - plural noun not ending in "s"

Homophone - their/there/they're

Hyphen - 2 words acting as one

Relative pronouns - who/whom/whose/whoever/whomever/that/which ("that" and "which" can be subject or object and are used only with objects and animals; "who" and "whom" are used with people; "who" is subject; "whom" is object)

Parallel construction - needed for clarity

NOTE - Teach coordinating conjunctions (FANBOYS - for, and, nor, but, or, yet so)

B - this is the **earthy** tale of love impending **nuptials** trickery mistaken identities passion and celebration which involves fairies sprites noblemen and **hard-handed** laborers that takes place in the ancient kingdom of athens greece where mens words were the law and women were **subjugated** to there will

C -   This is the **earthy** tale of love, impending **nuptials**, trickery, mistaken identities, passion, and celebration which involves fairies, sprites, noblemen, and **hard-handed** laborers. It takes place in the ancient kingdom of Athens, Greece, where men's words were the law, and women were **subjugated** to their will.

➥ **SUGGESTION:**

The common homophones like "their/there/they're" will sometimes be misspelled, sometimes spelled correctly. I do this to keep students on their toes. My students complain that they have to think. They never know if I'm going to misspell a homophone or not. Once, after misspelling "their" in at least five previous Caught'ya sentences, I spelled it correctly. My students were upset. By that time, though, most of them were correctly using that particular homophone in their writing!

---

2. ❤ jovial, ❤ mirthful, ❤ commences, comely, ❤ pageantry •

Paragraph - now talking about specific plot

Commas - appositives

Verb tense - present tense into past needed for introduction to story

Capital letters - titles

Subject/verb agreement - compound subject needs plural verb

Hyphens - 3 words serving as one

Homophones - there/their/they're

Possessive pronouns - my, your, his, her, its, our, their

Pronouns - discuss different types

B - our **jovial** and **mirthful** story **commences** when theseus the duke of athens and his bride to be hippolyta the **comely** queen of the amazons was planning the **pageantry** for there forthcoming wedding

C -   Our **jovial** and **mirthful** story **commences** when Theseus, the Duke of Athens, and his bride-to-be, Hippolyta, the **comely** Queen of the Amazons, were planning the **pageantry** for their forthcoming wedding.

B = suggested sentence for the board or overhead   C = sentence written correctly   LD = literary device

3. ❤ **nuptial** (adj.), ❤ **hence** •

No paragraph - continuation of same speaker and same subject

Commas - interrupter; date, non-restrictive modifier (extra information)

No comma after "red-blooded" - 2nd adjective denotes age

Verb tense - narrator begins to recount story in past tense

Hyphens - 2 words as one adjective

Homophones - their/there/they're

Possessive pronouns - my, your, his, her, its, our, their

B - they were impatient as would be any red blooded middle aged couple for theyre **nuptial** day to arrive five days **hence** on may 1 1600

C - They were impatient, as would be any red-blooded middle-aged couple, for their **nuptial** day to arrive five days **hence**, on May 1, 1600.

4. **devise** (verb) •

LD - alliteration (d,d,d); **play on words** (Philostrate/ Philistine)

No paragraph - continuation

Commas - appositive

Verb tense - pluperfect

Capitalization - title

Pronoun - object of infinitive, not subject; reverse order

Homophones - their/there/they're

Infinitives

Parts of speech - use of word as different parts of speech (devise)

B - theseus had just ordered philostrate his master of revelry to **devise** some diversion to distract he and hippolyta until their wedding day

C - Theseus had just ordered Philostrate, his Master of Revelry, to **devise** some diversion to distract Hippolyta and him until their wedding day.

5. ❤ **pert,** ❤ **pomp,** ❤ **reveling** (revel, revels), ❤ **noble,** ❤ **woo,** ❤ **strife** •

LD - metaphor; double entendre and symbol ("wooed me with your sword," sword being a rapier and a symbol for a male organ); **historical allusion** ("Let's stop the strife..."); **use of slang** ("have a blast")

2 paragraphs - different persons speaking

Commas - interjection; direct address; appositive; introductory word or phrase ("yes"); set off "too" with commas; direct address; 2 adj. before a noun and 2nd one is not age, color, size, or linked to noun

Quotation

Possessive pronouns - my, your, his, her, its, our, their

Run-on sentence without periods

Verb tense - present tense needed in conversation

Hyphens - 3 words acting as one

Contractions - discuss apostrophes in contractions vs. possessives (only for nouns)

Adjectives vs. adverbs - "good" as adjective and "well" as adverb

Compound predicate

Often confused prepositions - between/among

Numbers - write out to 99

Homophone - our/are

No comma before "and have a blast" - not a compound sentence (no subject)

Infinitives and infinitive phrases - discuss use

B - ah hippolyta my **pert** and noble bride to be let us marry with **pomp** and much **reveling**. in other words let us have a jolly good time of it too. yes my wise and **noble** mate to be you won me in battle you **wooed** me with your sword   lets make a merry joyous thing of our wedding lets stop the **strife** among are 2 nations and have a blast

C -   "Ah, Hippolyta, my **pert** and noble bride-to-be, let us marry with **pomp** and much **reveling**. In other words, let us have a jolly, good time of it, too."

"Yes, my wise and **noble** mate-to-be, you won me in battle. You **wooed** me with your sword. Let's make a merry, joyous thing of our wedding. Let's stop the **strife** and have a blast!"

B = *suggested sentence for the board or overhead*   **C** = *sentence written correctly*   **LD** = *literary device*

6. ❤ prodigious •

LD - alliteration (p,p)

Paragraph - subject change

Commas - optional after introductory adverb; adjective clause with relative pronoun

Verb tense - need for past tense as story continues

Pronouns - overuse as subject unclear in new paragraph

Homophone - two/to/too

Irregular verbs - lie/lay/has lain and lay/laid/has laid

Transitive vs. intransitive verbs - discuss difference

Commas - appositive (adjective clause with relative pronoun)

Coordinating conjunctions - Do not begin a sentence with one.

Relative pronouns - who/whom/whose/whoever/ whomever/that/which ("that" and "which" can be subject or object and are used only with objects and animals; "who" and "whom" are used with people; "who" is subject; "whom" is object)

Possessive pronouns - my, your, his, her, its, our, their

Pronouns - discuss various uses

No comma after two - 2nd adj. denotes age

Misplaced modifier - Egeus laid problem to rest, not his daughter

Numbers - write out to 99

Punctuation - use dash (or colon or even a comma) to denote break; avoid overuse of dashes

NOTE - Warn students of need to rewrite for clarity

B - and suddenly they were interrupted by the arrival of egeus an angry father who lay before his ruler his rebellious daughter and the 2 young men who professed to love her a **prodigious** problem

C -   Suddenly, Theseus and Hippolyta were interrupted by the arrival of Egeus, an angry father, who laid a **prodigious** problem before his ruler — his rebellious daughter and the two young men who professed to love her.

7. ❤ waxed, diminutive, ❤ wooed (past participial of "woo")

LD - slang (dudes)

No paragraph - same person continuing to speak

Commas - introductory subordinate clause; appositive; extra information (non-restrictive modifier)

Complex sentence - discuss differences among simple, compound, complex, and compound/complex sentences.

Incorrect verb tense - story in past tense

Verb tense - note correct use of conditional; warn of over-use and incorrect use as a substitute for the past tense

Comparisons - angry/angrier/angriest

No comma before Hermia - single word appositive closely related to the preceding word

No comma before 2nd "and" - not compound sentence

Hyphens - 3 words as one

Often confused words - accept/except

Numbers - write out to 99

Voice - avoid passive voice "was being wooed"

NOTE - Teach subordinating conjunctions (after, although, as — when, while, where — how — if — than — even though — because, before — until, unless— since, so that - **A White Bus**)

• •

B - as egeus **waxed** angrier and angrier he explains that his daughter hermia a **diminutive** ball of fire is being **wooed** by two dudes lysander and demetrius and she would not except his choice of the 2

C - As Egeus **waxed** angrier and angrier, he explained that his daughter Hermia, a **diminutive** ball-of-fire, was being **wooed** by two dudes, Lysander and Demetrius, and she would not accept his choice of the two.

B = suggested sentence for the board or overhead   *C = sentence written correctly*   *LD = literary device*

8. tokens, ❤ feigning, ❤ cunning ••

LD - use of aphorism and idiom ("stolen her heart")

Paragraph - new person speaking

Commas - direct address; quote; participial phrase, compound sentence; quote

Quotation - interrupted quote (note punctuation)

Possessive pronouns - my, your, his, her, its, our, their

Run-on sentence - 2nd sentence is a run-on with "and"

Irregular comparisons - some/more/most

Verbs - avoid use of passive voice

Compound sentence to correct non-parallel construction ("He has.....,and he has...)

Verb tense - use of present tense (conversation) and past tense (narrator)

Parallel construction - needed for clarity ("poems [n]...tokens [n]...sung [v]")

No comma before "Hermia" - restrictive modifier since he could have had more than one disobedient daughter; word closely related to preceding word

Homophone - presents/presence

Verb tense - use of present tense in conversation

NOTE - Teach coordinating conjunctions (for, and, nor, but, or, yet, so — FAN BOYS)

B - my noble lord my most disobedient daughter hermia has been bewitched by Lysander Egeus said. this Lysander has sent her poems and love **tokens** and he has sung under her window **feigning** love and he has stolen her heart with presents and **cunning** he continued

C - "My noble lord, Lysander has bewitched my most disobedient daughter Hermia," Egeus said. "This Lysander has sent her poems and love **tokens**. He has sung under her window, **feigning** love, and he has stolen her heart with presents and **cunning**," he continued.

➥ SUGGESTION:

I suggest having your students memorize the coordinating and subordinating conjunctions. It is not hard. Use the suggested acronyms, put the words to a beat, and students will learn them quickly. Simply repeat them each time one shows up in a Caught'ya. In this painless manner, the conjunctions will be memorized. Once the conjunctions are memorized, students then can learn comma placement.

9. trinkets, ❤ knave (noun), brandished ••

LD - anecdote; idiomatic expression ("pretty penny")

No paragraph - same person continuing to speak

Commas - interjection; quote

Quotation

Run-on sentence - conjunctions used instead of punctuation

Coordinating conjunctions - Do not begin a sentence with one.

Complex sentence - subordinate clause (.."as he brandished"); no comma when subordinate clause is located at the end of the sentence

Possession - singular noun ending in "s"

Verb tense error - story in past tense

NOTE - Review the subordinating conjunctions here.

B - and in fact he has sent hermia so many **trinkets** she could open a gift shop and make a pretty penny this **knave** so convinced her that she defied me and gave me this note Egeus concluded his complaint as he **brandished** a short note under theseuss nose

C - "In fact, he has sent Hermia so many **trinkets** she could open a gift shop and make a pretty penny. This **knave** so convinced her that she defied me and gave me this note," Egeus concluded his complaint as he **brandished** a short note under Theseus's nose.

B = *suggested sentence for the board or overhead*   *C* = *sentence written correctly*   *LD* = *literary device*

10. ♥ abide, dolorous •

Paragraph - body of letter

Commas - greeting; compound sentence; closing

Letter format - friendly letter

Common spelling errors - "cannot" is one word

Compound sentence - "I cannot.....heart lies"

Run on sentence - lack of punctuation

Verb tense - present tense needed in conversation

Often confused words - accept/except

Irregular verbs - lie/lay/has lain and lay/laid/has laid

Colon - to indicate break before letter

Relative pronouns - who/whom/whose/whoever/whomever/that/which ("that" and "which" can be subject or object and are used only with objects and animals; "who" and "whom" are used with people; "who" is subject; "whom" is object)

Homophones - your/you're

Capitalization - greeting and closing of letter; "I"

Coordinating conjunctions - review

B - the letter read

dearest father

    i can not except demetrius as my mate for my heart lies with lysander i will not **abide** being married to a man that i do not love

              youre **dolorous** daughter

              hermia

C - The letter read:

Dearest Father,

    I cannot accept Demetrius as my mate, for my heart lies with Lysander. I will not **abide** being married to a man whom I do not love.

            Your **dolorous** daughter,

            Hermia

11. **audaciously, supplicated, wayward** •

Paragraph - new person speaking

Commas - quote; interjection; direct address; interrupted quote; subordinate clause at beginning of sentence (adverb out of place); participial phrase

Interrupted quotation

Pronouns - overuse of pronouns in new paragraph make meaning unclear

Capitalization - "Duke" is a title used as a name.

Strong, action verbs - encourage use

Verb tense - narrator in past and conversation in present

Homophones - two/to/too; their/there/they're

Relative pronouns - adjective clause with relative pronoun "which"

Plural vs. possessives - "fathers"

Complex sentence - "If she does..."

Subordinating conjunctions - review

Often confused words - then/than ("then" is an adverb and "than" is a conjunction used to compare)

B - then he **audaciously supplicated** his ruler ah my duke he said I beg you to enforce the athenian law which gives fathers' absolute power over there **wayward** daughter's. if she does not wed demetrius I may according to our law put her too death

C - Then Egeus **audaciously supplicated** his ruler, "Ah, my Duke," he said, " I beg you to enforce the Athenian law which gives fathers absolute power over their **wayward** daughters. If Hermia does not wed Demetrius, I may, according to our law, put her to death."

---

12. ❤ palpable ●

LD - simile

2 Paragraphs - different persons speaking

Commas - quote; direct address; interrupter

Quotation - note location of question mark

Punctuation - use of exclamation mark for emphasis

Contractions

Pronouns -"I" as subject and "me" as object; put "I" last; object used after preposition; "he" as subject and "him" as object; put yourself last

Plural vs. possessive noun - confusion

Conjunctions - Do not begin a sentence with one.

Homophone - your/you're

Possessive pronouns

Capitalization - do not capitalize "God" as it is not a specific one.

NOTE - Teach prepositions. Use list in the Appendix of this book.

B - you wouldnt. me and lysander love each other sobbed hermia in **palpable** distress. you dont understand what is between I and him. and what do you have to say for yourself Hermia asked Theseus. your father of course should be like a god to you

C - "You wouldn't! Lysander and I love each other," sobbed Hermia in **palpable** distress. "You don't understand what is between him and me."

"What do you have to say for yourself, Hermia?" asked Theseus. "Your father, of course, should be like a god to you."

13. ❤ entreat, ❤ befall , ❤ beseeched ●

LD - conversation; metaphor; use of symbol and play on words ("unwished yoke")

Paragraph - new person speaking

Commas - compound sentence; quote

Quotation

Possessive pronouns - my, your, his, her, its, our, their

Capitalization - always capitalize "I;" title of person must be capitalized

Compound predicate

Run-on sentence - conjunction "and" used instead of punctuation

Homophone - its/it's

Pronouns - "me" as object

Complex and compound sentences - Review different types of sentences.

Subject-pronoun agreement - "family....its"

Collective nouns and pronouns - review common ones (see Appendix)

B - i **entreat** your grace to pardon me for loving and beg you to tell me what may **befall** me if i refuse to marry Demetrius and my family will not give me its approval and I do not want to carry any unwished yoke hermia **beseeched**

C - "I **entreat** your Grace to pardon me for loving and beg you to tell me what may **befall** me if I refuse to marry Demetrius. My family will not give me its approval, and I do not want to carry any unwished yoke," Hermia **beseeched**.

➥ **SUGGESTION:**
Since all nine comma rules have been introduced in the previous Caught'yas, this might be a good point to pause and review them all together. You can find a list of them under "Comma Rules" in the Appendix of this book.

B = suggested sentence for the board or overhead   C = sentence written correctly   LD = literary device

14. ❤ **audacious** •

LD - historical allusion (to Greek law)

Paragraph - new person speaking

Commas - introductory word ("well"); direct address; quote; quote

Quotation

Possessive pronouns - my, your, his, her, its, our, their

Infinitives

Homophone - your/you're; to/too/two

Complex sentence - no comma as subordinate clause is at end of sentence

Pronouns - always put yourself last

Possession - singular noun

B - well **audacious** hermia your father has the right to put you to death or to send you to a convent away from all men if you do not obey his will returned theseus. you have until my and hippolytas wedding day to decide your own fate he concluded

C -   "Well, **audacious** Hermia, your father has the right to put you to death or to send you to a convent away from all men if you do not obey his will," returned Theseus. "You have until Hippolyta's and my wedding day to decide your own fate," he concluded.

15. ❤ **woe, thwarted** •

LD - literary allusion; use of aphorism ("The course of true....")

3 Paragraphs - different people speaking

Commas - direct address; introductory subordinate clause; interrupted quote; participial phrase; interrupted quote; interjection; two adjectives when 2nd is not age, color, or linked to noun; appositive ("Romeo..."); quote

Quotation - note punctuation in continued (interrupted) quote

Often confused words - then/than ("then" is an adverb and "than" is a conjunction used to compare); accept/except

Possession - singular noun

Pronouns - "I" as subject and "me" as object and correct order

Subject/verb agreement - compound subject needs plural verb

Hyphen - 2 words acting as one

Negatives

Verb tense - incorrect use, story in past ("added")

Adverbs vs. adjectives - incorrect use of "smooth" (adjective) instead of "smoothly" (adverb)

B - hermia if you does not accept the man of my choice egeus maintained grasping at the dukes second punishment than you will die unwed in a convent. oh **woe** sobbed hermia. me and lysander is like the classic tale of the star crossed **thwarted** lovers romeo and juliet. the course of true love never did run smooth adds lysander

C -   "Hermia, if you do not accept the man of my choice," Egeus maintained, grasping at the Duke's second punishment, "then you will die unwed in a convent."

   "Oh, **woe**," sobbed Hermia. "Lysander and I are like the classic tale of the star-crossed, **thwarted** lovers, Romeo and Juliet."

   "The course of true love never did run smoothly," added Lysander.

➡ **SUGGESTION:**

This is a good spot to review the eight parts of speech and their various functions since all eight are represented in Caught'ya #15 — noun, interjection, preposition, pronoun, adverb, verb, adjective, conjunction. I put up a large sign in the window of my classroom that says NIPPAVAC. This, of course, is an acronym of the parts of speech. We chant these a few times until my students learn them. Once learned, they can be more easily applied to sentences.

B = suggested sentence for the board or overhead   *C = sentence written correctly*   *LD = literary device*

16. ❤ odorous, cad, unrequited ●

LD - simile

Paragraph - new person speaking (narrator)

Commas - interrupter; appositive; participial phrase

Indirect quotation - no quotes with "that"

Verb tense error - story in past tense

Gerund phrase - "after winning..." used as a noun

Indefinite articles - "an" used before vowel

Verb tense - use of pluperfect tense ("had wooed," "had jilted") to denote previous action

Splitting verbs - avoid splitting of helping verb and verb ("had first wooed")

Punctuation - no comma before second "and" as not a compound sentence (no subject)

Often confused words - then/than ("then" is an adverb and "than" is a conjunction used to compare)

Pronouns - possessives; object of preposition; discuss different types and uses

Strong verbs - use frequently

B - lysander politely argues that he was the equal of demetrius and that in fact demetrius first had wooed another fair maiden helena. lysander continued to explain that demetrius after winning helena had jilted her like a **odorous cad** and than pursued hermia. he abandoned poor helena to her **unrequited** love

C -   Lysander politely argued that he was the equal of Demetrius and that, in fact, Demetrius first had wooed another fair maiden, Helena. Lysander continued to explain that Demetrius, after winning Helena, had jilted her like an **odorous cad** and then pursued Hermia. He abandoned poor Helena to her **unrequited** love.

17. ❤ austere ●

LD - narrator aside (comment injected into story); **simile; alliteration**

Paragraph - narrator changed pace

Commas - adjective series

Verb tense - correct use of tense switch (present for narrator aside)

Like vs. as - "like" is used only with nouns in a direct comparison; "as" is needed in comparatives ("as fast as...")

Irregular comparisons - bad/worse/worst; good/better/best

Capitalization - titles

Titles - Discuss rules for underlining vs. putting quotation marks around titles. Whole longer works like books, magazines, and record albums are underlined and smaller parts of the whole that are shorter like poems, articles, and songs are put into quotes.

Run on sentence - conjunction "and" substituted for punctuation

Possession - singular noun

Hyphen - two words acting as one ("pig-headed)

Subject-verb agreement - "group" is singular

Punctuation - no comma after "concerned" - not a compound sentence

Collective noun/verb agreement - collective nouns always singular

Verb tense - note correct use of conditional

Homophones -your/you're; its/it's

B - this is worser than a soap opera like days of your lives lysander loved hermia and demetrius loved hermia and helena adored demetrius and hermias father was a pig headed opinionated **austere** man where his daughters were concerned and would never bend. this group of athenians were like a wild herd of warthogs with each animal running in its own direction

C -   This is worse than a soap opera like <u>Days of Your Lives</u>! Lysander loved Hermia. Demetrius loved Hermia. Helena adored Demetrius. Hermia's father was a pig-headed, opinionated, **austere** man where his daughters were concerned and would never bend. This group of Athenians was like a wild herd of warthogs with each animal running in its own direction.

➥ **SUGGESTION:**

It is often a good idea to have students memorize the main prepositions (there are over forty of them). Students can do this painlessly, memorizing a few each day until the entire list is learned. My students make up a dance to them. Once learned, prepositions can be correctly used in places like titles, and students find it easier to understand that prepositional phrases are really adjectives and adverbs.

B = *suggested sentence for the board or overhead*   *C* = *sentence written correctly*   *LD* = *literary device*

18. ❤ **lamentable** •

Paragraph - place and subject change

Commas - noun series; compound sentence

Sentence structure - need to add subject to fragment

Often confused words - then/than ("then" is an adverb and "than" is a conjunction used to compare)

Pronouns - "he" as subject/"him" as object

Verb tense - use of pluperfect tense to refer to preceding action

Possession - singular noun

Plural vs. possessive noun - families/family's

Incorrect verb tense - story in past tense

Homophone - heard/herd

B - theseus then left with hippolyta egeus and demetrius following him had herd enough of this **lamentable** families squabble and he wanted to discuss business with egeus and demetrius. lysander and hermia are left alone.

C -   Theseus then left with Hippolyta, Egeus, and Demetrius following him. He had heard enough of this **lamentable** family's squabble, and he wanted to discuss business with Egeus and Demetrius. Lysander and Hermia were left alone.

19. ❤ **paramour,** ❤ **visage** •

LD - deliberate use of non-sequator

Paragraph - new person speaking

Quotation - note punctuation in quote that ends in a question

Commas - quote; direct address

Often confused prepositions - between/among (between 2; among 3 or more)

Often confused words - affect/effect ("affect" to change; "effect" to cause or a cause)

Pronouns - "us" as object/"we" as subject

Relative pronouns - who/whom/whose/whoever/whomever/that/which ("that" and "which" can be subject or object and are used only with objects and animals; "who" and "whom" are used with people; "who" is subject; "whom" is object)

Possessive pronouns - my, your, his, her, its, our, their

Intensifier - "so"

B - why are you so pale my love asked Lysander of his **paramour**. among us we can solve this problem that effects us so profoundly. Your **visage** is so lovely

C -   "Why are you so pale, my love?" asked Lysander of his **paramour**. "Between us we can solve this problem that affects us so profoundly. Your **visage** is so lovely."

B = suggested sentence for the board or overhead   *C = sentence written correctly*   ***LD** = literary device*

20. ♥ uttered •

LD - literary allusion

Paragraph - new person speaking

Commas - interjection; direct address; compound sentence; quote; non-restrictive modifier; quote

Pronouns - "me" as object and "I" as subject; position of subject pronouns; possessive; pronoun order

Capitalization - always capitalize "I"

Titles - Title of play needs to be in quotes.

Verb tense - subjunctive mood needed in "if" clause

Punctuation - no comma after "love" - not a compound sentence (no subject)

Prepositions - review

NOTE - Review rules for underlining vs. putting quotation marks around titles - whole longer works like books, magazines, and record albums are underlined and smaller parts of the whole that are shorter like poems, articles and songs are put into quotes

B - oh my sweet Lysander woe is i. me and you cannot marry. my strict father will not allow it and i do not love demetrius. i am in the same position as juliet hermia said again referring to that classic tale romeo and juliet. I shall have to marry someone I do not love or spend the rest of my life in a convent. if only I was a boy she **uttered** with a sigh

C -   "Oh, my sweet Lysander, woe is me. You and I cannot marry. My strict father will not allow it, and I do not love Demetrius. I am in the same position as Juliet," Hermia said, again referring to that classic tale, "Romeo and Juliet." "I shall have to marry someone I do not love or spend the rest of my life in a convent. If only I were a boy," she **uttered** with a sigh.

➥ SUGGESTION:

This is a good point for a discussion of the difference between a phrase and a clause. See Appendix for explanation.

21. intrepid ♥ shrewd, abode, jurisdiction, ♥ stealth •

LD - slang; historical reference

Paragraph - new person speaking

Commas - quote; two adjectives where 2nd is not age, color, or linked to noun; verb series

Quotations

Capitalization - always capitalize "I"

Articles - "an" before a vowel or silent "h"

Possessive pronouns - my, your, his, her, its, our, their

Pronouns - discuss different types and their uses

Contraction

Compound predicate

Possession - singular noun

Often confused words - affect/effect ("effect" as a verb meaning "to cause, to bring about")

B - i have a awesome idea said the **intrepid shrewd** clever lysander. my wealthy aunt has a **abode** outside the **jurisdiction** of athenian law. lets leave our respective homes in **stealth** meet in the woods and elope to my aunts house to be married. we will effect our own future

C -   "I have an awesome idea," said the **intrepid, shrewd** Lysander. "My wealthy aunt has an **abode** outside the **jurisdiction** of Athenian law. Let's leave our respective homes in **stealth**, meet in the woods, and elope to my aunt's house to be married. We will effect our own future."

22. ♥ gallant •

LD - hyperbole ("dearest....")

Paragraph - new person speaking

Commas - interjection; adjective series that is also a direct address; compound sentence

Quotation - punctuation with exclamation mark

Capitalization - capitalize "I" (Note that from here on, this will no longer be listed.)

Verb tense - use of future tense with "will" to indicate definite future action

Intensifier - "wonderfully" used as an adjective

Punctuation - need for exclamation mark for emphasis after hyperbole

B - oh my dearest best most wonderfully **gallant** love I will meet you and we will wed said hermia

C -   "Oh, my dearest, best, most wonderfully **gallant** love, I will meet you, and we will wed!" said Hermia.

B = *suggested sentence for the board or overhead*   **C** = *sentence written correctly*   **LD** = *literary device*

23. ❤ **naught, timidity** ●

LD - description (note use of strong, action verbs)

Paragraph - narrator speaking

Commas - appositive

Homophone - who's/whose

Often confused words - then/than ("then" is an adverb and "than" is a conjunction used to compare)

Relative pronoun - adjective clause with relative pronoun "whose"

Verb tense - use of pluperfect

Punctuation - no comma between "poor" and "young" (2nd adj. is age) as well as "lovely" and "blond" (2nd adj. is color)

Punctuation - use of semicolon in a series of related sentences

Possessive pronouns - my, your, his, her, its, our, their

Strong verbs - needed in description

NOTE - This would be a good place to discuss the 3 uses of semicolons - sentence series, compound sentence instead of conjunction, list after a colon if commas present.

B - just then helena the poor young lady whos love for demetrius had come to **naught** appeared. helenas lovely blond hair hung limp in her distress. her usually tall figure stooped in sorrow and her natural **timidity** made her voice hesitant and faint

C -   Just then Helena, the poor young lady whose love for Demetrius had come to **naught**, appeared. Helena's lovely blond hair hung limp in her distress; her usually tall figure stooped in sorrow; and her natural **timidity** made her voice hesitant and faint.

24. ❤ **enmity** ●

Paragraph - change of emphasis

Commas - interrupter ("surprisingly"); introductory word or phrase ("in fact")

Incorrect verb-tense switch - story in past tense

Possession - singular noun

Spelling rule - "i" before "e" except after "c" and neighbor and weigh are weird

Relative pronouns - who/whom/whose/whoever/ whomever/that/which ("that" and "which" can be subject or object and are used only with objects and animals; "who" and "whom" are used with people; "who" is subject; "whom" is object)

Pronouns - use of "her" as possessive or object and "she" as subject

Reflexive pronouns - use of "herself" for clarity

Infinitives - review difference between infinitive use of "to" and preposition "to"

Possession - singular noun ending in "s"

Prepositions - review

B - now hermia is helenas best freind. helena surprisingly bore no **enmity** for her friend which was supposed to marry the man she herself loved. in fact she beseeched hermia and lysander to tell her how to win demetrius love

C -   Now Hermia was Helena's best friend. Helena, surprisingly, bore no **enmity** for her friend who was supposed to marry the man she herself loved. In fact, she beseeched Hermia and Lysander to tell her how to win Demetrius's love.

B = suggested sentence for the board or overhead   C = sentence written correctly   LD = literary device

25. ♥ paragon •••

LD - satire, personification; use of aphorism; narrator aside ("The plot thickens!"); **foreshadowing**

3 Paragraphs - narrator, person speaking, narrator

Commas - participial phrase ("informing her"); 2 subordinate clauses at beginning of sentence (adverb out of place); quote

Quotations

Subject/verb agreement - "we" needs plural verb

Often confused prepositions - between/among (between 2; among 3 or more)

Pronouns - possessive

Complex sentence - no comma before "so that" (not a compound sentence but a subordinate clause at end of sentence

Plural vs. possessive noun - lovers/lover's/lovers'

Often confused words - then/than ("then" is an adverb and "than" is a conjunction used to compare)

Verb tense - correct use of present tense to indicate a narrator aside

Pronouns - excessive use of pronouns makes meaning unclear; need to add nouns

Numbers - write out to 99

B - they tried to comfort helena informing her of there plans to elope. perhaps when we is wed demetrius will turn his affection once again to you. if this does not work maybe between the three of us we can come up with a plan to transform him into a **paragon** of a suitor hermia said. helena than decided to inform demetrius of the impending elopement so that she could go with him in pursuit of the 2 lovers. the plot thickens

C - Hermia and Lysander tried to comfort Helena, informing her of their plans to elope.

"Perhaps when we are wed, Demetrius will turn his affection once again to you. If this does not work, maybe among the three of us we can come up with a plan to transform Demetrius into a **paragon** of a suitor," Hermia said.

Helena then decided to inform Demetrius of the impending elopement so that she could go with him in pursuit of the two lovers. The plot thickens.

26. clandestine •••

LD - subplot

Paragraph - narrator speaking with place and subject change

Commas - introductory subordinate clause (adverb) series (3 of them); appositive

Parallel construction - need to add "while" for clarity

Transitions - used to indicate place and subject change

Complex sentences - review

Homophone - their/there/they're

Possessive pronouns - my, your, his, her, its, our, their

Possession - singular noun that ends in "s"

Prepositions - go over prepositions and uses thereof

B - while theseus and hippolyta anticipated their wedding celebration hermia and lysander planned there **clandestine** elopement and helena plotted to win demetriuss love a meeting took place in town at the house of peter quince the carpenter

C - While Theseus and Hippolyta anticipated their wedding celebration, while Hermia and Lysander planned their **clandestine** elopement, and while Helena plotted to win Demetrius's love, a meeting took place in town at the house of Peter Quince, the carpenter.

B = suggested sentence for the board or overhead   **C** = sentence written correctly   **LD** = literary device

27. cohorts, to divvy up •

LD - subplot; irony (town tradesmen putting on a play for duke); **play on words** (names of trades people); **double entendre** ("act together")

No paragraph - continuation

Commas - noun series

Possession - singular nouns, one ending in "s"

Spelling rule - if word ends in consonant/vowel/consonant and a suffix is added, double the consonant ("wedding")

Demonstrative adjectives - this/that/these/those

Antecedent/pronoun agreement - collective noun "troupe" needs singular possessive pronoun

Collective nouns - review

Hyphen - two words acting as one ("would-be")

Homophone - its/it's

NOTE - A discussion here about collective nouns and problems with agreement would be appropriate.

B - quince and his **cohorts** nick bottom flute snug snout and robin starveling were **divvying up** parts and setting a time for a rehearsal for a short play they wished to perform in honor of theseus and hippolytas wedding. this troupe of would be actors had trouble getting their act together

C - Quince and his **cohorts**, Nick Bottom, Flute, Snug, Snout, and Robin Starveling, were **divvying up** parts and setting a time for a rehearsal for a short play they wished to perform in honor of Theseus's and Hippolyta's wedding. This troupe of would-be actors had trouble getting its act together.

28. bumptious, ❤ lofty •

LD - sarcasm and oxymoron ("most lamentable comedy"); **description**

No paragraph - continuation

Commas - appositive; two adjectives; introductory subordinate clause

Relative pronouns - who/whom/whose/whoever/whomever/that/which ("that" and "which" can be subject or object and are used only with objects and animals; "who" and "whom" are used with people; "who" is subject; "whom" is object)

Punctuation - note comma placement inside quote even though quote is short

Adjective clause - note use of relative pronoun

Indirect quotation - avoidance of quotes with "that"

Punctuation - use of quotes to denote character's actual words even though this is not a direct quotation

B - the planning of this amateurish play was hampered by the weaver nick bottom. he was the clumsy offensively **bumptious** man not known for **lofty** thoughts that tried to take over the meeting. while Bottom was cast as the hero in this "most lamentable comedy" he also said that he could play the part of the heroine

C - The planning of this amateurish play was hampered by the weaver Nick Bottom. He was the clumsy, offensively **bumptious** man not known for **lofty** thoughts who tried to take over the meeting. While Bottom was cast as the hero in this "most lamentable comedy," he also said that he could play the part of the heroine.

29. falsetto, versatility, prowess •

LD - onomatopoeia; character development in action and dialogue; description

Paragraph - new person speaking

Commas - direct address; quote; appositive; 2 adjectives; quote; participial phrase; compound sentence

Quotation (interrupted)

Adjective clause - note use of relative pronoun

Splitting verbs - avoid splitting helping verb and main verb ("can also play")

Adverb and adjective usage - "bad" as adjective, "badly" as adverb, plus placement of adverb

B - let me play the heroine thisbe said bottom a man whose name fit his personality in a lovely **falsetto** voice. i can also play the part of the lion he growled trying to show his **versatility** and **prowess** as an actor for he wanted more parts bad. grrrr

C - "Let me play the heroine, Thisbe," said Bottom, a man whose name fit his personality, in a lovely, **falsetto** voice. "I also can play the part of the lion," he growled, trying to show his **versatility** and **prowess** as an actor, for he badly wanted more parts. "Grrrr."

B = suggested sentence for the board or overhead   *C = sentence written correctly*   *LD = literary device*

30. confrère ●

LD - humor; irony (Quince's cajoling)**; sarcasm** ("a man whose name....."); **use of foreign language for effect**

Paragraph - new person speaking

Commas - word or phrase at beginning ("no"); direct address; appositive; noun series; direct address

Quotation

Intensifier - use of "so" as an intensifier with adverb

Hyphen - 2 words acting as one

Adjective and adverb usage - "well" as adverb and "good" as adjective

B - no bottom you will play no part but that of pyramus the hero. pyramus is a sweet faced man a proper man a most lovely gentlemanly man. this is why only you can play the part my **confrère** confided quince. you will play it so good

C - "No, Bottom, you will play no part but that of Pyramus, the hero. Pyramus is a sweet-faced man, a proper man, a most lovely, gentlemanly man. This is why only you can play the part, my **confrère**," confided Quince. "You will play it so well."

31. rustic, ❤ valorous, bucolic   ● ● ● ● ● ● ● ● ● ● ● ● ● ● ❤ ● ❤ ● ● ●

LD - literary allusion; setting; foreshadowing

Paragraph - return to narrator speaking

Commas - optional comma with introductory adverb; noun series; appositive; use of "themselves" for emphasis

Punctuation - parentheses needed for a clarification outside action

Prefixes and suffixes - use of suffix "ment" to create noun ("agreement")

Voice - passive vs. active voice (avoid passive if at all possible)

Quotation vs. underlining - title of story needs to be in quotes

Comma placement - comma always goes inside quotation marks.

Reflexive pronouns - "themselves;" correct form needed

Verb tense - note correct use of conditional; warn of misuse

NOTE - This is a good place to review once again the rules for underlining vs. putting quotation marks around titles - whole longer works like books, magazines, and record albums are underlined and smaller parts of the whole that are shorter like poems, articles and songs are put into quotes

B - finally the parts in the play the rehearsal time and the rehearsal place the very same woods where Lysander and Hermia planned to meet were all resolved. the **rustic** actors themselves at last were in agreement. the play was to be based on the story pyramus and thisbe a classic tale of tragic misunderstandings. the **valorous** but **bucolic** actors theirselves would make it a comedy

C -   Finally, the parts in the play, the rehearsal time, and the rehearsal place (the very same woods where Lysander and Hermia planned to meet) were all resolved. The **rustic** actors themselves at last were in agreement. The play was to be based on the story "Pyramus and Thisbe," a classic tale of tragic misunderstandings. The **valorous** but **bucolic** actors, themselves, would make it a comedy.

➥ SUGGESTION:

If your students are unfamiliar with the story "Pyramus and Thisbe," this would be a good time to read it or assign a group of students to find out the plot.

---

32. ♥ **frolicked** ••

LD - fantasy and unreality; subplot #2; narrator aside

Paragraph - place change

Commas - introductory subordinate clause; introductory word or phrase; appositive

Plural rules - "elf" to "elves", "fairy" to "fairies" (see Appendix for plural rules)

Punctuation - parentheses needed for clarification outside action in narrator aside

Sentence structure - fragment needs to be made into a sentence

Subordinating conjunctions and subordinate clauses - review here

Possessive pronouns - my, your, his, her, its, our, their

B - as all this was taking place the elfs and fairys **frolicked** in the forest. yes the same forest where everyone else had planned to meet that evening. they awaited the arrival of titania the queen of the pixies and her court

C -   As all this was taking place, the elves and fairies **frolicked** in the forest (Yes, it was the same forest where everyone else had planned to meet that evening.) They awaited the arrival of Titania, the Queen of the Pixies, and her court.

33. **convened, waggish,** ♥ **mortals** ••

LD - elaboration of fantasy; oxymoron ("seriously waggish")

No paragraph - continuation

Commas - three appositives; "too" meaning also (always set off by commas)

Often confused prepositions - between/among

Plural rules - consonant "y" singular nouns change the "y" to "i" and add "es;" "f" changes to "v" and add "es"

Adjective clauses - note use of relative pronoun

Spelling rule - if word ends in vowel/consonant and a suffix is added, double the consonant ("waggish")

Relative pronouns - who/whom/whose/whoever/ whomever/that/which ("that" and "which" can be subject or object and are used only with objects and animals; "who" and "whom" are used with people; "who" is subject; "whom" is object)

Punctuation - need parentheses for clarification

Verb tense error - story in past tense

Infinitive phrase - "about to arrive"

Homophone - to/too/two

B - among the **convened** fairies in the forest was the seriously **waggish** elf puck that liked to play tricks on **mortals** non fairys in order to amuse his king oberon. all is complicated by the fact that oberon the pixie king was about to arrive in that same forest too

C - Among the **convened** fairies in the forest was the seriously **waggish** elf, Puck, who liked to play tricks on **mortals** (non fairies) in order to amuse his king, Oberon. All was complicated by the fact that Oberon, the Pixie King, was about to arrive in that same forest, too.

B = suggested sentence for the board or overhead   C = sentence written correctly   LD = literary device

34. ♥ wrath, ♥ knavish (adj.) ●

LD - conversation; telling action description within dialogue; rhyme

2 Paragraphs - 2 people speaking

Commas - quote; appositive; quote

Quotations

Verb tense - future tense to indicate definite future action

Run on sentence - lack of punctuation

Homophones - no/know, its/it's, your/you're

Contractions

Comparisons - angry/angrier/angriest

Relative pronouns - "whom" needed as object of preposition

Possessive pronouns - my, your, his, her, its, our, their

Pronouns - review various types

Gerund phrase - acts as a noun ("Being bad...")

B - the king will frolic here tonight we must be careful to keep the queen from his sight. oberon is full of **wrath** for the queen and she for him puck warned the other pixies. i dont no which one is angrier. you are that **knavish** sprite puck from who mortal maidens run in fear. you are the one who the town blames for all its mishaps. being bad is youre favorite sport one pixie said

C - "The king will frolic here tonight. We must be careful to keep the queen from his sight. Oberon is full of **wrath** for the queen and she for him," Puck warned the other pixies. "I don't know which one is angrier."

"You are that **knavish** sprite, Puck, from whom mortal maidens run in fear. You are the one whom the town blames for all its mishaps. Being bad is your favorite sport," one pixie said.

35. lugubrious ●

LD - anadiplosis ("mortals. Mortals.."); **anecdote** (to establish character); **humor** (referring to drunks)

Paragraph - new person speaking

Commas - quote; interjection; interrupter ("as they tell...") that is a qualifier; for clarity to separate extra information ("even with mortals")

Quotation

Pronouns - "I" needed as subject with verb of being

Incorrect word use -"gots" not a word

Possessive pronouns - my, your, his, her, its, our, their

Common spelling errors - "a lot" as 2 words

Prepositions - review

B - that is me boasted puck. oh we gots to get our kicks somewhere even with mortals. mortals as they tell **lugubrious** tales and then fall off their stools provide alot of laughs

C - "That is I," boasted Puck. "Oh, we have to get our kicks somewhere, even with mortals. Mortals, as they tell **lugubrious** tales and then fall off their stools, provide a lot of laughs."

➡ **SUGGESTION:**

This is a good spot to review the eight parts of speech and their various functions since all eight are represented in Caught'ya #35. (NIPPAVAC)

36. discord ●

LD - slang ("ticked")

Paragraph - new speaker (narrator)

Commas - appositive; introductory prepositional phrase; introductory phrase ("in fact")

Homophone - write/right

Compound subject

Compound predicate

Often confused words - accept/except

Parallel construction - needed for clarity ("for...for")

Capitalization - name of country

Prepositional phrases - used as adverbs and adjectives

Repetition - eliminate redundancy ("each other")

B - now puck was write. titania and oberon her mate were not exactly on the best of terms. in plain words they were ticked at each other. in fact titania was barely speaking to oberon accept to yell at him. they blamed each other for the **discord** and for stealing an indian boy from each other

C - Now Puck was right. Titania and Oberon, her mate, were not exactly on the best of terms. In plain words, they were ticked at each other. In fact, Titania was barely speaking to Oberon except to yell at him. They blamed each other for the **discord** and for stealing an Indian boy.

➡ **SUGGESTION:**

This might be a good place to review the nine comma rules once again.

B = *suggested sentence for the board or overhead*   **C** = *sentence written correctly*   **LD** = *literary device*

37. entourage, tapestry •

LD - **metaphor** ("tapestry of a .... tale"); **personification** ("sparks began...)

Paragraph - time change-

Commas - for emphasis with introductory adverb ("suddenly"); introductory subordinate clause (complex sentence); compound sentence

Incorrect verb tense - story in past

Possessive pronouns - my, your, his, her, its, our, their

Types of sentences - review compound and complex sentences

Comparatives - some/more/most

B - suddenly just as titania with her court entered the forest from one direction oberon and his **entourage** arrived from the opposite direction. the sparks begin to fly and the **tapestry** of a complicated tale became even more interwoven

C -   Suddenly, just as Titania with her court entered the forest from one direction, Oberon and his **entourage** arrived from the opposite direction.   The sparks began to fly, and the **tapestry** of a complicated tale became even more interwoven.

38. philanderer, amorous, lanky •

LD - **oxymoron** ("faithful philanderer"); **historical allusion** ("Amazon"); **double entendre** ("loved...word")

Paragraph - new person speaking

Commas - quote; 2 adjectives; for clarity ("of all mortals")

Quotation

Run-on sentence - conjunction "and" used instead of punctuation

Homophone - sense/since/cents

Common spelling errors - foreigner

Unusual plurals - woman/women

Incorrect word usage - use "should have" not "should of" (with a verb a preposition makes no sense)

Pronoun use - "I" as subject and "me" as object

B - you faithful **philanderer** accused titania and you loved hippolyta in all senses of the word and you were **amorous** with a tall **lanky** foriegner of all mortal women and you should of been devoted to me

C - "You faithful **philanderer**," accused Titania. "You loved Hippolyta in all senses of the word. You were **amorous** with a tall, **lanky** foreigner, of all mortal women! You should have been devoted to me."

39. chide, dalliance •

Paragraph - new person speaking

Commas - direct address

Quotation

Punctuation - use of exclamation mark for emphasis

Punctuation - question mark needed

Complex sentence - no comma needed before "when" as subordinate clause at end of sentence

Often confused prepositions - between/among (between 2; among 3 or more)

Contraction

Pronouns - "her" and "me" as objects; "she" and "I" as subjects; "I" and "me" go last

B - for shame titania retorted oberon. how can you **chide** me for my **dalliance** with hippolyta when you went after theseus. you dont understand the relationship among me and her

C - "For shame, Titania!" retorted Oberon. "How can you **chide** me for my **dalliance** with Hippolyta when you went after Theseus. You don't understand the relationship between her and me."

---

40. ❤ **taunted,** ❤ **perchance** ●

LD - conversation

3 Paragraphs - conversation

Commas - interjection; noun series; quote

Quotations

Sentence structure - deliberate use of fragment as a quote

Demonstrative adjectives - this/that/these/those

Punctuation - note punctuation of question

Often confused comparisons - fewer/less ("fewer" can be counted; "less" is a vague, uncountable amount)

Semicolon - use in compound sentence instead of conjunction ("I will stay" is implied)

Possession - singular noun ending in "s"

Complex sentence - no comma as subordinate clause at end of sentence

Pronouns - "her" as object or possessive and "she" as subject

NOTE - Discuss 3 uses of semicolons - in a series of independent clauses, in a compound sentence instead of a conjunction, and after a colon (for clarity) if the list uses commas.

B - ah jealousy lies and rumors **taunted** titania. how long do you plan to remain in this woods asked oberon. **perchance** less than five days perhaps more. i may stay until after theseus wedding day flung titania as her and her entourage left the grove

C - "Ah, jealousy, lies, and rumors," **taunted** Titania.

"How long do you plan to remain in these woods?" asked Oberon.

"**Perchance** fewer than five days; perhaps more. I may stay until after Theseus's wedding day," flung Titania as she and her entourage left the grove.

41. roguish, ❤ **chronicled** ●

LD - tale within a tale; anecdote

Paragraph - narrator speaking

Commas - 2 adverbial phrases at beginning of sentence; quote

Quotation

Spelling rule - if word ends in consonant/vowel/consonant and a suffix is added, double the consonant ("plotted")

Often confused comparisons - fewer/less ("fewer" can be counted; "less" is a vague, uncountable amount)

Often confused words - then/than ("then" is an adverb and "than" is a conjunction used to compare)

B - oberon ploted his revenge against titania. he recounted the old tale of cupid to the **roguish** puck. one night less then a year ago I saw a strange and wonderful sight he **chronicled**

C - Oberon plotted his revenge against Titania. He recounted the old tale of Cupid to the **roguish** Puck. "One night, less than a year ago, I saw a strange and wonderful sight," he **chronicled**.

42. ❤ **pate** ●

LD - description within narrative; anecdote

No paragraph - continuation

Commas - appositive; participial phrase; 3 adjectives where 2nd is not age or color but 3rd adjective is linked to noun; compound sentence; introductory word

Quotation that is continued in new paragraph and thus no quotes at end of first paragraph

Run-on sentence - punctuation needed

Hyphen - 2 words acting as one

Homophone - taught/taut

Complex sentence - adjective clause using "which"

Punctuation - no end quote as quotation will be continued in the next paragraph

B - cupid that little sprite with a baby bald **pate** kept his bow taught and his arrow cocked he flew between earth and the moon trying to strike a young beautiful mortal girl he released the arrow but it missed the heart of the girl instead it struck a mild white flower which turned purple with desire *(Quote continued tomorrow.)*

C - "Cupid, that little sprite with a baby-bald **pate**, kept his bow taut and his arrow cocked. He flew between earth and the moon, trying to strike a young, beautiful mortal girl. He released the arrow, but it missed the heart of the girl. Instead, it struck a milk-white flower which turned purple with desire.

---

43. ❤ regale ●●

LD - anecdote

2 Paragraph - time change, subject change

Commas - introductory adverbial phrase; quote; quote; subordinate clause at beginning; extra information for clarity

Quotation - note punctuation in continued (interrupted) quote; note no quotation marks needed at end of paragraph when quote is continued in next paragraph

Homophone - its/it's

Antecedent/pronoun agreement - "a sleeper" is singular and needs singular object pronoun

Pronouns - "him" and "her" as direct object pronouns

Verb tense - subjunctive mood needed with "if" clause ("may")

Gerund - "awakening" (a verb form used as a noun)

Complex sentence - no comma after "flower" as "so that" is a subordinating conjunction, not a coordinating conjunction

Punctuation - no quotation marks after "awakening" because quotation is continued in next paragraph

B - from that time on that flower was magical oberon continued to **regale** his listener and if its nectar is dropped onto the eyelids of a sleeper mortal or fairy it will make them fall instantly in love with the first living creature seen after awakening. fetch me that flower so that i may play a trick on titania

C - "From that time on, that flower was magical," Oberon continued to **regale** his listener, "and if its nectar is dropped onto the eyelids of a sleeper, mortal or fairy, it will make him or her fall instantly in love with the first living creature seen after awakening.

"Fetch me that flower so that I may play a trick on Titania."

44. ❤ contrived, antics ●●

LD - play on words ("I'm gone...")

2 Paragraphs - 2 different people speaking

Commas - quote; quote

Quotation

Run-on sentence - conjunction "and" used instead of punctuation

Contraction

Coordinating conjunctions - do not begin a sentence with one

Possession - singular noun

Complex sentence - no comma after "Oberon" as subordinate clause is at the end of sentence

Homophone - where/were

Prepositions - avoid ending a sentence with a preposition (eliminate "at")

B - im gone grinned puck. and i shall become invisible to watch titanias **contrived antics** said oberon as he faded from sight and she will not know where i am at

C - "I'm gone," grinned Puck.

"I shall become invisible to watch Titania's **contrived antics**," said Oberon as he faded from sight. "She will not know where I am."

45. ❤ witty, denouement ●●●

LD - establishment of setting

Paragraph - narrator again

Commas - introductory subordinate clause; qualifier as interrupter ("with Helena...")

Possessive pronouns - my, your, his, her, its, our, their

Subordinating conjunctions - review

Prepositions - review

B - while oberon was plotting his **witty** scheme to blackmail titania demetrius with helena in hot pursuit right behind him ran into the same clearing where oberon was waiting for the **denouement** of his trickery

C - While Oberon was plotting his **witty** scheme to blackmail Titania, Demetrius, with Helena in hot pursuit right behind him, ran into the same clearing where Oberon was waiting for the **denouement** of his trickery.

B = *suggested sentence for the board or overhead*   *C* = *sentence written correctly*   *LD* = *literary device*

46. dastardly, ♥ sinister, disdain •

LD - alliteration ("dastardly Demetrius")

No paragraph

Commas - interrupter; verb series; 2 adjectives with 2nd not age, color or linked to noun

Homophone - fair/fare

Often confused verbs - lose/loose

Possession - singular noun ending in "s"

Compound predicate

Run-on sentence - conjunction "and" substituted for needed punctuation

Spelling rule - if word ends in consonant/vowel/consonant and a suffix is added, double the consonant ("planned")

B - fare and usually timid helena still hoped to win demetrius love. demetrius on the other hand planed to kill lysander capture hermia and loose the pesky helena in the woods and poor misguided helena still loved the **dastardly** demetrius despite his **sinister** threats and obvious **disdain** for her

C - Fair and usually timid Helena still hoped to win Demetrius's love. Demetrius, on the other hand, planned to kill Lysander, capture Hermia, and lose the pesky Helena in the woods. Poor, misguided Helena still loved the **dastardly** Demetrius despite his **sinister** threats and obvious **disdain** for her.

47. ♥ vile, ♥ varlet, wombat, daft •

LD - narrator aside ("What a lovesick..."); **alliteration** (vile..varlet); **use of aphorism and personification** ("love is blind")

Paragraph - narrator aside

Commas - 2 adjectives; compound sentence

Quotation

Verb tenses - correct use of verb-tense switch with aside

Punctuation - use of exclamation for emphasis

Homophone - vile/vial

Like vs. as - "like" compares nouns and "as" precedes a verbal phrase or sentence

Pronouns - incorrect pronoun use in the phrase "as daft as he" as the verb "is" is implied

Comparisons - daft/more daft than/most daft

Coordinating conjunctions - do not begin a sentence with one unless for effect

B - what a lovesick fool. demetrius is a **vile** unfeeling **varlet** but love is blind as the proverbial **wombat**. and perhaps she is as **daft** as him

C -   What a lovesick fool! Demetrius is a **vile**, unfeeling **varlet**, but love is blind like the proverbial **wombat**. Perhaps she is as **daft** as he.

48. ♥ vexatious, scoffed •

Paragraph - new person speaking

Commas - direct address; quote

Quotation

Run-on sentence - lack of punctuation

Complex sentence - no comma before "as" since subordinate clause at end of sentence

Verb tense - story in past tense

Often confused words - further/farther ("farther" refers to measurable distance)

B - get away from me you **vexatious** female you make me sick when I look at you **scoffed** demetrius as he runs further into the woods

C -   "Get away from me, you **vexatious** female. You make me sick when I look at you," **scoffed** Demetrius as he ran farther into the woods.

B = suggested sentence for the board or overhead   C = sentence written correctly   LD = literary device

49. ♥ spurn, glen ●

LD - literary allusion ("Daphne and Apollo..."); **allusion to mythology** ("griffin"); **motif** ("Use me....griffin"); **paradox** ("heaven...hell"); **quote within a quote; monologue; metaphor** ("deer chasing the lion...")

Paragraph - new person speaking

Comma - repetitive phrase ("the dove.."); quote

Quotation

Verbs - use of imperative and strong verbs

Sentence structure - note use of short, simple sentences for effect

Contraction

Sentence structure - avoid fragment by removing the word "only"

Complex sentence - no comma after "Helena" as subordinate clause at end

B - use me as your spaniel. **spurn** me. strike me. only let me be with you. i will change the story of daphne and apollo and will chase you. it will be the deer chasing the lion the dove chasing the griffin. ill follow you and make a heaven of my hell huffed Helena as she chased demetrius through the woods away from the **glen** where oberon stood invisible

C - "Use me as your spaniel. **Spurn** me. Strike me. Let me be with you. I will change the story of Daphne and Apollo and will chase you. It will be the deer chasing the lion, the dove chasing the griffin. I'll follow you and make a heaven of my hell," huffed Helena as she chased Demetrius through the woods away from the **glen** where Oberon stood invisible.

50. ♥ idle (adj.), debacle, ♥ enthralled ●

Paragraph - new person speaking

Commas - interjection; direct address; 2 adjectives; introductory subordinate clause; quote

Quotation

Irregular verb - did/done/has done

Verbs - incorrect use of "done" since "done" is a past participle and requires "have" before it

Complex sentence - no comma after Oberon - subordinate clause at end

Pronouns - note correct use of object pronoun "him" with preposition

B - oh my poor lovesick maiden before this **idle** youth leaves this forest i shall see to it that he will seek your love promised oberon as he observed this **debacle** . he will be **enthralled** and madly in love with you before i am done with him he chortled

C - "Oh, my poor, lovesick maiden, before this **idle** youth leaves this forest, I shall see to it that he will seek your love," promised Oberon as he observed this **debacle**. "He will be **enthralled** and madly in love with you before I am done with him," he chortled.

➡ **SUGGESTION:**

This is a good spot to review the eight parts of speech and their various functions since all eight are represented in Caught'ya #50 (adverb is subordinate clause).

51. knoll ●

LD - description (strong verb) **within dialogue; substitute synonym to avoid repetition** ("flower" and "blossom" and "blooms); **naturalistic detail**

2 paragraphs - narrator and Oberon speaking

Commas - direct address; quote

Quotation

Often confused words - then/than ("then" is an adverb and "than" is a conjunction used to compare)

Adjectives vs. adverbs - "good" is adjective and "well" is adverb

One run-on sentence

Strong verbs - encourage use

Direct and indirect objects - discuss differences and use ("Give it to me..")

Subject/verb agreement - "canopy" is singular and needs singular verb

B - puck then returned with the magical flower. you did good. give it to me puck. i have much use for this blossom. I will find titania this very night. she sleeps by a **knoll** where violets and lovely blooms grow a canopy of woodbine and roses arch over her favorite spot oberon said

C - Puck then returned with the magical flower.

"You did well. Give it to me, Puck. I have much use for this blossom. I will find Titania this very night. She sleeps by a **knoll** where violets and lovely blooms grow. A canopy of woodbine and roses arches over her favorite spot," Oberon said.

B = suggested sentence for the board or overhead   *C = sentence written correctly*   *LD = literary device*

52. ♥ canker, ♥ anoint •

LD - substitute synonym to avoid repetition ("lady" and "maiden"); **double entendre and sarcasm** ("canker"); **metaphor and personification** ("canker on the rear...")

No paragraph at beginning (continuing a quote) then paragraph when Oberon commands

Commas - direct address; introductory subordinate clause; introductory subordinate clause

Quotation - no quotation marks after "true" since quote is picked up in next paragraph

Verbs - use of imperative

Contraction

Comparatives and superlatives - bad/worse/worst, good/better/best

Indefinite articles - "an" before a vowel or silent "h"

No comma before "so that" - subordinating conjunction not coordinating

Complex sentence - no comma before "when" as subordinate clause is at end of sentence

B - there she will sleep. ill put some of the juice of this in her eyes and make her worst nightmare come true. puck you go and find a athenian youth in the forest. their will be a sweet lady near him. when this **canker** on the rear of humanity sleeps for the night **anoint** his eyes so that when he wakes he may fall in love with the maiden

C - "There she will sleep. I'll put some of the juice of this in her eyes and make her worst nightmare come true.

   "Puck, you go and find an Athenian youth in the forest. There will be a sweet lady near him. When this **canker** on the rear of humanity sleeps for the night, **anoint** his eyes so that when he wakes, he may fall in love with the maiden."

➡ **SUGGESTION:**

This would be a good point for a midterm exam. You can type up as a test Caught'yas #53 - #58 for a good review of most of what your students have been practicing up to here. Type them together, without numbers as one, long Caught'ya for editing and correction.

---

53. rascality •

Paragraph - narrator

Commas - introductory subordinate clause; list of verbs

Homophone - their/there/they're

Possessive pronouns - my, your, his, her, its, our, their

Irregular verbs - lie/lay/has lain and lay/laid/has laid

Transitive vs. intransitive verbs - lie/lay/has lain and lay/laid/has laid

Word use - discuss judicious use of the word "all"

B - as puck and oberon left on theyre respective errands of **rascality** titania arrived at her favorite sleeping place with her entourage sent away all her sprites and laid down to sleep

C -   As Puck and Oberon left on their respective errands of **rascality**, Titania arrived at her favorite sleeping place with her entourage, sent away all her sprites, and lay down to sleep.

54. ♥ stealthily •

LD - foreshadowing and building of suspense

No paragraph to begin (continued); paragraph for Oberon's quote

Commas - direct address; elaboration ("be it...."); quote

Quotation

Punctuation - note use of "or" instead of commas in a list

Plural vs. possessive nouns - confusion

Possession - singular noun

Homophone -your/you're

Pronouns - "I" as subject and "me" as object

B - oberon **stealthily** entered and squeezed the flower juices on titanias eyelids.

whatever you see when you awake dear titania be it bear or cat or pig you will love it with all your heart. wake when some vile thing is near oberon taunted. what is in store for you will amuse puck and i

C - Oberon **stealthily** entered and squeezed the flower juices on Titania's eyelids.

   "Whatever you see when you awake, dear Titania, be it bear or cat or pig, you will love it with all your heart. Wake when some vile thing is near," Oberon taunted. "What is in store for you will amuse Puck and me."

B = suggested sentence for the board or overhead   *C = sentence written correctly*   **LD** = *literary device*

55. ❤ keen, ❤ troth •

Paragraph - place and subject change

Commas - introductory adverb and adverbial phrase; infinitive phrase

Optional comma for one-word introductory adverb

Gerund phrase - "being forbidden" used as noun

Homophone - their/there/they're

Irregular verbs - lie/lay/has lain and lay/laid/has laid

Transitive vs. intransitive verbs - discuss

Often confused comparisons - fewer/less ("fewer" can be counted; "less" is a vague, uncountable amount)

B - meanwhile nearby in that very same woods lysander and hermia met in secret. exhausted by all the trauma of the day and the **keen** disappointment at being forbidden to marry they pledged their **troth** to one another and laid down to sleep. in order to preserve her modesty hermia laid a few feet away from her love

C -   Meanwhile, nearby in that very same woods, Lysander and Hermia met in secret. Exhausted by all the trauma of the day and the **keen** disappointment at being forbidden to marry, they pledged their **troth** to one another and lay down to sleep. In order to preserve her modesty, Hermia lay a few feet away from her love.

56. impish •

Paragraph - time and subject change

Commas - long introductory adverbial phrase; appositive

Often confused comparisons - fewer/less ("fewer" can be counted; "less" is a vague, uncountable amount)

Often confused words - then/than ("then" is an adverb and "than" is a conjunction used to compare)

Numbers - write out to 99

Hyphen - 2 words acting as one

Misplaced modifier - Puck is the sprite, not the scene

Homophone - to/too/two, sense/cents

Spelling - pronunciation with double consonant

B - in less than 2 minutes after the too would be lovers fell asleep puck appeared on the scene that **impish** sprite with a bizarre sense of humor

C -   In fewer than two minutes after the two would-be lovers fell asleep, Puck, that **impish** sprite with a bizarre sense of humor, appeared on the scene.

57. alacrity •

Paragraph - new person speaking

Commas - quote

Quotation

Relative pronouns - who/whom/whose/whoever/ whomever/that/which ("that" and "which" can be subject or object and are used only with objects and animals; "who" and "whom" are used with people; "who" is subject; "whom" is object)

Prepositions - do not end a sentence with one

Verb tense - future with "will"

Deliberate splitting of verb ("will quickly put") - other way awkward

Possession - singular noun

Spelling rule - if word ends in consonant/vowel/consonant and a suffix is added, double the consonant ("dripped")

B - this must be the athenian youth and maid that oberon spoke of. i will quickly put the flower juice in his eyes and return to oberon with **alacrity** he said as he driped the potion by mistake onto lysanders eyelids

C -   "This must be the Athenian youth and maid of whom Oberon spoke. I will quickly put the flower juice in his eyes and return to Oberon with **alacrity**," he said as he dripped the potion by mistake onto Lysander's eyelids.

B = *suggested sentence for the board or overhead*   **C** = *sentence written correctly*   **LD** = *literary device*

58. latter, former, ♥ dissembling •••

Paragraph - narrator

Commas - introductory subordinate clause; participial phrase ("latter still running"); appositive

Incorrect verb-tense switch - story in past

Commonly confused words - breathe/breath

Spelling rule - if a word ends in consonant/vowel/consonant, double the last consonant if you add a suffix ("stopped")

Compound predicate

B - as puck departs demetrius and poor helena arrived the **latter** still running after the **former**. helena was out of breathe and stoped. demetrius the **dissembling** cad took advantage of her exhaustion and sped away

C -   As Puck departed, Demetrius and poor Helena arrived, the **latter** still running after the **former**. Helena was out of breath and stopped. Demetrius, the **dissembling** cad, took advantage of her exhaustion and sped away.

59. espied •••

LD - use of aphorism ("head-over-heels")

No paragraph

Commas - verb series

Irregular verbs - raise/rise

Transitive vs. intransitive verbs - discuss difference

Hyphen - 3 words used as one

Pronouns - review different types and uses

B - lysander awoke at the noise raised himself up **espied** helena and fell head over heels in love with her

C - Lysander awoke at the noise, raised himself up, **espied** Helena, and fell head-over-heels in love with her.

60. beau, ♥ plenitude •••

LD - narrator aside (stepping out of story to make comment); **foreshadowing**

Paragraph - narrator aside

Commas - introductory word; compound sentence; interrupting adverbial phrase ("in one mad..."); interrupter

Common spelling error - truly

2 Run-on sentences - lack of punctuation

Verb tense - correct verb-tense switch for narrator's aside

Punctuation - use of exclamation point for emphasis

Irregular comparatives - bad/worse/worst and good/better/best

Demonstrative adjectives - this/that/these/those

Incorrect word use - "tonight" (implying present tense) cannot be used when the story is in the past tense

NOTE - Review prepositions

B - truely this is worser than the worst soap opera lysander now loved helena and poor hermia in one mad moment had lost her **beau**. this was not the end of the mischief however oberon and puck still had a **plenitude** of trouble to stir up tonight

C -   Truly, this is worse than the worst soap opera! Lysander now loved Helena, and poor Hermia, in one mad moment, had lost her **beau**. This was not the end of the mischief, however. Oberon and Puck still had a **plenitude** of trouble to stir up that night.

B = *suggested sentence for the board or overhead*   *C* = *sentence written correctly*   *LD* = *literary device*

61. ♥ fawned ●

LD - hyperbole; alliteration ("lustfully lunged")

Paragraph - new person speaking

Commas - interjection; adjective series; interrupted quote; quote

Quotation

Relative pronouns - "which" is never used with people; "whom" is needed as direct object

Negatives - review correct use

Irregular verb - see/saw/have seen ("seen" is the past participle and must be with a form of the verb "to have")

Complex sentence - subordinate clause at end so no comma is needed ("as he...")

B - oh sweet wonderful comely perfect helena **fawned** the newly lovesick lysander i never seen a more desirable and lovely girl. you are the one which i love he said as he lustfully lunged for her

C - "Oh, sweet, wonderful, comely, perfect Helena," **fawned** the newly lovesick Lysander, "I never saw a more desirable and lovely girl. You are the one whom I love," he said as he lustfully lunged for her.

➥ **SUGGESTION:**

This is a good spot to review the eight parts of speech and their various functions since all eight are represented in Caught'ya #61.

62. ♥ mockery ●

Paragraph - new person speaking

Quotation

Homophone - here/hear

Incorrect verb tense - story in past tense

Run-on sentence - lack of punctuation

Punctuation - question in quote

B - what is happening hear helena asked as she tries to push lysander away what is this **mockery** of love

C - "What is happening here?" Helena asked as she tried to push Lysander away. "What is this **mockery** of love?"

63. ♥ beseeched ●

Paragraph - new person speaking

Commas - direct address; compound sentence; quote

Quotation

Irregular verb - see/saw/have seen ("seen" is the past participle and must be with a form of the verb "to have")

Irregular verbs - lie/lay/has lain, lying and lay/laid/has laid, laying

Transitive vs. intransitive verbs - review

Possession - singular noun

B - help me lysander for I have had a terrible dream. tell me that you still love me and not helena hermia **beseeched** lysander as she awoke and seen helena laying in lysanders arms

C - "Help me, Lysander, for I have had a terrible dream. Tell me that you still love me and not Helena," Hermia **beseeched** Lysander as she awoke and saw Helena lying in Lysander's arms.

64. ♥ bower ●

LD - foreshadowing

Paragraph - narrator

Commas - introductory subordinate clause; introductory subordinate clause

Pronouns - use of too many pronouns makes meaning unclear

Verb tense - incorrect use of conditional tense as substitute for past tense ("would sleep," "would awake"); correct use of conditional tense ("would love") to indicate possible future action; use of pluperfect

Punctuation - dash needed to separate modifier from entire phrase and indicate break

Subordinating and coordinating conjunctions - review

B - while this switching of alliances was taking place titania would sleep on peacefully in her flowery **bower** a disaster waiting to happen. he had placed the potion on her eyelids. when she would awake she would love the first creature she would see

C - While this switching of alliances was taking place, Titania slept on peacefully in her flowery **bower** — a disaster waiting to happen. Oberon had placed the potion on her eyelids. When Titania awoke, she would love the first creature she would see.

B = suggested sentence for the board or overhead　　C = sentence written correctly　　LD = literary device

65. ♥ **buffoon** •••

Paragraph - subject change

Comma - introductory subordinate clause; introductory adjective phrase

Punctuation - quotes around name of a play

Misplaced modifier - Peter Quince and troupe are unaware, not Thisbe

Homophone - their/there/they're

Possessive pronouns - my, your, his, her, its, our, their

Punctuation - period inside quotation mark even though quote is short

Like vs. as - "like" used only in direct comparisons of 2 nouns; "as if" needed here in subjunctive mood

Reflexive pronouns - use correct forms ("themselves")

NOTE - Review the rules of putting quotes vs. underlining for books, plays, etc.

B - as titania slept the local **buffoons** arrived to practice there play. peter quince and his troupe conducted their disastrous rehearsal of pyramus and thisbe unaware of her royal presence like they had the hole forest to theirselves

C -   As Titania slept, the local **buffoons** arrived to practice their play. Unaware of her royal presence, Peter Quince and his troupe conducted their disastrous rehearsal of "Pyramus and Thisbe" as if they had the whole forest to themselves.

66. a plethora of, patrician •••

No paragraph; paragraph for new person speaking

Commas - long introductory adverb; appositive; 2 adjectives; quote

Quotation

Homophone - no/know

Punctuation - dashes needed for aside comment and deliberate fragment; warn students not to overuse

Irregular verb - raise/rise

Transitive and intransitive verbs - review

Possessive pronouns - my, your, his, her, its, our, their

Reflexive pronouns - myself, yourself, himself, herself, ourselves, themselves

Compound predicate in last sentence

B - no sooner had the rehearsal begun when bottom the weaver interrupted the proceedings something he did **a plethora of** times. the refined **patrician** ladies will be frightened when pyramus rises his sword and kills himself he protested

C - No sooner had the rehearsal begun, when Bottom, the weaver, interrupted the proceedings — something he did **a plethora of** times.

"The refined, **patrician** ladies will be frightened when Pyramus raises his sword and kills himself," he protested.

67. interjected ••

LD - oxymoron ("love tragedy")

2 Paragraphs - conversation

Commas - quote; introductory word; quote; extra information

Quotation

Contraction

Homophone - no/know, assure/insure, allusion/illusion

Commonly confused words - assurance/insurance.

Pronouns - "I" is the subject pronoun; must use subject pronouns with verb of being

Subject/verb agreement - "he" is singular and needs singular verb "kills"

Reflexive and intensive pronouns - "himself" (do not use in place of personal pronouns and do not use incorrect forms)

B - well leave that part out reassured quince. no i have a better idea **interjected** bottom. you write a prologue that will insure the audience that pyramus is only me nick bottom and that it is only an allusion that he kill hisself

C -   "We'll leave that part out," reassured Quince.

"No, I have a better idea," **interjected** Bottom. "You write a prologue that will assure the audience that Pyramus is only I, Nick Bottom, and that it is an illusion that he kills himself."

B = *suggested sentence for the board or overhead*   *C* = *sentence written correctly*   *LD* = *literary device*

68. redoubtable ●

LD - anadiplosis ("one, one"), **oxymoron** ("love tragedy")

Paragraph - narrator speaking

Commas - adverb out of place ("one after...")

Punctuation - dash needed to separate a list and indicate a break

Contraction

Colon - use before a series of questions

Punctuation - question mark needed

Reflexive pronouns - themselves not "theirselves;" use correct forms

NOTE - You may wish to discuss other common abbreviations here as well.

B - the **redoubtable** bottom and his cohorts launched objections such as this one one after another wouldnt the lion frighten the ladies should someone play the moon what to do for the wall. the actors theirselves made a comedy of this love tragedy

C -   The **redoubtable** Bottom and his cohorts launched objections such as this one, one after another: Wouldn't the lion frighten the ladies? Should someone play the moon? What should they do for the wall? The actors themselves made a comedy of this love tragedy.

69. elucidate ●

LD - use of idiom

Paragraph - new topic

Plural rules - consonant "y" to "ies"

Underlining - use of underline or italics for emphasis (*"really," " feel"*)

Contraction

Indirect quotation - no quotes with "that"

Punctuation - quotes needed around idiom and falsehood

Homophone - threw/through

B - snout suggested adding yet another prologue to **elucidate** to the ladys that the lion was not really a lion. he also maintained that he didnt feel the part he had been assigned. bottom added his two cents again by saying that snout could be the wall threw which pyramus and thisbe talked

C -   Snout suggested adding yet another prologue to **elucidate** to the ladies that the lion was not *really* a lion. He also maintained that he didn't *feel* the part he had been assigned. Bottom added his "two cents" again by saying that Snout could be the wall through which Pyramus and Thisbe talked.

70. travesty, burlesque, sham ●

LD - use of repeated synonyms to make a point; implied humor; foreshadowing

No paragraph; paragraph - scene change

Commas - introductory subordinate clause; adverbial phrase out of place ("unseen...")

Spelling rule - if word ends in consonant/vowel/consonant and a suffix is added, double the consonant ("plotted")

Incorrect verb tense - story in past tense

Voice - avoid passive voice that is used here (active always better)

B - the entire rehearsal was a **travesty** of errors. while this **burlesque** of a rehearsal was being enacted puck unseen to the actors comes on the scene. he listened to the **sham** of a play and ploted mischief

C - The entire rehearsal was a **travesty** of errors.

     While this **burlesque** of a rehearsal was being enacted, Puck, unseen to the actors, came on the scene. He listened to the **sham** of a play and plotted mischief.

---

71. dulcet, orating, rotund, corpulent •

LD - sarcasm; narrator's aside ("This was certainly an appropriate...")

No paragraph

Commas - 2 adjectives; subordinate clauses at beginning; long introductory adverbial phrase; 2 adjectives

Relative pronouns - who/whom/whose/whoever/whomever/that/which ("that" and "which" can be subject or object and are used only with objects and animals; "who" and "whom" are used with people; "who" is subject; "whom" is object)

Parentheses - used here for further explanation

Pronouns - meaning unclear by overuse of pronouns (insert noun)

Possession - singular noun

Indefinite articles - "an" precedes a vowel or silent "h"

B - when bottom made a grand stage exit behind some bushes puck followed him. at the same moment that flute whom played **dulcet** thisbe was **orating** he transformed bottoms **rotund corpulent** head into that of an ass. this was certainly a appropriate transformation

C - When Bottom made a grand, stage exit behind some bushes, Puck followed him. At the same moment that Flute (who played **dulcet** Thisbe) was **orating**, Puck transformed Bottom's **rotund, corpulent** head into that of an ass. This was certainly an appropriate transformation.

72. metamorphosis •

LD - onomatopoeia

Paragraph - Bottom speaks

Commas - introductory adjective phrase; long introductory gerund phrase

Quotation

Placement of modifier - awkward ("unaware...")

Prepositions - review

Misplaced modifier - awkwardly split up ("singing loudly")

Possessive pronouns - my, your, his, her, its, our, their

Pronouns - discuss various types (possessive, object, subject in this Caught'ya)

Punctuation - use of exclamation mark for drama

Warn of need to rewrite

B - bottom unaware of the **metamorphosis** of his head thought his fellow actors were playing a trick on him when they dispersed in fear at the sight of him. in order to demonstrate his fearlessness he walked up and down singing loudly heehaw. heehaw

C -   Unaware of the **metamorphosis** of his head, Bottom thought his fellow actors were playing a trick on him when they dispersed in fear at the sight of him. Singing loudly in order to demonstrate his fearlessness, he walked up and down. "Heehaw! Heehaw!"

73. pondered, ponderous •

LD - play on word "ponder;" soliloquy; irony ("angel:)

2 Paragraphs - new person speaking; narrator

Commas - participial phrase; interrupter

Quotation - note punctuation of question

Spelling rule - if word ends in consonant/vowel/consonant and a suffix is added, double the consonant ("hidden")

Verb tense - need for pluperfect tense since the flower had done its work before

Homophone - its/it's

Possessive pronouns - my, your, his, her, its, our, their

Verb tense - need for pluperfect tense for action that preceded paragraph

B - this loud braying awakened titania from her hiden bower. what angel wakes me from my flowery bed she **pondered**, admiring the **ponderous** song. titania was indeed bewitched. the magical flower did its work

C -   This loud braying awakened Titania from her hidden bower. "What angel wakes me from my flowery bed?" she **pondered**, admiring the **ponderous** song.

Titania was, indeed, bewitched. The magical flower had done its work.

---

74. enjoined •

No paragraph; paragraph for direct quotation

Commas - modifier as interrupter; interjection; direct address; quote

Quotation

Hyphen - 2 words acting as one

Irregular verb - lead/led/has led

Pronouns - too many pronouns for clarity (insert some nouns)

Possessive pronouns - my, your, his, her, its, our, their

Pronouns - discuss various types

B - the minute she saw him ass head and all she fell instantly and madly in love with him. oberon had his revenge. oh my dear pixies lead this gentle mortal to my bower and tend to his every need she **enjoined** her entourage

C - The minute she saw Bottom, ass-head and all, Titania fell instantly and madly in love with him. Oberon had his revenge.

"Oh, my dear pixies, lead this gentle mortal to my bower and tend to his every need," Titania **enjoined** her entourage.

75. paradigm, pulchritudinous, bumpkin •

LD - humor; double entendre ("ass" referring to Bottom's head and personality)

2 Paragraphs - narrator with place change; new person speaking

Commas - Long introductory adverbial phrase (2 prepositional phrases at beginning); appositive; quote; compound sentence

Quotation

Relative pronouns - who/whom/whose/whoever/ whomever/that/which ("that" and "which" can be subject or object and are used only with objects and animals; "who" and "whom" are used with people; "who" is subject; "whom" is object)

Possessive pronouns - my, your, his, her, its, our, their

Pronouns - review types and uses

Indefinite articles - "an" precedes a vowel or silent "h"

B - in another part of the wood puck that **paradigm** of mischief was regaling oberon with the results of his various pranks. **pulchritudinous** titania is in love with a monster puck tittered. i found a **bumpkin** that was trying to act the part of pyramus in a play and i turned his head into that of a ass

C -   In another part of the wood, Puck, that **paradigm** of mischief, was regaling Oberon with the results of his various pranks.

"**Pulchritudinous** Titania is in love with a monster," Puck tittered. "I found a **bumpkin** who was trying to act the part of Pyramus in a play, and I turned his head into that of an ass."

76. devise (verb) •

LD - double entendre ("ass"); **simile**

No paragraph (key word "continued"); paragraph when Oberon speaks

Commas - introductory participial phrase; quote

Quotation

Punctuation - quote within a quote; quotes needed to indicate falsehood (Bottom is not really a donkey.)

Often confused words - then/than ("then" is an adverb and "than" is a conjunction used to compare)

Irregular plurals - goose/geese

Homophone - hear/here

Possession - singular noun ending in "s"

Irregular comparatives - good/better/best

Antecedent/pronoun agreement of collective noun - "flock" is singular, therefore one has to use "it" to refer to it

Collective nouns - discuss collective nouns like "flock" and how they are singular

Punctuation - question mark needed in interrogative

B - puck continued with his recital. upon seeing this ass the other actors fled the scene faster than a flock of wild geese when they hear a guns report. this is gooder than i could **devise** said oberon in delight. what about the athenian cad

C - Puck continued with his recital. "Upon seeing this 'ass,' the other actors fled the scene faster than a flock of wild geese when it hears a gun's report."

"This is better than I could **devise**," said Oberon in delight. "What about the Athenian cad?"

B = *suggested sentence for the board or overhead*   **C** = *sentence written correctly*   **LD** = *literary device*

77. corroborated, rejoined ●●

LD - play on words ("change of heart"); **conversation**

3 Paragraphs - conversation

Commas - quote; quote; compound sentence ("This is the same..."); quote

Quotations

Punctuation - use of exclamation for effect in single word sentence

Homophones - hear/here, its/it's

Contraction

Comparison - handsome/handsomer/handsomest

Often confused words - then/than ("then" is an adverb and "than" is a conjunction used to compare)

Pronouns - improper pronoun use since" he" is subject and "him" is object ("than he *is*" — "is" is implied); note various types used in this Caught'ya

B - i put the juice in his eyes as he was sleeping puck **corroborated**. wait hear comes that same athenian whispered oberon as demetrius and hermia appeared. lets listen to see if he has had a change of heart. this is the same woman but its not the same man **rejoined** puck. this one is handsomer than him

C - "I put the juice in his eyes as he was sleeping," Puck **corroborated**.

"Wait! Here comes that same Athenian," whispered Oberon as Demetrius and Hermia appeared. "Let's listen to see if he has had a change of heart."

"This is the same woman, but it's not the same man," **rejoined** Puck. "This one is handsomer than he."

78. ❤ rebuke, cur ●●

LD - quick repartée; repetition of synonyms to make a point ("hound...dog...cur")

5 Paragraphs - conversation

Commas - interjection; direct address; direct address; direct address

Quotations

Quotations with question marks - note punctuation

Relative pronouns - who/whom/whose/whoever/ whomever/that/which ("that" and "which" can be subject or object and are used only with objects and animals; "who" and "whom" are used with people; "who" is subject; "whom" is object)

Verb tense - incorrect use of pluperfect rather than conditional to indicate possible future action

Possessive pronouns - my, your, his, her, its, our, their

Homophone - your/you're

B - what have you done with my lysander asked Hermia. why do you **rebuke** me which loves you so asked demetrius. where is he. ah good demetrius will you give him to me. i had rather give his carcass to my hounds. out dog. out **cur**. your trying my patience

C - "What have you done with my Lysander?" asked Hermia.

"Why do you **rebuke** me who loves you so?" asked Demetrius.

"Where is he? Ah, good Demetrius, will you give him to me?"

"I would rather give his carcass to my hounds."

"Out, dog! Out, **cur**! You're trying my patience."

79. ❤ surfeit ●●

Paragraph - narrator

Commas - introductory subordinate clause; adjective phrase

Indirect quotation - no quotes with "that"

Pronouns - too many pronouns for clarity (nouns needed)

Pronouns - use of "her" as possessive and as object

Misplaced modifier - Demetrius, not the sleep, is heavy with woe

Irregular verbs - lie/lay/has lain, lay/laid/has laid, sleep/slept

Transitive vs. intransitive verbs - review

B - after she accused him of killing lysander he assured her that he was not dead. she left in search of her lost love. he laid down and slept heavy with a **surfeit** of woe

C - After Hermia accused Demetrius of killing Lysander, Demetrius assured her that Lysander was not dead. Hermia left in search of her lost love. Demetrius, heavy with a **surfeit** of woe, lay down and slept.

B = *suggested sentence for the board or overhead*   *C* = *sentence written correctly*   *LD* = *literary device*

80. misbegotten, erring •

LD - quote within a quote

Paragraph - new person speaking

Commas - interjection; direct address; appositive as another direct address; verb series; quote

Quotation

Indefinite articles - "an" is used preceding a vowel

Irregular verbs - lie/lay/has lain and lay/laid/has laid

Transitive vs. intransitive verbs - review

Punctuation - use of italics or underline for emphasis

Imperative sentences - subject implied

Contraction

Punctuation - use of quotation marks to denote improperly written phrase (using "wrong to right" as a noun); quote within a quote

Homophones - write/right, hear/here, your/you're

Gerund - "erring" used as a noun

B - oh puck you **misbegotten** excuse for a elf what have you done asked oberon angrily. you have lain the love juice on the eyes of a true lover. go back into the woods find this helena and bring her here. ill put wrong to right to correct your **erring**

C - "Oh, Puck, you **misbegotten** excuse for an elf, what have you done?" asked Oberon angrily. "You have laid the love juice on the eyes of a *true* lover. Go back into the woods, find this Helena, and bring her here. I'll put 'wrong to right' to correct your **erring**."

➥ **SUGGESTION:**

This is a another good spot to review the eight parts of speech and their various functions since all eight are represented in Caught'ya #80.

81. orbs, erroneous •

Paragraph - return to narrator

Commas - Introductory subordinate clause

Possession - singular noun that ends in "s"

Relative pronouns - "who" needed as subject

Possessive pronouns - my, your, his, her, its, our, their

Punctuation - use of parentheses to review information (could use commas)

B - as puck left oberon put the juice in demetrius **orbs**. puck soon returned with news of helena whom was nearby. he told oberon of lysander the **erroneous** recipient of the love juice who was pleading with helena for her love

C -   As Puck left, Oberon put the juice in Demetrius's **orbs**. Puck soon returned with news of Helena who was nearby. He told Oberon of Lysander (the **erroneous** recipient of the love juice) who was pleading with Helena for her love.

82. nincompoops •

LD - slightly changed very familiar quote from Shakespeare ("What fools these mortals be.")

Paragraph - new person speaking

Commas - quote

Quotation

Demonstrative adjectives - this/that/these/those

Infinitive use - note that use of infinitive with subject as in Shakespeare's day is incorrect today

Complex sentence - no comma before subordinate clause at end of sentence

Incorrect verb tense - story is in past

B - what **nincompoops** these mortals be observed puck as lysander and helena arrive on the scene

C - "What **nincompoops** these mortals are," observed Puck as Lysander and Helena arrived on the scene.

B = suggested sentence for the board or overhead   C = sentence written correctly   LD = literary device

83. expeditiously ●

LD - hyperbole, play on words

Paragraph - narrator again

Commas - adjective list

Spelling rule - if a word ends in consonant/vowel/consonant and you add a suffix, you need to double the final consonant ("stepped")

Run-on sentence - lack of punctuation

Splitting infinitives - never split infinitives (*Star Trek* was wrong — "To boldly go.." should be "To go boldly...")

Splitting verbs - do not split verbs and helping verbs ("now would have")

Verb tense - note use of conditional tense; warn of misuse instead of past tense

Numbers - write out to 99

Negatives - discuss negatives and use of negative words

B - puck and oberon **expeditiously** steped behind a tree to happily watch the proceedings puck was delighted that poor bereft lamentable helena would now have 2 suitors instead of none

C -   Puck and Oberon **expeditiously** stepped behind a tree to watch the proceedings happily. Puck was delighted that poor, bereft, lamentable Helena now would have two suitors instead of none.

84. dispassionate ●

No paragraph - narrator continues

Commas - introductory word; introductory subordinate clause; verb series

Incorrect verb-tense switch - story in past tense

Parallel construction - verb series in past tense so participle is inappropriate

Possessive pronouns - my, your, his, her, its, our, their

B - indeed as lysander is wooing a **dispassionate** helena demetrius wakes up saw helena trying to kiss her hand and professes his love for her

C - Indeed, as Lysander was wooing a **dispassionate** Helena, Demetrius woke up, saw Helena, tried to kiss her hand, and professed his love for her.

85. divine, buss, simpered ●

LD - hyperbole, alliteration
("beautiful....buss....bliss...")

Paragraph - new person speaking

Commas - interjection; direct addresses in a noun series; quote

Quotation

Often confused words - then/than

B - oh my goddess my nymph my **divine** love i want to give your beautiful lips a **buss**. than i will be in bliss **simpered** demetrius

C -   "Oh, my goddess, my nymph, my **divine** love, I want to give your beautiful lips a **buss**. Then I will be in bliss," **simpered** Demetrius

➥ **SUGGESTION:**

If you have not yet done so, this is an excellent point to review the nine comma rules since so many of them have been included in Caught'yas #84 and #85. A copy of these rules can be found in the Appendix.

86. ❤ confounded ●

Paragraph - narrator again

Comma - introductory participial phrase

Verb tense - need for pluperfect tense when you go anterior to current past action

Homophones - there/their/they're

Negatives - no double negatives ("had been none" or "hadn't been any")

Numbers - write out to 99

B - **confounded** by all this professed love when recently their wasnt none helena doubted the sincerity of the 2 gentlemen

C -   **Confounded** by all this professed love when recently there had been none, Helena doubted the sincerity of the two gentlemen.

B = *suggested sentence for the board or overhead*   ***C*** = *sentence written correctly*   ***LD*** = *literary device*

87. guano ●●●

LD - euphemism (using less offensive "bat guano" for something stronger)

Paragraph - new person speaking

Commas - interjection; interjection; direct address; pause before phrase for clarity

Quotation

Punctuation - use of exclamation for emphasis in curse

Pronoun use - "I" as subject and "me" as object ("you love......me")

Punctuation.- question mark needed in interrogative

B - oh hell oh bat **guano** stomped helena in anger. you are all making fun of me. do you hate me so much that you join to mock me. you lysander and demetrius both love hermia not i

C - "Oh, Hell! Oh, bat **guano**!" stomped Helena in anger. "You are all making fun of me. Do you hate me so much that you join to mock me? You, Lysander and Demetrius, both love Hermia, not me."

88. reiterated ●●●

2 Paragraphs - 2 different speakers

Commas - direct address; quote; direct address; quote

Quotations

Homophone - its/it's

B - helena my love its not so protested lysander. helena my beauty I love you so **reiterated** demetrius

C - "Helena, my love, it's not so," protested Lysander.

"Helena, my beauty, I love you so," **reiterated** Demetrius.

89. entreated (past participle), flaxen ●●●●●●●●●●●●●●●●●●●●●●●●●●●●●●●●●●●

LD - aphorism ("to the quick")

2 Paragraphs - 2 different speakers

Commas - long introductory adverb that is a prepositional phrase (optional); direct address; 2 adjectives; participial phrase

Quotations

Hyphen - 2 words acting as one

Contraction

Multiple parts of speech - note multiple parts of speech of the word "quick" (adverb, adjective, and here used as a noun)

B - at this moment hermia found them. why don't you love me anymore lysander hermia **entreated** with palpable distress. my love is for the beauteous **flaxen** haired helena. i hate the sight of you now answered lysander wounding hermia to the quick

C - At this moment, Hermia found them. "Why don't you love me anymore, Lysander?" Hermia **entreated** with palpable distress.

"My love is for the beauteous, **flaxen**-haired Helena. I hate the sight of you now," answered Lysander, wounding Hermia to the quick.

90. ❤ confederacy ●●

Paragraph - new person speaking

Commas - interjection; "too" meaning "also;" direct address; noun series

Quotation

Punctuation - need exclamation mark for emphasis (she "cried"); need for dash for elaboration of noun series and to indicate break and deliberate fragment;

Sentence structure - deliberate use of fragment for emphasis

Possession - plural noun ending in "s"

Possessive vs. plural nouns

Plurals - review basic rules (see **Appendix**)

B - oh she is one of this **confederacy** too cried helena. oh my best friend after all we have shared the schooldays the friendship the sisters vows the childish games and the childhood innocence

C - "Oh, she is one of this **confederacy**, too!" cried Helena. "Oh, my best friend, after all we have shared — the schooldays, the friendship, the sisters' vows, the childish games, and the childhood innocence."

B = suggested sentence for the board or overhead   *C = sentence written correctly*   *LD = literary device*

91. deride (verb) •

LD - similes

No paragraph - continued quote

Commas - quote; repetition in different words (two long predicate-noun phrases)

Quotation

Incorrect verb tense - story in past tense

Pronouns - use "I" as subject and "me" as object; word order (place yourself last)

Numbers - write out to 99

Plural rules - consonant "y" ("y" changes to "i" and "es" is added)

Inversion - note inversion of subject and verb in interrogative

Punctuation - need for question mark in interrogative

B - she continues me and you grew up together. we were like 2 berrys molded on one stem 2 bodies with one heart. how can you **deride** me so

C - She continued, "You and I grew up together. We were like two berries molded on one stem, two bodies with one heart. How can you **deride** me so?"

92. bereft •

Paragraph - narrator

Comma - appositive (non-restrictive modifier)

Spelling rule - "i" before "e" except after "c" and neighbor and weigh are weird

Pronouns - "she" as subject; "her" as possessive pronoun

Pronouns - review various types; too many for clarity

Subject/verb agreement - compound subject takes plural verb

No comma in last sentence - not compound sentence (no subject)

B - hermia did not understand what all this was about. her and her closest freind helena was no longer on speaking terms. her and her love were no longer going to be wed. poor hermia was **bereft** of her love and weary with sorrow

C -   Hermia did not understand what all this was about. She and her closest friend, Helena, were no longer on speaking terms. Hermia and her love were no longer going to be wed. Poor Hermia was **bereft** of her love and weary with sorrow.

93. vixen, docile, acquiescent •

LD - double entendre ("puppet")

Paragraph - time change

Commas - optional comma after introductory single-word adverb; for clarity in adjective clause with relative pronoun because it is really an aside; noun series; adjective clause with relative pronoun

Quotation marks: needed around untruths

Spelling rule - "i" before "e".....

Relative pronouns - "who" needed as subject

Homophone - to/too/two

Numbers - write out to 99

Plural rules of irregular nouns - review rules of plurals that do not end in "s"

B - finally lysander called Hermia who was very short a dwarf a **vixen** and a acorn. this was to much for hermia to bear. she accused her former freind of stealing lysander. helena whom was usually **docile** and **acquiescent** called hermia a puppet of the 2 mens

C -   Finally, Lysander called Hermia, who was very short, a "dwarf," a "**vixen**," and an "acorn." This was too much for Hermia to bear. She accused her former friend of stealing Lysander. Helena, who was usually **docile** and **acquiescent**, called Hermia a "puppet" of the two men.

B = *suggested sentence for the board or overhead*   **C** = *sentence written correctly*   **LD** = *literary device*

94. diminutive, stature ●●●

No paragraph

Commas - 2 adjectives; compound sentence; appositive; compound sentence

Hyphen - Put a hyphen after the prefix "ex" if the noun does not begin with a vowel or "C," "P," "Q," "S," or "T" ("friend" does not begin with those letters, so the hyphen is needed). If the noun begins with those letters, the "ex" is added to it as one word — no hyphen, no break.

Punctuation - use of quotation marks when referring to a word or letter

Punctuation - comma inside quote (even in one-word quote)

Parallel construction - need for clarity ("to...to")

B - hermia thought that her tall fair ex friend had been making fun of her **diminutive stature** by using the word puppet and she started to quarrel. hermia a real spitfire was about to scratch helena and pulled her hair but timid helena backed away

C - Hermia thought that her tall, fair ex-friend had been making fun of her **diminutive stature** by using the word "puppet," and she started to quarrel. Hermia, a real spitfire, was about to scratch Helena and to pull her hair, but timid Helena backed away.

95. striplings ●●●

LD - play on words (hilt)

Paragraph - change of action

Commas - optional comma after "this for clarity; "compound sentence; appositive

Often confused words - then/than

Homophone - their/there/they're, to/too/two

Numbers - write out to 99

Plural rule - words ending in consonant and "y" to "i" and add "es"

B - both **striplings** rushed to protect helena. in doing this they antagonized each other even more than usual and lysander angry to the hilt challenged demetrius to a duel. they drew there swords and left the 2 ladys

C - Both **striplings** rushed to protect Helena. In doing this, they antagonized each other even more than usual, and Lysander, angry to the hilt, challenged Demetrius to a duel. They drew their swords and left the two ladies.

96. volatile, virago, fracas, fray ●●●

LD - alliteration ("volatile virago"); **anadiplosis** ("alone...alone")

Paragraph - change focus

Commas - long introductory adverb; appositive; participial phrase as interrupter; two phrases together (repetition of first word); interrupter "that was"

Plurals - plural of nouns not ending in "s"

Incorrect verb tense - story in past tense

Often confused words - accept/except

B - with the men gone hermia that **volatile virago** blamed helena for the entire **fracas**. helena not wanting to get into a **fray** runs off. hermia was left alone in the glen alone that was except for puck and oberon

C - With the men gone, Hermia, that **volatile virago**, blamed Helena for the entire **fracas**. Helena, not wanting to get into a **fray**, ran off. Hermia was left alone in the glen, alone, that was, except for Puck and Oberon.

B = suggested sentence for the board or overhead   *C = sentence written correctly*   *LD = literary device*

97. ❤ **contriving, strife, implored, petty** ●

2 Paragraphs - subject change; new person speaking

Commas - direct address; appositive; quote; interrupter

Quotation

Homophones - their/there/they're, to/too/two, no/know

Verb tense - need for pluperfect tense to denote previous action

Often confused words - affect/effect ("affect" to change; "effect" to cause or a cause)

Possession - singular noun

Collective nouns - possessive adjective/noun agreement ("everyone" is singular)

Common collective nouns/pronouns - review (everyone, no one, group, family, troop, etc.)

Hyphen - 2 words acting as one

Spelling rule - "i" before "e" except after "c..."

B - oberon blamed puck for **contriving** all the **strife** that effected everyones lives. he was convinced there had been to much mischief making. please beleive me oberon king of shadows i made a mistake. you no how all these athenians dress alike puck **implored**. i must admit though that i enjoyed watching all the **petty** squabbles

C -   Oberon blamed Puck for **contriving** all the **strife** that had affected everyone's life. He was convinced there had been too much mischief-making.

   "Please believe me, Oberon, King of Shadows, I made a mistake. You know how all these Athenians dress alike," Puck **implored**. "I must admit, though, that I enjoyed watching all the **petty** squabbles."

98. enervated ●

Paragraph - narrator with subject change

Comma - for clarity in elaboration

Often confused words - then/than ("then" is an adverb and "than" is a conjunction used to compare)

Possessive pronouns - my, your, his, her, its, our, their

Articles - "an" before a vowel or a silent "h"

Possession - plural noun ending in "s"

Misplaced modifier - herb was put into eyes

Verb tense - note correct use of conditional

Homophone - its/it's

Sentence structure - review

NOTE: Warn of need to rewrite

B - oberon decided to set things right both in his life with titania and in the mortals lives. he ordered puck to lead lysander and demetrius around in circles until they were **enervated** enough to sleep. then puck was to put an herb that would remove the spell of the love juice and let nature take its course into lysanders eyes

C -   Oberon decided to set things right, both in his life with Titania and in the mortals' lives. He ordered Puck to lead Lysander and Demetrius around in circles until they were **enervated** enough to sleep. Then Puck was to put into Lysander's eyes an herb that would remove the spell of the love juice and let nature take its course.

99. simultaneously ●

No paragraph

Commas - introductory subordinate clause (adverb out of place); interrupter adverb ("in the same...")

Verb tense - note correct use of conditional tense (Students often misuse and overuse conditional, substituting it for past tense.)

Hyphen - 2 words acting as one

B - while puck was performing his duties oberon **simultaneously** would release titania from her infatuation with the ass pated bottom

C - While Puck was performing his duties, Oberon, **simultaneously**, would release Titania from her infatuation with the ass-pated Bottom.

B = *suggested sentence for the board or overhead*   *C* = *sentence written correctly*   *LD* = *literary device*

100. impenetrable, miasma, ploy ●

LD - sarcasm

Paragraph - new action

Commas - 2 adjectives; participial phrase; compound sentence; noun series

No comma before "so" - subordinating rather than coordinating conjunction

Plural vs. possessive nouns - review difference (used incorrectly here)

Irregular verbs - lie/lay/has lain and lay/laid/has laid

Verb tense - note correct use of conditional to indicate possible future action

Reflexive pronouns - use correct form ("themselves")

Possessive pronoun - her (note same form as object pronoun)

Hyphen - 2 words acting as one

Plural rule - most nouns ending in "f" change "f" to "v" and add "es"

Punctuation - use of quotes to denote sarcasm and falsehood

B - puck flooded the glade with a dense **impenetrable miasma** so that the lover's would dash about blindly searching for each other until they tired theirselves out. his **ploy** worked and the four mortals' laid down to sleep. it was at this point that titania her donkey headed love and her elfe's entered the scene

C -   Puck flooded the glade with a dense, **impenetrable miasma** so that the lovers would dash about, blindly searching for each other until they tired themselves out. His **ploy** worked, and the four mortals lay down to sleep. It was at this point that Titania, her donkey-headed "love," and her elves entered the scene.

101. enamored ●

LD - onomatopoeia; humor

Paragraph - subject change

Commas - verb series; 2 adjectives; compound sentence

Coordinating conjunctions - wrong to begin a sentence with a conjunction except for effect

Sentence combining - needed for smoothness

Negatives - no double negative ("wanted none" or "didn't want any")

Contraction (if used)

Possession - singular noun

Plural rule - change "f" to "v" and add "es"

Punctuation - quotes around direct quote, especially a made-up sound

B - and titania was still **enamored** of bottom. she crowned his head with flowers. she kissed his long rather hairy ears. she caressed him. bottom didnt want none of this but he did like being waited upon by titanias little elves and hee hawed his approval

C -   Titania was still **enamored** of Bottom. She crowned his head with flowers, kissed his long, rather hairy ears, and caressed him. Bottom wanted none of this, but he did like being waited upon by Titania's little elves and "hee hawed" his approval.

102. Philistine, paramour, enfolded ●

LD - historical and Biblical reference (A "Philistine" now refers to a person who is hostile to culture. Originally, this refers to the rather barbaric kingdom of Philistia which existed from 950 to 700 BC in the area of what today is Israel.)

No paragraph

Commas - appositive; optional comma after introductory single-word adverb "suddenly;" modifier as interrupter

Possession - singular noun

Irregular verbs - lie/lay/has lain and lay/laid/has laid

Transitive and intransitive verbs - review

Punctuation - use of quotes to denote sarcasm and falsehood

B - bottom ever the **Philistine** in his tastes asked for clattering music and hay. suddenly he felt drowsy he laid down and fell asleep in titanias arms titania her **paramour enfolded** in her arms lay down her head and slept as well

C - Bottom, ever the **Philistine** in his tastes, asked for clattering music and hay. Suddenly he felt drowsy. He lay down and fell asleep in Titania's arms. Titania, her "**paramour**" **enfolded** in her arms, laid down her head and slept as well.

---

103. bucolic ●

LD - double entendre (ass)

2 Paragraphs - narrator and Oberon

Commas - quote; direct address

Quotation

Punctuation - optional comma for clarification in adjective clause ("who now loved")

Parentheses - use for clarification

Parentheses around clarification by narrator

Relative pronouns - who/whom/whose/whoever/ whomever/that/which ("that" and "which" can be subject or object and are used only with objects and animals; "who" and "whom" are used with people; "who" is subject; "whom" is object)

Capitalization - title of person

Verb tense - future tense to indicate definite future action

Possession - singular noun

B - oberon then arrived at this **bucolic** and placid scene. he felt remorse over the dispute of the possession of the indian boy a changeling and pity for titania that now loved an ass. i will release the fairy queen said oberon as he put the antidote into titanias eyes. now my sweet titania awaken

C - Oberon then arrived at this **bucolic** and placid scene. He felt remorse over the dispute of the possession of the Indian boy (a changeling) and pity for Titania, who now loved an ass.

   "I will release the Fairy Queen," said Oberon as he put the antidote into Titania's eyes. "Now, my sweet Titania, awaken."

104. ❤ enamored ●

Paragraph - only one as first part leads into quote of new person speaking

Commas - verb series; direct address

Quotation

Irregular verb - review see/saw/have seen

B - titania awoke saw bottom in her arms and said my oberon what visions I have seen. i dreamed that i was **enamored** of a donkey

C - Titania awoke, saw Bottom in her arms, and said, "My Oberon, what visions I have seen. I dreamed that I was **enamored** of a donkey."

105. ❤ loathe ●

LD - humor (tongue-in-cheek)

2 Paragraphs - conversation

Commas - participle; quote; interjection; direct address

Quotation

Punctuation - need for question mark in interrogative

Irregular verbs - lie/lay/has lain and lay/laid/has laid

Homophone - your/you're

Possession - singular noun ending in "s"

Plural vs. possessive noun - asses/ass's

Plural rule - add "es" to nouns ending in "s," "x," "ch," "sh," or "z"

Word misuse - "off of" is not proper English; "of" is redundant and awkward

B - oberon responded pointing. their lies your love. how did all this come to pass queried titania. oh how i **loathe** this asses visage now. how could i have loved such a creature. puck take the asses head off of this bumpkin

C - Oberon responded, pointing, "There lies your love."

   "How did all this come to pass?" queried Titania. "Oh, how I **loathe** this ass's visage now. How could I have loved such a creature? Puck, take the ass's head off this bumpkin."

106. cavort ●

Paragraph - new person speaking

Comma - quote

Quotation

Possession - plural noun

Demonstrative adjectives - this/that/these/those

Irregular verbs - lie/lay/has lain and lay/laid/has laid

Homophone - hear/here; where/were

Possession - singular noun

B - let us dance in the palace at midnight to bless the aristocrats marriage. let us now **cavort** hear near where those sleepers lay said oberon as he took titanias hand

C - "Let us dance in the palace at midnight to bless the aristocrats' marriage. Let us now **cavort** here near where these sleepers lie," said Oberon as he took Titania's hand.

B = *suggested sentence for the board or overhead*   **C** = *sentence written correctly*   **LD** = *literary device*

107. ululated, ♥ amity •

LD - naturalistic detail; description

Paragraph - narrator's description

Commas - introductory subordinate clause; noun series

Plural rules - consonant before "y," change "y" to "i" and add "es"

Homophones - threw/through, their/there/they're

Possessive pronouns - my, your, his, her, its, our, their

Parallel construction - needed for clarity ("where....where")

Verb tense - need for pluperfect tense in last sentence for action that happened before this paragraph

B - as dawn broke over the tops of the trees and the morning lark began to sing the sound of a hunting horn **ululated** through the forest. theseus hippolyta egeus and the entire athenian court passed threw the place where the other mortals still slept and the fairys had just celebrated the renewal of there **amity**

C - As dawn broke over the tops of the trees and the morning lark began to sing, the sound of a hunting horn **ululated** through the forest. Theseus, Hippolyta, Egeus, and the entire Athenian court passed through the place where the other mortals still slept and where the fairies had just celebrated the renewal of their **amity**.

108. recalcitrant •

No paragraph - continuation; paragraph - new speaker

Commas - compound sentence; non-restrictive modifier; interjection; interrupted quote

Quotation

Possessive pronouns - my, your, his, her, its, our, their

Contraction

Incorrect word use - "gots" not a word (use "must give" or "has to give")

Parallel construction - needed for clarity ("ing...ing")

Punctuation - question mark needed in interrogative

B - theseus saw the sleeping girls and egeus recognized helena and his **recalcitrant** daughter hermia. ah said theseus isnt this the day hermia gots to give me her decision about marrying demetrius or go to live in a convent he asked

C - Theseus saw the sleeping girls, and Egeus recognized Helena and his **recalcitrant** daughter, Hermia.

"Ah, " said Theseus, "Isn't this the day Hermia must give me her decision about marrying Demetrius or about going to live in a convent?" he asked.

109. dauntless •

No paragraph with Theseus continuing; paragraph for narrator

Commas - Direct address; quote; elaboration and therefore extra information

Quotation

Irregular verbs - lie/lay/has lain and lay/laid/has laid

Like vs. as - use of "as if" (with subjunctive) instead of "like" (for comparison)

Verb tense - subjunctive mood needed in "if" clause

Spelling rules - "ie" or "ei"

Spelling rules - review all

B - hunter awaken these **dauntless** maidens and their intrepid striplings with your horns theseus commanded. the young people awoke and kneeled before theseus. he asked them how they came to be laying there together like they were friends without the enmity of the past

C - "Hunter, awaken these **dauntless** maidens and their intrepid striplings with your horns," Theseus commanded.

The young people awoke and knelt before Theseus. He asked them how they came to be lying there together as if they were friends, without the enmity of the past.

110. reparation •

Paragraph - subject change

Commas - participial phrase; elaboration; quote

Indirect quotation - no quotes with "that"

Quotation

Verb tense - need for pluperfect tense (action precedes current action which is already in past)

Possession - plural noun ending in "s"

Pronouns - "I" as subject and "me" as object

B - egeus demanded **reparation** from lysander saying that the latter had intended to steal his daughter from the man of her parents choice. this lysander is against my daughter and i no matter how much love he professes he said

C - Egeus demanded **reparation** from Lysander, saying that the latter had intended to steal his daughter from the man of her parents' choice. "This Lysander is against my daughter and me, no matter how much love he professes," he said.

B = suggested sentence for the board or overhead   *C = sentence written correctly*   *LD = literary device*

111. forged, ❤ doted ●

LD - simile

Paragraph - subject change

Commas - long introductory adverb; participial phrase; quote

Quotation

Often confused comparisons - fewer/less ("fewer" can be counted; "less" is a vague, uncountable amount)

Often confused words - then/than ("then" is an adverb and "than" is a conjunction used to compare)

Numbers - write out to 99

Incorrect pronoun use - "she" and "I" as subject; "her and "me" as object

Homophone - our/are

Punctuation - use of quotation marks to denote falsehood

Punctuation - quote within a quote

Odd word usage - "but" to mean "only"

B - in less then 2 heartbeats demetrius spoke up his original love for helena **forged** even stronger by the juice of the flower. my love for hermia melted as snow does from the fields in spring. i love helena. me and her **doted** on each other in are childhood. my supposed love for hermia was but a temporary sickness he said

C -   In fewer than two heartbeats, Demetrius spoke up, his original love for Helena **forged** even stronger by the juice of the flower. "My love for Hermia melted as snow does from the fields in spring. I love Helena. She and I **doted** on each other in our childhood. My supposed 'love' for Hermia was but a temporary sickness," he said.

112. to issue an edict ●

Paragraph - subject change

Commas - participial phrase as interrupter

Indirect quotation - no quotes with "that"

Homophone - piece/peace

Numbers - write out to 99

Pronouns - incorrect pronoun use ("he" as subject and "him" as object of preposition)

B - theseus desiring peace for his forthcoming nuptials overruled egeus and **issued his edict** that the 2 couples should join with hippolyta and he in a triple wedding

C -   Theseus, desiring peace for his forthcoming nuptials, overruled Egeus and **issued his edict** that the two couples should join with him and Hippolyta in a triple wedding.

113. disconcerted ●

LD - simile

No paragraph

Incorrect verb tense - story in past

Verb tense - need for pluperfect tense for what happened prior to this

Verb tense - need for subjunctive mood ("as if") instead of straight comparison ("like") to express doubt or uncertainty

Homophone - their/there/they're

Plural rules - consonant "y" words change to "ies"

B - theseus and the court all leave the forest and returned to athens. the lovers followed him. they were still **disconcerted** by what took place in the forest during the night. it was like a fog clouded theyre memorys

C - Theseus and the court all left the forest and returned to Athens. The lovers followed him. They were still **disconcerted** by what had taken place in the forest during the night. It was as if a fog clouded their memories.

B = *suggested sentence for the board or overhead*   *C* = *sentence written correctly*   *LD* = *literary device*

114. **hapless, sans** (French word - without) ●

LD - play on words ("drama crime")

Paragraph - place and subject change

Commas - optional comma after "meanwhile; adjective phrase ("now sans...")

Splitting verbs - deliberate splitting of verb and helping verb to avoid awkwardness ("was only vaguely aware")

Transition - needed to indicate change

Hyphen

Possession - singular noun

Common spelling error - occur

Verb tense - note use of pluperfect to refer to previous action

Spelling rule - if word ends in consonant/vowel/consonant and a suffix is added, double the consonant ("occurred")

B - meanwhile the **hapless** bottom now **sans** ass head woke up alone in titanias bower. he was only vaguely aware of what had occurred the previous night and thought that he was still awaiting his cue as pyramus

C - Meanwhile, the **hapless** Bottom, now **sans** ass-head, woke up alone in Titania's bower. He was only vaguely aware of what had occurred the previous night and thought that he was still awaiting his cue as Pyramus.

115. ❤ **ballad** (in Shakespeare it is "ballet"), **bolster** ●

LD - humor ("drama crime"); **sarcasm** ("in true Bottom style"); **paradox and pun** ("Bottom's dream..."); **quote within a quote**

No paragraph

Commas - introductory participial phrase; introductory adverbial phrase

Quotation - said by narrator but words are Bottom's

Punctuation - use of quotation marks to denote play on words; use of quotation marks for double meaning of name "Bottom;" quote within a quote in direct quotation from Bottom; need parentheses around narrator's clarification

Dangling modifier - Bottom's mind did not discover - he did.

Titles - review rules for underlining vs. putting quotation marks around titles (whole, longer works like books, magazines, and record albums are underlined; smaller parts of the whole like poems, articles and songs are put into quotes)

Possession - singular noun

No commas around Quince - single word closely related to the preceding word and restrictive modifier (necessary because he has more than one friend)

B - discovering that his cohorts in "drama crime" were missing his mind tried to recall the nights adventures. in true bottom style he thought that perhaps his friend quince might want to make a **ballad** of his dream to be called bottoms dream because it had no bottom to **bolster** his part in the play

C - Discovering that his cohorts in "drama crime" were missing, Bottom tried to recall the night's adventures. In true "Bottom" style, he thought that perhaps his friend Quince might want to make a **ballad** of his "dream" (to be called "'Bottom's Dream' because it had no bottom") to **bolster** his part in the play.

116. **thespians** ●

No paragraph

Commas - around "too" meaning "also"

Often confused words - then/than ("then" is an adverb and "than" is a conjunction used to compare)

Possessive pronouns - my, your, his, her, its, our, their

B - bottom too than departed the forest in pursuit of his fellow **thespians**

C - Bottom, too, then departed the forest in pursuit of his fellow **thespians**.

B = suggested sentence for the board or overhead   *C = sentence written correctly*   *LD = literary device*

117. ❤ shed (verb), mirth, ineptitude ●

LD - play on words (Philostrate/Philistine)**; oxymoron** ("tears of mirth")

Paragraph - place and subject change

Commas - long introductory adverbial phrase; interrupter; participial phrase; noun series; appositive

Possession - plural noun

Possession - singular noun

Punctuation - quotes around play (A review of quotation marks vs. underlining would fit here. See Caught'ya #115.)

Verb tense - use of pluperfect tense needed for action that preceded this paragraph

Parallel construction - preposition "of"

B - at the aristocrats palace the triple marriage was conducted. that evenings entertainment was of course the play pyramus and thisbe performed by none other than quince bottom and company. philostrate the master of revels recommended it as he saw the play and **shed** tears of **mirth** over the **ineptitude** of the dialogue and the actors

C -   At the aristocrats' palace, the triple marriage was conducted. That evening's entertainment was, of course, the play "Pyramus and Thisbe," performed by none other than Quince, Bottom, and company. Philostrate, the Master of Revels, recommended it as he had seen the play and had **shed** tears of **mirth** over the **ineptitude** of the dialogue and of the actors.

118. deplorable, execrable ●

Paragraph - subject change

No commas

Incorrect verb tense - story in past tense

Often confused words - then/than ("then" is an adverb and "than" is a conjunction used to compare)

Misplaced modifier - synopsis is of plot, not the verse

B - the play began with a **deplorable** prologue with quince so nervous that he interrupts himself and said the opposite of what he intended. the characters then gave a short synopsis in **execrable** verse of the plot

C -   The play began with a **deplorable** prologue with Quince so nervous that he interrupted himself and said the opposite of what he intended. The characters then gave a short synopsis of the plot in **execrable** verse.

119. avowed ●

No paragraph; paragraph - change of focus

Comma - appositive; before "etc."

Indirect quotation - no quotes with "that"

Abbreviations - "etc." (review all common abbreviations.)

Punctuation - only one period if abbreviation is at end of sentence

Verb tense - note correct use

Run-on sentence - lack of punctuation

Homophone - their/there/they're

B - snug as the lion reassured the audience that he was only snug and that he would not bite them. moonshine forgot his part and **avowed** that his lantern was the moon and that he was the man in the moon etc from there the play progressed downhill in quality

C - Snug, as the Lion, reassured the audience that he was only Snug and that he would not bite them. Moonshine forgot his part and **avowed** that his lantern was the moon and that he was the man in the moon, etc.

From there the play progressed downhill in quality.

120. resurrection ●

LD - narrator aside

No paragraph; paragraph - narrator's advice

Commas - long introductory adverbs (2 prepositional phrases); participial phrase

Punctuation - use of quotation marks to denote something not really true

Article "an" precedes vowel or a silent "h"

Irregular verb - leap/leapt

Homophones - hear/here; tail/tale

B - at the end after the double suicide of pyramus and thisbe bottom performing an instant **resurrection** leaped up from the dead to ask theseus if he wanted to watch a dance or hear an epilogue. theseus and the rest could take no more of this travesty of a play and opted for the dance. the three couples retired at last. you will have to take the final exam to read the end of this tail

C - At the end, after the double "suicide" of Pyramus and Thisbe, Bottom, performing an instant **resurrection**, leapt up from the "dead" to ask Theseus if he wanted to watch a dance or hear an epilogue. Theseus and the rest could take no more of this travesty of a play and opted for the dance. The three couples retired at last.

You will have to take the final exam to read the end of this tale.

End-of-the-year Caught'ya Test

Directions:

Be very careful. You will receive no hints for this test, except that there are eight paragraphs, only one misplaced modifier, and one run-on sentence. Other than in the run-on sentence, all end punctuation has been provided.

Edit this story as best you can on this paper. Use the paragraph sign to indicate the need for a paragraph. Use proofreading symbols for mechanical corrections. Write in corrections of misspelled words. Rewrite sentences where the meanings are unclear. Then rewrite the entire test correctly on your own paper. This is what your teacher will grade.

When you reach the end of the test, do the following: write the numbers 1 to 20 on the back of your paper and tell the part of speech of each word in the last sentence of the story (treat "never fear" as one word). After you have finished the entire test, go back and check your work several times. Good editors always do. Good luck! This is a difficult test with many errors to find.

the dénouement of the story

after the three couples had retired puck appeared and spoke. the fun and games are finished and not a tiny furry mouse shall effect this hallowed house and the lovers are back with their correct mates and the awful thespians have produced there play and all is right in the world of fantasy too he declared. as puck speaks oberon titania and all their entourage arrived at theseus castle too. they also were not quite ready for the nights merriment to end. and they want more partys. lets all gather around the fire with the elfs and dance and sing to bless this house and the newly married couples. more than one and fewer then 4 may they find happiness as me and you have titania said oberon. yes lets sing and dance to bless this place hand in hand acceded titania who had thoroughly forgiven oberon. among us me and you are in agreement. let the couples lay in there beds while we ensure their continued happiness. than oberon added to titanias comment as they left the palace. yes may the 3 couples forever be in love and may they have many healthy children. let us leave and take our rest as well. we have done good this evening my dear. let us retire too. its you that i love. puck said i sure hope that the mortals never recall what really happened last night or i am in trouble like borachio in shakespeares play much ado about nothing. thus all ended good except that the trades people that put on that awful play were planing to produce another spectacle based on bottoms dream. never fear with glee oberon and his elfin freinds already were happily planning there strategy to sabotage the would be actors.

End-of-the-year Caught'ya Test Key

Teachers: *This is an extremely difficult test. It covers a year's worth of material. You might want to have a review before the test. On the day of the test, read the test out loud to your students to give them hints of where to paragraph and punctuate. Remind your students to number their papers from 1 to 20 on the back and write the part of speech of each word in the last sentence. Since there are over one hundred errors in this test, depending on how you count the misplaced modifier, you might want to grade it on a percentage basis. Those of you who teach ninth or tenth grade might want to help out your students by counting the possible errors in each line and writing these numbers in the margin before you photocopy the test for your students. Because it is so difficult to count errors correctly, you might want to triple-check your figures.*

The Dénouement of the Story

After the three couples had retired, Puck appeared and spoke.

"The fun and games are finished. Not a tiny, furry mouse shall affect this hallowed house. The lovers are back with their correct mates. The awful thespians have produced their play, and all is right in the world of fantasy, too" he declared.

As Puck spoke, Oberon, Titania, and all their entourage arrived at Theseus's castle, too. They also were not quite ready for the night's merriment to end. They wanted more parties.

"Let's all gather around the fire with the elves and dance and sing to bless this house and the newly-married couples. More than one and fewer than four, may they find happiness as you and I have, Titania," said Oberon.

"Yes, let's sing and dance hand in hand to bless this place," acceded Titania who had thoroughly forgiven Oberon. "Between us, you and I are in agreement. Let the couples lie in their beds while we ensure their continued happiness."

Then Oberon added to Titania's comment as they left the palace, "Yes, may the three couples forever be in love, and may they have many healthy children. Let us leave and take our rest as well. We have done well this evening, my dear. Let us retire, too. It's you whom I love."

Puck said, " I sure hope that the mortals never recall what really happened last night, or I am in trouble like Borachio in Shakespeare's play <u>Much Ado About Nothing</u>.

Thus, all ended well except that the trades people who had put on that awful play were planning to produce another spectacle based on Bottom's dream. Never fear, with glee Oberon and his elfin friends already happily were planning their strategy to sabotage the would-be actors.

Chapter 6

Twelfth Night of Mischief
or
What You Will Doubled

What is included in this chapter:

Twelfth Night
As told in caught'ya sentences

Below is the story shown in its entirety (not broken up into individual Caught'yas), exactly as it appears in the corrected Caught'yas (**C**). This should give you a quick look at the complexity of the sentences, at the vocabulary (in bold), and at the skills addressed in the Caught'yas of this story so that you can see if it is appropriate for your students. You will notice, for example, that the Caught'yas for this story are longer, more complex, and more difficult than the Caught'yas of the other two stories. The plot also is harder to follow because of its convolutions, subplots, and number of main characters.

Please note that this story has been written in the past tense instead of the historic present as many teachers of honors and advanced placement classes espouse when students write about literature. I did this for four reasons. One, this is not intended as a summary, but rather as an original story. Two, in my opinion, the story was clearer in the past tense. Three, having the story in the past tense let me use the present tense in quotes and in narrator asides and the pluperfect in references to past actions. And four, and most significant, this story is a teaching tool for grammar, mechanics, and usage, not for literary style, and all the verb tenses needed to be represented for recognition and practice.

It is assumed that your students can recognize proper nouns, common capitalizations, regular verbs, and end punctuation. Therefore, in the interests of space, these are not mentioned in the list to the left of each Caught'ya.

I suggest that you begin the year by showing the movie or reading the story on the next few pages. Hollywood just came out with a modern version of the play! Because this tale is broken up into daily sentences and because Shakespeare's plots tend to be more convoluted than the most enigmatic soap opera, students need to know where the story is headed. I piloted the Caught'yas of *Much Ado About Nothing* with my gifted eighth graders, and they loved it. After a month of doing Caught'yas and swearing in "Shakespearean," they begged to see the movie (I, of course, acquiesced). After seeing the movie (and loving it), about a third of my students bought the book on their own and read it for pleasure! As one enthusiastic student put it, "Shakespeare rules!"

Twelfth Night of Mischief or What You Will Doubled

This tale of trickery, mistaken identity, **unrequited** love, mischief, and a **bizarre** love triangle takes place in Illyria, an ancient Roman province along the east coast of the Adriatic Sea. Now, Illyria was a beautiful place of cliffs that seemed to dive into the blue-green sea and of almost constant sunshine. Illyria, like most nations in the ancient times of the Roman Empire, was ruled by a duke, the **benign** and gentlemanly Orsino. Orsino loved (or thought he loved) Lady Olivia, a rich countess, but she **spurned** the advances of everyone.

One day in his palace that overlooked the sea, Duke Orsino, surrounded by the sound of his musicians' songs, **pined** for the elusive, **divine** Olivia. The duke was in love, and he was in a **whimsical** mood, made more so by the lyrical **timbre** of the music. Being a romantic man, Duke Orsino expounded to the page Curio on the emotions that the music evoked.

"Music is the food of love," he mused. "It comes over my ears like a sweet sound that breathes on a field of fragrant violets," the Duke continued, **waxing** poetic in his rapture and in his distress at his spurned love for the **beguiling** Olivia.

Curio, the bold page, asked his **sovereign**, "Wouldn't you like to go hunting, my lord? It might take your mind off the fair Olivia. We could hunt for hart," Curio suggested.

"I would like to hunt Olivia's heart," Orsino punned. "It is I who resemble the hart, and my desire for Olivia is the **fell** and cruel hound that tears me apart," he **expounded**.

In the midst of Orsino's **mellifluous, melancholy** dialogue, Valentine, another one of the duke's pages, arrived with a **surfeit** of bad news. Orsino had sent Valentine, **aptly** named for his role in this story, to Olivia to inform her of Orsino's ardor. Orsino, the foolish **sage**, had sent a love letter to Olivia, hoping to win her favor. It was a short, grand letter except that it was full of **hyperbole** and professed love.

The letter read as follows:

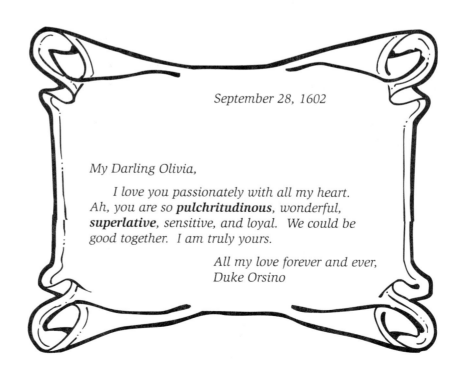

September 28, 1602

My Darling Olivia,

I love you passionately with all my heart. Ah, you are so **pulchritudinous**, *wonderful,* **superlative**, *sensitive, and loyal. We could be good together. I am truly yours.*

All my love forever and ever,
Duke Orsino

"I beg you, my lord, I do not wish to tell you this news," **beseeched** Valentine. "Sit down first."

"Come on, lad, tell me what news you received," begged Orsino who was, of course, on **tenterhooks** to hear from his love.

Valentine replied, "Olivia herself did not see me. I saw her handmaiden instead. The maid said that Olivia plans to mourn her recently-deceased brother for seven years."

"Seven years!" exclaimed Orsino in awe. "What a **virtuous** lady. She would make a devoted and faithful lover. I should have **wooed** her even harder," he moaned.

Meanwhile, somewhere by the seashore, a sea captain, a young lady, and a **motley** bunch of sailors were having a discussion. They had been shipwrecked nearby, and all had barely escaped drowning. The young, **nubile** maiden Viola was concerned for the fate of her twin brother, Sebastian.

"Where are we, my dear captain? What happened to my twin brother? He and I are very close, and I look just like him. If I lived, perhaps he did, too. What do you think?" asked Viola who was **disquieted** and very affected by the fact that her brother was not there.

"You and I and all these sailors are in Illyria, Madame," replied the captain. "I know because my **siblings** and I grew up here. When the ship wrecked itself on these fell rocks, it split in two pieces. I saw your twin brother, Sebastian, lash himself to the mast, but the mast and he were swept out to sea.

"He was like Arion (a Greek poet and musician who so charmed the dolphins with his **ethereal** music that one saved him from drowning) on his dolphin, only Sebastian was riding a mast into the waves," the captain concluded.

"He must be alive," insisted Viola, **mollified** by the thought that her twin had last been seen **animate**. "If I thought he weren't, I would try to raise him from the depths. My family is everything to me. I must effect his rescue."

The captain then dashed Viola's hopes. "There is a strong possibility that only you and I and these few sailors who now stand around us survived the wreck. The rest of the crew is probably dead," he **lugubriously** concluded. "Among us, we did well to survive."

"Who rules this country?" asked Viola.

"A noble duke whose name is as **meritorious** as his nature," replied the captain.

"What's his name, then?"

"Orsino."

"Ah, I know of him," said Viola. "He was a bachelor at that time. Is he still unwed?"

"Well, he was a month ago," **rejoined** the captain. "I saw him last on August 26, 1602. I remember it as if it were yesterday. According to gossip, he seeks the love of the fair Olivia.

"Within the past year, however, Olivia has lost her father and her brother," the Captain continued. "She was a **virtuous** maid who really was affected by her family's **demise**. Since then, she totally has **abjured** men's sight and company."

"In other words, Orsino won't have any luck," stated Viola. "Oh, until my own circumstances improve, I would like to be a servant for that poor, **bereft** lady who shares my sorrow, but I know that would be impossible if she is **sequestering** herself.

"Captain, I will pay you well if you will help me **ingratiate** myself to this Duke Orsino. I will present myself to him as a **eunuch**," Viola decided, "and sing and serve him well until my brother is found."

"I shall remain **mute**, and your secret will lie safe with me. No one will know in his or her wildest dream that you are a woman," promised the Captain as they walked to the Duke's palace.

Meanwhile, at Olivia's house, Olivia's uncle, Sir Toby **Belch**, was criticizing his niece to her serving maid, Maria. Now, Sir Belch was a man who was known for frequently **quaffing** spirits until he was quite intoxicated; that night was no exception. This was why Sir Toby Belch's name was so **apt**. He was a sober **sot** who belched **vociferously** when he drank a lot. Sir Belch had one other **egregious** fault. He delighted in playing tricks on people, especially on obnoxious people.

Sir Belch thought that his only niece, Olivia, was taking this mourning of her brother too far. He did not want Olivia to go any further in her **melodramatic melancholy**.

Maria, on the other hand, **upbraided** Sir Belch for his **slovenly** ways. "You will go to perdition for your Godless ways," she **vociferated**. "You are nothing but a **tosspot**. It's a shame! If I were you, I would mend my ways. Really, Sir Belch," Maria continued, "you must come in earlier. Your niece hates the hours you keep, and your quaffing will undo you. Yesterday I heard my lady talking of a foolish knight whom you brought in one night to woo her. You **fatuous** sot, what were you thinking?"

"Who? Sir Andrew Aguecheek?" asked Sir Belch **fervently**. "He's tall and rich, plays the violoncello, and speaks several languages. He's a real catch. Do you have some ale?"

"Sir Aguecheek is a Narcissus-like **knave**, a **lecher**, a 'quarreler,' a gambler, and a coward who drinks nightly with you, Sir Belch, and then lies **inebriated** on the floor," accused Maria. "He, like you, probably never will **amend** his **heathen** ways," she concluded. "Ah, here comes the **dissembling** drunkard now."

"Ah, Sir Toby Belch, my friend. Bless you, Maria, you fair **shrew**," Sir Aguecheek said in greeting.

"Sweet Sir Aguecheek, you, too, Sir," answered Sir Belch.

Maria and Sir Aguecheek exchanged a few insults and jests, with Sir Aguecheek coming off the worse for wear. She upbraided him for his lechery and, with her **rapier wit**, made **aspersions** to his drinking. It was clear that she **abhorred** the fellow.

With Maria gone, the two tosspots, Sir Belch and Sir Aguecheek, conspired. They discussed Sir Aguecheek's chances as Olivia's suitor which Sir Aguecheek thought were less than his two hunting dogs' chances to **articulate** words in French. During the course of the conversation, Sir Aguecheek **bemoaned** his lack of wit and blamed it on the fact that he was, as he said, "a great eater of beef." He could not understand Sir Belch's use of French and whined that he wished that he had **bestowed** as much time in study as he had in gambling, dancing, **wenching**, and fencing. Being a **hedonist** who was a slave to his immediate desires and not able to wait for anything, Sir Aguecheek was ready to give up his pursuit of Olivia and quit Illyria.

Sir Belch persuaded his friend to stay for another month. "There will be no fewer than ten parties held next month. And masquerade balls. And **a plethora of** drink!" he argued. "Everyone in town will host his or her own party."

Sir Aguecheek agreed to stay with the promise of a lot of such **revels**. (Is this a **portend** of an ulterior motive for Sir Belch's fervor in convincing his friend to stay?)

Viola, a **shrewd, sagacious** lady in disguise as a young man, quickly ingratiated herself into the Duke's household. Valentine and the Duke immediately took a fancy to "him." Viola used a boy's name Cesario to disguise her sex further.

"Cesario, you are about to move up in **stature** in the Duke's service," said Valentine to the disguised Viola.

"Does this mean that he is inconsistent in his favors?" queried Viola who had already fallen in love with Duke Orsino.

"Hush, **stripling**, here he comes," warned Valentine.

"Cesario, I trust you. In the brief time you have been with us, I have **divulged** my secret soul to you. Therefore, I ask you to effect a change in Olivia's affection for me. Do not leave her door until she agrees to see you. When you see her, speak of me," Orsino commanded Viola. Orsino continued, "Win her for me, my friend. Make **clamorous** sounds. Be persistent. Woo her for me in my **stead**. Do not return to me without a lot of good news. Do well, Cesario, for I **languish** of love."

Viola was **disconcerted** by the idea of wooing Olivia for Orsino, the man whom she secretly loved. "Oh, **woe** is me. If I woo her successfully for him, then she, not I, would be his wife. She is no more deserving than I. I never should have disguised myself as a man."

While Viola was fretting further about her dilemma, the **redoubtable** Maria and Feste, the jester, were exchanging **barbs**. Feste, as usual, had been late. Maria threatened that Olivia would hang him for his **transgressions**.

"Many a good hanging prevented a bad marriage," Feste retorted. "You know," Feste continued to Maria, "if Sir Toby Belch were to give up his drinking, you, who are such an intelligent and **droll** piece of Eve's flesh, and he might be interested in each other."

"Go away again, you **implacable rogue**," said Maria as she left the room.

Feste rejoined, "Remember what Quinapalus, the Greek, said. 'Better a witty fool than a foolish wit.'"

As Maria left the room, Olivia and the arrogant, **churlish** Malvolio entered. Their **miens** were serious, and they talked very **gravely**. As soon as Olivia saw the fool, she asked him to leave.

"I will not go, Madame, for I am not the fool; you are," Feste retorted.

"Prove it," countered Olivia.

"**Dexterously**, good lady. You mourn your brother. Is his soul in Hell?"

Olivia answered, "No, Fool, it is in heaven."

"Then only a fool would mourn, my Madonna, for heaven is a wonderful place," concluded Feste.

"You lighten my mood with your **levity**, dear Feste."

While Olivia's spirits were raised a lot by Feste's jesting, the humorless and **haughty** Malvolio was not amused. This pompous and arrogant "fool" maintained that the jester was a weak man, weak as his wit. Needless to say, Feste held his own in the verbal **parry**. Malvolio was the *real* fool!

Now, this is the point where the plot thickens like pudding burbling and blupping on the stove.

Inserting herself between the two verbally sparring men in order to speak to Olivia, Maria informed her **disconsolate** mistress that a young gentleman wanted to speak with her. This stripling was none other than Viola in disguise as Cesario, and Olivia wanted to send "him" away. Olivia sent Maria and Malvolio to chase away the would-be **swain**. Sir Toby Belch, the uncle who drank a lot, staggered into the room. He was as drunk as a skunk.

Olivia, who loved her uncle even though he drank no fewer than two bottles of spirits a day, sent Feste to accompany Sir Belch to ensure his safety.

Malvolio returned to **impart** the news to Olivia that the young fellow at the door was *very* insistent, would not take "no" for an answer, and threatened to remain by her door like a "supporter to a bench" until she gave her **approbation** to see him.

"What does he look like? From where is he ? How old is he? Who is he?" **queried** Olivia whose resolve had weakened with the report of the young man's persistence. "Oh, I should have combed my hair better."

"He is all right. He's not old enough for a man and not young enough for a boy. He's very **dapper**," replied Malvolio.

"Oh, all right, let him in," Olivia sighed.

Olivia put a veil over her face the moment Viola, still disguised as Cesario, entered the room.

"Oh, most radiant, exquisite, and unmatchable beauty.....," Viola began her prepared speech, but Olivia interrupted her.

"Who are you?" Olivia asked. This mysterious, fair-faced youth **enthralled** her.

Viola dodged with **finesse** all Olivia's probes at her identity and background. She kept trying to resume her speech and pressed Orsino's suit for Olivia's hand in marriage. Viola so **enraptured** Olivia with her fair words and wit that Olivia soon sent everyone else out of the room. Viola even persuaded Olivia to unveil herself.

During the course of their social **intercourse**, Viola **lamented**, "Your beauty is so overwhelming that it would be very cruel of you to carry your **comeliness** to the grave and leave the world no copy." Viola continued, **reiterating** Orsino's love, "Orsino loves you with all his heart."

"Love? Orsino can't really love me. He doesn't truly know me, nor does he understand me, so his love can't be very **profound**," Olivia maintained.

"I still do not wish to see Orsino, but on the other hand, Cesario, if you wish to come again, I would be most happy to see you," Olivia **coyly** said, for she was already falling in love with the "young man."

Ah, what a pickled plot! Viola adores Orsino. Orsino **idolizes** Olivia. Olivia **adulates** Cesario. Cesario is really Viola and vice versa. This is, indeed, an **uncanny** love triangle. But, wait! It will get even more bizarre.

Intrigued with Cesario, Olivia's fertile mind manufactured a **ruse**, a **subterfuge** designed to lure the "young man," whom she found so cute, to another **rendezvous**.

"Malvolio, run after Cesario and give him this ring that he must have left," Olivia lied as she handed Malvolio one of her rings. "Tell Cesario that if he returns tomorrow, I will inform him in great detail why Orsino is not an **apposite** suitor."

While all these **embroiling** love triangles were taking place in the **regal** households, two people were meeting somewhere among the many tall sand dunes on the coast of Illyria: Sebastian and Captain Antonio. Sebastian, if you recall, was the twin brother of Viola who was **masquerading** as Cesario. He *had* survived the maelstrom and the shipwreck. Captain Antonio had rescued him from the jaws of death. Sebastian was not a happy camper. He thought that his beloved twin sister, Viola, had drowned and felt bad that he had survived when she had not. He cursed his "**malignant** fate."

"You should have let me drown," he said.

Sebastian decided to go to Duke Orsino's court. Even though he had many enemies there, Captain Antonio resolved to go with Sebastian as his **minion**.

"After all," he reasoned, "after the horror of the shipwreck, the dangers of the court will be like a sport."

This is worse than the **convoluted** story in Middlemarch by George Elliot (who was a woman writing as if she were a man).

While Sebastian and the **staunch** Antonio were trekking across the hills and pine forests of Illyria and were soon to complicate matters further at Orsino's palace, a foul-tempered, churlish Malvolio **accosted** Viola.

"You left this ring with the Countess Olivia, you canker-blossom," vociferated the **peevish** Malvolio with venom in his voice.

"I didn't leave a ring," Viola insisted

Malvolio threw down the ring. "If it is worth stooping for, there it lies."

The **surly** Malvolio delivered the rest of his message in the same manner as a snarling dog with a snout full of porcupine quills. Viola quickly figured out Olivia's ploy and realized that Olivia must have lost her heart to "Cesario."

Viola bemoaned the tangle. "Oh, what will become of this? As a man, I am loved by this woman. As a woman, I love the man who loves the woman who loves me as a 'man.' It's too **obfuscated** a knot for me to untie."

After midnight as the troubled Viola lay tossing and turning in her bed, Sir Toby Belch and Sir Andrew Aguecheek were getting **intoxicated**. In their inebriated state, each sang, laughed, argued, and called for Maria, Olivia's maid, to bring him more wine. Sir Belch even launched into a drunken **diatribe** that made no sense whatsoever except to another sot. Hearing the revelry, Feste, the jester, joined the party. Their singing and **caterwauling** woke Maria and everyone else who lay **abed** in his or her chamber.

"My lady has called up her steward, Malvolio, to throw you out, " Maria warned as the three drunks insulted Malvolio, a man whom none among the three sots liked; then the three **inebriates** continued their **salacious** attack.

"Malvolio is an earth-vexing **dandiprat** and an **impotent** fool," said Sir Belch.

At this "**astute**" observation, the three drunks launched into a **bawdy** song, each singing a phrase.

"Three merry men are we."

"There dwelt a man in Babylon, lady, lady."

"On the twelfth day of December...," sang all of the tosspots who were oblivious to the fact that Malvolio had just entered the room.

Malvolio was **choleric**. "Have you no wit, manners, nor **couth**? You turn my lady's house into a saloon. Have you no remorse for your behavior?" he raged. "And you, Maria," Malvolio turned on the **hapless** maid, "how can you allow such **misbehavior**?" he continued, scandalized. "Their obnoxious behavior will be reported immediately. Olivia will toss them out even if Sir Belch is **consanguineous**," he continued with righteous indignation as he stormed out of the room.

The group of tosspots then plotted with Maria's help to **gull** the pompous, **puritanical** Malvolio into making a total "fool" of himself.

"I will send him a lot of **epistles** of love in which I praise the following: the color of his beard; the shape of his leg; the manner of his **gait**; as well as the "beauty" of his eyes, his forehead, and his complexion," Maria planned. "I can write like a lady when I wish."

"That fool-born horse's **posterior** will think the letters come from my niece. He'll think that she's in love with him," chortled Sir Belch, so delighted to make a donkey's **derrière** out of his **nemesis** that he took another drink in celebration.

The next morning at Duke Orsino's palace, Orsino engaged in another of his increasingly frequent **discourses** with Viola, who was still in disguise. The latter was only too happy to comply.

Viola and Orsino talked again of love.

"If ever you love, boy, remember me, for I am the **quintessential** man in love," Orsino **mused**. "No man pursues his woman as passionately as I."

"I love someone, too, my Lord," boldly confessed Viola.

"Tell me."

"She is a lot like you," **proffered** Viola.

"How old is she?"

"About your age, my Lord," dared Viola.

Orsino (a real sexist like most of the men of his time) kept insisting on several points: a woman should marry a man older than she; women by nature were not able to love with the **vigor** of men; men needed to marry much younger women, for women were like roses that bloom briefly and then fade. (How unflattering!)

This Orsino was quite a **bigot** who did not feel that women were his equal and who loved a female with whom he never had conversed.

Why did Viola love this **bombastic ignoramus**? Ah well, love knows no reason.

Orsino felt positively **paternal** towards Viola, much to Viola's dismay. Viola, in desperation, became even bolder, telling Orsino that women could love as passionately as men.

"My father had a daughter," Viola bravely began, "who loved a man with the same intensity as I. My sister died, and I am now all the daughters of my father's house and all the sons, too," she said **enigmatically**.

Orsino then gave Viola a jewel and **bade** her to go again to Olivia's house.

"Do not take 'no' for an answer. I will have her love," he declared in the typical **machismo** fashion of the time.

A few days later the **diabolical** plan of revenge was enacted in Olivia's garden. Sir Belch and Sir Aguecheek hid behind a hedge. As soon as they spotted Malvolio entering the garden, Maria darted out and dropped the letter on the path where Malvolio couldn't miss it.

Now Malvolio, it seemed, had already contemplated the **plausibility** that Olivia was falling in love with him. Hadn't he heard her say that if ever she should choose a husband, it would be someone like Malvolio?

Musing about his possible future with Olivia, Malvolio spied the note. "Ah, this looks as if it were written by my **dulcet** lady, Olivia," he said.

The letter read:

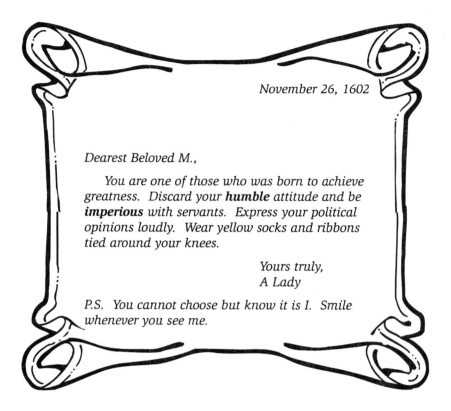

November 26, 1602

Dearest Beloved M.,

*You are one of those who was born to achieve greatness. Discard your **humble** attitude and be **imperious** with servants. Express your political opinions loudly. Wear yellow socks and ribbons tied around your knees.*

Yours truly,
A Lady

P.S. You cannot choose but know it is I. Smile whenever you see me.

"It is I whom she loves," **suspired** Malvolio as he fell hook, line, sinker, and yellow socks for the trick. "I shall do as my beloved asks."

Behind the **bracken**, the conspirators chortled as they contemplated the results of their plot. Everyone wanted to voice his opinion.

"I would like to marry this **wench** Maria who thought of this droll trick," said Sir Belch, little knowing how **prophetic** his words would prove to be and that he soon would be an ex-bachelor.

Meanwhile, Viola, still disguised as Cesario, went again to Olivia's house to plead Orsino's case for marriage. While Viola was waiting in the garden, Sir Belch and Sir Aguecheek joined her and concluded, after a lengthy conversation with the youth, that Cesario was a rare **courtier** who just might win Olivia's heart.

Olivia came to the garden, **euphoric** that Cesario had returned. She sent everyone else away to his or her room and talked to Viola. Olivia acknowledged the ruse of the ring and begged "him" to speak words of love to her. Viola, of course, did not.

Instead Viola **prevailed** upon Olivia one more time to consider Orsino instead.

"I have given my heart to no woman," Viola said **cryptically**.

Neither Duke Orsino nor Sir Aguecheek was having any luck in his pursuit of Olivia. Sir Aguecheek's friend Sir Belch, certain that no duel would ensue, **insinuated** that a duel with Cesario over Olivia's affections might be a good idea.

While all this intrigue was going on, Sebastian and Antonio reached the **hamlet**. Antonio, the sea captain who had saved him, gave the penniless Sebastian his own wallet, arranged to meet him later at a tavern, and then went to hide from his enemies while Sebastian explored the town.

Olivia already was making plans to **inveigle** Cesario to her side. She sent him an invitation for dinner.

"Oh, what will I serve him? Where is that Malvolio? He is usually such a perfect servant," she acknowledged. "Maria, go find him, please."

Malvolio, grinning, spouting nonsense, and wearing yellow socks and ribbons around his knees, soon joined Olivia. At almost every other word he uttered, he kissed her hand or blew her a **buss**. His appearance was no longer **dour**, nor was his **mien** sour. In fact, Malvolio appeared **deranged**. He **prattled** on and on as he smiled, blew kisses, and spouted bits of the letter he supposed that Olivia had written. Olivia thought he was "off his rocker." She **loathed** yellow socks and ribbons.

Suddenly, a servant announced Cesario's arrival at the door. Olivia quickly put the "mad" Malvolio into Maria's capable hands and sent all the servants away. The entire group had difficulty managing its "mad" **colleague**. Malvolio, per instructions in the epistle, was **rancorous** toward Sir Belch and **insolent** to the other servants. He drove them all to such desperation that they made plans to lock him up in a dark room, a common solution for handling a lunatic in Shakespearean times.

Viola again pleaded her master's suit. Olivia changed the topic, still trying to find out more about this charming young "man" and still pressing gifts on "him." Viola, however, finally did accept a diamond **brooch** that contained a miniature portrait of Olivia.

While Malvolio was reaping the rewards of poetic justice, Sir Aguecheek, in his usual **asinine** fashion, challenged Cesario to a sword fight. He did this in an absolutely **obtuse** and ridiculous-sounding letter.

Sir Belch delivered the message to Viola. "Sir Aguecheek is **implacable** and can get satisfaction only by killing you. He is a devil in a private **brawl**, having already killed a lot of men," he lied.

"Please, Sir Belch, seek this knight and discover what I have done to offend him," said Viola who was scared out of her wits.

Sir Belch then returned to Sir Aguecheek and **equivocated** again. "That Cesario, he's the very devil himself. I never have seen such a **rapacious** and skilled swordsman."

"I'll not **meddle** with the likes of him," concluded Sir Aguecheek, who was the **proverbial** coward. "I shouldn't have challenged him."

Sir Belch finally **taunted** both Sir Aguecheek and Cesario into drawing their swords. A real swordsman entered the garden — Captain Antonio. He mistook Viola for her twin brother, Sebastian. Now all **perdition** broke loose. A troop of officers arrived and arrested Antonio. Viola had hope that Sebastian was alive.

At this point in the story, the plot waxes **farcical**!

Sebastian arrived at the door of Olivia's **abode**. Sir Aguecheek saw him and assumed he was Cesario, the coward who had refused to fight, and attacked Sebastian. Sebastian made mincemeat out of Sir Aguecheek.

"You're a foolish fellow," Sebastian said. "If you don't leave me in peace, I'll really kick your *gluteus maximus*."

Olivia spied Sebastian and rendered Sebastian **dumbfounded** by asking him to marry her!

"Either I am mad, or this is a dream," Sebastian said with **incredulity**. "Yes, gorgeous lady, I will marry you," he said, for he had fallen instantly in love with this **comely** countess. "We have to find a priest."

The **irrepressible** mischief-maker, Feste, **dissembled** himself as a priest and went to Malvolio in his dark room. He tormented the servant, playing tricks with his mind. Malvolio, who kept maintaining that he was *not* **demented**, asked for pen and paper to write a letter to Olivia in order to **aver** his sanity.

"There is no darkness but ignorance," said Feste to himself. "Malvolio still thinks he has a chance with Olivia."

What a **puny ignoramus**! He is the real "fool"!

Sebastian was in seventh heaven. He sat in Olivia's lovely, **verdant** garden on a stone bench, waiting for the priest to arrive to marry him and Olivia. He delighted in his fate — a rich countess in love with him. As he sat there, surrounded by fragrant flowers and shrubs of all kinds, Sebastian wondered how it all had **transpired**. There was an **enigma** here.

Several problems still remained to be resolved. Everyone, except Sebastian and Viola, of course, was under the **misconception** that the twins were the same person. Antonio was still under arrest. Everyone had his or her doubts about Malvolio's sanity. Finally, the love triangle still existed, only now it was a "quintangle" with Sir Aguecheek and Malvolio also loving Olivia.

All the **protagonists**, including the hapless Antonio and his arresting officers, eventually came together in Olivia's lovely garden. Viola cleared Antonio by making Orsino (the one with whom Antonio had had his troubles over a sunken ship) see that Antonio was, indeed, a brave and honorable man. Orsino, who was spitting mad with **ire**, lit into Viola. In the heat of the moment, Viola confessed her love for Orsino.

You can imagine the shock this caused! Olivia, confusing the twins, thought it was her husband who loved Orsino and said as much. This *really* ticked off Orsino, who accused Viola of stealing Olivia's love.

"I am not married to Olivia," cried Viola (who still was **garbed** as Cesario). I love you, Orsino, with all my life."

Sir Aguecheek and Sir Belch, bloody from their fight with Sebastian, entered the crowded garden and accused Viola of **drubbing** them. At last the solution to the **conundrum** arrived — Sebastian. Captain Antonio, Sebastian's sailor friend, was amazed at the likeness between Viola and Sebastian.

"You're like an apple **cleft** in two," he said, amazed.

Finally, Viola revealed her **gender**, and everything was resolved. All practical jokes were confessed, and Orsino did an about-face and asked Viola to marry him.

The rest of the resolution to this convoluted tale, including Sir Belch's and Malvolio's fates, will be **divulged** in the final exam.

Teachers, see page 200 (End-of-the-year Caught'ya Test key) for the dénouement of this tale.

Vocabulary used in this story

1. unrequited, bizarre
2. benign, spurned, pined, divine
3. whimsical, timbre
4. ❤ waxing, ❤ beguiling
5. ❤ sovereign
6. ❤ fell, expounded
7. ❤ mellifluous, ❤ melancholy, ❤ surfeit, aptly
8. sage, hyperbole
9. pulchritudinous, superlative
10. ❤ beseeched, tenterhooks
11. virtuous, ❤ woo
12. ❤ motley, nubile
13. disquieted
14. siblings
15. ethereal
16. ❤ mollified, animate
17. lugubriously
18. meritorious
19. rejoined
20. ❤ virtuous, demise, ❤ abjured
21. bereft, sequestering
22. ingratiate, ❤ eunuch
23. ❤ mute,
24. ❤ belch, ❤ quaffing
25. ❤ apt, sot, vociferously, egregious
26. melodramatic, ❤ melancholy
27. ❤ upbraided, slovenly, vociferated (verb), ❤ tosspot
28. fatuous
29. fervently
30. ❤ knave, ❤ lecher, ❤ quarreler, inebriated
31. ❤ amend, ❤ heathen, ❤ dissembling
32. ❤ shrew
33. aspersions, ❤ rapier, ❤ wit, abhorred
34. articulate
35. bemoaned, bestowed, wenching
36. hedonist
37. a plethora of
38. revels, ❤ portend
39. shrewd, sagacious
40. stature, stripling
41. divulged
42. ❤ clamorous, stead, languish
43. disconcerted, ❤ woe
44. redoubtable, barbs, transgressions
45. ❤ droll
46. ❤ implacable, ❤ rogue
47. ❤ churlish, miens, ❤ gravely
48. ❤ dexterously
49. levity
50. haughty
51. parry
52. disconsolate
53. swain
54. impart, ❤ approbation
55. queried
56. dapper
57. enthralled
58. finesse
59. enraptured
60. intercourse, lamented, comeliness
61. reiterate, profound
62. coyly
63. idolizes, adulates, uncanny
64. ruse, subterfuge, rendezvous
65. apposite
66. embroiling, regal
67. masquerading
68. ❤ malignant
69. ❤ minion
70. convoluted
71. ❤ staunch, accosted
72. ❤ peevish
73. surly
74. obfuscated
75. intoxicated
76. diatribe, ❤ caterwauling, abed
77. inebriates, salacious
78. dandiprat, impotent, astute, bawdy
79. choleric, couth
80. hapless, misbehavior, ❤ consanguineous
81. ❤ gull, ❤ puritanical
82. ❤ epistle, ❤ gait
83. posterior, derrière, nemesis
84. discourses
85. quintessential, mused
86. proffered
87. vigor
88. bigot, bombastic, ignoramus
89. paternal
90. enigmatically
91. bade, machismo
92. diabolical
93. plausibility
94. dulcet
95. humble, imperious
96. suspired
97. bracken, wench, prophetic
98. ❤ courtier
99. euphoric
100. prevailed, cryptically
101. insinuated
102. hamlet
103. inveigle
104. buss, dour, mien
105. deranged, prattled, loathed
106. colleague
107. rancorous, insolent
108. brooch
109. asinine
110. ❤ implacable, ❤ brawl
111. equivocated, rapacious, ❤ meddle, proverbial
112. taunted, perdition
113. farcical, abode, gluteus maximus
114. dumbfounded, incredulity, comely
115. irrepressible, dissembled, demented, aver
116. ❤ puny, ignoramus
117. verdant
118. transpired, enigma
119. misconception
120. protagonists
121. ire
122. garbed
123. drubbing, conundrum, ❤ cleft
124. gender, divulged

Literary devices and writing conventions used in this story

Alliteration #26, 31, 39, 50, 106, 114

Anadiplosis #50, 61, 113

Anecdote #20

Aphorism (cliché) #10, 33, 39, 53, 62, 96, 117

Biblical allusion or reference #45, 48, 49

Building suspense and foreshadowing #25, 37, 38, 51, 63, 71, 90, 97, 100, 112

Character development in action and dialogue #2, 3, 4, 33, 35, 36, 49

Conversation #18, 72

Description #1, 2, 25

Description within action #50, 71, 117

Description within dialogue #20, 56

Double entendre #7, 24, 29, 32, 40, 47, 50, 72, 81

Establishment of setting and motif #1, 2, 12

Euphemism #27, 83, 112

Flashback #116 (brief from narrator)

Use of foreign language for effect # 64, 83, 91, 113 (Latin)

Historical allusion or reference #1, 107

Homily #88

Humor #25, 34, 49, 74, 104, 105

Hyperbole #9, #57, #60

Idiomatic expression #68, 73, 105, 124

Irony #24, 29, 41, 44, 57, 58, 62, 98, 103, 109

Literary allusion or reference #15, 18, 46, 70, 107

Use of made-up word #30 (from Shakespeare), #51, 119

Metaphor #4, 6, 110

Motif #1

Allusion to mythology #30

Narration #12

Narrator aside #2, 7, 38, 51, 63, 70, 87, 88, 116, 121

Naturalistic detail #71, 118

Onomatopoeia #51

Oxymoron #8, 25, 46

Personification #1, 4, 14, 67

Play on words #5, 27, 32, 46, 47, 48, 49, 50, 116

Pun #5

Use of direct quote #30, 44, 46, 54, 68

Repartée #48, 49, 78, 86

Repetition of word for effect #74

Use of rhyme for effect #69, 104

Sarcasm #50, 62, 78, 82, 109

Satire #104

Scene within a scene #109

Deliberate use of non sequitur #28, 29, 55

Simile #4, 6, 15, 51, 53, 54, 69, 73, 87, 123

Soliloquy #63

Subplot #12, 66, 81, 82, 83, 92, 93, 94, 95, 102, 110, 111, 112

Summary for clarification #119

Synecdoche #45, 58

Repeated use of synonyms to make a point #63, 77, 83

Substituting synonyms to avoid repetition #64

Use of symbol #110, 111

Tale within a tale #15

Caught'ya Sentences for Twelfth Night of Mischief or What You Will Doubled

1. unrequited, bizarre ●

LD - motif; description; historical reference; personification (cliffs diving into sea)

Paragraph - beginning of story

Commas - noun series; introductory word

Demonstrative adjectives - this/that/these/those

Verb tense - use of present tense to introduce, then switch to tense of story

Articles - use "an" with words that begin with vowels or silent "h"

Parallel construction - 2 prepositional phrases ("of cliffs...of constant.....")

Hyphen - two words acting as one

B - this tale of trickery mistaken identity **unrequited** love mischief and a **bizarre** love triangle takes place in illyria a ancient roman province along the east coast of the adriatic sea. now illyria was a beautiful place of cliffs that seemed to dive into the blue green sea and almost constant sunshine

C - This tale of trickery, mistaken identity, **unrequited** love, mischief, and a **bizarre** love triangle takes place in Illyria, an ancient Roman province along the east coast of the Adriatic Sea. Now, Illyria was a beautiful place of cliffs that seemed to dive into the blue-green sea and of almost constant sunshine.

2. benign, spurned, pined, divine ●

LD - character development; description; narrator aside; establishment of setting

2 Paragraphs -1st for change of topic; 2nd for change of place and time

Commas - appositive; appositive; compound sentence ("countess, but"); long introductory adverb; participial phrase; 2 adjectives together and second is not age, color, or linked to noun

Capitalization - name of former empire

Punctuation - use of parenthesis for narrator aside where the narrator steps out of the story

Collective noun - "everyone" as a singular noun

Possession - plural noun ending in "s"

Strong verb use - "loved," "spurned," "pined"

B - illyria like most nations in the ancient times of the roman empire was ruled by a duke the **benign** and gentlemanly orsino. orsino loved or thought he loved lady olivia a rich countess but she **spurned** the advances of everyone. one day in his palace that overlooked the sea duke orsino surrounded by the sound of his musicians songs **pined** for the elusive **divine** olivia

C - Illyria, like most nations in the ancient times of the Roman Empire, was ruled by a duke, the **benign** and gentlemanly Orsino. Orsino loved (or thought he loved) Lady Olivia, a rich countess, but she **spurned** the advances of everyone.

One day in his palace that overlooked the sea, Duke Orsino, surrounded by the sound of his musicians' songs, **pined** for the elusive, **divine** Olivia.

3. whimsical, timbre ●

LD - character development

No paragraph - continuation

Commas - compound sentence; participial phrase; gerund phrase ("being..."); unnecessary modifier

No commas around "Curio" - a single-word appositive related to the preceding word; also a restrictive modifier (necessary) since Orsino has more than one page

Gerund - verb form used as a noun ("Being")

NOTE: Teach coordinating conjunctions - **f**or, **a**nd, **n**or, **b**ut, **o**r, **y**et, **s**o — **FAN BOYS**

B - the duke was in love and he was in a **whimsical** mood made more so by the lyrical **timbre** of the music. being a romantic man duke orsino expounded to his page curio on the emotions that the music evoked

C - The duke was in love, and he was in a **whimsical** mood, made more so by the lyrical **timbre** of the music. Being a romantic man, Duke Orsino expounded to his page Curio on the emotions that the music evoked.

B = *suggested sentence for the board or overhead*   **C** = *sentence written correctly*   **LD** = *literary device*

4. ❤ waxing, ❤ beguiling   •

LD - personification ("sound that breathes"); **metaphor** ("music is...."); **simile** ("like the sweet sound..."); **character development in dialogue**

Paragraph - different person speaking

Commas - quote; quote; participial phrase

Quotation

"Like" vs. "as" - "like" used only in a direct comparison and must be followed by a noun

Spelling rule - "i" before "e" except after "c" and neighbor and weigh are weird

Parallel structure needed - "in his"

B - music is the food of love he mused. it comes over my ears like a sweet sound that breathes on a feild of fragrant violets the duke continued **waxing** poetic in his rapture and distress at his spurned love for the **beguiling** olivia

C -   "Music is the food of love," he mused. "It comes over my ears like a sweet sound that breathes on a field of fragrant violets," the Duke continued, **waxing** poetic in his rapture and in his distress at his spurned love for the **beguiling** Olivia.

5. ❤ sovereign   •

LD - play on words; pun

2 Paragraphs - 2 persons speaking

Commas - appositive; quote; quote; quote

Quotations

Run-on sentence - Curio's quote

Punctuation - question marks needed in interrogative

Verb tense - correct use of conditional tense (students misuse this tense in place of the past tense)

Spelling rule - words that end in a consonant/vowel/consonant double the second consonant when a suffix is added ("punned")

B - curio the bold page asked his **sovereign** wouldn't you like to go hunting my lord it might take your mind off the fair olivia we could hunt for hart curio suggested. i would like to hunt olivias heart orsino puned

C -   Curio, the bold page, asked his **sovereign**, "Wouldn't you like to go hunting, my lord? It might take your mind off the fair Olivia. We could hunt for hart," Curio suggested.

     "I would like to hunt Olivia's heart," Orsino punned.

6. ❤ fell, expounded   •

LD - simile, metaphor

No paragraph - continuation

Commas - compound sentence; quote

Quotation

Pronouns - "I" as subject and "me" as object

Relative pronouns - who/whom/whose/whoever/whomever/that/which ("that" and "which" can be subject or object and are used only with objects and animals; "who" and "whom" are used with people; "who" is subject; "whom" is object)

Possessive pronouns - my, your, his, her, its, our, their

Subject/verb agreement - "I.... .resemble," "desire....is," "hound....tears..."

Compound sentence - review type of sentence

Coordinating conjunctions and rules for compound sentences - review

NOTE: This is a good place, right in the beginning of the year to review the types of pronouns and their various functions. See the Appendix for a brief summary of each type.

B - it is me that resembles the hart and my desire for olivia are the **fell** and cruel hound that tear me apart he **expounded**

C - "It is I who resemble the hart, and my desire for Olivia is the **fell** and cruel hound that tears me apart," he **expounded**.

B = *suggested sentence for the board or overhead*   **C** = *sentence written correctly*   **LD** = *literary device*

7. ❤ mellifluous, ❤ melancholy, ❤ surfeit, aptly ●

LD - double entendre (the name "Valentine"); **narrator aside**

Paragraph - subject change

Commas - long introductory adverb (with 2 prepositional phrases); appositive; narrator aside

Possession - singular nouns

Pronouns - too many for clarity

Verb tense - use of pluperfect to denote action that took place anterior to this paragraph

NOTE: Teach the prepositions if your students do not already know them. You can find a list under "Prepositions" in the Appendix of this book.

B - in the midst of orsinos **mellifluous melancholy** dialogue valentine another one of the dukes pages arrived with a **surfeit** of bad news. orsino had sent valentine **aptly** named for his role in this story to olivia to inform her of his ardor

C -   In the midst of Orsino's **mellifluous, melancholy** dialogue, Valentine, another one of the duke's pages, arrived with a **surfeit** of bad news. Orsino had sent Valentine, **aptly** named for his role in this story, to Olivia to inform her of Orsino's ardor.

➡ SUGGESTION:

It is often a good idea to have students memorize the main prepositions (if they have not already done so). You can do this painlessly, memorizing a few each day until the entire list is learned. My students chant them, complete with hand signals. Once learned, prepositions can be correctly used in places like titles, and students find it easier to understand that prepositional phrases are really adjectives and adverbs.

8. sage, hyperbole ●

LD - oxymoron ("foolish sage" and "short, grand letter" if you consider the French meaning of "grand")

No paragraph - continuation

Commas - appositive; participial phrase; 2 adjectives where 2nd is not age, color, or linked to noun

Run-on sentence - lack of punctuation

Verb tense - use of pluperfect tense to denote action anterior to this paragraph

Often confused words - accept/except

B - orsino the foolish **sage** had sent a love letter to olivia hoping to win her favor it was a short grand letter accept that it was full of **hyperbole** and professed love the letter read

C - Orsino, the foolish **sage**, had sent a love letter to Olivia, hoping to win her favor. It was a short, grand letter except that it was full of **hyperbole** and professed love.

9. pulchritudinous, superlative ●

LD - hyperbole

2 Paragraphs - introduction and then letter

Commas - greeting; predicate adjective series; closing

Use of colon before a list or referent - not after a verb

Letter format - friendly letter

Greeting - no indentation

Closing - no capitals except in first word

Adjective vs. adverb - "good" as adjective and "well" as adverb

Common spelling error - "truly"

B - the letter read as follows

september 28 1602

my darling olivia i love you passionately with all my heart. ah you are so **pulchritudinous** wonderful **superlative** sensitive and loyal. we could be good together. i am truely yours. all my love forever and ever duke orsino

C -   The letter read as follows:

September 28, 1602

My Darling Olivia,

     I love you passionately with all my heart. Ah, you are so **pulchritudinous**, wonderful, **superlative**, sensitive, and loyal. We could be good together. I am truly yours.

All my love forever and ever,
Duke Orsino

➡ SUGGESTION:

This is a good spot to review the eight parts of speech and their various functions since all eight are represented in Caught'ya #9 — noun, interjection, preposition, pronoun, adverb, verb, adjective, conjunction. I put up a large sign in the window of my classroom that says NIPPAVAC. This, of course, is an acronym of the parts of speech. We chant these a few times until my students learn them. Once learned, they can be more easily applied to sentences.

B = suggested sentence for the board or overhead   C = sentence written correctly   LD = literary device

10. ❤ **beseeched, tenterhooks** •

LD - aphorism ("on tenterhooks")

2 Paragraphs - 2 people speaking

Commas - direct address; quote; direct address; interrupter

Quotations

Transitive vs. intransitive verbs - "sit" is intransitive; "set" is transitive and must take an object

Irregular verbs - sit and set

Spelling rules - "i" before "e" except after "c" and neighbor and weigh are weird; words that end in a consonant/vowel/consonant double the second consonant when a suffix is added ("begged")

Relative pronouns - who/whom/whose/whoever/whomever/that/which ("that" and "which" can be subject or object and are used only with objects and animals; "who" and "whom" are used with people; "who" is subject; "whom" is object)

Possessive pronouns - my, your, his, her, its, our, their

B - i beg you my lord i do not wish to tell you this news **beseeched** valentine. set down first. come on lad tell me what news you recieved beged orsino whom was of course on **tenterhooks** to hear from his love

C -   "I beg you, my lord, I do not wish to tell you this news," **beseeched** Valentine. "Sit down first."

    "Come on, lad, tell me what news you received," begged Orsino who was, of course, on **tenterhooks** to hear from his love.

11. **virtuous, ❤ woo** •

2 Paragraphs - 2 people speaking

Commas - quote; optional before demonstrative pronoun "herself;" quote

Quotations

Irregular verb - see/saw/have seen

Indirect quotation - not exact words if spoken

Numbers - write out to 99

Use of adverb as intensifier ("recently...")

Hyphen - intensifier and adjective acting as one word

Punctuation - use of italics for emphasis; exclamation mark for emphasis

Incorrect word use - "should have" not "should of" since you need a verb, not a preposition

Comparisons - hard/harder/hardest

B - valentine replied olivia herself did not see me. i seen her handmaiden instead. the maid said that olivia plans to mourn her recently deceased brother for 7 years. *seven years* exclaimed orsino in awe. what a **virtuous** lady. she would make a devoted and faithful lover. i should of **wooed** her even more hard he moaned

C -   Valentine replied, "Olivia herself did not see me. I saw her handmaiden instead. The maid said that Olivia plans to mourn her recently-deceased brother for seven years."

    "Seven years!" exclaimed Orsino in awe. "What a **virtuous** lady. She would make a devoted and faithful lover. I should have **wooed** her even harder," he moaned.

B = *suggested sentence for the board or overhead*   *C* = *sentence written correctly*   *LD* = *literary device*

12. ❤ motley, nubile   •

LD - narration; subplot; establishment of setting

Paragraph - place and subject change

Commas - 2 introductory adverbs; list of nouns; compound sentence; 2 adjectives; appositive (non-restrictive modifier)

Compound sentence - review

Compound subject

Prepositions - review

Collective nouns - "bunch" must be treated as singular (bunch is or was)

Subject/verb agreement - In this case "bunch" is followed by the plural form of the verb because the "bunch" are also joined by the captain and young lady.

No commas around "Viola" - a single-word appositive closely related to preceding word; also a restrictive modifier

NOTE: Collective nouns are difficult for students to grasp at any age. It might be a good idea to review the common ones here. A list can be found in the Appendix.

B - meanwhile somewhere by the seashore a sea captain a young lady and a **motley** bunch of sailors were having a discussion. they had been shipwrecked nearby and all had barely escaped drowning. the young **nubile** maiden viola was concerned for the fate of her twin brother sebastian

C -   Meanwhile, somewhere by the seashore, a sea captain, a young lady, and a **motley** bunch of sailors were having a discussion. They had been shipwrecked nearby, and all had barely escaped drowning. The young, **nubile** maiden Viola was concerned for the fate of her twin brother, Sebastian.

13. disquieted   •

Paragraph - new person speaking

Commas - direct address; compound sentence; introductory subordinate clause (adverb out of place); "too" meaning "also"

Quotation

Interrogatives - question marks needed

Run-on sentence - lack of punctuation

Commonly confused words - where/were

Subordinate clause - review

Often confused words - affect/effect ("affect" to change; "effect" to cause or a cause)

Pronouns - "I" as subject and "me" as object

Relative pronouns - who/whom ("who" as subject and "whom" as object)

Irregular verb - to be

Homophone - their/there/they're

B - where are we my dear captain what happened to my brother me and him are very close and I look just like him if i lived perhaps he did too what do you think asked viola which was **disquieted** and very effected by the fact that her brother be not their

C -   "Where are we, my dear captain? What happened to my twin brother? He and I are very close, and I look just like him. If I lived, perhaps he did, too. What do you think?" asked Viola who was **disquieted** and very affected by the fact that her brother was not there.

➥ **SUGGESTIONS:**

Try confusing your students by slipping in a correct homophone now and then. It drives them crazy, and forces them to think.

This is another good spot for a general pronoun review. I find that drawing simple charts on the board, putting each type of pronoun in a separate box, helps students recognize them more readily. I point out the pronouns whose forms repeat (like "her" as a possessive and as an object pronoun).

B = suggested sentence for the board or overhead   C = sentence written correctly   LD = literary device

14. siblings ●

LD - personification ("ship wrecked itself")

Paragraph - new person speaking

Commas - direct address; quote; introductory subordinate clause (adverb out of place and long introductory adverb); appositive; compound sentence

Compound subject

Quotation - Note no end quotation marks as quote continued in next paragraph.

Pronouns - "I" as subject and "me" as object with "I" placed last; "he" as subject and "him" as object

Adjectives - this/that/these/those; review 3 uses of adjectives

Homophones - piece/peace, know/no, your/you're

Spelling rule - "i" before "e" except after "c".......

Possessive pronouns

Non-restrictive modifiers - In this case Viola has only one twin brother, so it is not necessary to supply his name.

Sentence structure - review the differences between compound and complex sentences

B - me and you and all these sailors are in illyria madame replied the captain. i no because me and my **siblings** grew up here. when the ship wrecked itself on these fell rocks it split in two pieces. i saw youre twin brother sebastian lash himself to the mast but the mast and him were swept out to sea *(to be continued in the next Caught'ya)*

C - "You and I and all these sailors are in Illyria, Madame," replied the captain. "I know because my **siblings** and I grew up here. When the ship wrecked itself on these fell rocks, it split in two pieces. I saw your twin brother, Sebastian, lash himself to the mast, but the mast and he were swept out to sea. *(to be continued in the next Caught'ya)*

15. ethereal ●

LD - literary allusion; simile; tale within a tale

Paragraph - change to comparison

Commas - "only" is used as conjunction in compound sentence; quote

Quotation

Punctuation - use of parentheses for added information (commas or dashes would also be all right)

Relative pronouns - who/whom/whose/whoever/ whomever/that/which ("that" and "which" can be subject or object and are used only with objects and animals; "who" and "whom" are used with people; "who" is subject; "whom" is object)

B - he was like arion a greek poet and musician that so charmed the dolphins with his **ethereal** music that one saved him from drowning on his dolphin only sebastian was riding a mast into the waves the captain concluded

C - "He was like Arion (a Greek poet and musician who so charmed the dolphins with his **ethereal** music that one saved him from drowning) on his dolphin, only Sebastian was riding a mast into the waves," the captain concluded.

➥ **SUGGESTION:**

This is a good point to hold a discussion on the difference between a clause and a phrase. See the Appendix for more information on the subject.

16. ❤ mollified, animate ●

Paragraph - new person speaking

Commas - quote; participial phrase; introductory subordinate clause

Quotation

Verb tense - use of pluperfect; subjunctive needed in "if" clause to express a condition that is impossible

Homophone - seen/scene

Irregular verb -rise/raise

Collective nouns - "family" is singular,

Often confused words - affect/effect ("affect" to change; "effect" to cause)

B - he must be alive insisted viola **mollified** by the thought that her twin had last been seen **animate**. if i thought he wasnt i would try to rise him from the depths. my family are everything to me. i must affect his rescue

C - "He must be alive," insisted Viola, **mollified** by the thought that her twin had last been seen **animate**. "If I thought he weren't, I would try to raise him from the depths. My family is everything to me. I must effect his rescue."

B = suggested sentence for the board or overhead   *C = sentence written correctly*   *LD = literary device*

17. lugubriously ●

Paragraph

Commas - quote; introductory phrase at beginning

Quotation

Pronouns - too many pronouns make meaning unclear (noun needed in each paragraph)

Often confused words - then/than ("then" is an adverb and "than" is a conjunction used to compare)

Possession - singular noun

Homophone - their/there/they're

Relative pronouns - who/whom/whose/whoever/whomever/that/which ("that" and "which" can be subject or object and are used only with objects and animals; "who" and "whom" are used with people; "who" is subject; "whom" is object)

Collective nouns ("rest" and "crew") treated as singular and need singular verbs and adjectives

Pronouns - "I" as subject and "me" as object; mention "I" last in a series

Adjective vs. adverb - "good" as adjective and "well" as adverb

Use of infinitive

Often confused prepositions - between/among ("between" for 2; "among" for 3 or more)

B - the captain than dashed her hopes. theyre is a strong possibility that only me and you and these few sailors that now stand around us survived the wreck. the rest of the crew are probably dead he **lugubriously** concluded. between us we did good to survive

C -   The captain then dashed Viola's hopes. "There is a strong possibility that only you and I and these few sailors who now stand around us survived the wreck. The rest of the crew is probably dead," he **lugubriously** concluded. "Among us, we did well to survive."

18. meritorious ●

LD - conversation; literary reference (Orsino)

5 Paragraphs - conversation

Commas - quote; extraneous word ('then'); interjection; quote

Quotations

Punctuation - quotations with question mark

Relative pronouns - who/whom/whose/whoever/whomever/that/which ("that" and "which" can be subject or object and are used only with objects and animals; "who" and "whom" are used with people; "who" is subject; "whom" is object)

Interrogative pronouns - who/what

Homophones - who's/whose and no/know

Contraction

Use of inversion - indicates interrogative

Indentation - use of indention only in order to indicate who is speaking

Punctuation - periods and commas *always* go inside quotation mark (no exception)

B - who rules this country asked viola. a noble duke whos name is as **meritorious** as his nature replied the captain. whats his name then. orsino. ah i no of him said viola. he was a bachelor at that time. is he still unwed

C -   "Who rules this country?" asked Viola.

      "A noble duke whose name is as **meritorious** as his nature," replied the captain.

      "What's his name, then?"

      "Orsino."

      "Ah, I know of him," said Viola. "He was a bachelor at that time. Is he still unwed?"

B = *suggested sentence for the board or overhead*   **C** = *sentence written correctly*   **LD** = *literary device*

19. rejoined •

Paragraph - new person speaking

Commas - introductory word or phrase like "yes," "no," "well;" quote; date; introductory prepositional phrase ("according to" is a preposition)

Quotation - ño end quotation marks as continued in next paragraph

Like vs. as - incorrect use of "like" ("Like" is used only in a direct comparison between two nouns or pronouns.)

Verb tense - need for subjunctive in "if" clause

Coordinating conjunctions - for, and, nor, but, or, yet, so **FANBOYS** (Do not begin a sentence with one.)

Homophone -fair/fare

B - well he was a month ago **rejoined** the captain. i saw him last on august 26 1602. i remember it like it was yesterday. but according to gossip he seeks the love of the fare olivia *(to be continued in next Caught'ya)*

C -   "Well, he was a month ago," **rejoined** the captain. "I saw him last on August 26, 1602. I remember it as if it were yesterday. According to gossip, he seeks the love of the fair Olivia.

↪ **SUGGESTION:**

Since all nine comma rules have been introduced in the previous Caught'yas, this might be a good point to pause and review them all together. You can find a copy of the rules, with examples to illustrate each, in the Appendix of this book under the heading "Comma Rules."

---

20. ♥ **virtuous, demise,** ♥ **abjured** •

LD - description within dialogue; anecdote (story about Olivia)

Paragraph - time change

Commas - interrupter; quote; introductory adverbial clause (optional)

Quotation

Incorrect verb tense switch - story in past

Splitting verbs - don't

Possession - singular collective noun

Confusing plural with possessive nouns

Relative pronouns - who/whom ("who" as subject and "whom" as object)

Common spelling error - since

Possession - plural noun that does not end in "s" takes "'s"

Often confused words - affect/effect

B - within the past year however olivia has lost her father and her brother the captain continues. she was a **virtuous** maid whom was really affected by her families **demise**. sence then she has totally **abjured** mens sight and company

C -   "Within the past year, however, Olivia has lost her father and her brother," the Captain continued. "She was a **virtuous** maid who really was affected by her family's **demise**. Since then, she totally has **abjured** men's sight and company."

B = *suggested sentence for the board or overhead*   *C* = *sentence written correctly*   *LD* = *literary device*

21. bereft, sequestering

Paragraph - new person speaking

Commas - introductory word or phrase; quote; interjection; subordinate clause at beginning; 2 adjectives where 2nd is not age, color, or linked to noun; compound sentence

Quotation - no end quotation mark due to continuation in next paragraph

Semicolons - could substitute one for some of the 4 commas in the first sentence

Contraction

Common spelling error - until

Relative pronouns - who/whom/whose/whoever/whomever/that/which ("that" and "which" can be subject or object and are used only with objects and animals; "who" and "whom" are used with people; "who" is subject; "whom" is object)

Verb tense - correct use of conditional tense

Dangling modifier - adverb in awkward place

Homophone - no/know

Complex sentence - no comma after "impossible" as subordinate clause is at end

NOTE: Review subordinating conjunctions (after, although, **as** — when, while, where — how — if — than — even though — because, before — until, unless — since, so that — **A White Bus**)

B - in other words orsino wont have any luck stated viola. oh i would like to be a servant for that poor **bereft** lady that shares my sorrow untill my own circumstances improve but i no that would be impossible if she is **sequestering** herself *(to be continued in the next Caught'ya)*

C -   "In other words, Orsino won't have any luck," stated Viola. "Oh, until my own circumstances improve, I would like to be a servant for that poor, **bereft** lady who shares my sorrow, but I know that would be impossible if she is **sequestering** herself. *(to be continued in the next Caught'ya)*

➥ SUGGESTION:

This is another good spot to review the eight parts of speech since all eight are represented in Caught'ya #21.

➥ SUGGESTION:

I suggest having your students memorize the coordinating and subordinating conjunctions. It is not hard. Use the suggested acronyms, put the words to a beat, and students will learn them quickly. Simply repeat them each time one shows up in a Caught'ya. In this painless manner, the conjunctions will be memorized. Once the conjunctions are memorized, students then can learn comma placement and compound and complex sentences.

---

*B = suggested sentence for the board or overhead   C = sentence written correctly   **LD** = literary device*

22. ingratiate, ♥ eunuch •

Paragraph - new topic

Commas - direct address; quote

Quotation - note punctuation in a new paragraph that continues a quotation

Adjective vs. adverb - "good" as adjective and "well" as adverb

Verb tense - use of future tense

Homophone - to/too/two

Complex sentence - no comma after "him" as subordinate clause is at end

Irregular verb - find/found/has been found ("be found" incorrect form)

Common spelling error - until

Possessive pronouns

Subordinating conjunctions - review

B - captain i will pay you good if you will help me **ingratiate** myself to this duke orsino. i will present myself to him as a **eunuch** viola decided and sing too him and serve him good until my brother be found

C -   "Captain, I will pay you well if you will help me **ingratiate** myself to this Duke Orsino. I will present myself to him as a **eunuch**," Viola decided, "and sing and serve him well until my brother is found."

➡ SUGGESTION:

From now on, every time you encounter a subordinate clause, it is a good idea to review the subordinating conjunctions and the rules for punctuating such a clause. Once your students understand this simple comma rule (comma if clause is at beginning of sentence and no comma if it is at the end), this common mistake will miraculously disappear from their writing.

23. ♥ mute •

Paragraph - new person speaking

Commas - compound sentence

Quotation

Irregular verbs - lie/lay/has lain and lay/laid/has laid

Transitive vs. intransitive verbs - review

Common spelling errors - "no one" is two words; so are "a lot" and "all right"

Subject/ pronoun agreement - "no one" is a singular noun; "their" is plural

Subject/verb agreement - you are

Regular comparatives - wild/wilder/wildest

Complex sentence - no comma after "captain" as subordinate clause at end of sentence

B - i shall remain **mute** and your secret will lay safe with me. noone will know in their most wild dream that you is a woman promised the captain as they walked to the dukes palace

C -   "I shall remain **mute**, and your secret will lie safe with me. No one will know in his or her wildest dream that you are a woman," promised the Captain as they walked to the Duke's palace.

B = *suggested sentence for the board or overhead*   *C* = *sentence written correctly*   *LD* = *literary device*

24. ❤ belch, ❤ quaffing ●●●

LD - double entendre and irony (name of uncle who drinks too much and belches a lot)

Paragraph - narrator with place change

Commas - 2 introductory adverbs; appositive; appositive (non-restrictive modifier as she has only one maid so name is not necessary); introductory word or phrase

Transition - needed to indicate change

Possession - singular noun

Semicolon - may use in compound sentence instead of conjunction

Uses of semicolon - in a series of independent clauses, in a compound sentence instead of a conjunction, and after a colon (for clarity) if the list uses commas

Spelling rule - "i" before "e".....

Relative pronouns - who/whom/whose/whoever/ whomever/that/which ("that" and "which" can be subject or object and are used only with objects and animals; "who" and "whom" are used with people; "who" is subject; "whom" is object)

Common spelling error - until

Homophones - quit/quite/quiet, no/know

Incorrect word use - "tonight" (story in the past tense; "tonight" and "today" require present tense)

B - meanwhile at olivias house olivias uncle sir toby **belch** was criticizing his neice to her serving maid maria. now sir belch was a man that was known for frequently **quaffing** spirits untill he was quit intoxicated tonight was no exception

C -   Meanwhile, at Olivia's house, Olivia's uncle, Sir Toby **Belch**, was criticizing his niece to her serving maid, Maria. Now, Sir Belch was a man who was known for frequently **quaffing** spirits until he was quite intoxicated; that night was no exception.

25. ❤ apt, sot, vociferously, egregious ●●●●●●●●●●●●●●●●●●●●●●●●●●●●●●●●●●●

LD - humor; description; building suspense; oxymoron ("sober sot")

No paragraph

Comma - elaboration (extra information)

Possession - singular noun

Run-on sentence - lack of punctuation

Relative pronouns - who/whom/whose/whoever/ whomever/that/which ("that" and "which" can be subject or object and are used only with objects and animals; "who" and "whom" are used with people; "who" is subject; "whom" is object)

Common spelling error - "a lot" is 2 words; so are "all right" and "no one"

Parallel construction - "on people"

B - this was why sir toby belchs name was so **apt** he was a sober **sot** that belched **vociferously** when he drank alot sir belch had one other **egregious** fault he delighted in playing tricks on people especially on obnoxious people

C - This was why Sir Toby Belch's name was so **apt**. He was a sober **sot** who belched **vociferously** when he drank a lot. Sir Belch had one other **egregious** fault. He delighted in playing tricks on people, especially on obnoxious people.

26. melodramatic, ❤ melancholy ●●

LD - alliteration (m, m, m)

Paragraph - subject change

Commas - appositive (non-restrictive modifier as he has only one niece)

Indirect quotation - avoidance of quotes by use of "that"

Spelling rule - "I" before "e" except after "c" and neighbor and weigh are weird

Homophone - to/too/two

Often confused words - farther/further ("farther" indicates a measurable distance)

B - sir belch thought that his only niece olivia was taking this mourning of her brother to far. he did not want olivia to go any farther in her **melodramatic melancholy**

C -   Sir Belch thought that his only niece, Olivia, was taking this mourning of her brother too far. He did not want Olivia to go any further in her **melodramatic melancholy**.

B = *suggested sentence for the board or overhead*   **C** = *sentence written correctly*   **LD** = *literary device*

27. ♥ **upbraided, slovenly, vociferated** (verb), ♥ **tosspot** •

LD - play on words ("tosspot" meaning 1) to be a drunk and 2) a pot in which to vomit); **euphemism** ("perdition" for "Hell")

Paragraph - new person speaking

Commas - interrupter; quote; introductory subordinate clause ("if" clause)

Quotation

Incorrect verb-tense switch - story in past

Homophone - your/you're, its/it's

Possessive pronouns - my, your, his, her, its, our, their

Capitalization - always capitalize "God"

Verb tense - subjunctive with "if" clause ("If I were you..."); correct use of conditional

B - maria on the other hand **upbraided** sir belch for his **slovenly** ways. you will go to perdition for youre godless ways she **vociferated**. you are nothing but a **tosspot**. its a shame. if i was you i would mend my ways (to be continued in the next Caught'ya)

C - Maria, on the other hand, **upbraided** Sir Belch for his **slovenly** ways. "You will go to perdition for your Godless ways," she **vociferated**. "You are nothing but a **tosspot**. It's a shame! If I were you, I would mend my ways. *(Continued in the next Caught'ya)*

28. fatuous •

LD - deliberate *non sequitur* (talking of drinking and then wooing)

No paragraph - continuation

Commas - direct address; interrupted quote; compound sentence; direct address

Quotation - interrupted (note punctuation)

Preposition - avoid ending a sentence with one

Adverbs - awkward placement of adverb "yesterday"

Spelling rules - if word ends in consonant/vowel/ consonant and a suffix is added, double the consonant ("quaffing"); "i" before "e" except after "c". . .

Relative pronouns - who/whom/whose/whoever/ whomever/that/which ("that" and "which" can be subject or object and are used only with objects and animals; "who" and "whom" are used with people; "who" is subject; "whom" is object)

Voice - discuss active vs. passive voice (avoid passive)

Types of sentences - review simple, compound, complex, and compound/complex sentences

B - really sir belch maria continued you must come in earlier. your niece hates the hours you keep and your quafing will do you in. i heard my lady talking yesterday of a foolish knight which you brought in one night to woo her. you **fatuous** sot what were you thinking

C - Really, Sir Belch," Maria continued, "you must come in earlier. Your niece hates the hours you keep, and your quaffing will undo you. Yesterday I heard my lady talking of a foolish knight whom you brought in one night to woo her. You **fatuous** sot, what were you thinking?"

29. fervently •

LD - double entendre and irony (the name "Aguecheek"); **deliberate use of** *non sequitur*

Paragraph - new person speaking

Commas - verb series

Quotation

Interrogative pronouns - why, what, which, who, whom ("who" is subject)

Incorrect verb-tense switch - story in past tense

Run-on sentence - lack of punctuation

Sentence combining - combine into a series for more clarity

Contractions

Pronouns - only in a noun can an apostrophe show possession; pronouns are never contracted nor ever take an apostrophe

B - who sir andrew aguecheek asks sir belch **fervently** hes tall hes rich he plays the violoncello he speaks several languages hes a real catch do you have some ale

C - "Who? Sir Andrew Aguecheek?" asked Sir Belch **fervently**. "He's tall and rich, plays the violoncello, and speaks several languages. He's a real catch. Do you have some ale?"

B = suggested sentence for the board or overhead   *C = sentence written correctly*   *LD = literary device*

30. ❤ knave, ❤ lecher, ❤ quarreler, inebriated ●

LD - use of direct quote; reference to mythology (Narcissus was concerned only with his looks); **use of made-up word**

Paragraph - new person speaking

Commas - noun series; quote

Quotation

Hyphen - 2 words acting as one

Relative pronouns - who/whom/whose/whoever/ whomever/that/which ("that" and "which" can be subject or object and are used only with objects and animals; "who" and "whom" are used with people; "who" is subject; "whom" is object)

Quote within a quote

Punctuation - use of quotation marks around archaic or made-up word; placement of comma inside single quote

Often confused words - then/than ("then" is an adverb and "than" is a conjunction used to compare)

Irregular verbs - lie/lay/has lain and lay/laid/has laid

Transitive vs. intransitive verbs - review

B - sir aguecheek is a Narcissus-like **knave**, a **lecher**, a "**quarreler**" a gambler and a coward that drinks nightly with you sir belch and then lays **inebriated** on the floor accused maria

C -   "Sir Aguecheek is a Narcissus-like **knave**, a **lecher**, a '**quarreler**,' a gambler, and a coward who drinks nightly with you, Sir Belch, and then lies **inebriated** on the floor," accused Maria.

31. ❤ amend, ❤ heathen, ❤ dissembling ●

LD - alliteration

No paragraph - continuation

Commas - interrupter; quote; interjection

Quotation

Splitting verbs - avoid if possible; avoid splitting infinitives as well

Homophone - hear/here

Parts of speech - review the 8 parts

B - he like you will probably never **amend** his **heathen** ways she concluded. ah hear comes the **dissembling** drunkard now

C - "He, like you, probably never will **amend** his **heathen** ways," she concluded. "Ah, here comes the **dissembling** drunkard now."

➥ **SUGGESTION:**

This is another good spot to review the eight parts of speech since all eight are represented in Caught'ya #31.

32. ❤ shrew ●

LD - play on words (Aguecheek also means a tick in the cheek, often caused by excessive drinking); **double entendre** ("shrew")

2 Paragraphs - 2 different speakers

Commas - interjection; direct address; direct address; quote; direct address; use of "too" meaning also; direct address; quote

Quotation

Spelling rules - "i" before "e"....

Homophone - to/too/two

Capitalization - title

B - ah sir toby belch my friend. bless you maria you fair **shrew** sir aguecheek said in greeting. sweet sir aguecheek you to sir answered sir belch

C -   "Ah, Sir Toby Belch, my friend. Bless you, Maria, you fair **shrew**," Sir Aguecheek said in greeting.

    "Sweet Sir Aguecheek, you, too, Sir," answered Sir Belch.

B = suggested sentence for the board or overhead   C = sentence written correctly   LD = literary device

33. ❤ rapier, ❤ wit, aspersions, abhorred　• •

LD - aphorism (worse for wear); **character development**

Paragraph - narrator again

Commas - for clarity in out-of-place adverbial phrases

Run-on sentence - lack of punctuation

Verb tense - incorrect use of conditional tense as a substitute for past tense

Pronoun use - overuse of pronouns makes meaning unclear

Misplaced modifier - She made aspersions with her wit, not his drinking.

Indirect quotation - avoidance of quotes with use of "that"

Prepositions - review

B - she and he would exchange a few insults and jests with him coming off the worse for wear she would upbraid him for his lechery and would make **aspersions** to his drinking with her **rapier wit**. it was clear that she **abhorred** the fellow

C -　Maria and Sir Aguecheek exchanged a few insults and jests, with Sir Aguecheek coming off the worse for wear. She upbraided him for his lechery and, with her **rapier wit**, made **aspersions** to his drinking. It was clear that she **abhorred** the fellow.

34. articulate　• •

LD - humor

Paragraph - subject change

Commas - introductory prepositional phrase (adverb); appositive

Numbers - write out to 99

Verb tense - incorrect use of conditional tense instead of past tense

Possession - singular noun

Often confused words - fewer/less ("fewer" can be counted; "less" is a vague, uncountable amount)

Often confused words - then/than ("then" is an adverb; "than" is a conjunction used to compare)

Possession - plural noun ending in "s"

Capitalization - names of countries and languages

B - with maria gone the 2 tosspots sir belch and sir aguecheek would conspire. they would discuss sir aguecheeks chances as olivias suitor which sir aguecheek thought fewer then his 2 hunting dogs chances to **articulate** words in french.

C -　With Maria gone, the two tosspots, Sir Belch and Sir Aguecheek, conspired. They discussed Sir Aguecheek's chances as Olivia's suitor which Sir Aguecheek thought were less than his two hunting dogs' chances to **articulate** words in French.

35. bemoaned, bestowed, wenching　• •

LD - character development

No paragraph - continuation

Commas - long introductory adverb; quote; noun series

Compound verb

Verb tense - use of pluperfect tense to denote action anterior to this paragraph

No comma after "wit" - not a compound sentence (no subject)

Punctuation - use of quote during narration

Possession - singular noun

Capitalization - cities, states, counties, countries

Indirect quotation - avoidance of quotes with use of "that"

Comparisons - "as much.....as"

Parallel construction - needed in series (gerunds)

Use of strong verbs

B - during the course of the conversation sir aguecheek **bemoaned** his lack of wit and blamed it on the fact that he was as he said a great eater of beef. he could not understand sir belchs use of french and whined that he wished that he had **bestowed** as much time in study as he had in gambling dance **wenching** and fencing

C - During the course of the conversation, Sir Aguecheek **bemoaned** his lack of wit and blamed it on the fact that he was, as he said, "a great eater of beef." He could not understand Sir Belch's use of French and whined that he wished that he had **bestowed** as much time in study as he had in gambling, dancing, **wenching**, and fencing.

B = *suggested sentence for the board or overhead*　　*C* = *sentence written correctly*　　*LD* = *literary device*

36. hedonist ●

LD - character development

No paragraph - continuation

Comma - introductory gerund phrase

Relative pronouns - who/whom/whose/whoever/whomever/that/which ("that" and "which" can be subject or object and are used only with objects and animals; "who" and "whom" are used with people; "who" is subject; "whom" is object)

Complex sentence with relative pronoun - "who" is needed as subject

Homophone - quit/quiet/quite

B - being a **hedonist** which was a slave to his immediate desires and not able to wait for anything sir aguecheek was ready to give up his pursuit of olivia and quite illyria

C - Being a **hedonist** who was a slave to his immediate desires and not able to wait for anything, Sir Aguecheek was ready to give up his pursuit of Olivia and quit Illyria.

37. a plethora of ●

LD - building suspense

Paragraph - new person speaking

Quotation

Coordinating conjunctions - deliberate use of "and" to begin a fragment for conversational effect

Sentence structure - use of fragment for effect

Often confused words - fewer/less ("fewer" can be counted; "less" is a vague, uncountable amount)

Plural rules - consonant "y" changed to "i" and add "es"

Punctuation - use of exclamation for emphasis

Subject/possessive pronoun agreement - "everyone" is singular, collective noun

Collective nouns and pronouns - discuss

B - sir belch persuaded his friend to stay for another month. their will be no less than ten partys held next month and masquerade balls and **a plethora of** drink he argued. everyone in town will host their own party

C - Sir Belch persuaded his friend to stay for another month. "There will be no fewer than ten parties held next month. And masquerade balls. And **a plethora of** drink!" he argued. "Everyone in town will host his or her own party."

38. revels, ♥ portend ●

LD - narrator aside; building suspense

Paragraph - narrator again

No commas

Incorrect verb-tense switch - story in past ("agreed")

Common spelling errors - "a lot" is 2 words, so are "all right" and "no one"

Punctuation - use of parentheses for narrator aside

Correct use of verb-tense switch - indicates narrator aside ("is this...")

Spelling rules - "i" before "e"...

Possession - singular noun

B - sir aguecheek agrees to stay with the promise of alot of such **revels**. is this a **portend** of an ulterior motive for his fervor in convincing his freind to stay

C - Sir Aguecheek agreed to stay with the promise of a lot of such **revels**. (Is this a **portend** of an ulterior motive for Sir Belch's fervor in convincing his friend to stay?)

B = *suggested sentence for the board or overhead*   **C** = *sentence written correctly*   **LD** = *literary device*

39. shrewd, sagacious ●

LD - alliteration; aphorism

Paragraph - subject change

Commas - appositive; 2 adjectives

Possession - singular noun

Misplaced modifier - Viola disguised herself, not the household

Punctuation - quotes around "him" to indicate deceptive role; placement of period inside quote even though quote is only one word

Verb tense - use of pluperfect to denote action anterior to this paragraph

Pronouns - "him" as object of preposition

No commas around Cesario - restrictive modifier

Often confused words - further/farther

Splitting infinitives - avoid splitting infinitives (The *Star Trek* announcer was wrong. It is never "to boldly go" but instead "to go boldly." Here it is "to disguise her sex further.")

B - viola a **shrewd sagacious** lady quickly ingratiated herself into the dukes household in disguise as a young man. valentine and the duke immediately took a fancy to him. viola used a boys name cesario to further disguise her sex

C -   Viola, a **shrewd, sagacious** lady in disguise as a young man, quickly ingratiated herself into the Duke's household. Valentine and the Duke immediately took a fancy to "him." Viola used a boy's name Cesario to disguise her sex further.

40. stature, stripling ●

LD - double entendre ("inconsistent in his favors")

3 Paragraphs - 3 different speakers

Commas - direct address; quote; direct address; quote

Quotations

Possession - singular noun

Interrogative - question mark goes inside quote

Possessive pronoun - his

Relative pronouns - who/whom/whose/whoever/ whomever/that/which ("that" and "which" can be subject or object and are used only with objects and animals; "who" and "whom" are used with people; "who" is subject; "whom" is object)

Homophone - hear/here

Pronouns - review types and use

B - cesario you are about to move up in **stature** in the dukes service said valentine to the disguised viola. does this mean that he is inconsistent in his favors queried viola who had already fallen in love with duke orsino. hush **stripling** here he comes warned valentine

C -   "Cesario, you are about to move up in **stature** in the Duke's service," said Valentine to the disguised Viola.

   "Does this mean that he is inconsistent in his favors?" queried Viola who had already fallen in love with Duke Orsino.

   "Hush, **stripling**, here he comes," warned Valentine.

➡ **SUGGESTION:**

This is another good spot to review the eight parts of speech since all eight are represented in Caught'ya #40.

---

41. divulged •••

LD - irony (Viola is forced to curry Olivia's favor for the Duke whom she herself loves.)

Paragraph - new person speaking

Commas - direct address; long introductory adverb; introductory word or phrase; introductory subordinate clause (adverb out of place)

Quotation

Imperative sentences - subjects implied

Homophone - soul/sole

Pronouns - use of too many pronouns for clarity

Often confused words - affect/effect ("affect" to change; "effect" to cause of a cause)

Possession - singular noun

Common spelling error - until

Subordinating conjunctions and subordinate clauses - review

B - cesario i trust you. in the brief time you have been with us i have **divulged** my secret sole to you. therefore i ask you to affect a change in Olivias affection for me. do not leave her door untill she agrees to see you. when you see her speak of me orsino commanded viola

C - "Cesario, I trust you. In the brief time you have been with us, I have **divulged** my secret soul to you. Therefore, I ask you to effect a change in Olivia's affection for me. Do not leave her door until she agrees to see you. When you see her, speak of me," Orsino commanded Viola.

42. ❤ clamorous, stead, languish ••••••••••••••••••••••••••••

No paragraph - continued

Commas - quote; direct address; direct address; compound sentence

Quotation

Imperative sentences - subjects implied

Spelling rules - "i" before "e".....

Common spelling errors - "a lot" is 2 words; "all right" is also 2 words

Adjective vs. adverb - "good" as adjective; "well" as adverb

B - orsino continued win her for me my freind. make **clamorous** sounds. be persistent. woo her for me in my **stead**. do not return to me without alot of good news. do good cesario for i **languish** of love

C - Orsino continued, "Win her for me, my friend. Make **clamorous** sounds. Be persistent. Woo her for me in my **stead**. Do not return to me without a lot of good news. Do well, Cesario, for I **languish** of love."

43. disconcerted, ❤ woe ••••••••••••••••••••••••••••••••••

Paragraph - new subject

Commas - appositive; interjection; introductory subordinate clause; interrupter for clarification

Quotation

Pronouns - "I" as subject and "me" as object

Relative pronouns - "whom" needed as object of verb "loved"

Subordinating conjunctions and complex sentences - review

Often confused words - then/than ("then" is an adverb; "than" is a conjunction used to compare)

Verb tense - use conditional or subjunctive with "if" clause

Splitting verbs - avoid

Pronouns - the use of "I" in last sentence ("am" is implied)

Incorrect word use - "Should have" not "should of" should be used since "should" needs to be followed by a helping verb, not a preposition; "of" makes no sense here as there is no object.

Negatives - avoid double negative

Like vs. as - incorrect use of "like" ("Like" is used only in a direct comparison between two nouns or pronouns.)

B - viola was **disconcerted** by the idea of wooing olivia for orsino the man who she secretly loved. oh **woe** is i. if i woo her successfully for him than her not me will be his wife. she is no more deserving then me. I shouldnt never of disguised myself like a man

C - Viola was **disconcerted** by the idea of wooing Olivia for Orsino, the man whom she secretly loved. "Oh, **woe** is me. If I woo her successfully for him, then she, not I, would be his wife. She is no more deserving than I. I never should have disguised myself as a man."

B = *suggested sentence for the board or overhead*   **C** = *sentence written correctly*   **LD** = *literary device*

44. redoubtable, barbs, transgressions ●

LD - irony (Feste's statement), **direct quote from Shakespeare**

2 Paragraphs - 2 persons speaking (narrator and Feste)

Commas - introductory subordinate clause; appositive; interrupter; quote

Quotation

Splitting verbs - don't

Often confused words - farther/further ("farther" indicates a measurable distance)

Spelling rule - if word ends in consonant/vowel/consonant and a suffix is added, double the consonant ("fretting")

Prepositions - review

B - while viola was further freting about her dilemma the **redoubtable** maria and feste the jester were exchanging **barbs**. feste as usual had been late. maria threatened that olivia would hang him for his **transgressions**. feste retorted many a good hanging prevented a bad marriage

C - While Viola was fretting further about her dilemma, the **redoubtable** Maria and Feste, the jester, were exchanging **barbs**. Feste, as usual, had been late. Maria threatened that Olivia would hang him for his **transgressions**.

"Many a good hanging prevented a bad marriage," Feste retorted.

45. ♥ droll ●

LD - biblical allusion; synecdoche ("flesh" for a whole woman)

No paragraph - continuation

Commas - continued quote; introductory subordinate clause; adjective clause with relative pronoun as interrupter

Continued (interrupted) quote - punctuation

Homophones - no/know; piece/peace

Incorrect verb-tense switch - story in past ("continued")

Verb tense - need for subjunctive in "if" clause

Relative pronouns - who/whom/whose/whoever/whomever/that/which ("that" and "which" can be subject or object and are used only with objects and animals; "who" and "whom" are used with people; "who" is subject; "whom" is object)

Subject/verb agreement - you are

Irregular verb - to be

Pronouns - "he" as subject and "him" as object

Possession - singular noun

B - you no feste continues to Maria if sir toby belch gave up his drinking you who is such an intelligent and **droll** peace of eves flesh and him might be interested in each other

C - "You know," Feste continued to Maria, "if Sir Toby Belch were to give up his drinking, you, who are such an intelligent and **droll** piece of Eve's flesh, and he might be interested in each other."

46. ♥ implacable, ♥ rogue ●

LD - play on words; use of quote ("Better a witty....."); **literary reference** ("remember..."); **oxymoron** ("witty fool" and "foolish wit")

2 Paragraphs - 2 persons speaking

Commas - direct address; quote; quote; appositive; quote

Quotations

Punctuation - quote within a quote

Verb tense - past necessary in quote when referring to action anterior to now

Irregular comparisons - good/better/best

Capitalization - "Fool" refers to a specific job

Often confused words - then/than ("then" is an adverb; "than" is a conjunction used to compare)

B - go away again you **implacable rogue** said maria as she left the room. feste rejoined remember what quinapalus the greek said better a witty fool then a foolish wit

C - "Go away again, you **implacable rogue**," said Maria as she left the room.

Feste rejoined, "Remember what Quinapalus, the Greek, said. 'Better a witty fool than a foolish wit.'"

B = suggested sentence for the board or overhead   C = sentence written correctly   LD = literary device

47. ❤ churlish, miens, ❤ gravely ●

LD - play on words ("Malvolio" meaning "bad wishes" for the nasty person in the story); **double entendre** ("fool")

Paragraph - subject change

Commas - introductory subordinate clause; 2 adjectives; compound sentence introductory subordinate clause

Prepositions - avoid ending a sentence with one if at all possible

Homophone - their/there/they're

Spelling rule - "i" before "e".....

Capitalization - "Fool" is a specific job

Incorrect verb-tense switch - story in past

Types of sentences - review compound and complex sentences

B - as maria left the room olivia and the arrogant **churlish** malvolio came in. there **miens** were serious and they talked very **gravely**. as soon as olivia sees the fool she asks him to leave

C -   As Maria left the room, Olivia and the arrogant, **churlish** Malvolio entered. Their **miens** were serious, and they talked very **gravely**. As soon as Olivia saw the fool, she asked him to leave.

---

48. ❤ dexterously ●

LD - play on words (fool); **repartée; biblical reference**

3 Paragraphs - conversation

Commas - direct address; compound sentence; quote; direct address

Quotations

Semicolon - review 3 uses of semicolon (in a series of independent clauses, in a compound sentence instead of a conjunction as in this Caught'ya, and after a colon for clarity if the list uses commas)

Sentence structure - deliberate use of fragment in conversation

Inversion - to indicate interrogative

B - i will not go madame for i am not the fool you are feste retorted. prove it countered olivia. **dexterously** good lady. you mourn your brother. is his soul in hell

C -   "I will not go, Madame, for I am not the fool; you are," Feste retorted.

"Prove it," countered Olivia.

"**Dexterously**, good lady. You mourn your brother. Is his soul in Hell?"

---

49. levity ●

LD - continued play on words (fool as name and as idiot); **repartée; biblical references; development of character in conversation; humor**

4 Paragraphs - conversation

Commas - quote; direct address; direct address; compound sentence; quote; direct address

Quotations

Capitalization - "Fool" specifies a particular person; "Madonna" refers to person

Often confused words - then/than ("then" is an adverb; "than" is a conjunction used to compare)

Homophone - your/you're

B - olivia answered no fool it is in heaven. then only a fool would mourn my madonna for heaven is a wonderful place concluded feste. you lighten my mood with youre **levity** dear feste

C -   Olivia answered, "No, Fool, it is in heaven."

"Then only a fool would mourn, my Madonna, for heaven is a wonderful place," concluded Feste.

"You lighten my mood with your **levity**, dear Feste."

B = suggested sentence for the board or overhead   *C = sentence written correctly*   *LD = literary device*

50. haughty •

LD - sarcasm; alliteration (h,h and w,w,w); **description within action; anadiplosis** ("weak, man, weak"); **play on words** ("jesting"); **double entendre**

Paragraph - narrator again

Commas - introductory subordinate clause; extra descriptive phrase

Clauses vs. phrases - review the difference between

Irregular verb - raise/rise

Common spelling errors - "a lot" is 2 words and so is "all right"

Possession - singular nouns

Punctuation - use of quotation marks to denote sarcasm and double meaning

B - while olivias spirits were raised alot by festes jesting the humorless and **haughty** malvolio was not amused. this pompous and arrogant fool maintained that the jester was a weak man weak as his wit

C -   While Olivia's spirits were raised a lot by Feste's jesting, the humorless and **haughty** Malvolio was not amused. This pompous and arrogant "fool" maintained that the jester was a weak man, weak as his wit.

51. parry •

LD - narrator aside; simile; building of suspense; onomatopoeia and use of made-up words ("burbling and blupping")

No paragraph - continuation; paragraph for a narrator aside

Commas - introductory phrase; introductory word

Incorrect verb-tense switch

Punctuation - italics for emphasis

Verb tense - use of present tense to indicate narrator aside

"Like" vs. "as" - "like" needed in direct comparison

Word misuse - never use "is when" ("when" is a subordinating conjunction, not a predicate adjective)

B - needless to say feste holds his own in the verbal **parry**. malvolio was the real fool! now this is when the plot thickens like pudding burbling and blupping on the stove.

C - Needless to say, Feste held his own in the verbal **parry**. Malvolio was the *real* fool!

Now, this is the point where the plot thickens like pudding burbling and blupping on the stove.

B = suggested sentence for the board or overhead   C = sentence written correctly   LD = literary device

52. disconsolate •

Paragraph - subject change

Commas - long introductory participial phrase; compound sentence

Often confused prepositions - between/among ("between" for 2; "among" for 3 or more)

Numbers - write out to 99

Pronouns - "she" as subject and "her" as object or possessive

Dangling modifier - Maria is inserting herself, not Olivia

Indirect quotation - avoidance of quote with "that"

No comma after "handsome" - 2nd adjective is age

Demonstrative adjectives - this/that/these/those

Use of "none" as a qualifier or comparative

Often confused words - then/than ("then" is an adverb and "than" is a conjunction used to compare)

Quotation marks around "him" - "he" is really a "she" (a falsehood)

NOTE: Warn of the need to change the sentence around for clarity

B - inserting herself among the 2 verbally sparring men in order to speak to olivia her **disconsolate** mistress was informed by maria that a handsome young gentleman wanted to speak with she. that stripling was no other than viola in disguise as cesario and olivia wanted to send him away

C -   Inserting herself between the two verbally sparring men in order to speak to Olivia, Maria informed her **disconsolate** mistress that a young gentleman wanted to speak with her. This stripling was none other than Viola in disguise as Cesario, and Olivia wanted to send "him" away.

➥ **SUGGESTION:**

This would be a good point for a mid-term exam. You can type up as a test Caught'yas #53 to #57 for a good review of much of what your students have been practicing up to this point. Type the five Caught'yas together, without numbers or breaks, as one, long Caught'ya.

---

53. swain •

LD - aphorism, simile ("as drunk...")

No paragraph - continuation; new action paragraph

Commas - appositive; adjective clause with relative pronoun

Homophones - to/too/two, ensure/insure

Hyphen in "would-be"- two words are acting as one

Relative pronouns - who/whom/whose/whoever/ whomever/that/which ("that" and "which" can be subject or object and are used only with objects and animals; "who" and "whom" are used with people; "who" is subject; "whom" is object)

Misplaced modifier - need new sentence for clarity

Common spelling errors - "a lot" is 2 words; "all right" is also 2 words

Like vs. as - incorrect use of "like" ("Like" is used only in a direct comparison between two nouns or pronouns.)

Often confused words - fewer/less ("fewer" can be counted; "less" is a vague, uncountable amount)

Numbers - write out to 99

Plural vs. possessive nouns

Use of infinitives

B - olivia sent maria and malvolio too chase away the would be **swain**. sir toby belch the uncle that drank alot staggered into the room drunk like a skunk. olivia who loved her uncle even though he drank no less than 2 bottles' of spirits' a day sent feste to accompany sir belch to insure his safety

C - Olivia sent Maria and Malvolio to chase away the would-be **swain**. Sir Toby Belch, the uncle who drank a lot, staggered into the room. He was drunk as a skunk.

Olivia, who loved her uncle even though he drank no fewer than two bottles of spirits a day, sent Feste to accompany Sir Belch to ensure his safety.

B = suggested sentence for the board or overhead   C = sentence written correctly   LD = literary device

54. impart, ❤ approbation ●

LD - use of quote; simile

Paragraph - subject change

Commas - verb series

Compound verbs

Incorrect verb-tense switch - story in past

Punctuation - use of italics for emphasis

Punctuation - quotation marks needed around word used by itself ("no")

Punctuation - use of quotes around direct words of Cesario ("supporter to a bench")

Common spelling error - until

Complex sentence - no commas before "until" (subordinate clause at end of sentence)

B - malvolio returned to **impart** the news to olivia that the young fellow at the door was *very* insistent would not take no for an answer, and threatens to remain by her door like a "supporter to a bench" untill she gave her **approbation** to see him.

C -   Malvolio returned to **impart** the news to Olivia that the young fellow at the door was *very* insistent, would not take "no" for an answer, and threatened to remain by her door like a "supporter to a bench" until she gave her **approbation** to see him.

55. queried ●

LD - Deliberate use of non sequitur

Paragraph - new person speaking

Commas - interjection

Quotation - note punctuation of question

Punctuation - need question marks in interrogatives

Preposition - avoid ending a sentence with one if possible

Homophone - whose/who's

Relative pronouns - "who" is needed as subject of verb of being

Verb tense - use of pluperfect to refer to action anterior to this paragraph

Possession - singular noun

Common spelling error - persistence

Word misuse - "should have" not "should of" ("should" needs a helping verb; "of" is a preposition and makes no sense)

Irregular comparisons - good/better/best; worse/worst

B - what does he look like. where is he from.   how old is he. whom is he **queried** olivia whos resolve had weakened with the report of the young mans persistence. oh i should of combed my hair better.

C -   "What does he look like? From where is he ? How old is he? Who is he?" **queried** Olivia whose resolve had weakened with the report of the young man's persistence. "Oh, I should have combed my hair better."

(SUGGESTION:

This is another good spot to review the eight parts of speech since all eight are represented in Caught'yas #55 and #56.

---

56. dapper ●

LD - description in dialogue

2 Paragraphs - 2 persons speaking

Commas - quote; 2 interjections

Quotations

Run-on sentence - lack of punctuation

Common spelling error - "all right" not "alright"

Contractions

Parallel construction - needed for clarity ("not.....not")

B - hes alright hes not old enough for a man and not young enough for a boy hes very **dapper** replied malvolio. oh alright let him in olivia sighed

C -   "He is (*or he's*) all right. He's not old enough for a man and not young enough for a boy. He's very **dapper**," replied Malvolio.

   "Oh, all right, let him in," Olivia sighed.

B = suggested sentence for the board or overhead   C = sentence written correctly   LD = literary device

57. enthralled •

LD - hyperbole; irony

3 Paragraphs - narrator; 2 different speakers

Commas - participial phrase; interjection; direct address; adjective series; quote; compound sentence; participial phrase; 2 adjectives and second is not age, color, or linked

Quotation

Sentence structure - deliberate use of fragment in quotation

Punctuation - need for dots to indicate sentence left off in middle

Relative pronouns - "who" needed as subject of verb of being

Hyphen - 2 words acting as one

Homophone - fair/fare; veil/vale

B - olivia put a veil over her face just as viola still disguised as cesario entered the room. oh most radiant exquisite and unmatchable beauty viola began her prepared speech but olivia interrupted her. whom are you olivia asked. this mysterious fare faced youth **enthralled** her

C -   Olivia put a veil over her face the moment Viola, still disguised as Cesario, entered the room.

"Oh, most radiant, exquisite, and unmatchable beauty.....," Viola began her prepared speech, but Olivia interrupted her.

"Who are you?" Olivia asked. This mysterious, fair-faced youth **enthralled** her.

58. finesse •

LD - irony (Viola wants Orsino for herself and is forced to woo Olivia for him); **synecdoche** ("Olivia's hand" refers to the whole of Olivia)

Paragraph - narrator again

No commas

Possession - singular nouns

Plural vs. possessive nouns

Run-on sentence - lack of punctuation

Misplaced modifier - "with finesse" tells how she dodged

No comma after "speech" - not a compound sentence

Prepositions - review

B - viola dodged all olivias probes at her identity and background with **finesse** she kept trying to resume her speech and pressed orsinos suit for olivias hand in marriage

C -   Viola dodged with **finesse** all Olivia's probes at her identity and background. She kept trying to resume her speech and pressed Orsino's suit for Olivia's hand in marriage.

59. enraptured •

No paragraph - continuation

Pronouns -too many used here for clarity

Homophone - fair/fare

Collective nouns and pronouns - "everyone"

Reflexive pronouns - myself, yourself, himself, herself, ourselves, themselves (correct form needed)

B - she so **enraptured** her with her fair words and wit that she soon sent everyone else out of the room. she even persuaded her to unveil her

C - Viola so **enraptured** Olivia with her fair words and wit that Olivia soon sent everyone else out of the room. Viola even persuaded Olivia to unveil herself.

60. intercourse, lamented, comeliness •

LD - hyperbole

Paragraph - new person speaking

Commas - long introductory adverb; quote

Quotation

Homophones - their/there/they're, your/you're, know/no

Possessive pronouns

Compound verb

Negatives - avoid double negatives

B - during the course of there social **intercourse** viola **lamented** youre beauty is so overwhelming that it would be very cruel of you to carry your **comeliness** to the grave and not leave the world know copy

C -   During the course of their social **intercourse**, Viola **lamented**, "Your beauty is so overwhelming that it would be very cruel of you to carry your **comeliness** to the grave and leave the world no copy." (*or "not leave the world any copy."*)

B = *suggested sentence for the board or overhead*   *C* = *sentence written correctly*   *LD* = *literary device*

61. reiterate, profound •

LD - anadiplosis

No paragraph - continuation; paragraph when Olivia speaks

Commas - quote; participial phrase; compound sentence; quote

Quotation

Possession - singular noun

Sentence structure - deliberate use of one-word fragment

Negatives - use "nor" with negatives and reverse subject/verb; discuss

Homophone - no/know

Contractions

Spelling of common word - truly

B - orsino loves you with all his heart viola continued **reiterating** orsinos love. love orsino cant really love me. he doesnt truely no me or understand me so his love cant be very **profound** olivia maintained

C - Viola continued, **reiterating** Orsino's love, "Orsino loves you with all his heart."

"Love? Orsino can't really love me. He doesn't truly know me, nor does he understand me, so his love can't be very **profound**," Olivia maintained.

62. coyly •

LD - aphorism; sarcasm (another falling in love at nothing); **irony**

Paragraph - new topic, same speaker

Commas - compound sentence; interrupter; direct address, subordinate clause; quote; compound sentence

Quotation

Italics - use of italics for emphasis

Verb tense - correct use of conditional; remind not to use as substitute for past tense

Punctuation - use of quotation marks to denote irony, sarcasm, or falsehood ("young man"); period inside quote, even short one

B - i still do not wish to see orsino but on the other hand cesario if you wish to come again i would be most happy to see you olivia **coyly** said for she was already falling in love with the young man

C - "I still do not wish to see Orsino, but on the other hand, Cesario, if you wish to come again, I would be most happy to see you," Olivia **coyly** said, for she was already falling in love with the "young man."

63. idolizes, adulates, uncanny •

LD - repeated use of synonyms to make a point; soliloquy of narrator; narrator aside; building suspense and foreshadowing

Paragraph - narrator aside

Commas - interjection; interrupter; after a coordinating conjunction used as an interjection ("but")

Sentence structure - deliberate use of fragment

Punctuation - use of exclamation marks for emphasis

Verb tense - correct use of present tense (narrator steps out of story)

B - ah what a pickled plot. viola adores orsino. orsino **idolizes** olivia. olivia **adulates** cesario. cesario is really viola and vice versa. this is indeed an **uncanny** love triangle. but wait. it gets even more bizarre

C - Ah, what a pickled plot! Viola adores Orsino. Orsino **idolizes** Olivia. Olivia **adulates** Cesario. Cesario is really Viola and vice versa. This is, indeed, an **uncanny** love triangle. But, wait! It will get even more bizarre.

B = suggested sentence for the board or overhead   *C = sentence written correctly*   *LD = literary device*

64. ruse, subterfuge, rendezvous •

LD - substituting synonyms to avoid repetition; use of foreign word

Paragraph - subject change

Commas - extra information (non-restrictive modifier); adjective clause with relative pronoun

Dangling modifier - it is the ruse that is the subterfuge, not Olivia's mind

Incorrect verb-tense switch

Punctuation - use of quotes to denote confusion ("young man")

Infinitives

Relative pronouns - who/whom/whose/whoever/ whomever/that/which ("that" and "which" can be subject or object and are used only with objects and animals; "who" and "whom" are used with people; "who" is subject; "whom" is object)

B - intrigued with cesario olivia manufactures a **ruse** with her fertile mind a **subterfuge** designed to lure the young man who she found so cute to another **rendezvous**

C -   Intrigued with Cesario, Olivia's fertile mind manufactured a **ruse**, a **subterfuge** designed to lure the "young man," whom she found so cute, to another **rendezvous**.

65. apposite •

Paragraph - new person speaking

Commas - direct address; quote; introductory subordinate clause

Quotation

Verb tense - "if" clause needs subjunctive or future tense

Imperative sentence - subject implied

Word use - use of "that" instead of commas

Article - use "an" before a vowel or a silent "h"

B - malvolio run after cesario and give him this ring that he must have left olivia lied as she handed malvolio one of her rings. tell cesario that if he returns tomorrow i will inform him in great detail why orsino is not a **apposite** suitor

C -   "Malvolio, run after Cesario and give him this ring that he must have left," Olivia lied as she handed Malvolio one of her rings. "Tell Cesario that if he returns tomorrow, I will inform him in great detail why Orsino is not an **apposite** suitor."

66. embroiling, regal •

LD - subplot

Paragraph - new place, new people, subplot

Commas - introductory subordinate clause

No comma needed - between adjectives "embroiling" and "love" ("love" is linked to noun); between "many" and "tall" ("tall" linked to noun "sand dunes")

Numbers - write out to 99

Often confused prepositions - between/among ("between" 2; "among" 3 or more)

Punctuation - use colon or dash for separate list or break

Colons - use before a list

Semi colons: review 3 uses (in a series of independent clauses, in a compound sentence instead of a conjunction, and after a colon for clarity if the list uses commas)

B - while all these **embroiling** love triangles were taking place in the **regal** households 2 people were meeting somewhere between the many tall sand dunes on the coast of illyria sebastian and captain antonio

C -   While all these **embroiling** love triangles were taking place in the **regal** households, two people were meeting somewhere among the many tall sand dunes on the coast of Illyria: Sebastian and Captain Antonio. *(or use a dash instead of colon)*

B = *suggested sentence for the board or overhead*   **C** = *sentence written correctly*   **LD** = *literary device*

67. masquerading •

LD - personification

No paragraph - continuation

Commas - interrupter

Incorrect verb-tense switch - story in past

Relative pronouns - "who" needed as subject

Pronouns - review subject vs. object pronouns

Use of italics - for emphasis

Verb tense - use of pluperfect tense needed for previous action

B - sebastian if you recall is the twin brother of viola that was **masquerading** as cesario. he had survived the maelstrom and the shipwreck. captain antonio rescued him from the jaws of death

C - Sebastian, if you recall, was the twin brother of Viola who was **masquerading** as Cesario. He _had_ survived the maelstrom and the shipwreck. Captain Antonio had rescued him from the jaws of death.

68. ♥ malignant •

LD - idiomatic expression; use of a direct quote

No paragraph; paragraph when Sebastian speaks

Commas - appositive; quote

Quotation

No comma between "beloved" and "twin" - second adjective is linked to noun

Adjectives vs. adverbs - use of "bad" as adjective or predicate adjective with verbs of being (to be/to feel); "badly" is adverb

Punctuation - use of quotation marks around obvious direct quote from Shakespeare

Incorrect word use - "should have" not "should of" since it is a helping verb (preposition doesn't make sense)

B - sebastian was not a happy camper. he thought that his beloved twin sister viola had drowned and felt badly that he had survived when she had not. he cursed his "**malignant** fate." you should of let me drown he said

C - Sebastian was not a happy camper. He thought that his beloved twin sister, Viola, had drowned and felt bad that he had survived when she had not. He cursed his "**malignant** fate."

"You should have let me drown," he said.

69. ♥ minion •

LD - rhyme; simile

2 Paragraphs - narrator then Captain speaking

Commas - introductory subordinate clause; continued (interrupted) quote and introductory phrase; continued quote; long introductory adverb

Quotation - continued (interrupted) so note punctuation

Possession - singular noun

Homophone - there/their/they're

Like vs. as - "as" means "in the role of" and is not a comparison

Verb tense - Incorrect use of conditional tense (future needed)

B - sebastian decided to go to duke orsinos court. even though he had many enemies there captain antonio resolved to go with sebastian like his **minion**. after all he reasoned after the horror of the shipwreck the dangers of the court would be like a sport

C - Sebastian decided to go to Duke Orsino's court. Even though he had many enemies there, Captain Antonio resolved to go with Sebastian as his **minion**.

"After all," he reasoned, " after the horror of the shipwreck, the dangers of the court will be like a sport."

70. convoluted •

LD - literary reference; narrator aside

Paragraph - narrator aside

Verb tense - correct use of present tense in narrator aside

Often confused words - then/than

Titles - underline title of book

Punctuation - use of parentheses for extraneous information

Relative pronouns - who/whom/whose/whoever/whomever/that/which ("that" and "which" can be subject or object and are used only with objects and animals; "who" and "whom" are used with people; "who" is subject; "whom" is object)

Like vs. as - "as if" needed since this is not a comparison; "like" used as a direct comparison and must be followed by a noun

Verb tense - use of subjunctive mood in "if" clause

NOTE: Review rule of thumb for underlining long works and putting quotation marks around shorter ones.

B - this is worse then the **convoluted** story in middlemarch by george elliot who was a woman writing like she was a man.

C -   This is worse than the **convoluted** story in <u>Middlemarch</u> by George Elliot (who was a woman writing as if she were a man).

➡ SUGGESTION:

This is a good place to teach a mini-lesson on what to underline and what to surround with quotation marks. The rule of thumb is to underline the title of a book and anything that takes over an hour to read, listen to, or watch. You also underline the main topic (like a magazine or encyclopedia or record album) and put quotation marks around the sub-topics (like the articles or a single song on the album).

71. ❤ staunch, accosted •

LD - description within action; naturalistic detail; foreshadowing

Paragraph - place and subject change

Commas - introductory subordinate clause; 2 adjectives

Confused words - further/farther

Splitting infinitives - The *Star Trek* announcer was wrong. It is never "to boldly go" but instead "to go boldly." Here it is "to complicate matters further."

Possession - singular noun

Hyphen - 2 words acting as one

Voice - avoid passive voice

B - while sebastian and the **staunch** antonio were trekking across the hills and pine forests of illyria and were soon to farther complicate matters at orsinos palace viola was **accosted** by a foul tempered churlish malvolio.

C -   While Sebastian and the **staunch** Antonio were trekking across the hills and pine forests of Illyria and were soon to complicate matters further at Orsino's palace, a foul-tempered, churlish Malvolio **accosted** Viola.

B = *suggested sentence for the board or overhead*   *C* = *sentence written correctly*   *LD* = *literary device*

72. ♥ peevish •••

LD - conversation; double entendre ("canker-blossom")

3 Paragraphs - conversation

Commas - direct address; quote; introductory subordinate clause

Hyphen - 2 words acting as one ("canker-blossom")

Coordinating conjunction - avoid beginning a sentence with one

Contraction

Homophone - through/threw

Irregular verbs - lie/lay/has lain and lay/laid/has laid

Transitive vs. intransitive verbs - review

B - you left this ring with the countess olivia you canker blossom vociferated the **peevish** malvolio with venom in his voice. but i didnt leave a ring viola insisted. malvolio through down the ring. if it is worth stooping for theyre it lays

C -   "You left this ring with the Countess Olivia, you canker-blossom," vociferated the **peevish** Malvolio with venom in his voice.

"I didn't leave a ring," Viola insisted

Malvolio threw down the ring. "If it is worth stooping for, there it lies."

➥ **SUGGESTION:**

This would be a good spot to review the coordinating and subordinating conjunctions, their uses and restrictions.

---

73. surly •••

LD - simile; idiomatic expression ("lost her heart")

Paragraph - narrator again

Like vs. as - use "as" instead of "like" ("in the same manner as")

Possession - singular noun

Incorrect word usage - "must have" and not "must of" since "have" is a helping verb for "lost"

Homophone - to/too/two

Punctuation - quotes needed around "Cesario" since it is a pseudonym

Punctuation - period inside quote even though it is a one-word quote

B - the **surly** malvolio delivered the rest of his message in the same manner as a snarling dog with a snout full of porcupine quills. viola quickly figured out olivias ploy and realized that olivia must of lost her heart too cesario

C -   The **surly** Malvolio delivered the rest of his message in the same manner as a snarling dog with a snout full of porcupine quills. Viola quickly figured out Olivia's ploy and realized that Olivia must have lost her heart to "Cesario."

74. obfuscated ••

LD - deliberate repetition of word for effect; humor

Paragraph - new person speaking

Commas - quote; interjection; introductory phrase; introductory phrase

Punctuation - quotation with introduction

Question marks needed

Punctuation - quotation marks needed to indicate falsehood; quote within a quote

Homophone - its/it's, to/too/two

Relative pronouns - "who" needed as subject

Pronouns - "I" as subject and "me" as object (of preposition here)

B - viola bemoaned the tangle oh what will become of this. as a man i am loved by this woman. as a woman i love the man who loves the woman whom loves me as a man. its to **obfuscated** a knot for i to untie

C -   Viola bemoaned the tangle. "Oh, what will become of this? As a man, I am loved by this woman. As a woman, I love the man who loves the woman who loves me as a 'man.' It's too **obfuscated** a knot for me to untie."

B = suggested sentence for the board or overhead   C = sentence written correctly   LD = literary device

75. intoxicated ●

Paragraph - narrator again

Commas - optional comma after introductory adverb; introductory adverb followed by a introductory subordinate clause; long introductory adverb; verb series; appositive

Subject/verb agreement - compound subject needs plural verb; "each" needs singular verb

Irregular verbs - lie/lay/has lain and lay/laid/has laid (Remember, something has to get laid....")

Transitive vs. intransitive verbs - review

Spelling rule - if word ends in consonant/vowel/consonant and a suffix is added, double the consonant ("getting")

Possession - singular noun

Homophone - their/there/they're, to/too/two

Antecedent/pronoun agreement - "each.........his"

B - after midnight as the troubled viola laid tossing and turning in her bed sir toby belch and sir andrew aguecheek was geting **intoxicated**. in there inebriated state each sang laughed argued and called for maria olivias maid too bring them more wine

C -   After midnight as the troubled Viola lay tossing and turning in her bed, Sir Toby Belch and Sir Andrew Aguecheek were getting **intoxicated**. In their inebriated state, each sang, laughed, argued, and called for Maria, Olivia's maid, to bring him more wine.

76. diatribe, ♥ caterwauling, abed ●

No paragraph

Commas - introductory participial phrase; appositive

Homophones - cents/sense, their/there/they're

Often confused words - accept/except

Irregular verbs - lie/lay/has lain and lay/laid/has laid

Transitive vs. intransitive verbs - review

Collective noun/pronoun agreement - "everyone...his or her" as "everyone" is singular

Relative pronouns - "who" needed as subject

B - sir belch even launched into a drunken **diatribe** that made no cents whatsoever accept to another sot. hearing the revelry feste the jester joined the party. theyre singing and **caterwauling** woke maria and everyone else who laid **abed** in their chamber

C - Sir Belch even launched into a drunken **diatribe** that made no sense whatsoever except to another sot. Hearing the revelry, Feste, the jester, joined the party. Their singing and **caterwauling** woke Maria and everyone else who lay **abed** in his or her chamber.

77. inebriates, salacious ●

LD - repeated use of synonyms to make point (he was *really* drunk)

Paragraph - new person speaking

Commas - appositive; quote; appositive

Quotation

Numbers - write out to 99

Relative pronouns - "whom" needed as object

Often confused prepositions - among/between

Often confused words - then/than

Homophone - their/there/they're

Incorrect verb-tense switch

Semicolon - use of semicolon in compound sentence

B - my lady has called up her steward malvolio to throw you out maria warned as the 3 drunks insulted malvolio a man who none between the 3 sots liked and then the three **inebriates** continued there **salacious** attack

C -   "My lady has called up her steward, Malvolio, to throw you out, " Maria warned as the three drunks insulted Malvolio, a man whom none among the three sots liked; then the three **inebriates** continued their **salacious** attack.

B = *suggested sentence for the board or overhead*   *C* = *sentence written correctly*   *LD* = *literary device*

78. dandiprat, impotent, astute, bawdy •

LD - repartée; sarcasm ("astute observation")

5 Paragraphs - conversation

Commas - quote; long introductory adverb; direct addresses; extra information; quote

Quotations - use of indentation only to denote new person speaking

Punctuation - need for quotation marks around sarcasm or falsehood

Use of intent only to indicate person speaking

Numbers - write out to 99

Article "an" with a noun beginning with a vowel or a silent "h"

Hyphen - 2 words acting as one

Pronouns - "we" as subject and "us" as object

Homophone - to/too/two

Subject/verb agreement - "each.....was"

Verb tense - pluperfect needed to refer to previous action

B - malvolio is a earth vexing **dandiprat** and an **impotent** fool said sir belch. at this **astute** observation the 3 drunks launched into a **bawdy** song each singing a phrase. three merry men are us. there dwelt a man in babylon lady lady. on the twelfth day of december... sang all of the tosspots who was oblivious too the fact that malvolio just entered the room

C -   "Malvolio is an earth-vexing **dandiprat** and an **impotent** fool," said Sir Belch.

At this "**astute**" observation, the three drunks launched into a **bawdy** song, each singing a phrase.

"Three merry men are we."

"There dwelt a man in Babylon, lady, lady."

"On the twelfth day of December...," sang all of the tosspots who were oblivious to the fact that Malvolio had just entered the room.

79. choleric, couth •

Paragraph - new person speaking

Commas - noun series

Quotation - note punctuation of quote with question

Inversion - use for question

Punctuation - question marks needed in interrogatives

Parallel construction - negative "no" should be followed by negative "nor"

Possession - singular noun

Apostrophes - plurals vs. possessive nouns

B - malvolio was **choleric**. have you no wit manners or **couth**. you turn my ladies house into a saloon. have you no remorse for your behavior he raged

C -   Malvolio was **choleric**. "Have you no wit, manners, nor **couth**? You turn my lady's house into a saloon. Have you no remorse for your behavior?" he raged.

80. hapless, misbehavior, ♥ consanguineous •

No paragraph - continuation

Commas - direct address; quote; continued quote; participial; quote

Quotation - continued (interrupted) quote

Coordinating conjunction - deliberate misuse for effect and conversation

Homophone - their/there/they're

Complex sentence - no comma before "as" (subordinate clause at end of sentence)

B - and you maria malvolio turned on the **hapless** maid how can you allow such **misbehavior** he continued scandalized. theyre obnoxious behavior will be reported immediately. olivia will toss them out even if sir belch is **consanguineous** he continued with righteous indignation as he stormed out of the room

C - "And you, Maria," Malvolio turned on the **hapless** maid, "how can you allow such **misbehavior**?" he continued, scandalized. "Their obnoxious behavior will be reported immediately. Olivia will toss them out even if Sir Belch is **consanguineous**," he continued with righteous indignation as he stormed out of the room.

---

81. ❤ gull, ❤ puritanical ●

LD - subplot begins; double entendre

Paragraph - subject change

Comma - 2 adjectives where 2nd is not age, color, or linked

Often confused words - then/than

Spelling rule - if word ends in consonant/vowel/consonant and a suffix is added, double the consonant ("plotted")

Possession - singular noun

Punctuation - use of quotation marks to denote double entendre

B - the group of tosspots than ploted with marias help to **gull** the pompous **puritanical** malvolio into making a total fool of himself.

C -   The group of tosspots then plotted with Maria's help to **gull** the pompous, **puritanical** Malvolio into making a total "fool" of himself.

82. ❤ epistles, ❤ gait ●

LD - subplot continues; sarcasm

Paragraph - new person speaking

Commas - noun series; quote

Common spelling errors - "a lot," "all right," and "no one" are 2 words

Colon - use to set off a list (never put a colon after a verb)

Semicolons - use for clarity when commas are present in a list set off by a colon

Punctuation - use of quotation marks to denote sarcasm

Homophone - write/right/rite

Prepositions - avoid ending sentences with them if at all possible

NOTE: Review 3 uses of semicolon - in a series of independent clauses, in a compound sentence instead of a conjunction, and after a colon (for clarity) if the list uses commas.

B - i will send him alot of **epistles** of love in which i praise the following the color of his beard the shape of his leg the manner of his **gait** as well as the beauty of his eyes his forehead and his complexion maria planned. i can rite like a lady when i wish to

C -   "I will send him a lot of **epistles** of love in which I praise the following: the color of his beard; the shape of his leg; the manner of his **gait**; as well as the "beauty" of his eyes, his forehead, and his complexion," Maria planned. "I can write like a lady when I wish."

83. posterior, derrière, nemesis ●

LD - use of foreign word; repetition of synonyms for emphasis; euphemism ("derrière" substituted for a stronger term)**; subplot**

Paragraph - new person speaking

Commas - quote; participial phrase

Demonstrative adjectives - this/that/these/those

Hyphen -2 words acting as one

Possession - singular noun

Verb tense - use of future tense

Spelling rule - "i" before "e" except after "c" and neighbor and weigh are weird

Contractions

Possession vs. plural nouns - singular noun ending in "y"

Accents - accent needed on French word

B - that fool born horses **posterior** will think the letters come from my neice. hell think that shes in love with him chortled sir belch so delighted to make a donkeys **derrière** out of his **nemesis** that he took another drink in celebration

C -   "That fool-born horse's **posterior** will think the letters come from my niece. He'll think that she's in love with him," chortled Sir Belch, so delighted to make a donkey's **derrière** out of his **nemesis** that he took another drink in celebration.

↪ **SUGGESTION:**

Since there are many prepositions in Caught'ya #83, this might be a good point once again to review prepositions, their functions, and their capitalization.

B = suggested sentence for the board or overhead   C = sentence written correctly   LD = literary device

84. discourses •

Paragraph - narrator again

Commas - 2 introductory adverbs together; non-restrictive modifier

Possession - singular noun

Homophones - to/too/two

Relative pronouns - "who" needed as subject

Often confused words - former/latter

B - the next morning at duke orsinos palace orsino engaged in another of his increasingly frequent **discourses** with viola whom was still in disguise. the latter was only to happy to comply

C - The next morning at Duke Orsino's palace, Orsino engaged in another of his increasingly frequent **discourses** with Viola, who was still in disguise. The latter was only too happy to comply.

↪ **SUGGESTION:**

Caught'ya #85 would be an excellent one to diagram. There are two simple sentences. Periodical practice in diagramming helps students to "see" the function of each part of the sentence. After reviewing diagramming, I like to take part of a Caught'ya at least once a week and require that students diagram it.

85. quintessential, mused •

2 Paragraphs - subject change; new person speaking

Commas - direct address; compound sentence; quote

Quotation

Antecedent/pronoun agreement - "no man (singular)...his (singular)"

Pronouns - subject pronoun "I" needed (verb "do" is implied)

B - viola and orsino talked again of love. if ever you love boy remember me for i am the **quintessential** man in love orsino **mused**. no man pursues their woman as passionately as me.

C - Viola and Orsino talked again of love.

"If ever you love, boy, remember me, for I am the **quintessential** man in love," Orsino **mused**. "No man pursues his woman as passionately as I."

86. proffered •

LD - repartée

5 Paragraphs - conversation

Commas - set off "too" by commas if it means "also;" direct address; quote; quote; direct address; quote

Quotations - use of indentation only in order to indicate new person speaking

Homophone - to/too/two

Common spelling errors - "a lot" is 2 words, so are "all right" and "no one"

Punctuation - need question mark in interrogative

Sentence structure - deliberate use of fragment in conversation to make it more realistic

B - i love someone to my lord boldly confessed viola. tell me. she is alot like you **proffered** viola. how old is she. about your age my lord dared viola

C - "I love someone, too, my Lord," boldly confessed Viola.

"Tell me."

"She is a lot like you," **proffered** Viola.

"How old is she?"

"About your age, my Lord," dared Viola.

B = *suggested sentence for the board or overhead*   *C* = *sentence written correctly*   *LD* = *literary device*

87. vigor ●

LD - narrator aside; simile

Paragraph - narrator again

Commas - compound sentence

Punctuation - use of parentheses for narrator comment (2 times); use of colon to set off a list (never put a colon after a verb)

Semicolons - needed for clarity when commas are present in a list set off by a colon; 3 uses(in a series of independent clauses, in a compound sentence instead of a conjunction, and after a colon for clarity if the list uses commas)

Often confused words - then/than

Pronouns - "she" is subject and in a comparison the verb is implied ("than she is")

Regular comparisons - young/younger/youngest

Verb tense - use of present tense in comparison

Punctuation - exclamation needed at end for emphasis

NOTE: Warn of need to set off narrator aside in order to make it identifiable

B - orsino a real sexist like most of the men of his time kept insisting on several points a woman should marry a man older then her women by nature were not able to love with the **vigor** of men men needed to marry much younger women for women were like roses that bloom briefly and then fade. how unflattering

C -   Orsino (a real sexist like most of the men of his time) kept insisting on several points: a woman should marry a man older than she; women by nature were not able to love with the **vigor** of men; men needed to marry much younger women, for women were like roses that bloom briefly and then fade. (How unflattering!)

88. bigot, bombastic ignoramus ●

LD - use of homily ("love knows no reason"); **narrator aside**

2 Paragraphs - 2nd for narrator aside

Commas - interjection; introductory phrase (interjection and word)

Homophone - quite/quiet/quite, no/know

Relative pronouns - who/whom/whose/whoever/ whomever/that/which ("that" and "which" can be subject or object and are used only with objects and animals; "who" and "whom" are used with people; "who" is subject; "whom" is object)

Splitting verbs - avoid splitting helping verb and verb if at all possible

Verb tense - use of pluperfect tense

Inversion - use in question

Demonstrative adjectives - this/that/these/those

Punctuation - question mark needed in interrogative

Verb tense - correct use of present tense in aside

Homophone - no/know

B - this orsino was quit a **bigot** whom did not feel that women were his equal and who loved a female with which he had never conversed. why did viola love this **bombastic ignoramus**. ah well love knows no reason.

C -   This Orsino was quite a **bigot** who did not feel that women were his equal and who loved a female with whom he never had conversed.

     Why did Viola love this **bombastic ignoramus**? Ah well, love knows no reason.

89. paternal ●

Paragraph - subject change

Commas - introductory phrase out of place ("much to..."); interrupter; participial phrase

Possession - singular noun

Irregular verb - become/became

Incorrect verb-tense switch

Comparison - bold/bolder/boldest

B - orsino felt positively **paternal** toward viola much to violas dismay. viola in desperation becomes even bolder telling orsino that women could love as passionately as men

C -   Orsino felt positively **paternal** towards Viola, much to Viola's dismay. Viola, in desperation, became even bolder, telling Orsino that women could love as passionately as men.

B = suggested sentence for the board or overhead   C = sentence written correctly   LD = literary device

90. enigmatically ●

LD - building suspense

Paragraph - new person speaking

Commas - interrupted quote; compound sentence; "too" meaning "also"; quote

Quotation

Relative pronouns - "who" needed as subject

Pronoun - subject pronoun "I" needed (verb "love" is implied)

Possessive vs. plural noun - possessive confused with plural

Possession - singular noun

Homophone - to/too/two

B - my father had a daughter viola bravely began that loved a man with the same intensity as me. my sister died and i am now all the daughters of my fathers house and all the sons too she said **enigmatically**

C - "My father had a daughter," Viola bravely began, "who loved a man with the same intensity as I. My sister died, and I am now all the daughters of my father's house and all the sons, too," she said **enigmatically**.

91. bade, machismo ●

LD - use of foreign word

2 Paragraphs - narrator; new person speaking

Commas - quote

Quotation

Often confused words - then/than

No comma after "jewel" - not a compound sentence (no subject)

Splitting infinitives - never split infinitives as done on *Star Trek*

Possession - singular noun

Punctuation - quotation marks what is said (or could be said) out loud; quote within a quote

Italics - for emphasis

B - orsino than gave viola a jewel and **bade** her to again go to olivias house. do not take no for an answer. i will have her love he declared in the typical **machismo** fashion of the time

C -   Orsino then gave Viola a jewel and **bade** her to go again to Olivia's house.

   "Do not take 'no' for an answer. I will have her love," he declared in the typical **machismo** fashion of the time.

92. diabolical ●

LD - back to subplot

Paragraph - time change

Commas - optional comma after introductory adverb; introductory subordinate clause

Possession - singular noun

Spelling rule - if word ends in consonant/vowel/consonant and a suffix is added, double the consonant ("spotted," "dropped")

Compound subjects and compound verbs

Homophone - where/were

Negatives - avoid double negatives

Contraction

B - a few days later the **diabolical** plan of revenge was enacted in olivias garden. sir belch and sir aguecheek hid behind a hedge. as soon as they spoted malvolio entering the garden maria darted out and droped the letter on the path were malvolio couldnt not miss it

C -   A few days later the **diabolical** plan of revenge was enacted in Olivia's garden. Sir Belch and Sir Aguecheek hid behind a hedge. As soon as they spotted Malvolio entering the garden, Maria darted out and dropped the letter on the path where Malvolio couldn't miss it.

---

93. plausibility ●

LD - subplot continued

Paragraph - subject change

Commas - interrupter; introductory subordinate clause

Incorrect verb-tense use - interrupter needs to remain in past tense

Verb tense - need for pluperfect to refer to action previous to the story.

Negatives - never use a double negative

Contractions

Indirect quotation - use of "that" to avoid quotation marks

Irregular verb - choose/chose

Verb tense - use of subjunctive mood in "if" clause

B - now malvolio it seems already contemplated the **plausibility** that olivia was falling in love with him. hadnt he not heard her say that if she should ever chose a husband it would be someone like malvolio

C -   Now Malvolio, it seemed, had already contemplated the **plausibility** that Olivia was falling in love with him. Hadn't he heard her say that if ever she should choose a husband, it would be someone like Malvolio?

94. dulcet ●

LD - subplot continues

2 Paragraphs - Malvolio; narrator

Commas - introductory participial phrase; interjection; non-restrictive modifier; quote

Quotation

Dangling modifier - "the note" did not do the musing, Malvolio did

Verb tense - need for subjunctive in "if" clause

Spelling rule - if word ends in consonant/vowel/consonant and a suffix is added, double the consonant ("written")

Colon - needed as break before letter

B - musing about his possible future with olivia the note was spied by malvolio. ah this looks as if it was writen by my **dulcet** lady olivia he said. the letter read

C -   Musing about his possible future with Olivia, Malvolio spied the note. "Ah, this looks as if it were written by my **dulcet** lady, Olivia," he said.

The letter read:

95. humble, imperious ●

LD - subplot

Paragraph - body of letter

Commas - date; greeting; closing

Letter format - friendly letter

Greeting - do not indent

Demonstrative adjectives - this/that/these/those

Relative pronouns - who/whom/whose/whoever/ whomever/that/which ("that" and "which" can be subject or object and are used only with objects and animals; "who" and "whom" are used with people; "who" is subject; "whom" is object)

Homophones - to/too/two, your/you're, no/know

Imperative sentences - subjects implied

Incorrect word use - need adverb not adjective

Common spelling error - truly

Abbreviation of "post script" - This would be a good time to review common abbreviations like the postal abbreviations of states.

Irregular verb - choose/chose

Pronouns - "I" needed as subject with verbs of being even if in predicate

B - november 26 1602   dearest beloved m   you are one of these that was born too achieve greatness. discard your **humble** attitude and be **imperious** with servants. express your political opinions loud. wear yellow socks and ribbons tied around youre knees. yours truely   a lady   ps   you can not choose but no it is me. smile whenever you see me

C -   November 26, 1602

Dearest Beloved M.,

    You are one of those who was born to achieve greatness. Discard your **humble** attitude and be **imperious** with servants. Express your political opinions loudly. Wear yellow socks and ribbons tied around your knees.

                    Yours truly,
                    A Lady

P.S.   You cannot choose but know it is I. Smile whenever you see me.

B = suggested sentence for the board or overhead   C = sentence written correctly   LD = literary device

96. suspired (from the French for "sigh" - it is used in literary English) •

LD - aphorism

Paragraph - new person speaking

Commas - quote; noun series

Quotation

Pronoun - "I" must be used with verbs of being

Relative pronouns - "whom" needed as object

Verb tense - correct use of future tense

Like vs. as - use "like" only in direct comparison of 2 nouns (never with a verb phrase)

B - it is me who she loves **suspired** malvolio as he fell hook line sinker and yellow socks for the trick. i shall do like my beloved asks

C - "It is I whom she loves," **suspired** Malvolio as he fell hook, line, sinker, and yellow socks for the trick. "I shall do as my beloved asks."

97. bracken, wench, prophetic •

LD - foreshadowing for the purpose of **building suspense**

2 Paragraphs - narrator; new person speaking

Commas - optional after introductory adverb; quote; participial phrase

Quotation

Homophone - their/there/they're

Antecedent/pronoun agreement - "Everyone... his..." since "everyone" is a collective noun and therefore singular

Collective nouns - review

Relative pronouns - "who" needed as subject of "thought"

Splitting verbs - avoid splitting helping verb and verb if at all possible

Hyphen - Put a hyphen after the prefix "ex" if the noun does not begin with a vowel or "C," "P," "Q," "S," or "T" ("bachelor" does not begin with those letters, so the hyphen is needed). If the noun begins with those letters, the "ex" is added to it as one word — no hyphen, no break.

B - behind the **bracken** the conspirators chortled as they contemplated the results of there plot. everyone wanted to voice their opinion. i would like to marry this **wench** maria that thought of this droll trick said sir belch little knowing how **prophetic** his words would prove to be and that he would soon be an ex bachelor

C - Behind the **bracken**, the conspirators chortled as they contemplated the results of their plot. Everyone wanted to voice his opinion.

"I would like to marry this **wench** Maria who thought of this droll trick," said Sir Belch, little knowing how **prophetic** his words would prove to be and that he soon would be an ex-bachelor.

98. ♥ courtier •

LD - irony

Paragraph - place and subject change

Commas - optional comma after transitional adverb; appositive; subordinate clause at beginning; adverb as interrupter (awkward to have long adverb in middle)

Transitions - needed for subject and place change

Possession - singular nouns

Relative pronouns - "who" needed as subject of "win;" "that" not used with people

Splitting verbs - avoid if at all possible

B - meanwhile viola still disguised as cesario went again to olivias house to plead orsinos case for marriage. while viola was waiting in the garden sir belch and sir aguecheek joined her and concluded after a lengthy conversation with the youth that cesario was a rare **courtier** that might just win olivias heart

C - Meanwhile, Viola, still disguised as Cesario, went again to Olivia's house to plead Orsino's case for marriage. While Viola was waiting in the garden, Sir Belch and Sir Aguecheek joined her and concluded, after a lengthy conversation with the youth, that Cesario was a rare **courtier** who just might win Olivia's heart.

B = suggested sentence for the board or overhead   C = sentence written correctly   LD = literary device

99. euphoric •

Paragraph - Subject change

Commas - participial phrase; interrupter

Pronouns - overuse of pronouns makes meaning unclear

Antecedent/pronoun agreement - "Everyone ....his or her..." since "everyone" is a collective noun and therefore singular

Collective nouns/pronouns - review common ones

Punctuation - quotes around "him" to denote a deceptive term

B - she came to the garden **euphoric** that cesario had returned. she sent everyone else away to their room and talked to viola. she acknowledged the ruse of the ring and begged him to speak words of love to her. she of course did not

C -   Olivia came to the garden, **euphoric** that Cesario had returned. She sent everyone else away to his or her room and talked to Viola. Olivia acknowledged the ruse of the ring and begged "him" to speak words of love to her. Viola, of course, did not.

100. prevailed, cryptically •

LD - building suspense

2 Paragraphs - subject change; new person speaking

Comma - quote

Quotation

Voice - use active voice whenever possible

Negatives - avoid double negatives

B - instead viola **prevailed** upon olivia one more time to consider orsino instead.

 my heart has not been given to no woman viola said **cryptically**

C -   Instead Viola **prevailed** upon Olivia one more time to consider Orsino instead.

   "I have given my heart to no woman," Viola said **cryptically**.

101. insinuated •

Paragraph - place and subject change

Commas - pause around extra information in a phrase for clarification

Parallel construction - negative "neither" must be followed by negative "nor" (correlative conjunction)

Subject/verb agreement - "neither...nor" indicates each subject is taken singularly (correlative conjunction)

Splitting verbs - avoid

Antecedent/pronoun agreement - "neither...nor...his" (correlative conjunction)

Spelling rule - "i" before "e" except after "c" and neighbor and weigh are weird

No comma after "friend" - single word closely related to the preceding word (and restrictive modifier as he has many friends)

Misplaced modifier - Sir Belch was certain, not the idea

Possession - singular nouns

Homophone - no/know

Prepositions - review

B - neither duke orsino or sir aguecheek were having any luck in their pursuit of olivia. sir aguecheeks friend sir belch **insinuated** that a duel with cesario over olivias affections might be a good idea certain that know duel would ensue

C -   Neither Duke Orsino nor Sir Aguecheek was having any luck in his pursuit of Olivia. Sir Aguecheek's friend Sir Belch, certain that no duel would ensue, **insinuated** that a duel with Cesario over Olivia's affections might be a good idea.

B = *suggested sentence for the board or overhead*   **C** = *sentence written correctly*   **LD** = *literary device*

102. hamlet ●

LD - subplot

Paragraph - place and subject change

Commas - introductory subordinate clause; appositive; verb series

Transition - needed to indicate place and subject change

Relative pronouns - "who" needed as subject of "had saved"

Verb tense - use pluperfect since Antonio had saved him before this story began

Possessive vs. plural nouns - enemy's/enemies

Often confused words - then/than

B - while all this intrigue was going on sebastian and antonio reached the **hamlet**. antonio the sea captain that saved him gave the penniless sebastian his own wallet arranged to meet him later at a tavern and than went to hide from his enemys while sebastian explored the town

C -   While all this intrigue was going on, Sebastian and Antonio reached the **hamlet**. Antonio, the sea captain who had saved him, gave the penniless Sebastian his own wallet, arranged to meet him later at a tavern, and then went to hide from his enemies while Sebastian explored the town.

103. inveigle ●

LD - irony ("He is such a perfect servant...")

2 Paragraphs - narrator and Olivia

Commas - interjection; quote; direct address; extra, unnecessary word

Quotation

Punctuation - need for question marks in interrogative

Direct and indirect objects - review

B - olivia was already making plans to **inveigle** cesario to her side. she sent him a invitation for dinner. oh what will i serve him. were is that malvolio. he is usually such a perfect servant she acknowledged. maria go find him please

C -   Olivia already was making plans to **inveigle** Cesario to her side. She sent him an invitation for dinner.

"Oh, what will I serve him? Where is that Malvolio? He is usually such a perfect servant," she acknowledged. "Maria, go find him, please."

(**SUGGESTION:**

This might be a good place to discuss or review direct vs. indirect objects. These are not really an issue in English, but when your students study a foreign language like French or Spanish, they will need to differentiate between them.

104. buss, dour, mien ●

LD - satire; humor; rhyme

Paragraph - return to narrator

Commas - series of participles; long introductory adverb; compound sentence with "nor"

Parallel construction - for clarity ("grinning...spouting....wearing")

Negatives - parallel negatives needed ("no longer... nor")

B - malvolio grinning spouting nonsense and he wore yellow socks and ribbons around his knees soon joined olivia. at almost every other word he uttered he kissed her hand or blew her a **buss**. his appearance was no longer **dour** or his **mien** sour

C -   Malvolio, grinning, spouting nonsense, and wearing yellow socks and ribbons around his knees, soon joined Olivia. At almost every other word he uttered, he kissed her hand or blew her a **buss**. His appearance was no longer **dour**, nor was his **mien** sour.

B = suggested sentence for the board or overhead   *C = sentence written correctly*   *LD = literary device*

105. deranged, prattled, loathed   •••

LD - idiomatic expression; humor

No paragraph - continuation

Commas - introductory phrase; verb series

Parallel construction - past tense of verbs ("smiled...blew....spouted")

Verb tense - need for pluperfect tense for action anterior to paragraph

Complex sentence - subordinate clause at end of sentence (no comma)

Punctuation - use of quotation marks in idiomatic expression ("off his rocker")

Plural vs. possessive nouns - confused

B - in fact malvolio appeared **deranged**. he **prattled** on and on as he smiled blew kisses' and spouting bits of the letter he supposed that olivia wrote. olivia thought he was off his rocker. she **loathed** yellow socks' and ribbon's

C - In fact, Malvolio appeared **deranged**. He **prattled** on and on as he smiled, blew kisses, and spouted bits of the letter he supposed that Olivia had written. Olivia thought he was "off his rocker." She **loathed** yellow socks and ribbons.

106. colleague   •••

LD - alliteration

Paragraph - new action

Comma - optional comma for introductory adverb

Possession - singular nouns

Punctuation - use of quotes around opposite, denoting incorrect information on part of protagonists

Collective nouns - review

Antecedent/pronoun agreement - "group" requires singular possessive pronoun

Homophone - its/it's

B - suddenly a servant announced cesarios arrival at the door. olivia quickly put the mad malvolio into marias capable hands and sent all the servants away. the entire group had difficulty managing their mad **colleague**

C -   Suddenly, a servant announced Cesario's arrival at the door. Olivia quickly put the "mad" Malvolio into Maria's capable hands and sent all the servants away. The entire group had difficulty managing its "mad" **colleague**.

107. rancorous, insolent   •••

LD - historical allusion; literary allusion

No paragraph

Commas - interrupter; extra information for clarity

Indirect quotation - avoidance of quotes with "that"

B - malvolio per instructions in the epistle was **rancorous** toward sir belch and **insolent** to the other servants. he drove them all to such desperation that they made plans to lock him up in a dark room a common solution for handling a lunatic in shakespearean times

C - Malvolio, per instructions in the epistle, was **rancorous** toward Sir Belch and **insolent** to the other servants. He drove them all to such desperation that they made plans to lock him up in a dark room, a common solution for handling a lunatic in Shakespearean times.

108. brooch   •••

Paragraph - subject change

Commas - participial phrase; interrupter

Possession - singular noun

Punctuation - use of quotes to indicate falsehood

Word use - "that" as subject of adjective clause

Often confused words - accept/except

Splitting verbs - don't

B - viola again pleaded her masters suit. olivia changed the topic still trying to find out more about this charming young man and still pressing gifts on him. viola did however finally except a diamond **brooch** that contained a miniature portrait of olivia

C -   Viola again pleaded her master's suit. Olivia changed the topic, still trying to find out more about this charming young "man" and still pressing gifts on "him." Viola, however, finally did accept a diamond **brooch** that contained a miniature portrait of Olivia.

B = suggested sentence for the board or overhead   C = sentence written correctly   LD = literary device

109. asinine ●

LD - sarcasm; irony; scene within a scene

Paragraph - subject and place change

Commas - introductory subordinate clause; interrupter

Transition - needed to indicate change

Misplaced modifier - the fight was not in the letter so meaning is unclear

Sentence structure - new sentence needed for clarity

Hyphen - 2 words acting as one

Intensifier - "absolutely" as an adverb modifying an adjective

B - while malvolio was reaping the rewards of poetic justice sir aguecheek in his usual **asinine** fashion challenged cesario to a sword fight in an absolutely **obtuse** and ridiculous sounding letter

C -   While Malvolio was reaping the rewards of poetic justice, Sir Aguecheek, in his usual **asinine** fashion, challenged Cesario to a sword fight. He did this in an absolutely **obtuse** and ridiculous-sounding letter.

110. ❤ **implacable,** ❤ **brawl** ●

LD - use of symbol (devil)**; metaphor; subplot again**

2 Paragraphs - conversation

Commas - participial phrase; quote; introductory word; direct address; quote

Quotation

Common spelling error - a lot

Verb splitting - avoid

Deliberate verb splitting - "already" sounds awkward if put before "having" so we bend the rule

Repetition - avoid repetition of word "out" (Note that there are many ways to solve this.)

Pronouns - review types and uses

B - sir belch delivered the message to viola. sir aguecheek is **implacable** and can only get satisfaction by killing you. he is a devil in a private **brawl** having already killed alot of men he lied. please sir belch seek out this knight and find out what i have done to offend him said viola who was scared out of her wits

C -   Sir Belch delivered the message to Viola. "Sir Aguecheek is **implacable** and can get satisfaction only by killing you. He is a devil in a private **brawl**, having already killed a lot of men," he lied.

   "Please, Sir Belch, seek this knight and discover what I have done to offend him," said Viola who was scared out of her wits.

111. equivocated, rapacious, ❤ **meddle, proverbial** ● ● ● ● ● ● ● ● ● ● ● ● ● ● ● ● ● ● ●

LD - subplot continued; use of symbol

2 Paragraphs - 2 different speakers

Commas - repetition of subject ("Cesario, he")

Quotation

Contractions

Irregular verb - see/saw/has seen

Splitting verbs - avoid

Relative pronouns - "who" needed as subject of "was"

Incorrect word use - "shouldn't have challenged" is a verb (using a preposition wouldn't make sense)

B - sir belch then returned to sir aguecheek and **equivocated** again. that cesario hes the very devil himself. i never seen such a **rapacious** and skilled swordsman. ill not **meddle** with the likes of him concluded sir aguecheek whom was the **proverbial** coward. i shouldnt of challenged him

C -   Sir Belch then returned to Sir Aguecheek and **equivocated** again. "That Cesario, he's the very devil himself. I never have seen such a **rapacious** and skilled swordsman."

   "I'll not **meddle** with the likes of him," concluded Sir Aguecheek, who was the **proverbial** coward. "I shouldn't have challenged him."

B = suggested sentence for the board or overhead   C = sentence written correctly   LD = literary device

112. taunted; perdition •

LD - subplot; building suspense; euphemism ("perdition" instead of stronger term)

Paragraph - return to narrator

Comma - non-restrictive modifier

Run-on sentence - lack of punctuation

Homophone -their/there/they're

Punctuation - use of dash for separation and a break for thought (and effect); warn students away from dash overuse

Collective nouns - troop; discussion and review

Antecedent/pronoun agreement - It sounds weird, but it is correct to use "it" since "troop" is a singular collective noun ("It arrested..."). It is better to change the sentences to avoid the awkwardness.

B - sir belch finally **taunted** both sir aguecheek and cesario into drawing their swords. a real swordsman entered the garden captain antonio. he mistook viola for her twin brother sebastian. now all **perdition** broke loose a troop of officers arrived they arrested antonio viola had hope that sebastian was alive

C -   Sir Belch finally **taunted** both Sir Aguecheek and Cesario into drawing their swords. A real swordsman entered the garden — Captain Antonio. He mistook Viola for her twin brother, Sebastian. Now all **perdition** broke loose. A troop of officers arrived and arrested Antonio. Viola had hope that Sebastian was alive.

113. farcical, abode, gluteus maximus •

LD - use of foreign language (Latin) **in order to repeat word again; anadiplosis**

3 Paragraphs - narrator, narrator, Sebastian

Commas - long introductory adverb with 2 prepositional phrases; appositive; quote; introductory subordinate clause

Quotation

Punctuation - use of exclamation mark for emphasis

Relative pronouns - who/whom/whose/whoever/ whomever/that/which ("that" and "which" can be subject or object and are used only with objects and animals; "who" and "whom" are used with people; "who" is subject; "whom" is object)

Homophones - your/you're

Possessive pronouns

Contractions

Homophones - piece/peace, your/you're

Italics - needed for Latin word

B - at this point in the story the plot waxes **farcical**. sebastian arrived at the door of olivias **abode**. sir aguecheek saw him and assumed he was cesario the coward that had refused to fight and attacked sebastian. sebastian made mincemeat out of sir aguecheek. your a foolish fellow Sebastian said. if you dont leave me in piece ill really kick youre ***gluteus maximus***

C -   At this point in the story, the plot waxes **farcical**!

Sebastian arrived at the door of Olivia's **abode**. Sir Aguecheek saw him and assumed he was Cesario, the coward who had refused to fight, and attacked Sebastian. Sebastian made mincemeat out of Sir Aguecheek.

"You're a foolish fellow," Sebastian said. "If you don't leave me in peace, I'll really kick your ***gluteus maximus***."

114. dumbfounded, incredulity, comely •

LD - alliteration (c,c,c);

2 Paragraphs - narrator; new person speaking

Commas - compound sentence; introductory word; direct address; quote; compound sentence

Interrupted (continued) quote - the compound sentence is interrupted

Correlative conjunctions - "either....or"

Incorrect verb tense - need for pluperfect to refer to previous action

Incorrect word usage - "gots" not a word

Irregular verb - get/got/has gotten (discourage use of the last in writing)

Spelling rule - "i" before "e" except after "c" and neighbor and weigh are weird

B - olivia spied sebastian and rendered sebastian **dumbfounded** by asking him to marry her. either i am mad or this is a dream sebastian said with **incredulity**. yes gorgeous lady i will marry you he said for he fell instantly in love with this **comely** countess. we gots to find a preist

C -   Olivia spied Sebastian and rendered Sebastian **dumbfounded** by asking him to marry her!

"Either I am mad, or this is a dream," Sebastian said with **incredulity**. "Yes, gorgeous lady, I will marry you," he said, for he had fallen instantly in love with this **comely** countess. "We have to find a priest."

B = *suggested sentence for the board or overhead*   **C** = *sentence written correctly*   **LD** = *literary device*

115. irrepressible, dissembled, demented, aver •

Paragraph - narrator

Commas - appositive; participial phrase; adjective phrase with relative pronoun

Hyphen - 2 words acting as one

Spelling rule - "i" before "e"....

Relative pronouns - "who" needed as subject

Indirect quote - avoidance of quotes with "that"

Italics - emphasis

B - the **irrepressible** mischief maker feste **dissembled** himself as a preist and went to malvolio in his dark room. he tormented the servant playing tricks with his mind. malvolio who kept maintaining that he was not **demented** asked for pen and paper to write a letter to olivia in order to **aver** his sanity

C -   The **irrepressible** mischief-maker, Feste, **dissembled** himself as a priest and went to Malvolio in his dark room. He tormented the servant, playing tricks with his mind. Malvolio, who kept maintaining that he was *not* **demented**, asked for pen and paper to write a letter to Olivia in order to **aver** his sanity.

116. ❤ puny, ignoramus •

LD - play on words; narrator aside; brief flashback

2 Paragraphs - 2nd for narrator aside

Comma - quote

Run-on sentence - lack of punctuation

Punctuation - need for quotes in play on words; placement of exclamation mark outside of quote for one word quotes; quote within a quote; need exclamation marks for Feste's statements (the first of which is also a deliberate fragment)

Incorrect verb-tense switch - Feste is speaking

B - there is no darkness but ignorance said feste to himself malvolio still thought he had a chance with olivia what a **puny ignoramus** he was the real fool

C - "There is no darkness but ignorance," said Feste to himself. "Malvolio still thinks he has a chance with Olivia."

What a **puny ignoramus**! He is the real "fool"!

117. verdant •

LD - aphorism; description within action

Paragraph - subject change

Comma - 2 adjectives; participial phrase

Possession - singular noun

Spelling rule - "i" before "e"...

Pronouns - "he" as subject and "him" as object ("to marry Olivia and him")

Punctuation - use of dash for break and effect and providing extra information (comma could also be used)

Sentence structure - fragment used deliberately after dash for emphasis

Possessive pronouns

B - sebastian was in seventh heaven. he sat in olivias lovely **verdant** garden on a stone bench waiting for the priest to arrive to marry he and olivia. he delighted in his fate a rich countess in love with him

C -   Sebastian was in seventh heaven. He sat in Olivia's lovely, **verdant** garden on a stone bench, waiting for the priest to arrive to marry him and Olivia. He delighted in his fate — a rich countess in love with him.

118. transpired, enigma •

LD - naturalistic detail

No paragraph

Commas - introductory subordinate clause; participial phrase in middle

Homophones - their/there/they're, hear/here

Irregular verbs - sit/set

Transitive vs. intransitive verbs - review

Incorrect verb tense - pluperfect needed as it transpired before he got to garden

Article - "an" before a vowel or a silent "h"

B - as he set theyre surrounded by fragrant flowers and shrubs of all kinds   sebastian wondered how it all **transpired**   there was a **enigma** hear

C - As he sat there, surrounded by fragrant flowers and shrubs of all kinds, Sebastian wondered how it all had **transpired**. There was an **enigma** here.

B = suggested sentence for the board or overhead   *C = sentence written correctly*   **LD** *= literary device*

119. misconception ●

LD - summary for clarification; use of made-up word

Paragraph - subject change

Commas - qualifier for "everyone" (also interrupter); interrupter optional comma after introductory adverb; use of "only" as a coordinating conjunction makes compound sentence

Often confused words - accept/except

Antecedent/pronoun agreement - "everyone" is singular so must use singular possessive pronoun "his/her"

Possession - singular noun

Coordinating conjunctions - avoid beginning a sentence with one unless for effect

Punctuation - need for quotes around made-up word

B - several problems still remained to be resolved. everyone except sebastian and viola of course was under the **misconception** that the twins were the same person. antonio was still under arrest. everyone had their doubts about malvolios sanity. and finally the love triangle still existed only now it was a quintangle with sir aguecheek and malvolio also loving olivia

C - Several problems still remained to be resolved. Everyone, except Sebastian and Viola, of course, was under the **misconception** that the twins were the same person. Antonio was still under arrest. Everyone had his or her doubts about Malvolio's sanity. Finally, the love triangle still existed, only now it was a "quintangle" with Sir Aguecheek and Malvolio also loving Olivia.

120. protagonists ●

LD - flashback

Paragraph - place and subject change

Commas - participial phrase; interrupter

Possession - singular noun

Punctuation - use of parentheses (commas are also O.K.) around flashback

Relative pronouns - "whom" needed as object

Verb form as adjective - "sunken" is adjective form, not "sunk"

Incorrect verb tense - pluperfect needed for action that preceded story

B - all the **protagonists** including the hapless antonio and his arresting officers eventually came together in olivias lovely garden. viola cleared antonio by making orsino the one with who antonio had his troubles over a sunk ship see that antonio was indeed a brave and honorable man

C - All the **protagonists**, including the hapless Antonio and his arresting officers, eventually came together in Olivia's lovely garden. Viola cleared Antonio by making Orsino (the one with whom Antonio had had his troubles over a sunken ship) see that Antonio was, indeed, a brave and honorable man.

121. ire ●

LD - idiomatic expression; narrator aside

No paragraph - continuation; paragraph - narrator aside

Commas - adjective clause with relative pronoun used as appositive; long introductory adverb with 2 prepositional phrases; participial phrase; non-restrictive adjective clause with relative pronoun

Punctuation - use of exclamation marks for emphasis

Relative pronouns - "who" needed as subject in both cases; "that" not used with people

Italics - emphasis (say word louder as you read)

Incorrect verb-tense switch - story in past

Possession - singular noun

B - orsino who was spitting mad with **ire** lit into viola. in the heat of the moment viola confessed her love for orsino. you can imagine the shock this caused. olivia confusing the twins thought it was her husband that loved orsino and said as much. this really ticked off orsino whom accuses viola of stealing olivias love

C - Orsino, who was spitting mad with **ire**, lit into Viola. In the heat of the moment, Viola confessed her love for Orsino.

You can imagine the shock this caused! Olivia, confusing the twins, thought it was her husband who loved Orsino and said as much. This *really* ticked off Orsino, who accused Viola of stealing Olivia's love.

B = suggested sentence for the board or overhead   C = sentence written correctly   LD = literary device

122. garbed •

Paragraph - new person speaking

Commas - quote; direct address

Relative pronouns - "who" needed as subject

Punctuation - use of parentheses for added information for clarity (commas would also be O.K.)

Splitting verbs - don't if at all possible

B - i am not married to olivia cried viola whom was still **garbed** as cesario. i love you orsino with all my life

C - "I am not married to Olivia," cried Viola (who still was **garbed** as Cesario). I love you, Orsino, with all my life."

123. drubbing, conundrum, ♥ cleft •

LD - simile

2 paragraphs - narrator; new person speaking

Commas - adjective phrase; quote; participle; appositive

Misplaced modifier - Sir Aguecheek and Sir Belch are bloody, not the garden

Spelling rules - if word ends in consonant/vowel/consonant and a suffix is added, double the consonant ("drubbing"); "i" before "e..."

Possession - singular noun

Punctuation - use of dash to indicate break

Often confused prepositions - among/between

Homophone - your/you're

B - sir aguecheek and sir Belch entered the crowded garden bloody from their fight with sebastian and accused viola of **drubbing** them. at last the solution to the **conundrum** arrived sebastian. captain antonio sebastians sailor friend was amazed at the likeness among viola and sebastian. your like an apple **cleft** in two he said amazed

C - Sir Aguecheek and Sir Belch, bloody from their fight with Sebastian, entered the crowded garden and accused Viola of **drubbing** them. At last the solution to the **conundrum** arrived — Sebastian. Captain Antonio, Sebastian's sailor friend, was amazed at the likeness between Viola and Sebastian.

"You're like an apple **cleft** in two," he said, amazed.

124. gender, divulged •

LD - idiomatic expression

2 Paragraphs - narrator; narrator's aside

Commas - optional comma after introductory adverb; compound sentence; compound sentence; participial phrase

Incorrect verb tense switch

Hyphen - 2 words acting as one

Plural rule - singular words ending in "es" (even though there isn't really one here)

Plural vs. possessive nouns - confused

Possession - singular noun

Verb tense - use of future tense for definite future action

B - finally viola reveals her **gender** and everything was resolved all practical jokes were confessed orsino did an about face and asked viola to marry him. the rest of the resolution to this convoluted tale including sir belches and malvolios fates will be **divulged** in the final exam

C - Finally, Viola revealed her **gender**, and everything was resolved. All practical jokes were confessed, and Orsino did an about-face and asked Viola to marry him.

The rest of the resolution to this convoluted tale, including Sir Belch's and Malvolio's fates, will be **divulged** in the final exam.

B = suggested sentence for the board or overhead   C = sentence written correctly   LD = literary device

End-of-the-Year Caught'ya Test

Directions:

Be very careful. You will receive no hints for this test, except that there are fourteen paragraphs, only one misplaced modifier, and one run-on sentence. Other than in the run-on sentence, all end punctuation has been provided.

Edit this story as best you can on this paper. Use the paragraph sign to indicate the need for a paragraph. Write in the proofreading symbols for all mechanical corrections. Write in corrections of misspelled words. Rewrite sentences where the meanings are unclear. Then rewrite the entire test correctly. This is what your teacher will grade.

When you reach the end of the test, do the following: write the numbers one to twenty-two on the back of your paper and tell the part of speech of each word in the last two sentences of the story. After you have finished the entire test, go back and check your work several times. Good editors always do.

the dénouement of the story

when everyone accept churlish foolish malvolio feste sir belch and sir aguecheek were in olivias garden and viola had revealed her gender the troubles were not quiet at there end. sebastian like he was stupid and hadnt been given enough clues realized that viola was his sister and chided her. you was betrothed to both a maid and a man! he concludes. viola we are now sisters said olivia since youre brother is my husband. do not be amazed at your sister broke in orsino. i should of picked up on her hints. she said to me many times that the person she loved was like me said orsino whom was delighted and amazed to find that his servant and trusted friend was indeed a beautiful young woman. give me your hand viola let me see you in womens clothing it is me that loves you. well said viola me and a sea captain conspired to have me dress as a man and work as youre servant. this captain has my clothes but he be held prisoner by malvolio. at that point whom should enter the garden but feste with malvolios letter the one he wrote to try too prove his sanity. its contents were read aloud by olivia whos reading in a fake voice made everyone shake theyre sides in laughter. malvolio heard everyones laughter as he entered the garden shaking with anger. madame you have done me wrong he said to olivia. me malvolio? no i dont think so objected olivia. malvolio waved the original letter the one that maria dropped in the garden at olivia. look at this letter. its in your handwriting. no malvolio its not said olivia. that is not my writing but it is alot like it. its marias handwriting. my uncle sir belch and her told me you were mad. perhaps this is there trick. alas poor fool they have hoodwinked you she concluded. captain antonio than accused viola of betraying him. orsino cleared up that misunderstanding by swearing that she had been in his service for 3 months as cesario. all however was still not resolved. sir belch and sir aguecheek entered the scene. among them they were complaining about their wounds accusing cesario of attacking and called for a surgeon. the surgeon couldnt come for he was drunk. finally sir belch realized what an intelligent woman maria was and married her. orsino recognized that he really had always loved viola. everything ended good except for malvolio and sir aguecheek that were the real fools.

End-of-the-year Caught'ya Test Key

Teachers: *This is an extremely difficult test. It covers a year's worth of material. You might want to have a review before the test. On the day of the test, read the test out loud to your students to give them hints of where to paragraph and punctuate. Remind your students to number their papers from one to twenty on the back and write the part of speech of each word in the last sentence. Since there are over one hundred errors in this test, depending on how you count the misplaced modifier, you might want to grade it on a percentage basis. Those of you who teach ninth or tenth grade might want to help out your students by counting the possible errors in each line and writing these numbers in the margin before you photocopy the test for your students. Because it is so difficult to count errors correctly, you might want to triple-check your figures.*

The Dénouement of the Story

When everyone except churlish, foolish Malvolio, Feste, Sir Belch, and Sir Aguecheek was in Olivia's garden, and Viola had revealed her gender, the troubles were not quite at their end. Sebastian, as if he were stupid and hadn't been given enough clues, realized that Viola was his sister and chided her.

"You were betrothed to both a maid and a man!" he concluded.

"Viola, we are now sisters," said Olivia, " since your brother is my husband."

"Do not be amazed at your sister," broke in Orsino. "I should have picked up on her hints. She said to me many times that the person she loved was like me," said Orsino, who was delighted and amazed to find that his servant and trusted friend was, indeed, a beautiful young woman. "Give me your hand, Viola, and let me see you in women's clothing. *[or "Give me your hand, Viola. Let me see you...."]* It is I who loves you."

"Well," said Viola, "a sea captain and I conspired to have me dress as a man and work as your servant. This captain has my clothes, but he is being held prisoner by Malvolio."

At that point who should enter the garden but Feste with Malvolio's letter (the one he had written to try to prove his sanity). *[Note: commas also would be acceptable.]* Its contents were read aloud by Olivia whose reading in a fake voice made everyone shake his or her sides in laughter.

Malvolio, shaking with anger, heard everyone's laughter as he entered the garden. "Madame, you have done me wrong," he said to Olivia.

"I, Malvolio? No, I don't think so," objected Olivia.

Malvolio waved the original letter (the one that Maria had dropped in the garden) *[Note: commas also would be acceptable.]* at Olivia. "Look at this letter. It's in your handwriting."

"No, Malvolio, it is *[or it's]* not," said Olivia. "That is not my writing, but it is a lot like it. It is Maria's handwriting. She and my uncle, Sir Belch, told me you were mad. Perhaps this is their trick. Alas, poor fool, they have hoodwinked you," she concluded.

Captain Antonio then accused Viola of betraying him. Orsino cleared up that misunderstanding by swearing that she had been in his service for three months as Cesario.

All, however, still was not resolved. Sir Belch and Sir Aguecheek entered the scene. Between them they were complaining about their wounds, accusing Cesario of attacking, and calling for a surgeon. The surgeon couldn't come, for he was drunk.

Finally, Sir Belch realized what an intelligent woman Maria was and married her. Orsino recognized that he really always had loved Viola. Everything ended well, but for Malvolio and Sir Aguecheek who were the real "fools."

Appendix

• •

Everything You Never Wanted to Know about

Grammar, Mechanics, and Usage

But I'm Going to Tell You Anyway

Introductory Notes

Those of us who are familiar with some topic or idea sometimes forget that not everyone else has the same knowledge. This is why I included this **Appendix**. Unless you have taught English for a year at eighth-grade level or higher, unless you have had a teacher somewhere along the way who has successfully taught you all the terms, or unless you have studied a grammar book from cover to cover and have kept up with all the changes, there is no way that you can know the rules of English grammar and usage and its many technical terms.

Complex as the language is, even we English teachers have trouble with some of the picky mechanical points of the language. We also disagree!

English is a fluid language. It changes with use. Thirty years ago we strewed commas with near abandon. Now we are eliminating many of them. People begin sentences with conjunctions. I have real trouble with this. Conjunctions are for joining ideas, not starting them. What teachers once called a dependent clause is now lumped under the heading of subordinate clause, and so on. Because of this, we all do not follow identical rules and terms, yet all of us still can be officially correct at the same time.

Do not be afraid to disagree with me. Many points of mechanics, especially the use of some commas, are highly debatable, extremely personal, and sometimes linked to a particular generation. When I participated in writing the English curriculum for the middle schools in my county, seven English teachers sat around a table and argued various points. Each of us always could find a book that would support a specific opinion. After a few hot debates, we finally had to agree to use one standard book for reference.

When Maupin House asked me to include a section that could serve as a reference for the grammar, mechanics, and usage terms, frankly, I was apprehensive. It seemed to be a dangerous task for one person to attempt. Grammar books are usually written by committees and still have errors in them. I solicited the help of my mother and several of my colleagues, all excellent grammarians, to ensure accuracy.

Do not feel inadequate or undereducated if you find yourself frequently referring to this Appendix. Many of you, like me, probably did not major in English in college and do not read grammar textbooks for pleasure. This **Appendix** will help you understand the whys and wherefores of a sentence so that you can explain it to your children in a way that makes sense to them. Once students understand the underlying concept of a rule, they can apply that rule to their own sentences when they write.

The terms are listed in alphabetical order for easier reference. If you do not fully understand a term used in one explanation, you can look it up under its own heading. All the terms that a non-English major might need for clarity are cross-referenced. Also included in the **Appendix** are some tips for teaching some of these concepts. I hope you find these suggestions useful. All of these teaching tips have proven successful with students.

Examples are included for each concept. If, after reading the explanation of a concept, you still do not feel comfortable with it, study the examples. Right here, I feel the need to apologize for the truly uninspired examples. The majority of them concerns my two dogs and one cat. They are always present when I write, like furry muses.

While I am aware that the current trend is to abandon the teaching of certain concepts and terms such as the parts of speech, as a foreign language teacher I know that students need to be familiar with these terms to learn the new language. If a student is aware of the difference, for example, between a subject pronoun and an object pronoun, then French pronouns do not hold much horror.

In my French classes, I often find myself having to teach the parts of speech just so my students and I can have a common frame of reference. It is hard enough to learn a different vocabulary in another language. If, in addition, students have to learn basic grammar terms as well, it makes the task much more difficult. The grammar of languages based on Indo-European is basically similar. The verb may come at the end of a sentence in German or at the end of a subordinate clause in Dutch, or there may be an extra verb tense to learn in Spanish and French. The basic concepts and parts of speech, however, are the same in all these languages.

I believe, too, in the teaching of sentence diagramming to help students to think and to use logic. Diagramming reaches some left-brain students who otherwise might never understand sentence structure.

After teaching rudimentary sentence diagramming through the Caught'yas, I almost can see the light bulb go on in some students' eyes. I do not believe, however, in teaching all the picky points of English like infinitive phrases, gerund phrases, etc. unless there is a reason for learning them, like learning the appropriate placement of commas.

Even then, when teaching the picky points is unavoidable, I advise trying to avoid using the abstruse, esoteric grammar terms. Instead, explain these points in simpler terms, using the eight parts of speech for reference. I don't say to students, for example, "If a participial phrase begins or interrupts a sentence, you need to set it off by commas. You need to know that a participial phrase is . . . " Even after you explain what a participial phrase is, your students probably are gazing out the window, minds elsewhere.

Try something like this instead. "See this phrase. What part of speech is it? An adjective? Right! You know the parts of speech! Well, look at it. It contains a form of a verb. If you see a group of words like this at the beginning of a sentence or in the middle of a sentence, you need to put commas after it or around it." That gets their attention because it is something that makes sense to them. I do mention the words "participial phrase" so that students may recognize the term in the future in case other English teachers use it, but I stress the concept and not the specific term.

Other examples: instead of talking about "gerunds," you can teach your students to use a verb or a verb phrase as a noun. In teaching verbs like "lie" and "lay," "sit" and "set," and "rise" and "raise," a teacher can explain the use of each verb by talking about verbs that take direct objects and verbs that do not, instead of introducing new labels "transitive" and "intransitive."

Basically, the bottom line is to write correctly, not to memorize the names for everything or to identify certain phrases or clauses. When a student writes a sentence, the labels are useless. The task of English teachers is not to teach rules and technical terms, but to teach correct writing and editing skills.

Those of you who teach basic-skills calsses will want to avoid the more complicated concepts anyway. Use your own judgement as to how much your students can comprehend and transfer to their writing. Each class is different. Each group has different needs. You know them best.

If you are writing your own sentences, you will want to keep this book open to the **Appendix** as you write. Make certain that you include in your story the grammar, mechanics, and usage that you know your students can grasp comfortably. The list is comprehensive so that this book can be used at any level. I hope that all of you find this **Appendix** a useful tool in teaching this beautiful language of ours.

Abbreviations

Most abbreviations are followed by a period.

Examples: Mr., Mrs.

If, however, all the letters of the abbre-viation are capitals, a period is not used.

Examples: NATO, USSR, USA

Usually abbreviations begin with a capital letter. Abbreviations of units of measure, however, do not begin with capital letters. They also do not require periods. The only exception is the abbreviation for inch.

Examples: mph, hp, l, km, and so on.

Exception: in.

Common abbreviations: Mr., Mrs., Ms., Dr., St., Rd., Ave., Co., Inc., days of the week, months of the year, A.M., P.M., O.K.,etc.

State abbreviations: The United States Postal Service now uses special abbreviations for each state. These are always two letters, both capitalized, without any periods. The postal code of twenty-nine states is the first two letters of the state. If the state has two words, the first letter of each word is used.

States that follow this rule: AL, AR, CA, CO, DE, FL, ID, IL, IN, MA, MI, NE, NH, NJ, NM, NY, NC, ND, OH, OK, OR, RI, SC, SD, UT, WA, WV, WI, and WY

Exceptions: Alaska (AK), Arizona (AZ), Connecticut (CT), Georgia (GA), Hawaii (HI), Iowa (IA), Kansas (KS), Kentucky (KY), Louisiana (LA), Maine (ME), Maryland (MD), Minnesota (MN), Mississippi (MS), Missouri (MO), Montana (MT), Nevada (NV), Pennsylvania (PA), Tennessee (TN), Texas (TX), Vermont (VT), and Virginia (VA).

Accept/Except

These two words often are confusing for students since they are so close in sound. Every time one of them appears in a Caught'ya, you can explain the difference.

1. Accept is a verb that means "to receive willingly."

Example: The fat Rottweiler surely **will accept** the bone.

2. Except is a preposition that means "excluding" or "other than." It also can be used as a verb that means "to leave out" or "exclude."

Examples: The fat Rottweiler eats everything **except** onions. (preposition)

The fire department will **except** men over seventy-two inches from that kind of duty. (verb)

Active vs Passive Verb Voices

1. **Active**: In the active voice, the subject does the action. Active voice is always better for more effective writing.

Example: The owner **pets** the happy dog on the head.

2. **Passive**: In the passive voice, the subject **receives** the action. Encourage students to try to avoid passive voice if at all possible. It weakens writing and often muddies the meaning in a sentence.

Example: The happy dog **was petted** on the head by the owner.

Adjective

An adjective describes a noun; it gives information about a noun.

Examples: ugly, pretty, big, little, this, four

An adjective answers one of the following three questions about a noun:

1) which one?

2) what kind?

3) how many?

Example: **The amazing English** teacher taught **two** grade levels. (which teacher? **the English** teacher; what kind of teacher? an **amazing** teacher; how many grade levels? **two** grade levels.)

Adjective Clauses

An adjective clause is any subordinate clause (a complete sentence made into an incomplete sentence by the addition of a subordinating conjunction) that acts as an adjective in a sentence.

Example: The house **where she lives** is filled with animals. ("She lives." would be a complete sentence without the addition of "where." "Where she lives" modifies the noun "house.")

Adjective clauses also can begin with a relative pronoun: who, whom, whose, which, that, where, or when.

Examples: The oven **which was small and dirty** could not be used.

This is the school **where my child is a student**.

The school **that my child attends** is a good one.

The teacher **who loves to laugh** has more fun.

Monday is the day **when we always write in our journals**.

The teacher **whom we admire** is retiring.

Jane Kiester, **whose dogs are obese**, teaches middle school.

Adverb

An adverb is any word, phrase or clause that tells more about a verb; many of the single word adverbs end in "ly."

An adverb also tells to what extent an adjective or another adverb is true (very, extremely, and so on). This is called an intensifier.

Examples: a **very** hungry dog, an **extremely** sleepy cat

An adverb answers one of the following six questions about a verb, an adjective, or another adverb: where, when, why, how, how often, or to what extent it happened.

Examples: Where? The students learned grammar **at home**. (phrase)

When? **Yesterday** the teacher was absent.

How? The students **quickly** intimidated the substitute.

How often? The student yawned **four times** during class. (phrase)

To what extent? The teacher was **very** angry. (modifies the adjective "angry")

Why? She yelled **because she was angry**. (clause)

Adverb Clauses

In the "olden days," an adverb clause was called an adverbial clause.

An adverb (or adverbial) clause is a subordinate clause that cannot stand on its own in a sentence. It acts as an adverb in a sentence.

Adverb clauses begin with a subordinating conjunction (see list under "Subordinating Conjunctions")

Examples: **Whenever the teacher taught grammar,** the students groaned. (When did the students groan? "Whenever the teacher . . .")

The students went home **when the last bell rang**. (When did the students go home? "when the bell rang.")

Affect/Effect

"Affect" and "effect" are two more words that many people confuse. If students have trouble with the correct use of these two words, use them in the Caught'yas and discuss their meanings.

1. Affect is a verb that means "to influence." It cannot be used as a noun.

Example: The eating habits of the fat Rottweiler will **affect** her girth.

2. Effect can be a noun or a verb. As a noun it means "the result of an action." As a verb it means "to cause to happen."

Examples: The **effect** of overeating is obvious in the width of the dog's belly. (noun)

The fat dog's owner **will effect** a new rule this week — no more scraps. (verb)

Agreement

1. **Antecedent and pronoun**: It is important that everything agrees in a sentence. If the subject is singular, then the pronoun used later in the sentence also must be singular. If the subject is plural, the pronoun should be plural.

Example of incorrect agreement: **Everyone** ate **their** pizza. (The indefinite pronoun "everyone" is singular and thus the possessive pronoun which refers to it also must be singular.

Examples of correct agreement: **Everyone** ate **his** or **her** pizza.

Each finished **his** or **her** lunch.

The **teachers** ate **their** lunch.

The **teacher** ate **his** lunch.

2. **Subject and verb**: If the subject is singular, then the verb must also be singular. If the subject is plural, then the verb must be plural.

Examples: The **dog bays** at the full moon. (singular)

The **dogs bay** at the full moon. (plural)

3. **Verbs in a story**: When writing a story an author must keep all the verbs in the same tense. If the story starts in the present tense, it must continue in the present tense (unless, of course, there is a flashback or a reference to something general). If a story begins in the past, it must remain in the past, and so on.

Among and Between

"Among" and "between" are two prepositions that students often confuse, but they cease to be a problem very quickly after you point out the difference.

1. **Between** refers to two people, things, or groups.

Example: The cat slept **between** the two huge dogs.

2. **Among** refers to more than two people, things, or groups.

Example: The foolish cat slept **among** the four dogs.

Antecedents (*See also* Collective Nouns)

These are the words that come before a given word in a sentence, as in "antecedent/pronoun agreement," and are referred to by the given word. Thus, they must agree with each other. If one is singular, the other also must be singular, etc.

Example: The **pack** (antecedent) of dogs forsook **its** (pronoun) mistress. ("**Pack**" is singular and thus must be followed by a singular pronoun.)

Apostrophes

1. Contractions always contain apostrophes. A contraction comprises two words that are combined into one by omitting one or more letters. (*See* Contractions for more information and examples.)

Common contractions: I'm, I've, can't, don't, haven't, isn't, it's, let's, they're, we're, we've, won't, you're

2. **Possessive nouns** always contain apostrophes. A possessive noun is a noun that shows ownership of something.

Singular: Always add 's to the noun.

Examples: The **dog's** growl is ferocious. (The growl belongs to the dog.)

The **glass's** rim is dirty. (The rim belongs to the glass.)

Plural: Add ' after the noun if the noun ends in "s."

Add 's to the noun if the plural does not end in "s."

Examples: The **dogs'** growls are ferocious. (Several dogs "own" their growls.)

The **children's** laughter fills the room. (Several children "own" the laughter.

3. **Plurals of letters**: Form the plural of single letters by adding apostrophe "s."

Examples: You will find more "**E's**" in words than any other letter.

She received all "**A's**" on her report card.

Appositive

An appositive is a noun or a noun phrase that means the same thing as the noun that comes before it.

Appositives are set off by commas if they occur in the middle or end of a sentence and are not necessary to the meaning of the sentence.

Examples: Dino, **the Doberman with the floppy ears**, loves to eat bananas.

The dog who craves bananas is Dino, **the Doberman with the floppy ears**.

Appositives are set off by commas if the appositive is extra information and is not needed to complete the meaning of the sentence.

Examples: Jane Kiester, **an English teacher at Westwood**, loves dogs.

Always by her side are her two dogs, **a wimpy Rottweiler and an oversized Doberman**.

Appositives are not set off by commas if the information given is needed to identify the noun.

Example: Mrs. Kiester's son **John** loves to tease his mother.

(There are no commas to set off this appositive because Mrs. Kiester has more than one son. The name is necessary to determine to which son the sentence refers. Technically, this is called a restrictive modifier. If Mrs. Kiester has only one son, the comma is needed because the information is *not* necessary. This is called a non-restrictive modifier.)

(*See* Modifiers and Misplaced Modifiers for more information and examples of restrictive and non-restrictive appositives.)

Articles

These are simply the three most commonly used adjectives. They are also called noun markers since they signal the arrival of a noun.

List of articles: a, an, the

1. Use "a" before a word that begins with a consonant.

Example: There is a lazy dog and a sleepy cat on the floor.

2. Use "an" before a word that begins with a vowel.

Example: **An** obnoxious black and white cat howled until someone let him out the door.

These three adjectives answer the question "which one?" (*See* Noun Markers.)

Bad and Badly

These words often cause confusion. "Bad" is the adjective and should modify a noun. "Badly" is the adverb and should tell about a verb.

Examples: The **bad** dog begged for forgiveness. (adjective tells what kind of dog)

The poor dog **badly** wanted a bone. (adverb tells to what extent it wanted the bone)

When a sense verb such as "feel" functions as a verb of being, it is often followed by a predicate adjective. Thus, one would use the adjective form after such a verb.

Example: I feel **bad**. (Not "I feel badly," since one would not say "I am badly."

Because and Since

If you never put a comma before "because" and "since," you will be right 98 percent of the time. While there are some exceptions to this, they are rare. The words "because" and "since" begin adverb clauses. An adverb clause that begins a sentence needs a comma, but an adverb clause that follows the independent clause usually does not need a comma. Saying the sentence aloud is a good test.

About the only exceptions to this would be with a quotation or in a series, in the case of "since" acting as a coordinating conjunction in a compound sentence, or in one of the few subordinate clauses that takes a comma for clarity.

Examples: **Because I like books about cats**, I read *The Literary Cat*. (adverb clause at the beginning of the sentence)

I read *The Literary Cat* **because I like books about cats**. (adverb clause that follows the independent clause)

Between (*See* Among and Between)

Bibliographical Forms

These do vary. Use the Modern Language Association form, and you will be safe. Most traditional grammar books have a large list explaining how to write any reference you may need in correct bibliographical form. Just make sure that you insist that students list the books, articles, etc. in their bibliographies in alphabetical order.

Business Letters (Correct Format)

> Sender's address
> Sender's city, state   zip
> Date

Receiver's name
Receiver's address
Receiver's city, state   zip

Dear Sir or Madam:

The bulk of the letter should be written in block style, skipping lines between paragraphs.

> Sincerely yours,
> Write name here in cursive.
> Print or type name here.

Capitalization

Capitalize the following:

1. Abbreviations (*See* Abbreviations for the exceptions.)
2. Beginnings of sentences
3. First word in the greeting and closing of a letter
4. I
5. Names of months and days and holidays
6. Proper nouns and proper adjectives
7. Titles of long works (*see* Titles)
   - Capitalize first and last words.
   - Capitalize all other words in title except prepositions, noun markers (a, an, the), and short conjunctions.

Chronological Order

In writing stories and paragraphs, it is important to narrate the action in a logical order. Chronological order maintains a sequence of time.

Clauses and Phrases

1. **Phrase**: Simply stated, a phrase is a group of words that serves as one part of speech (like a noun or an adjective or an adverb). It lacks a subject or a verb or both. Prepositional phrases are the most common. These are phrases that begin with a preposition and end with a noun (in the dog house).

Examples: in the dog house, to the store, filled with anger, rubbing his ears

2. **Clause**: A clause, on the other hand, is a group of words that contains a subject and a verb. With the removal of a subordinating conjunction that begins it, it could stand on its own as a sentence.

Example: because the dog is lazy (The subject is the word "dog." The verb is the word "is.")

Collective Nouns

Collective nouns are nouns that take a group of something (many) and make that group one thing.

Common collective nouns: crew, class, orchestra, chorus, committee, family, flock, herd, fleet, jury, group, team, majority.

1. Most collective nouns are singular and therefore require the singular form of the verb. Also, any pronoun that refers to such a collective noun must be singular.

Examples: A **flock** of big birds **flies** over her house every autumn. ("Fly" would be the plural form of the verb)

The **group** applauded its leader. "Its" is the singular pronoun; "their" is the plural pronoun and thus is incorrect. This is one of the most common mistakes that people make in speech and in writing.

The girl's **family** took **its** vacation in June.

2. A few collective nouns are plural.

Example: The **people** took **their** dogs to the veterinarian.

Colons

1. Use a colon before a list but never after a verb or a preposition.

Example: It is important to remember to bring the following to class: pencil, paper, and a big grin.

2. Use after the greeting in a business letter.

Examples: Dear Sir or Madam:

To Whom It May Concern:

3. Use a colon to separate the hour from the minute in telling time.

Examples: 5:45 P.M., 6:24 A.M.

4. If the wording that follows a colon forms a complete sentence, do not capitalize the first letter of the sentence.

Example: The question is as follows: do Dobermans like to eat broccoli?

Combining Sentences for Clearer, More Concise Writing

Combine two related sentences into one by making a compound subject and/or a compound verb or by adding an appositive. There are other ways to combine sentences. These are the most common.

Example: Change "The teacher hated spelling. Her students hated spelling." to "The teacher and her students hated spelling." (compound subject).

Change "The Rottweiler loved to sleep. She liked to lick her owner's face in the morning." (compound verb) to "The Rottweiler loved to sleep and liked to lick her owner's face in the morning."

Change "The Doberman had floppy ears. He also had a sweet disposition." to "The Doberman, who had floppy ears, had a sweet disposition." (adding an adjective clause)

Comma Rules

1. Use commas to separate items in a series. There are many different kinds of series, one for each part of speech except conjunctions.

Examples: The teacher **entered** the class, **wrote** on the board, and **sat** down at her desk. (verb series)

The teacher ate **apples, bananas, and cherries.** (noun series)

The **nice, kind**, and **beautiful** teacher assigned no homework for the weekend. (adjective series)

The teacher sat down **quickly, quietly,** and **with great dignity.** (adverb series)

He went **to the store, down the aisle**, and **into the vegetable section**. (prepositional phrase series)

She sat with **him, her,** and **them.** (series of pronouns)

Oh boy, wow, and **whoopee**, the teacher had a great class! (series of interjections)

You also can have a series of predicate nouns and adjectives. (These are just nouns and adjectives that are located after the predicate.)

2. Use commas between two or more adjectives that precede a noun unless one of the adjectives expresses a single idea with the noun (jet plane) or the last adjective tells color (green, etc.) or age (old, young).

Comma needed: The **cute, fuzzy** dog barked at everyone.

Comma omitted: The **cute brown** dog barked at everyone. (color adjective)

The **noisy jet** plane flew overhead. ("Jet plane" is one idea. The adjective is really part of the noun.)

The **ugly young** dog wolfed down its food. (age adjective).

The general "rule of thumb" in this comma rule is to use a comma if it sounds right to use the word "and" instead of a comma.

Examples: The old oaken bucket was covered with wet green moss. (No commas needed as it would be awkward to say "The old and oaken bucket was covered with wet and green moss.")

The **floppy-eared, lazy** Doberman slept all day. (Here you use a comma because it makes sense to say "The floppy-eared and lazy Doberman slept all day.")

3. Use commas to separate the simple sentences included in a compound sentence. (See Compound Sentences)

Example: The teacher wrote the sentence, and she put in a comma because the sentence was compound.

4. Use commas after words, phrases, and clauses that come at the beginning of sentences. "No" and "yes" are included here. They always are followed by a comma.

Examples: **No**, you may not turn in your homework late.

Yes, you may do extra work if you wish.

Wow, the student earned an A + on his test!

At the end of the phrase, there should be a comma.

If a subordinate clause is at the beginning of a sentence, you have to put a comma after it.

Suddenly, the teacher yelled. (This comma is often debated. Put a comma if a breath or a pause would help clarify the sentence or if you want to accentuate the adverb.)

Well, she said that she would come.

5. Use commas to separate interrupters such as parenthetical expressions, direct addresses, and unnecessary appositives in a sentence.

Examples: Parenthetical expression — The big dog, **of course**, was a wimp.

Direct address: You know, **parents**, it is important to write correctly.

Parents, you know it is important to write correctly.

Unnecessary appositive: My cat, **Skeeter**, likes to sit on my lap as I write. (I have only one cat; therefore his name is not necessary for the meaning of the sentence to be clear.)

My dog Dino has floppy ears. (No commas are needed because I have two dogs, and I need to identify to which dog I refer.)

6. Use commas to separate the month and the day from the year.

Example: September 15, 1945

7. Use commas between the city and the state and after the state as well if the address is within the sentence.

Example: The animal lover lives in **Gainesville, Florida**, and teaches English at a middle school.

8. Use commas after the greeting in friendly letters and after the closing in both friendly and business letters.

Examples: Dear Jane,

Sincerely yours,

9. Use commas with quotation marks to set off what is being said out loud.

Examples: "Get off my foot," she whimpered to the heavy dog.

She whimpered to the heavy dog, "Get off my foot."

"If you don't get off my foot," she said, "I'll step on yours."

Comparisons

Adjectives

1. If you are comparing two or more things and the adjective has fewer than three syllables, add "er" to the adjective.

Example: Florida is **warmer** than Maine in the winter.

2. If you are stating that something is the best (or worst), add "est" to the adjective if it has fewer than three syllables.

Example: Florida is the **warmest** state in the union.

3. Using "more" and "most"

Adjectives of three or more syllables almost always use the words more" or "the most" to state comparison.

Examples: The Rottweiler is **more obnoxious** than the Doberman.

The black and white cat is **the most obnoxious** of all of the animals in her menagerie.

4. When comparing persons or things in the same group, use the word "other."

Example: Jesse can run faster than **any other** boy in his club.

A few adjectives with irregular forms of comparison must be memorized: good-better-best; bad-worse-worst; many, much-more-most; little (quantity only)-less-least; far-farther-farthest.

Adverbs

1. If you are comparing two things, add "er" to the adverb. If you are saying that something is done better than anything else, add "est" to the adverb.

Examples: Planes travel faster than cars.

Rockets travel fastest of all.

2. Using "more" and "most"

There is no steadfast rule as to when you add "er" or "est" or when you use "more" or "most." The best suggestion I can make is to go with what sounds correct. Most adverbs of two or more syllables form comparisons with "more" or "most."

Example: comprehensively, more comprehensively, most comprehensively

Complex Sentences (*See* also Subordinate Clauses)

A complex sentence is a sentence that has one or more independent clauses (a group of words that makes sense by itself) and a subordinate clause (a group of words with a subject and a verb but which does not make sense by itself).

The important thing to remember about a complex sentence is that if the subordinate clause begins the sentence, a comma must follow it.

Example: Although the dog sat on her foot, she did not say a word. (subordinate clause, independent clause)

Compound Sentences

A compound sentence is composed of two complete sentences (related ideas only) joined together with a comma and a coordinating conjunction (and, or, nor, for, so, but, yet) or a semicolon.

Examples: The big dog sat on her foot, **and** she gazed up at her mistress with love. "The big dog sat on her foot" is a complete sentence. "She gazed up at her mistress with love" is a sentence.

I tell my students to put their finger over the coordinating conjunction and check whether there is a complete sentence on either side of the finger. If there are two sentences, a comma has to precede the conjunction because the sentence is compound.

Examples: The big dog licked his paw, **or** he licked his leg.

The big dog did not lick his paw, **nor** did he lick his leg.

The big dog sat on her foot, **for** he loved her.

The big dog ate too much, **so** he was rotund.

The big dog sat on her foot, **but** he didn't put his full weight on it.

The big dog sat on her foot, **yet** he still felt insecure.

Sometimes a compound sentence does not have a coordinating conjunction joining the two sentences. Instead, it has a semicolon.

Example: The big dog sat on her foot; it then licked her knee.

A compound sentence does not occur when the word "that" is included or implied after the word "so." "So that" is a subordinating conjunction of a subordinate clause. If a subordinate clause comes at the end of a sentence, there is no comma.

Examples: She grabbed the bone **so that** the other dog could not get it. ("**So that**" the other dog could not get it, she grabbed the bone.)

She gobbled her food **so** the other dog could not get it. ("That" is implied)

A compound imperative sentence **does not** take a comma because the subjects, while implied, are not stated.

Examples: Get off my feet and go lie down elsewhere. (to the dog)

Stop clawing my legs and settle down. (to the cat)

Compound Subjects and Compound Predicates

These should be recognized if only to ensure that the students know the meanings of the words "compound," "subject," and "predicate." These words appear on the standardized tests. I usually teach these in my diagramming unit. Diagramming makes compound subjects and predicates much clearer.

1. A compound subject is simply more than one thing or person doing the action.

Example: **Rottweilers** and **Dobermans** make wonderful pets.

2. A compound predicate is more than one verb supplying the action.

Example: Rottweilers **love** to eat and **enjoy** being petted.

Conjunctions

A conjunction is a word that joins words or groups of words together. Do not capitalize a conjunction in a title.

Example: The dog **and** the cat are friends.

1. **Coordinating conjunctions**: These are the conjunctions (joiners) which join two complete thoughts (independent clauses) together to form a compound sentence.

List of coordinating conjunctions: and, or, nor, for, so, but, yet.

It is a good idea to chant these with your students every time you encounter a compound sentence in a Caught'ya.

Example: She loves ice cream, **and** she loves candy, too.

Do not begin a sentence with a coordinating conjunction since they are supposed to join, not begin. Many authors of fiction ignore this rule. This is fine, and it can make for very effective writing. I have to enforce this rule with those students who begin almost every sentence with a conjunction.

2. **Correlative conjunctions**: These are used to join words or word groups. They appear in pairs.

Examples: **Either** you do your homework, **or** your grade will suffer.

Both Dobermans **and** Rottweilers make good companions.

List of correlative conjunctions: either/or, neither/nor, not only/but, both/and, just as/so.

3. **Subordinating conjunctions**: These conjunctions make a clause that was a complete sentence into a clause that cannot stand on its own. In other words, if a subordinating conjunction is placed before an independent clause (complete sentence), the clause becomes a dependent clause (subordinate clause).

Complete sentence: The dog licks the rug.

Dependent clause: **When** the dog licks the rug (no longer a complete sentence)

Subordinating conjunctions begin subordinate clauses. Always set off an intro-ductory adverb clause (another word for a subordinate clause since subordinate clauses act as adverbs) with a comma.

Examples: **After the cat fell asleep**, he twitched his whiskers.

As the man shouted, the two dogs cringed.

Common subordinating conjunctions: after, although, as, as if, as long as, as soon as, as though, because, before, even though, if, in order that, provided that, since, so that, than, till, unless, until, when, whenever, where, whereas, wherever, while.

Continued Quote

This is a sentence in a quote that is interrupted by identifying the speaker. It is important to recognize that when the quoted sentence continues, quotation marks are necessary, but the first letter should not be capitalized. This is also called an interrupted quote.

Example: "My Doberman is a lazy dog," she said, "but my Rottweiler is even lazier."

Contractions

A contraction is a word made by the shortening of two words into one, eliminating some letters in the process. The two words are then joined by an apostrophe.

1. Contractions can be made by shortening "not" to "n't" and adding to a verb. Sometimes the spelling of the verb changes as when "n't" is added to "shall," "will," or "can."

Examples: is not/isn't; does not/doesn't; cannot/can't; shall not/shan't; will not/won't.

2. It's and its

"Its" is a possessive pronoun that shows that "it" owns something.

Example: The dog ate its food.

"It's" is a contraction for "it is."

Example: **It's** a shame that she has so many animals to feed.

3. Contractions are also formed by joining nouns or pronouns with verbs.

Examples: I am/I'm; he is/he's; he had/he'd; you are/you're; she has/she's, let us/let's, they are/they're.

Avoid contractions in formal writing. Contractions render writing informal, and unless a writer is using dialogue or a truly informal style, the use of contractions probably should be avoided.

Dangling Participle

A dangling participle is a participle (present or past form of a verb) used as an adjective that is not adjacent to the noun that it modifies. Dangling participles should be avoided.

Example: **Snoring, the dog's nose** twitched. (The dog's nose did not do the snoring, the dog did. The word "dog" needs to follow the participle "snoring.")

Snoring, the dog twitched his nose.

Dashes
A dash can be used to show a break or a shift in thought or structure. It also can signal an afterthought.

Examples: Now, when I was a boy — (break)

I found her most — well, I didn't like her manner. (shift in structure)

The big Doberman — the one with the floppy ears —leans against walls and people. (break)

My floppy-eared Doberman often leans — you know, all Dobermans lean like that. (shift in thought)

It is important to limit the use of dashes when writing. Too many dashes make the writing seem confused and jerky.

Diagramming Sentences

Sentence diagramming takes every word in a sentence and places it, according to its use, in a diagram-like chart. It is a graphic picture of a sentence. Diagramming sentences is a good skill for students to learn because it forces them to think logically. Diagramming sentences also teaches students good puzzle-solving techniques and makes them practice their knowledge of the eight parts of speech.

If you want students to diagram a few Caught'yas for practice, look at the section on diagramming sentences in any traditional grammar text.

The example below shows how a diagram works for a compound sentence:

Dialogues

Begin a new paragraph every time a different person speaks. If a person's speech includes more than one paragraph at a time, do not put quotation marks at the end of the first paragraph. Begin the next paragraph with quotation marks.

Example: (end of paragraph) " . . . and the teacher is always there."

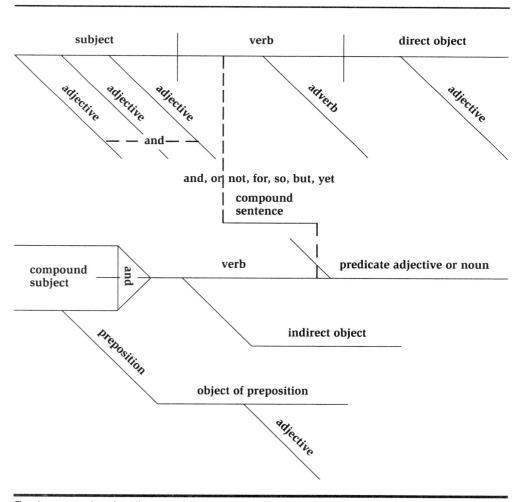

Basic example of a diagram for a compound sentence

(new paragraph) "Students, on the other hand . . . "

Punctuation of quotes: Put quotation marks around what is said aloud. Capitalize the first letter of a quote unless the quote is a continued one. Set off the quote by commas or by end punctuation. Always put all punctuation inside the quotation marks.

Examples: "Close the window, you outdoor fanatic," she whimpered. "I'm freezing in here."

"Please close the window," she said, "or I'll become an icicle."

She pleaded again, "Close that window."

"Will you please close the window?" she asked.

"Close that window!" she yelled.

Direct Address

A direct address occurs when the writer is speaking directly to someone, telling someone something, and naming that someone.

Direct addresses are also called interrupters because they interrupt the flow of a sentence. Always set a direct address off by commas.

Examples: **Dog**, get off my foot. (talking to the dog)

If you don't get off my foot, **dog**, you are in big trouble.

Get off my foot, dog.

Direct and Indirect Objects

1. **Direct objects** are nouns or pronouns that directly receive the action of the verb. They, therefore, follow only transitive verbs. Direct objects answer the question "whom" or "what" receives the action of the verb.

Examples: The dog licked the **teacher**. ("teacher" answers the question "whom")

Students should do all their **homework**. ("homework" answers the question "what")

The dog licked **me**. (whom)

2. **Indirect objects** are nouns or pronouns that indirectly receive the action. The action happens to them or for them, but the indirect object does not receive the action. This is an important concept to learn if anyone wants to learn a second language. Indirect objects follow only transitive verbs. You must have a direct object before you can have an indirect object. An indirect object answers the questions "to whom" or "for whom" the action is done. (In English, "to" usually is implied for an indirect object, making it more difficult to identify.)

Examples: The teacher gave [to] **the children** (indirect object) **a short homework assignment**. (direct object)

The dog gave [to] **me** (indirect object) **his paw**. (direct object)

End Marks (Punctuation)

Make sure each sentence has one!

1. Use a period at the end of a statement (a sentence that tells something).

Example: Dobermans can be sweet dogs.

2. Use an exclamation mark at the end of a sentence that expresses powerful emotion or strong feeling. You can also use an exclamation mark after an interjection of strong emotion so that the interjection stands all by itself.

Examples: Get out of here!

Wow! I really like that.

3. Use a question mark at the end of an interrogative sentence (a sentence that asks a question).

Example: Will you please get out of here?

Except (*See* Accept/Except)

EXCLAMATION MARKS (*See* End Marks)

Extraneous Capital Letters

Make sure that students eliminate them. Some students throw capital letters around in their writing without any rhyme or reason. If any students do this, put a stop to it.

Farther/Further

These two words are sometimes used incorrectly, but it is really very easy to tell the difference between the two and, therefore, an easy mistake to correct. Farther talks about physical distance. Further talks about everything else.

Examples: Mark can throw a ball **farther** than Jesse can.

We will discuss this **further** after dinner.

Fewer and Less

Few, fewer, and fewest should be used with things that can be counted. Little, less, and least should be used with things that cannot be counted.

Examples: **Fewer** students are interested in literature these days. (You can count students.)

I have less interest in Poodles than I do in Dobermans. (You cannot count an abstract concept like interest.)

Finding and Identifying

It is extremely important that students be able to find and identify the following:

1. **Eight parts of speech**: Noun, verb, adjective, adverb, conjunction, interjection, preposition, pronoun. (See each part of speech under its own heading.)

2. **Predicates**

Simple — The main verb or the main verb with a helping verb

Complete — the verb and its complements or modifiers (adverbs, adverb phrases).

3. **Subjects**

Simple — the noun or pronoun that does the action

Complete — the noun or pronoun that does the action and its modifiers (adjectives, adjective phrases)

4. **Synonyms for better writing**

Encourage students to use in their writing the vocabulary words of the Caught'yas and encourage them to use a thesaurus when they write.

Footnotes

Today, when a quote is used or referred to in the body of a paper, the trend is to list such a source in the bibliography rather than in footnotes or endnotes (footnotes at the end of a paper). The quote or reference in the text is followed by parentheses containing the author's name and the date of publication. When an author has published two sources within one year, list the title also.

Example: The section on footnotes in Kiester's book says that the trend is not to have footnotes or endnotes in a paper. **(Kiester, 1992)**

Fragments

A sentence fragment is an incomplete thought (either lacking in subject or verb) that is used and punctuated incorrectly as a complete sentence. This is an egregious error. Help students overcome this habit. If students write fragments, then they probably don't understand what a subject and verb are. Frame your discussions accordingly.

Examples: A rather chubby dog on the floor. (no verb)

Slept on the floor by her side. (no subject)

Sticking his paws into the air. (no verb or subject)

Friendly Letters (Correct Format)

> Sender's address
> Sender's city, state   zip
> Date

Dear Jane,

   The bulk of the letter goes here written without skipping lines between paragraphs.

> With love,
> Sign name here

Further (*See* Farther and Further)

Gerund

A gerund is a verb form that ends in "ing" and is used as a noun. A gerund can be used in any way that a noun can be used. Sometimes a gerund serves as the simple subject, direct object, or as the object of a preposition.

Examples: **Snorkeling** is my favorite sport. (subject)

I like **snorkeling**. (direct object)

I think of **snorkeling** a lot when I daydream. (object of the preposition)

Gerund Phrases

Depending on your point of view, gerund phrases are either fun or useless to learn. I believe that the understanding and recognizing of them serves no purpose since no placement of commas is involved. One of my colleagues, on the other hand, maintains that gerunds and gerund phrases are fun. She uses art work to teach the concept to her students. She may well be right.

A gerund phrase is a group of words that includes a gerund and other words that complete its meaning. It can be accompanied by an adjective, an adverb, a direct object, or a prepositional phrase.

A gerund phrase functions as a noun in a sentence. The gerund phrase can be a subject or an object.

Examples: **Speaking softly** was one of the rules. (subject)

She made **speaking softly** a requirement in her class. (object)

Good and Well

These two words often are confused.

1. "Good" is an adjective; it tells about the noun that must follow it.

Example: The **good** dog sat at her feet instead of on them. (adjective — tells what kind of dog)

2. "Well" is the adverb that modifies a verb; it often appears at the end of the sentence.

Examples: He did it **well**. (adverb — tells how he did it)

He did **well** on the test. (adverb — tells how he did)

You can, however, "feel good" because "feel" acts as a verb of being and thus "good" is a predicate adjective.

Example: **I feel good** when I pet my cat.

Helping Verbs

These verbs accompany a past or present participle in a sentence. My students and I call them "dead verbs" or "weak verbs." Help students limit them in their writing.

Common helping verbs: am, are, be, is, have, had, had been, has been, have, have been, was, were, will, and any form of "be" (such as could be, would be, might be, etc.).

Good writing uses strong verbs ("screamed" instead of "**was** screaming"). Look at literature!

Sense verbs (look, see, smell, feel, taste) can function as verbs of being or as action verbs.

Example: I **feel** loving today. (verb of being)

The boy **felt** the dog's broken leg. (action verb)

When a sense verb functions as a verb of being, it is often followed by a predicate adjective.

Example: I **feel** bad. (Not "I feel badly" since one would not say "I am badly.")

Homophones

Students need to be able to correctly use the most common ones.

Common homophones: there/their/they're; to/too/ two; your/you're; no/know; its/it's; right/rite/write; threw/ through; quiet/quit/quite; all ready/already; all together/ altogether; hole/whole; pair/pare/pear; whose/ who's

Hyphens

1. Use a hyphen to divide a word at the end of a line. Divide only at syllables. Check a dictionary for syllables.

Example: The two huge dogs ran **around** the yard and ter-rified the little girl.

2. Use a hyphen to separate the words in compound numbers from twenty-one to ninety-nine and in fractions that are used as adjectives.

Examples: The teacher had thirty-five pupils in the class.

They ate ten and one-half pizzas for lunch.

3. Use a hyphen in a compound noun that serves as an adjective. More simply stated, use with two or more words that express one thought and serve as one adjective. To test whether a hyphen is needed, simply see if each word alone makes sense in describing the noun.

Examples: an **up-to-the-minute** report

two **star-crossed** lovers

a very **well-known** man

bell-bottom trousers

4. Use a hyphen after the following prefixes: all-, ex-, self-.

Examples: all-knowing, ex-husband, self-deprecating

5. Use a hyphen to separate any prefix from a word that begins with a capital letter.

Example: **pre-Civil** War

Imperatives

Imperatives are sentences that are orders. The subject is omitted.

Examples: Get off my feet. (The subject of the dog has been left out.)

Do your homework now! (Again, the subject has been omitted.)

Compound imperative sentences do not take a comma because the subjects are not stated.

Example: Get off my feet and go lie down elsewhere.

Independent Clauses

An independent clause is a sentence within a sentence.

Example: **She petted the dog**, and **she kissed the cat**.

Indirect and Direct Objects (*See* Direct and Indirect Objects)

Indirect Quote

An indirect quote is really a reference to a direct quote. The use of the word "that" turns a direct quote into an indirect one. In an indirect quote, no quotation marks are necessary because a direct quote is being paraphrased. No comma is necessary either

Examples: The student said **that she was hot**.

He told me **that he had a lot of homework to do**.

We shouted to her **that we didn't want to walk the dogs**.

Infinitive

An infinitive is formed from the word "to" together with the basic form of a verb.

Examples: to go, to snore, to eat, to type

Do not split an infinitive with the adverb as in the introduction to the television show *Star Trek*.

Example of what to avoid: " . . . **to** boldly **go** where no one has been before." (Star Trek)

Correction: " . . . **to go** boldly where no one has been before."

You might want to explain the use of "to" as a part of a verb. Most students think it functions only as a preposition.

Infinitive Phrase

This is a group of words with an infinitive and the words that complete the meaning. An infinitive phrase can serve as a noun, an adjective, or an adverb.

Examples:

Noun — **To teach grammar** is sometimes fun. (noun, subject)

Most students hate **to study grammar**. (object)

The goal of my first book was **to make grammar fun**. (predicate noun)

Adjective — It is now time **to learn your grammar**.

Adverb — The dog turned around six times **to get ready for his nap**.

Intensifier

An intensifier is an adverb that tells to what extent an adjective or another adverb is true. The most common intensifiers are "very" and "extremely."

Examples: an **extremely** angry (adjective) cat

a **very** placid (adjective) dog

The cat wanted to sit on his mistress's lap **very** badly.(adverb)

She spoke **extremely** softly (adverb) because she was afraid to awaken the cat.

Interjection

An interjection is a word or group of words that expresses feeling (anger, surprise, happiness, pain, relief, grief).

Common interjections: ah, aha, awesome, bam, boom, bravo, good grief, goodness, hey, hooray, hurrah, oh, oh boy, oh dear, oh my, oh yes/no, okay, ouch, ow, phew, pow, shhh, ugh, uh oh, well, whee, whoopee, whoops, wow.

Interjections that are at the beginning of the sentence can be followed either by a comma or by an exclamation mark. If an interjection is followed by an exclamation mark, the next word must begin with a capital letter.

Examples: **Well**, what are you doing there?

Okay, let's finish going over your homework.

Wow! Those dogs are big.

Interrupted Quote (*See* Continued Quote)

Interrupters

An interrupter is any word, expression or phrase that interrupts the flow of a sentence. These can be appositives, direct addresses, parenthetical expressions, or any word, phrase, or clause that breaks the flow of a sentence.

Examples: The dog, **however**, refused to get off her foot.

The dog, **I think**, is stubborn.

The black and white cat, **by the way**, is obstreperous.

She loved her only cat, **Skeeter**, very much.

Intransitive Verbs

An intransitive verb never has a direct object. In a sentence where the verb is intransitive, the subject does the acting and does not do anything to anything or anyone else.

Examples: Dogs **bark**.

The teacher **sits** in the chair.

The class **sleeps** during long messages on the loud speaker.

The class **rises** with respect (dream on, fellow teachers) when the teacher enters the room.

The dog lies on the floor.

Introductory Words and Phrases

These are simply words and phrases that begin a sentence. The comma after some of these is hotly debated. Using commas makes sentences easier to understand because they signal a separation or a pause between parts. It sounds better to put a comma after an adverb that comes at the beginning of a sentence if that adverb has to do with time. It also helps clarify a sentence if one puts a comma after an introductory prepositional phrase that acts as an adverb and refers to time that has passed in some way.

1. **Adverb** (one-word adverbs): We commonly use a one-word adverb that indicates when the action (the verb) took place. Put a comma after it if you hear a pause when the sentence is spoken aloud.

Examples: **Meanwhile**, the dog's stomach growled.

Tomorrow, she will be fed again.

2. **Adverbial clauses** (subordinate clauses): A comma is needed after an adverbial clause that introduces a sentence.

Example: **After I feed the chubby Rottweiler**, I will feed the rotund Doberman.

3. **Participial phrases**: A comma is needed after a participial phrase that comes at the beginning of a sentence.

Example: **Traveling away from the city**, you can tour some of the beautiful antebellum homes in the country.

4. **Prepositional phrases**: The comma after these, too, is debatable. Many old-fashioned people, like my mother and I, put a comma after a longish prepositional phrase that comes at the beginning of a sentence, particularly if the phrase refers to time. This also can be called an "adverbial phrase."

Examples: **In about two weeks**, she will need to get her shots.

For a very long time, he will be able to exist on the food on the shelves.

A comma is needed after two or more prepositional phrases that follow each other at the beginning of a sentence.

Examples: **At the end of the day**, the fat dog tries to curl up on her "blankey" to go to sleep.

In one hour in the kitchen, the hungry dog will receive a dog biscuit.

In the fall of 1992, a presidential election was held in this country.

5. **Words**: A comma is needed to show a pause after an introductory word. The most common introductory words are "yes" and "no."'

Examples: **Yes**, it is necessary to have a comma after introductory words.

No, many dogs do not receive five dog biscuits a day.

Irregular Verb Forms

Instead of forcing students to memorize a list which somehow never transfers to their writing, I teach each verb as it comes up in students' writing. This makes it real to them. They know they made a mistake in a verb and are more receptive to learning the forms of that verb. Plus, overkill (there are so many irregular verbs) only confuses students.

Verbs to stress in Caught'yas: be, do, have, lay, lie, raise, rise, see, set, sit. If you want to teach a unit on irregular verbs, any traditional grammar book will have a complete list for you.

LAY/LIE

Few adults use these verbs correctly. Think about the trouble students must have with them!

1. **lay**: Lay, used in the present tense, always has an object, and **laid**, in the past tense always has an object. You lay something on the table. You can't "lay" yourself on the table. That would be awkward as well as ungrammatical.

Principal parts of "lay":

lay (present)

laid (past)

laid (past participle)

Examples: The dog **lay** his head in his owner's lap. (present)

The dog **laid** his head on the rug yesterday. (past)

The dog always **has laid** its bone beside its bed. (past participle)

2. **lie**: Lie means to recline. Lie never takes a direct object. You lie on a bed, but you can never "lie" something on that bed. The confusion **lies** when the past tense of **lie** is used; **lay** used as the past tense of **lie** does not take a direct object.

Principal parts of "lie":

lie (present)

lay (past)

lain (past participle)

Examples: The dog **lies** on the floor today. (present)

The dog **lay** on the floor yesterday. (past)

The dog **is lying** on the floor right now. (present participle)

The dog **has lain** on the floor every day of its life. (past participle)

Less and Fewer (*See* Fewer and Less)

Metaphors

A metaphor is a comparison of two unlike things without using "like" or "as."

Example: The tree **is a ballerina in green**.

Use metaphors in Caught'yas. Have your students write a "Metaphor Paper." (See the writing ideas in Chapter 5.) Encourage students to write metaphors. They make for beautiful writing. Emily Dickinson used metaphors in almost every poem. Metaphors are a wonderful tool to make writing more sophisticated.

Modifiers and Misplaced Modifiers

1. **Modifiers**: A modifier is simply another word for an adjective. A modifier may be classified as non-restrictive (non-essential) or restrictive (essential). A modifier can be a word, a phrase, or a clause.

An adjective, adjective phrase, or adjective clause is non-restrictive/non-essential when it is not necessary to the meaning of the sentence. The clause gives additional information. Use commas to set off non-restrictive modifiers.

Example: Dino, **who has floppy ears**, won a prize in obedience class. (The name of the dog has been identified, and it is not necessary to add more information about him.)

An adjective, adjective phrase, or adjective clause is restrictive/essential when it is necessary to the meaning of the sentence. Do not set off a restrictive modifier with commas.

Example: The dog **who won a prize in obedience class** has floppy ears. (This information is necessary since there are millions of dogs in the world.)

2. **Misplaced modifiers**: These are simply adjective phrases or clauses that are in the wrong place in a sentence so that they seem to modify the wrong noun. When you use modifiers in sentences, make sure that they are properly placed. The general rule to follow is this: place modifiers as close as possible to the sentence parts they modify.

Examples: The lady was watching her dog **driving down the road**. (The dog is not driving down the road; the lady is.)

Corrected sentence: Driving down the road, the lady was watching her dog.

After purchasing a skirt, her money was all gone. (The clause "her money was all gone" does not tell more about the skirt. It tells about the **person** "her" refers to and therefore should not come immediately after "skirt.")

Corrected sentence: **After purchasing a skirt**, she had no more money.

Negatives

A negative is a word that expresses the lack of something.

Common negatives: no, not, neither, never, nobody, none, no one, nothing, nowhere, barely, scarcely, hardly.

All you need to stress about negatives is the importance of avoiding the use of two negatives in the same sentence like "don't got no" or "don't have nobody." There should be only *one* negative word per sentence unless you are using the correlative conjunction "neither . . . nor."

Only one negative word is necessary to convey the meaning. There are two ways to correct a sentence with a double negative.

Example: The telephone **isn't no** new instrument.

Corrected sentence: The telephone is **no** new instrument. Or, The telephone is **not** a new instrument.

Noun

A noun is a person, a place, a thing, or an idea. It is important for students to recognize this part of speech and its function as a subject or object. Teach the difference between common and proper nouns.

Common nouns are terms for persons, places, things, or ideas.

Proper nouns are the names of particular persons, places, or things.

Examples:

Common nouns — girl, school, city

Proper nouns — Jane, Westwood School, Gainesville

Nouns have several functions in a sentence.

Subject — the person, place, or thing doing the action

Example: The **dog** yawned.

Direct object — the person, place, or thing who receives the action

Example: She stroked the **cat**.

Object of preposition — the person, place, or thing affected by the preposition

Example: He gave the bone to the **dog**.

Indirect object — the person, place, or thing for whom or to whom the action is done

Example: She gave the **dog** a big bone.("to" is implied)

Noun Clause

A noun clause is a subordinate clause which is used as a noun. It can be used as a subject, direct object, indirect object, predicate noun, or object of a preposition in a sentence.

Noun clauses usually begin with the following words: how, if, that, what, whatever, where, when, wherever, whether, which, whichever, who, whom, whoever, whomever, why.

Noun clauses take the place of a noun anywhere in a sentence that a noun can be used (subject, direct or indirect object, object of a preposition, predicate noun).

Examples:

Subject — **What the dog intended** was obvious.

Direct object — I still don't know **why he did it**.

Indirect object — Please give **whichever dog comes up to you** a pat under the chin.

Object of preposition — She tells her stories **to whoever will listen**.

Predicate noun — That is not **what the dog** intended to do.

Noun Markers

This is the term for the three demonstrative adjectives "a," "an," and "the." When I introduce these to the students, I first make my hand into a trumpet, "Toot-te-toot," and then announce, "Noun coming!!!!!!" Students quickly get the idea, and we move on to other things. Young students especially love the drama of the hand trumpet and seem to remember these three little words when they are presented in this fashion.

Example: The lady gave **an** old bone to **a** hungry dog.

Use "a" before a word that begins with a consonant and "an" before a word that begins with a vowel. These demonstrative adjectives are also called "articles." (*See* Articles)

Objects

There are two kinds of objects, direct and indirect. Objects are nouns, noun clauses, or noun phrases that receive the action of the verb either directly or indirectly. They answer the following questions:

1. whom? (direct object)
2. what? (direct object)
3. to or for whom? (indirect object)
4. to or for what? (indirect object)

For further information about objects and for examples, see Direct and Indirect Objects

Paragraphs

Discuss the need for a paragraph each time you do a Caught'ya. Correct paragraphing can be learned only through constant practice. While various writers may disagree as to the exact placement of a paragraph, there are some general rules.

1. In general, a new paragraph is needed if there has been a lapse of time, a change of subject, or a change of place. A paragraph is supposed to be about one basic idea. It needs a topic sentence and a concluding sentence (unless it is a quotation).

2. Use a new paragraph in conversations each time a new person speaks. This seems like such a simple thing to grasp, but students have a hard time learning it.

Example:

"Get out of here, you beastly dog!" cried the lady to the big brown Doberman cowering in the kitchen. "You're messing up my floor!"

"Rowrf, Rowrf!" barked back the dog as it slinked sheepishly away.

"Oh, come back here, you poor thing," called the lady. "I'm sorry I yelled at you."

"Rowrf!"

"I like you, too," said the lady.

Parallel Construction

Parallel structure are forms that use similar grammatical constructions. Similar forms of phrases, words, and clauses are used for items that are alike in a sentence.

Parallel construction means that if you begin with a word or a certain part of speech, you have to continue it if you have a series. It can, however, be implied, as in a series of infinitives.

Examples: The big Doberman likes **bananas, tomatoes**, and **broccoli**. (words — these are all nouns)

The two dogs liked **sleeping** and **eating**. (words — gerunds)

The chubby Rottweiler went **to her bowl, to her water dish**, and then **to her bed**. (phrases — prepositional)

She felt **that she was unloved** and **that she was unwanted** because there was no food in her bowl. (clauses)

He likes **to eat**, (to) **sleep**, and (to) **play**.

Parentheses
(As you may have noticed, I abuse these.)

Parentheses enclose information that isn't vital to the meaning of a sentence, but that is nevertheless important to include. Parentheses also can contain information that some of the readers of the sentence already know.

Examples: The author of this book (Jane Kiester) has a thing about dogs.

Emily Dickinson (1830-1886) is his favorite poet.

Frequent use of parentheses is not desirable. (Do as I say, not as I do.)

Parenthetical Expressions

Parenthetical expressions are phrases that are thrown into sentences as asides to the reader. They are not necessary to the meaning of the sentence and often interrupt a sentence's flow. Parenthetical expressions also are called interrupters.

Common parenthetical expressions: of course, however, for example, on the contrary, on the other hand, I suppose, in fact, by the way, in my opinion, to tell the truth, nevertheless, I believe, I think, etc.

Parenthetical expressions always are set off by commas no matter where they occur in a sentence.

Examples: The dog, **in fact**, was too chubby for her collar.

To tell the truth, two faithful dogs are a handful.

The cat, **however**, is quite a dapper fellow.

Cats are smarter than dogs, **of course**.

Participial Phrases (also called Participle Phrases)

These are groups of words that have the "ing," the "ed," or the special past form of the verb in them. In other words, they are phrases that contain a participle and its complement and modifiers. Participial phrases can come before or after the word that they modify and can give more information about a noun or an adjective. The participle will be present or past.

1. A present participle is the "ing" form of a verb. It can be used as an adjective by itself or in a participial or gerund phrase.

Examples: The **snoring** (adjective) **dog sleeping on the floor** (participial phrase) is the gentlest of animals.

Cramming before a test is a poor practice. (gerund phrase)

2. A **past participle** is the past tense form of a verb which usually ends in "ed." It can be used with a helping verb or can be used as an adjective or in a participial phrase.

Examples: The chef served the fish **fried in butter**.

That **trained** (adjective) dog who didn't learn anything has barked all morning long.

Participial phrases act as adjectives

Examples: **Rapidly gaining confidence**, the new teacher taught about participial phrases. (more about "teacher")

The new teacher, **feeling more sure of herself**, taught about participial phrases.

If the participial phrase begins the sentence or comes in the middle of the sentence, it usually is set off by commas. If, however, it is at the end of the sentence, it requires no comma.

Examples: **Groaning softly**, the dog kicked out in his sleep.

The dog, **groaning softly**, kicked out in his sleep.

She spied a dog **groaning softly in its sleep.**

Participle

A participle is just a fancy name for a verb form that is used as an adjective. It can be the present participial form of the verb ("–ing") or the past participial form of the verb (usually "–ed").

Examples: The **sleeping** dog blocked the doorway. (present)

A **trained** dog supposedly obeys better than an **untrained** one. (past)

(*See* Participial Phrases. *See also* Dangling Participle)

Parts of Speech

The eight parts of speech are the eight functional categories into which we can divide words. It is important that students learn the eight parts of speech to have a frame of reference and to have a way to understand the finer points of grammar.

The eight parts of speech: adjectives, adverbs, conjunctions, verbs, interjections, nouns, prepositions, pronouns.

Passive Voice (*See* Active vx. Passive Verb Voices)

Periods (*See* End Marks)

Plural

A plural is more than one of a noun. In the Caught'yas I covered the common mistakes students make. This is another skill that should be taught individually. When one of your students makes a mistake with the plural of a word, include that word or a similar word in a Caught'ya and teach it.

Basic plural rules.

1. Add "s" to most singular nouns.

Examples: dog-dogs; piano-pianos; monkey-monkeys; cat-cats.

2. Add "es" to singular nouns that end in ss, x, ch, sh, or z.

Examples: church-churches; mix-mixes; glass-glasses; buzz-buzzes; wish-wishes.

3. Most nouns that end in "o" add "s" in their plural form, but a few that end in "o" and are preceded by a consonant form their plurals with "es." Some can end in either one.

Examples: tomato-tomatoes, potato-potatoes; BUT hero-heros or heroes

4. Change singular nouns that end in a consonant and a "y" to plural by changing the "y" to an "i" and adding "es." This rule does not apply to proper nouns that end in a consonant and a "y."

Examples: party-parties; baby-babies; BUT Mary-Marys

5. To form the plural of some nouns that end in "f" or "fe," change the "f" to a "v" and add "es."

Examples: calf-calves; knife-knives

6. To form the plural of any proper name, no matter what the end letters, add "s."

Examples: Brady-Bradys; Finch-Finchs

7. There are so many exceptions to these rules that it boggles the mind. If you want a complete list, see a traditional grammar text. Few people can memorize a list one day and then apply it to their writing a month later. Plurals are best taught on the spur of the moment, at the time they are written incorrectly.

Examples: foot-feet; mouse-mice; deer-deer; child-children

Plurals vs. Possessives

For some reason, this is a skill many students find beyond them. No general explanations seem to clear up this problem. Only specific focuses help. I tell my students who put apostrophes on plural nouns to eliminate every apostrophe in their writing for a month. We then slowly put them back in possessives and in conjunctions. This works better than anything else I have tried. I also keep plugging away in the Caught'yas by frequently inserting apostrophes correctly and incorrectly in the sentence that is put on the board. This forces students to think each time– "Does that apostrophe belong there? Is the word plural or possessive?" This way, students eventually get the hang of it.

Possessive Nouns

A possessive noun is a noun (a person, place, or thing) that shows ownership of something. Ownership is shown by the use of an apostrophe.

Examples: the dog's bone, the dogs' bones

The rules of possessive nouns are quite simple for something that gives students such anguish.

1. **Singular possessive nouns**: Add "'s" to any singular possessive noun no matter what letter ends it.

Examples: glass's, dog's, cat's, box's, church's, calf's, child's

2. **Plural possessive nouns**: Add an apostrophe to all plural possessive nouns that end in "s."

Examples: glasses', dogs', cats', boxes', churches', calves'

Add "'s" to any plural noun that does not end in "s."

Examples: children's, men's, mice's

Predicate

A predicate is the verb in a sentence and all the words that modify it.

Example: The black and white cat **sat on his mistress's lap.**

Preposition

A preposition is a little word that, with its object, acts either as an adjective or as an adverb in a sentence.

Examples: in the doghouse, on the roof, under the bed

List of prepositions: aboard, about, above, across, after, against, along, among, around, at, before, behind, below, beneath, between, beyond, by, down, during, except, for, from, in, into, like, of, off, on, onto, over, past, since, through, throughout, to, toward, under, underneath, until, up, upon, with, within, without.

Students should memorize the basic list for quick reference. Repeated daily in class, these prepositions are learned in about three weeks. Teach the prepositions early in the year, write poems where every line has to begin with a different preposition, and refer to them often. Once students have memorized the prepositions, they can begin to use them more effectively and capitalize (or not) them correctly in titles.

Do not end a sentence with a preposition. It is uncouth! Do not capitalize a preposition in a title unless it is the first word of that title.

Prepositional Phrases

A prepositional phrase is a preposition and a noun or pronoun plus the adjectives that modify it. It is a group of words that functions as a single word. Prepositional phrases can serve as adjectives to modify a noun or as adverbs to modify a verb.

Examples: I gave a bone **to the dog**. (adverb)

The dog **with the floppy ears** ate the bone. (adjective)

An adjective phrase usually follows the word it modifies.

Example: The dog **on the right** is snoring.

An adverb phrase, like adverbs, may shift position.

Examples: **In the middle**, lies the cat.

The cat lies **in the middle**.

Pronouns

Pronouns are words that take the place of nouns and cause much trouble. They are hateful but necessary. If you think these are bad, try teaching French pronouns!

Especially stress the difference between subject and object pronouns.

Subject pronouns: I, you, he, she, it, we, they

Object pronouns: me, you, him, her, it, us, them.

Include in many Caught'yas "My friend and I did something." and "Someone did something to my friend and me."

Students experience much difficulty differentiating subject and object pronouns. They misuse them because they hear them misused all the time in common speech. Model the correct use as often as you can.

Examples of common errors: My friend and **me** went . . .

It is **me**.

She is better than **me**.

Correct examples: My friend and **I** went . . . ("I" is the subject of "went.")

It is **I**. (Implied here is "It is I who does something." "I" is a subject.)

She is better than **I** . . . (Again, something is implied. The word "am" has been left out. "I" is the subject of "am.")

Teach the correct use of the different kinds of pronouns. It is not the name of each that is important; it is recognizing the differences among them.

1. **Personal pronouns**: These are the subject and object pronouns listed above.

2. **Possessive pronouns**: These are pronouns that show ownership of something.

Singular possessive pronouns: my, mine, your, yours, his, her, hers, its

Plural possessive pronouns: our, ours, your, yours, their, theirs

3. **Interrogative pronouns**: These pronouns ask questions: why, what, which, who, whom.

4. **Demonstrative pronouns**: These pronouns point out people, places or things and highlight them: this, that, these, those.

5. **Indefinite pronouns**: These are pronouns that refer to a person or a thing that is not identified. Some indefinite pronouns are singular. Some are plural. Some can act either way.

Singular: another, anybody, anyone, anything, each, either, everybody, everyone, everything, neither, nobody, no one, none, nothing, other, one, somebody, someone, something

Plural: both, few, many, ones, others, several

Either: all, any, most, some

It is important to teach agreement with indefinite pronouns. Many students find it difficult to make a verb or another pronoun agree with the indefinite pronoun.

6. **Reflexive and intensive pronouns**: These usually end in "self" or "selves" and refer to the subject of the sentence. For your trivia information of the day, you need to know that reflexive pronouns are necessary to the meaning of a sentence and cannot be left out. Intensive pronouns, on the other hand, are not necessary and can be left out without hurting the meaning of a sentence.

Examples: The teacher knows **herself** very well. (reflexive)

The teacher **herself** washed the blackboard. (intensive)

7. **Relative pronouns**: These are the pronouns that modify a noun: who, which, that.

There are two big problems with pronouns — using the correct one and making the rest of the sentence agree with it.

Punctuation

Each kind of punctuation is listed under its own heading.

Question Marks (*See* End Marks)

Quotation Marks (In Uses Other Than Conversation)

Use quotation marks around words referred to or letters referred to in the context of a sentence. Use them also with words that are meant tongue-in-cheek.

Periods and commas always go inside quotation marks.

Examples: If you wish to make plural the word "party," take off the "y" and add "ies."

He loves the poem "Mother to Son."

The corpulent Rottweiler has been nicknamed "Miss Tub."

Exclamation marks and question marks go outside the quotation marks unless they are part of the words in quotation marks.

Examples: She got an "A"!

Did he give an extra bone to "Miss Tub"?

Quotations can be avoided with the use of the word "that." Instead of quotation marks, refer to what has been said with the word "that." *See* Indirect Quotes for more information.

Examples: She said that she was hungry and needed refreshments.

Despite her pleas, I told her that she was too chubby to get any more ice cream.

(*See also* Dialogues, Comma Rules, Indirect Quotes, and Titles))

Raise/Rise

These are two more verbs that confuse students. Again, as in "lie" and "lay" and "sit" and "set," one takes an object and the other does not.

1. Raise means "to lift or to grow." It requires an object that has to be "raised."

Example: The cat **raised** his tail and stormed off when no food was offered.

2. Rise means "to get up." It does not take an object.

Example: All students **rise** with a bow of respect when their English teacher enters the room.

Run Ons

A run on is a sentence that contains more than one thought. It goes on and on.

1. Sometimes run-on sentences simply lack punctuation.

Example: The dog lay on the floor she snored loudly.

Corrected: The dog lay on the floor. She snored loudly.

2. Sometimes run-on sentences are a group of sentences joined by coordinating conjunctions into one very long sentence.

Example: She lay on the floor, and she snored, but she didn't groan, and she wiggled her ears.

Corrected: She lay on the floor. She snored, but she didn't groan. She wiggled her ears.

Help your students avoid run ons.

Semicolons

A semicolon is a punctuation mark (;) that is used to separate parts of a sentence.

1. Use semicolons in compound sentences instead of using a conjunction and a comma.

Example: The black cat nuzzled the big dog; it is either very friendly or very stupid.

2. Use semicolons in lists where the use of a lot of commas makes meaning difficult.

Example: Learn the meanings of these homophones: there, their, they're; to, too, two; your, you're; no, know; and hear, here.

3. Use a semicolon to join two independent clauses (two sentences within a sentence) when the second clause begins with however, nevertheless, consequently, besides, therefore, moreover, or furthermore.

Example: The Rottweiler may lick faces; **however**, she is charming.

4. To avoid confusion, use a semicolon to separate two independent clauses that have many commas within one or both of them.

Example: My Rottweiler likes to eat tomatoes, broccoli, and cucumbers; my Doberman likes to eat fruit, dog food, and cookies.

Similes

A simile compares two unlike things and uses "like" or "as" in the comparison.

Examples: The cat sprawled on the rug **like a furry throw pillow**.

The leaves, **as agile as ballerinas**, seemed to dance in the wind.

Encourage students to use similes. I have included a plethora of them in the middle and high school Caught'yas so that students can learn to recognize and use them. Point them out to students. Practice coming up orally with other similes.

Simple Sentence

A simple sentence is a sentence with one subject and one predicate. In a simple sentence, the subject and/or the verb can be more than one thing, as in a compound subject or a compound predicate, but only one idea is expressed.

Examples: The wimpy **Rottweiler sat** on her owner's foot.

The wimpy **Rottweiler** and the brown **Doberman sat** by their owner's feet and **gazed** adoringly into their mistress's eyes. (Two subjects and two verbs, but it is still a simple sentence.)

Since (*See* Because and Since)

Set/Sit

These are two more verbs that students often use incorrectly.

1. Set means to put down. Set always takes an object. You set the sleeping cat in the chair or the milk on the table, but you never set yourself down anywhere. Tell students to think about it. You can't put your hands under your feet and lift your entire body up and set it down on something.

Example: The dumb Doberman set his bone down on the floor, and the chubby Rottweiler grabbed it from under his nose.

2. Sit means to place yourself in a seated position. Sit does not take an object. You sit down, but you never sit something down.

Example: The stupid dog always sits on its owner's foot.

Spelling Errors, The Most Common

1. All words with "ie" or "ei"

Examples: thief, relief, believe

weird, neighbor, receive

2. Plurals of nouns that end in "y"

Examples: parties, monkeys, babies

3. "A lot" (students write as one word)

Some teachers forbid the use of this in their classrooms. I agree. There are always ways to avoid the use of "a lot."

4. Doubling consonants in words that end in consonant/vowel/consonant plus a suffix that begins with a vowel (like "ed").

Examples: dropped, stopped, petted

5. Any grammar or spelling book will have a long list of commonly misspelled words, but very few people can memorize a long list of words and then remember the spelling of those words when they use them in their writing at a later date. It is better to attack these misspelled words as they appear in students' writings.

Spelling Rules

There are too many spelling rules and exceptions to the spelling rules to list here. See any standard spelling book for a discussion of this subject. The most common ones have been listed by the individual Caught'yas in which they appear.

Strong Verbs

These are verbs that are not helping verbs or sense verbs. They show rather than tell what is going on in a sentence. Use of these verbs fosters better writing. You will find the use of strong verbs in literature. There is even a language called E-Prime that is English minus the verb "to be." Try speaking or writing in E-Prime. The results are amazing, and the verb "to be" is only one of the "telling" verbs.

Examples: The dog **stretched** and **rolled** his big brown eyes at me.

He **ambled** to the door and **peeked** outside.

Dead verbs to avoid: to be — be, am, is, are, was, were; to have — has, have, had; become, became.

Sense verbs: sees, looks, feels, sounds, smells.

Any verb ending in "ing"

Subjects

A subject is the noun that performs the action in a sentence and everything that modifies it.

Example: The big black cat and his mistress like to snooze late on Saturday mornings.

Subject-Verb Agreement

Subject-verb agreement is very important to the coherence of a sentence. The subject of a sentence must agree as to whether it is singular or plural with the verb of the sentence.

If the subject is singular, then the verb should be singular. If the subject is plural, the verb should be plural.

Examples: **He think** he is right. (incorrect)

We goes to the circus every year.

Corrected examples: **He thinks** he is right.

We go to the circus every year.

Subordinate Clause

A subordinate clause is a part of a sentence that has a subject and a verb but cannot stand on its own to express a complete thought. A subordinate clause begins with a subordinating conjunction — a conjunction that makes the clause not a complete sentence. *See* Subordinating Conjunctions for a complete list them.

Examples: **When the teacher was funny**, the students laughed. ("The teacher was funny" is a complete sentence with a subject and a verb. If you add the subordinating conjunction "when," it can no longer stand on its own, and it needs the addition of an independent clause to form a complete sentence.)

While we sit here, I shall tell you my story.

I shall tell you my story **while we sit here**.

Subordinate clauses serve in a sentence as adverbs or adjectives. Subordinate clauses that are adverbs (adverb clauses) tell more about the verb and answer one of the following questions about a verb: when it happened, where it happened, how it happened, how often it happened, why it happened.

Examples: *See* Adverb Clauses.

Subordinate clauses that are adjectives (adjective clauses) tell more about a noun and answer one of the following questions about it: which one, what kind, how many.

Examples: *See* Adjective Clauses.

Punctuation of subordinate clauses is easy. Put a comma at the end of the clause if the clause begins the sentence. Do not put any commas if the clause does not begin the sentence.

Examples: **If you pet the dog**, you will get hairs on your suit.

You will get hairs on your suit **if you pet the dog**.

Subordinating Conjunctions

These are words that make something that was a complete sentence into an incomplete sentence. Subordinating conjunctions begin subordinate clauses (see above).

Example: **After** the cat fell asleep, he twitched his whiskers.

Common subordinating conjunctions: after, although, as, as if, as long as, as soon as, as though, because, before, even though, how, if, in order that, provided that, since, so that, than, till, unless, until, when, whenever, where, whereas, wherever, while.

Summarizing

To summarize something you write a condensed version of it. This is a skill that is necessary in almost any job. A repair man has to summarize each house call. A doctor has to summarize each patient's problems, and so on. It is a skill that is easily practiced with the Caught'yas. (See #9 of the General Writing Ideas in Chapter 5 for ideas to teach summarization skills.)

That

"That" is a relative or a demonstrative pronoun (depending on how it is used). Use "that" in an indirect quote to avoid the use of quotation marks.

Example: She said **that** she was going to feed the dogs.

Do not use "that" as a substitute for "who" or "whom." "That" refers to an object or a thing. "Who" and "whom" refer to people. This is an extremely common mistake.

Example: She is the one **whom** (not "that") I love.

Is feeding two hungry dogs **that** complicated?

She gave the dog the bone **that** seemed the biggest.

Titles

1. Underline titles of long works — books, magazines, newspapers, plays, movies, paintings, and long musical works.

2. Put quotation marks around short works — short stories, poems, chapters of books, magazine articles, songs. It also is important to recall that if a comma or a period follows the quoted work, it must be placed inside the quotation mark. If a question or an exclamation and the end punctuation is not a part of the cited work, then the question mark or the exclamation point goes outside the quotation mark.

Examples: Although she read the article "Sentence Diagramming," she still didn't understand the concept.

She read the article "Sentence Diagramming."

Did she read the article "Sentence Diagramming"?

3. Do not capitalize prepositions, noun markers, or conjunctions in a title unless they are the first word of the title.

Example: The (noun marker) Dog under (preposition) a (noun marker) Human Roof and (conjunction) the (noun marker) Cat on (preposition) the (noun marker) Lap

The Dog under a Human Roof and the Cat on the Lap

Ttransitive Verbs

A transitive verb takes a direct object. In other words, it always has to do something to something or someone.

Example: The dog **lay** his **head** on the carpet today.

The cat **set** his **paw** on the table before attacking the plate.

The dog **raised** his **paw** for inspection.

Verb Tense Shift in a Story

Make sure that students stick to the same tense they begin with in any story or paragraph they write. If a story starts in the present tense, it should remain in the present tense. If it begins in the past tense, it should continue in the past tense.

To practice this skill, I frequently have changed the verb tense in the Caught'ya sentences. All of the stories have been told in the past tense, so I sometimes put the verb in the present tense. In the margin I warn the teacher to make sure that the students practice correcting "verb tense shift."

Verbs

For lists of verbs and appropriate forms of regular and irregular verbs, please refer to a traditional grammar text. Otherwise, just correct students as they make the mistakes in their writing.The latter is more effective.

Try to keep students from splitting helping verbs and the participles that follow.

Example: The cat also **has lain** on the carpet all day. (Not "**has** also **lain**") all day.

While splitting helping verbs and the participles that follow is sometimes unavoidable, it is not correct English. Although more rigid grammarians disagree with me on this point, many of my colleagues and I believe that if avoiding the split creates an awkward sentence, the rule should be ignored.

Well (*See* Good and Well)

Who, Whoever, Whom, Whemever

These are relative or interrogative pronouns that are used to refer to people. These four pronouns are so misused in general parlance that to some students the correct form sounds incorrect! Simply correct students every time you hear an error in the use of these four pronouns. You may be making verbal corrections until students feel "grammatically abused," but the more students hear the correct way to use these pronouns, the more they will use them correctly.

Here's a general rule of thumb that works about 95 percent of the time. I tell my students to use "who" and "whoever" if the word after it is a verb. If the word is not a verb but a pronoun or a noun, then they must use "whom" or "whomever."

Another rule that often works even better is to substitute "he" or "she" for "who" and "him" or "her" for "whom" and see if it makes sense. These rules fail when you have one of those weird sentences or phrases that can be turned around like "Who I am" or when you have something else like "I think" between the subject and the verb. (She is the one who **I think** did it.)

1. **Who and whoever**: Used as interrogative pronouns, "who" and "whoever" are the subject of a simple or compound sentence. They should be followed by a verb, the thing that "who" does. Tell students, if they are in doubt, to try substituting "he" or "she" for "who" to see if it makes sense.

Examples: **Who is** that?

Who is sitting on my foot?

All right, **who ate** the dog food?

Whoever broke into the bag and ate the dog food is in big trouble.

Whoever is sitting on my foot had better get off.

Used as a relative pronoun, "who" and "whoever" may be the subject or the predicate noun of a clause.

Examples: **Whoever finishes first** will get extra ice cream for dessert. (subject)

We shall serve **whoever arrives first**. (predicate)

2. **Whom and whomever**: Whom and whomever are relative pronouns that serve as objects of sentences or clauses. They can be direct objects of a verb, indirect objects, or objects of a preposition. Tell students to try substituting "him" or "her" for "whom" to see if it sounds correct.

Examples: He is the one **whom** I love. (object of verb)

With **whom** did you go out last night? (object of preposition)

I will pick the one **whom** I want. (object of verb)

For **whom** does the lady buy diet dog food? (object of preposition)

3. **That**: Do not use "that" instead of "who" or "whom." "That" refers to objects or things. "Who" and "whom" refer to people.

Examples: (*See* That)

To reinforce the correct use of "who" and "whom," I tell students that I will give them one point extra credit (three of them erase a zero in my grade book) if they catch someone at home making a "who/whom" error. Students write down the offending sentence, coerce the person into adding a note that he/she did, in fact, make the error, and bring the paper to me. At first I was afraid that I would have angry parents, but it turned out that I received only positive phone calls from grateful parents who were delighted to see their children taking an interest in correct English grammar.

Bibliography

Black, Matthew. *Cliffs Notes on Shakespeare's "A Midsummer-Night's Dream."* Lincoln: Cliffs Notes Incorporated, 1995.

Black, Matthew, Ph.D. *Cliffs Notes on Shakespeare's "Much Ado about Nothing."* Lincoln: Cliffs Notes Incorporated, 1995.

Caplan, Rebakah and Deech, Catherine. *Showing Writing - A Training Program to Help Students Be Specific.* Berkeley: University of California Press, 1980.

Connors, R.J. and Lunsford, A.A.. "Frequency of Formal Errors in Current College Writing, or Ma and Pa Kettle Do Research, *College Composition and Communication* 39, 1988, pp 395-409.

Elgin, Suzette Haden. *The Great Grammar Myth.* National Writing Project Occasional Paper #5. Berkeley: University of California Press, 1982.

Elley, W. B., et al. *The Role of Grammar in a Secondary School Curriculum.* Wellington: N.Z.C.E.R., 1979.

Hacker, Diane. *A Writer's Reference.* Boston: Bedford Books, 1995.

Haley-James, Shirley and Stewig, John Warren. *Houghton Mifflin English.* Boston: Houghton Mifflin company, 1988.

Hill, Wayne and Öttchen, Cynthia. *Shakespeare's Insults. Educating Your Wit.* Cambridge: MainSail Press, 1993.

Hillegass, M.L.S. *Cliffs Notes on Shakespeare's "The Tempest."* Lincoln: Cliffs Notes Incorporated, 1995.

Kiester, Jane Bell. *Blowing Away the State Writing Assessment Test.* Gainesville: Maupin House Publishing, 1996.

Kiester, Jane Bell. *Caught'ya! Grammar with a Giggle.* Gainesville: Maupin House Publishing, 1990.

Kiester, Jane Bell. *Caught'ya Again! More Grammar with a Giggle.* Gainesville: Maupin House Publishing, 1993.

Laird, Charlton, preparer. *Webster's New World Thesaurus.* New York: Simon and Schuster, Inc., 1985.

Roberts, J. L., PhD. *Cliffs Notes on Shakespeare's "Twelfth Night."* Lincoln: Cliffs Notes Incorporated, 1995.

Shakespeare, William, Edited by Louis Wright and Virginia LaMar. *A Midsummer Night's Dream.* New York: Washington Square Press, 1968.

Shakespeare, William, edited by David L. Stevenson. *Much Ado about Nothing.* New York: Signet Classics, 1964.

Shakespeare, William, Edited by Barbara Mowat and Paul Werstine. *The Tempest.* New York: Washington Square Press, 1994.

Shakespeare, William, Edited by Barbara Mowat and Paul Werstine. *Twelfth Night.* New York: Washington Square Press, 1993.

Shertzer, Margaret. *The Elements of Grammar.* New York: Macmillan Publishing Company, 1996.

Sherwin, J. Stephen. *Four Problems in Teaching Egnlish: A Critique of Research.* Scranton: International Textbook Company, 1969.

Shuman, R. Baird. "What are the Priorities?" *Educational Leadership,* 1992.

Stein, Jess, Editor In Chief. *The Random House Dictionary of the English Language* (Unabridged Edition). New York: Random House, 1967.

Vail, Neil and Papenfuss, Joseph. *Daily Oral Language Level 7.* Racine: D.O.L. Publications, 1982.

Warriner, John, and Graham, Sheila Laws. *Warriner's English Grammar and Composition,* Complete Course. New York: Harcourt Brace Jovanovich, 1957.

Warriner, John, and Graham, Sheila Laws. *Warriner's English Grammar and Composition,* Third Course, New York: Harcourt Brace Jovanovich, 1977.